The Economics of Network Industries

This book introduces upper-level undergraduates, graduate students, and researchers to the latest developments in network economics, one of the fastest-growing fields in all industrial organization. Network industries include the Internet, e-mail, telephony, computer hardware and software, music and video players, and service operations in the banking, legal, and airlines industries among many others. The work offers an overview of the subject matter as well as investigations about specific industries. It conveys the essential features of how strategic interactions between firms are affected by network activity, as well as covering social interaction and its influence on consumers' choices of products and service. Virtually no calculus is used in the text, and each chapter ends with a series of exercises and selected references. The text may be used for both one- and two-semester courses.

Oz Shy is on the faculty of the Department of Economics at the University of Haifa, Israel. He has also taught at Tel Aviv University, the Stockholm School of Economics, the Universities of Michigan and Minnesota, Carleton College, and the State University of New York. Professor Shy's textbook *Industrial Organization: Theory and Applications* was published by MIT Press in 1996. He has written articles for the *Journal of Economics and Management Strategy* and the *International Journal of Industrial Economics*, among other leading publications.

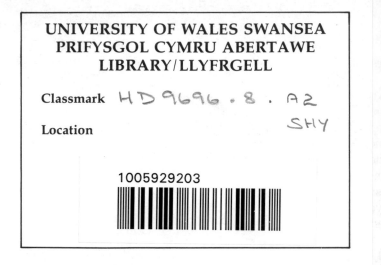
LONG LOAN

Items must be returned by the last date
stamped below or immediately if recalled.
To renew telephone 01792 295178.

BENTHYCIAD HIR

Dylid dychwelyd eitemau cyn y dyddiad a
stampiwyd olaf isod, neu ar unwaith os
gofynnir amdanynt yn ôl.
I adnewyddu ffôn 01792 295178.

The Economics of Network Industries

Oz Shy

University of Haifa

CAMBRIDGE
UNIVERSITY PRESS

PUBLISHED BY THE PRESS SYNDICATE OF THE UNIVERSITY OF CAMBRIDGE
The Pitt Building, Trumpington Street, Cambridge, United Kingdom

CAMBRIDGE UNIVERSITY PRESS
The Edinburgh Building, Cambridge CB2 2RU, UK
40 West 20th Street, New York, NY 10011-4211, USA
477 Williamstown Road, Port Melbourne, VIC 3207, Australia
Ruiz de Alarcón 13, 28014 Madrid, Spain
Dock House, The Waterfront, Cape Town 8001, South Africa

http://www.cambridge.org

First published 2001
Reprinted 2002

Printed in the United States of America

Typeface Computer Modern 10/12 pt.   *System* LaTeX 2_ε [AU]

A catalog record for this book is available from the British Library.

Library of Congress Cataloging in Publication Data

Shy, Oz.
  The economics of network industries / Oz Shy.
    p. cm.
  Includes bibliographical references and index.
  ISBN 0-521-80095-1 – ISBN 0-521-80500-7 (pb)
    1. Computer industry. 2. Computer networks. 3. Electronic data interchange. 4.
  Electronic commerce.   I. Title.

HD9696.8.A2 S55 2000
303.48′33—dc21   00-063044

ISBN 0 521 80095 1   hardback
ISBN 0 521 80500 7   paperback

For Sarah, Daniel, and Tianlai

Contents

Contents

Appendices

Preface

Motivation for Writing This Book

The motivation for writing this book grew from several years of research on the economics of network industries as well as from extensive teaching of undergraduate and graduate industrial organization courses at Haifa University, Swedish School of Economics (Hanken), Tel Aviv University, Stockholm School of Economics, the University of Michigan, and the State University of New York. I felt that the economics of networks is an important field in economics as it applies to a wide variety of industries that influence our life and will even become more influential in this millennium. In addition, it provides some link between consumer behavior and social interaction.

I chose to target this theoretical book for advanced undergraduate and beginning graduate students. I was guided by my belief that there should not be any necessary correlation between mathematical complexity and theoretical precision. That is, the purpose of this book is to bring to the advanced student the basic and the latest developments in this field in a very precise manner, but without resorting to advanced mathematical techniques.

The Level and Prerequisites

My intention is to make this book readable to undergraduates who have some training in intermediate-level microeconomics, although in some cases, such as in engineering school, even this training may not be needed. This course can be taught without using calculus. Occasionally, the student will have to have a very basic knowledge of what probability is and how to calculate the joint probability of two events in discrete spaces. Of course, students who have had a course in industrial organization will be familiar with most of the techniques used in this book, but taking such a course is definitely *not* a prerequisite.

To the Instructor

The instructor will find sufficient material in this book to fill at least a one-semester course, if not an entire year. This book is almost calculus free (all calculus topics could be skipped). All the analysis is game theoretic and therefore the course must start with the teaching of Game Theory given in the three appendices at the end of this book. I recommend spending two lectures on game theory given in Appendices A and B, which constitute the major tools of analysis used in this book. Appendix C defines the Undercut-proof equilibrium (UPE) concept, which is used commonly in this book, and therefore must be taught. Using the UPE facilitates the entire analysis of this book as it allows us to focus on non-calculus discrete models for which a Nash-Bertrand equilibrium does not exist.

It is advisable to follow the book in the order it is written. It is recommended that most sections in Chapter 2 be taught as they provide the basic definitions and the methodology used throughout the book.

At the end of each chapter and appendix, I have provided the student with several exercises. The instructor is strongly urged to assign exercises to students, in particular the exercises appearing at the end of the Game Theory chapters, Appendices A, B, and C. In general, the exercises at the end of each chapter attempt to motivate the student to understand and memorize the basic definitions associated with the various theories developed in that chapter.

Errors, Typos, and Errata Files

My experience with my first book, *Industrial Organization: Theory & Applications,* Cambridge, Mass.: The MIT Press, 1996, has been that it is near to impossible to publish a completely error-free book. Writing a book very much resembles writing a large piece of software. First, all software packages always contain some bugs which the author could not forecast. Second, just like software, 80% of the time is devoted to debugging the software. I will therefore make an effort to publish all errors known to me (if found) in this book.

Thus, errata files will be found on my home page, which is currently http://econ.haifa.ac.il/~ozshy and on the publisher's Internet site (with a link to my updated homepage and email addresses).

Typesetting and Acknowledgments

This book was typeset by the author using the LaTeX 2_ε document preparation software developed by Leslie Lamport (a special version of Donald Knuth's TeX program) and modified by the LaTeX3 Project Team.

The book was typeset during the months from April 1999 to July 2000 and was tested in classes taught at the Swedish School of Economics and Business Administration (Helsinki, Finland) and Haifa University (Haifa, Israel).

As boring as it may sound, the following cliché is the whole truth and nothing but the truth: Without the help of the people listed below, I would not have been able to complete writing this book! Foremost, I thank Sivan Frenkel (a Graduate Student at Haifa University) for reading the entire manuscript throughout the 1999 to 2000 academic year and for providing me with a wide variety of suggestions, corrections, and wise advice. In addition, I thank: Amit Gayer (Haifa University), Ugo Merlone (University of Torino), and Joerg Oechssler (University of Bonn), for most valuable corrections and suggestions during the process of writing this manuscript. I also thank a large number of exceptional international students at the Swedish School of Economics (Hanken) for the patience needed for reading and learning from the first draft of the manuscript during a crash course given in September to October 1999; and my undergraduate students at Haifa University and for their comments and corrections throughout a course delivered during the Fall 1999 semester.

During the preparation of the manuscript, I was very fortunate in working with Scott Parris of Cambridge University Press, to whom I owe many thanks for managing the project in the most efficient way. Scott has been fond of this project for several years, and his interest in this topic encouraged me to go ahead and write this book. Finally, I thank the entire Cambridge University Press team for a fast production of this book.

Haifa, Israel (September, 2000)
ozshy@econ.haifa.ac.il
http://econ.haifa.ac.il/~ozshy

Chapter 1

Introduction to Network Economics

1.1   Overview of Network Industries

This book is about markets. Not really a special type of market, since there are many markets for goods and services that satisfy the characteristics of what we call network products. These markets include the telephone, email, Internet, computer hardware, computer software, music players, music titles, video players, video movies, banking services, airline services, legal services, and many more. This book is also about social interaction and how it affects consumers' choices of products and services they buy.

The main characteristics of these markets which distinguish them from the market for grain, dairy products, apples, and treasury bonds are:

- Complementarity, compatibility and standards.

- Consumption externalities.

- Switching costs and lock-in.

- Significant economies of scale in production.

Complementarity, compatibility and standards

Computers are not useful without having monitors attached, or without having software installed. CD players are not useful without CD titles, just as cameras are not useful without films. Stereo receivers are useless without speakers or headphones, and airline companies will not be able to sell tickets without joining a particular reservation system. All these examples demonstrate that, unlike bread which can be consumed without wine or other types of food, the markets we analyze in this book supply goods that must be consumed together with other products (software and hardware). In the literature of economics, such goods and services are called *complements*. Complementarity means that consumers in these markets are shopping for *systems* (e.g., computers and software, cameras and film, music players and cassettes) rather than individual products. The fact that consumers are buying systems composed of hardware and software or complementary components allows firms to devise all sorts of strategies regarding competition with other firms. A natural question is to ask, for example, is whether firms benefit from designing machines that can work with machines produced by rival firms.

On the technical side, the next question to ask would be how complements are produced? In order to produce complementary products they must be *compatible*. The CD album must have the same specification as CD players, or otherwise it can't be played. A parallel port at the back of each computer must generate the same output voltage as the voltage required for inputting data into a printer attached to this port. Trains must fit on the tracks, and software must be workable with a given operating system. This means that complementary products must operate on the same *standard*. This creates the problem of *coordination* as how firms agree on the standards. The very fact that coordination is needed has the potential of creating some antitrust problems. As in some cases firms may need to coordinate their decisions and while doing that they may find themselves engaging in price fixing.

Complementarity turns to be a crucial factor in the markets for information goods. For example, people who subscribe to the *Private-Pilot* magazine are likely to be interested in fashion clothing catalogs, just like people who read the *New York Times* are likely to be interested in real-estate and interior decoration magazines. Advertising agencies have understood these complementarities for quite some time, and make use of these complementarities to attract more customers. For example, the publishers of real-estate magazines could benefit from purchasing the list of names and addresses of the subscribers to the *New York Times*, and send them sample copies to attract their attention. These information complementarities become more and more important with the increase in the use of the Internet for advertising and shopping purposes. For example, those who browse in commercial Internet sites offering toys for sale, such as www.etoys.com, are likely to be interested in browsing through Internet sites offering children clothing. Thus, the toy sites are likely to sell the list of their site visitors to children clothing stores.

Externalities

The reader should ask herself the following question: Would I subscribe to a telephone service knowing that nobody else subscribes to a telephone service? The answer should be: Of course not! What use will anyone have from having a telephone for which there is no one to talk to? Would people use e-mail knowing that nobody else does? Would people purchase fax machines knowing that nobody else has such a machine? These examples demonstrate that the utility derived from the consumption of these goods is affected by the number of other people using similar or compatible products. Note that this type of externalities is not found in the market for tomatoes, or the market for salt, as the consumption of these goods does not require compatibility with other consumers. Such externalities are sometimes referred to as *adoption or network externalities.*

The presence of these standard-adoption effects can profoundly affect market behavior of firms. The precise nature of the market outcome (e.g., consumers' adoption of a new standard) depends on how consumers form expectations on the size of the network of users. The reliance on joint-consumer expectations generates multiple equilibria where in one equilibrium all consumers adopt the new technology, whereas in the other no one adopts it. Both equilibria are "rational" from the consumers' viewpoint as they reflect the best response to the decisions made by all other consumers in the market. A good example for this behavior is the fax machine, which has been used in the 1950s by flight service stations to transmit weather maps every hour on the hour (transmission of single page took about one hour that time). However, fax machines remained a niche product until the mid-1980s. During a five-year period, the demand and supply of fax machines exploded. Before 1982 almost no one had a fax machine, but after 1987, the majority of businesses had one. The Internet exhibited the same pattern of adoption. The first e-mail message was sent in 1969, but adoption did not take off until the mid-1980s. The Internet did not take off until 1990, however, from 1990 Internet traffic more than doubles every year. All these examples raise a fundamental question, which is when to expect a new technology to catch on. A related question to ask is in the presence of adoption externalities, what should be the minimal number of users (the critical mass) needed for inducing all potential consumers to adopt the technology.

Switching costs and lock-in

Learning to master a particular operating system such as Windows, UNIX, DOS, or a Macintosh takes time (depending on the level of the user). It is an established fact that users are very much annoyed by having to switch between operating systems. To some consumers, switching operating systems is as hard as learning a new language. On the production side, producers heavily depend on the standards used in the production of other components of the system. For example, airline companies rely on spare parts and service provided by aircraft manufacturers. Switching costs are significant in service industries as well. Several estimates provided in this book show that the cost associated with switching between banks (i.e., closing an account in one bank, and opening an account and switching the activities to a different bank) could reach 6 percent of the average account balance. In all of these cases, we say that users are *locked-in*. Of course, lock-in is not an absolute term. The degree of lock-in is found by calculating the cost of switching to a different service or adopting a new technology, since these costs determine the degree in which users are locked in a given technology. We call these costs *switching costs*.

There are several types of switching costs that affect the degree of lock-in. Shapiro and Varian (1999) provide a nice classification of the various lock-ins.

Contracts: Users are sometimes locked into contracts for service, supplying parts, and buying spare parts. Switching costs amount to the damages and compensation that must be paid by the party who breaks the contract.

Training and learning: Consumers are trained to use products operating on a specific standard. Switching costs would include learning and training people, as well as lost productivity resulting from adopting a new system.

Data conversion: Each piece of software generates files that are saved using a particular digital format. Once a new software is introduced, a conversion software may be needed in order to be able to use it. Notice that the resulting switching cost increases over time as the collection of data may grow over time.

Search cost: One reason why people do not switch very often is that they would like to avoid the cost of searching and shopping for new products.

Loyalty cost: Switching technology may result in losing some benefits such as preferred customers' programs, for example, frequent-flyer mileage.

Switching costs affect price competition in two opposing ways. First, if consumers are already locked-in using a specific product, firms may raise prices knowing that consumers will not switch unless the price difference exceeds the switching cost to a competing brand. Second, if consumers are not locked in, brand-producing firms will compete intensively by offering discounts and free complimentary products and services in order to attract consumers who later on will be locked in the technology.

In the presence of switching costs, once the critical mass is achieved and the sales of the product take off, we say that the seller has accumulated an *installed base* of consumers, which is the number of consumers who are locked in the seller's technology. For example, AT&T's installed base is the number of customers subscribing to its long-distance service, where switching costs include the time and trouble associated with switching to, say, MCI's long-distance service.

Significant economies of scale

Software, or more generally any information has the highly noticeable production characteristic in which the production of the first copy involves a huge sunk cost (cost that cannot be recovered), whereas the second copy (third, fourth, and so on) costs almost nothing to reproduce. The cost of gathering the information for the Britannica encyclopedia involves more than one hundred years of research as well as the life-time work of a good number of authors. However, the cost of reproducing it on a set of CDs is less than five dollars. The cost of developing advanced software involves thousands of hours of programming time, however, the software can now be distributed without cost over the Internet. In economic terms, a very high fixed sunk cost, together with almost negligible marginal cost implies that the average cost function declines sharply with the number of copies sold out to consumers. This by itself means that a competitive equilibrium does not exist and that markets of this type will often be characterized by dominant leaders that capture most of the market.

Any student of intermediate microeconomics would clearly identify the major problem associated with modeling these markets, namely, that *these markets cannot function as competitive markets,* where by competitive we take the usual interpretation of price-taking behavior. Therefore the purpose of this book is to develop simple theories that would explain the behavior of companies in these noncompetitive markets.

1.2   Welfare Aspects

1.2.1   Government intervention

From our discussion in Section 1.1 it is clear that competitive equilibria do not exist in markets for network products and services. This implies that the First-Welfare Theorem of classical economics cannot be applied. Moreover, even if a competitive equilibrium exists, the existence of consumption and production externalities would make this theorem inapplicable. Therefore, market failures may occur in these markets.

The distortions leading to these misallocation of resources could be generated by noncompetitive behavior of firms, or by the consumption externalities, for example where the industry standardizes on the Pareto-inferior standard. Despite these market imperfections, while reading this book the reader must bear in mind that the *existence of market failures does not imply that government intervention is needed*. In fact the following examples illustrate that government intervention may make things even worse. The FCC's attempt to impose the CBS color TV standard in 1950 has left 200 consumers with unusable TV sets after the market has rejected the government-chosen standard and switched to NBC's NTSC standard which is used until this very day. For about twenty years the Japanese Ministry of International Trade and Industry (MITI) poured millions of dollars into the research and development of a standard for a high-definition television (HDTV). Finally, in 1990 one station started broadcasting high-definition programs for a few hours every night using MITI's MUSE standard. The MUSE standard suffered from one major problem, namely, that it was an analog standard that has already been considered outdated in the early 1990s. Today, the Japanese are switching to a digital standard. Both of these examples highlight the fact that government intervention can be harmful.

From this discussion, it is clear why government intervention in standard setting is undesirable. Yes, it is true that market failures occur where an industry standardizes on a second-best technology. However, there is no guarantee that government intervention would guarantee a first-best standard selection. In fact, since politicians are financed partly by firms, governments may end up imposing Pareto inferior standards. Therefore, despite the market failures recognized in this book, the reader must bear in mind that the author of this book does *not* advocate government intervention in standard settings!

1.2.2 "Natural" monopolies versus access pricing

It has been argued during the 1950s until the early 1980s, both in the academic world and by policy and decision makers that industries like telephony, mail/post, cable TV, electricity, gas, and transportation are subjected to strong economies of scale production patterns (see for example Section 3.1), and should therefore be termed as *natural monopolies*. The strong academic support for such a view has led governments to license only one company in a given region, and in many cases for the entire country. Thus, until the early 1980s, most counties licensed a single company called *Public Telephone and Telegraph (PTT)*) to provide telephony and mail deliveries. Cable TV in the U.S. and later in other countries followed the same pattern in which cable TV operators were given a geographical territory in which they were allowed to exercise a monopoly power. In order to avoid "excessive" monopoly charges, governments assigned regulating authorities and gave them a full power to determine prices based on production costs.

The major characteristic of natural monopolies is that these industries are subjected to strong economies of scale due to the significant investment in infrastructure needed to start the operation and a very small marginal cost for services produced over the existing infrastructure. More precisely, the idea behind natural monopolies is that it is a social waste to have each competing telephone company wiring its own network into each apartment building, where residents choose different carriers. Similarly, this argument held that it is socially undesirable to have more than one mail carrier reaching each neighborhood.

During the 1970s governments began realizing two major problems with the operations of these regulated service-providing ('natural') monopolies:

(a) Service was relatively poor and was not improving at the pace of technological advance made in these industries. For example, consumers did not benefit from the introduction of fast hand-writing recognizing mail sorters in the sense that delivery time did not improve and stamp prices did not fall.

(b) Regulators failed to control prices and other charges levied on consumers. Due to asymmetric information, the regulators failed to observe the true production cost faced by these service-providing firms, so these firms tended to inflate their reported production costs in order to lobby for high prices.

Thus, over the years governments began realizing that despite the significant economies of scale in production, competition may improve social welfare, or at least consumer welfare, who stand to gain a lot from improved service and reduced prices.

The deregulation of the airline industry in 1979, the 1982 break up of the world largest telephone company, AT&T, in the United States, and the deregulation of these industries in Europe in the 1990s confirmed the view that the introduction of competition into these industries is welfare improving. Moreover, whereas sharp welfare improvement on the consumer side was expected from competition, regulator found out that competition hardly worsened anything on the production side. More precisely, the natural monopoly theory argues that a multi-firm industry is inefficient, since each firm will end up operating on the downward sloping part of its average cost curve due to less than optimal scale of production. However, this prediction on the inefficiency of production of a multi-firm industry turned out to be false. How come? Well, as it turned out the introduction of *access pricing* (see Section 5.3) preserved the efficient large-scale use of existing infrastructure by letting all firms use the existing infrastructure while paying access charges to the firm that owns and maintains the infrastructure.

Access pricing is now practiced in all network industries. MCI, SPRINT, and AT&T pay access charges to local phone companies in the United States for the termination of long-distance phone calls originated by their customers. Airline and railroad companies pay access fees for using airport gates and railroad tracks owned and maintained by competing firms. Norwegian electric-power producers are able to sell electricity to German users by accessing the German infrastructure in order to deliver electricity to German homes and factories. All these examples demonstrate that the introduction of competition did not leave existing and newly constructed infrastructure underutilized. In fact, it turned out that the introduction of competition together with the regulators' demand that the existing infrastructure will be available for use by all competitors for "reasonable" access charges led to even more efficient utilization of infrastructure by having different companies providing substitute or complementary services. All this leads us to conclude that letting industries be controlled by the so-called "natural monopolies" was inefficient. In fact the name itself, natural monopoly, is problematic since a monopoly is one form of market structure that is maintained by government intervention or the persistence of patent rights. Clearly, there is nothing "natural" in the formation of monopolies. Therefore this term is likely to disappear from the language used by regulators and professional and academic economists.

1.3   References and the Scientific Literature

My experience with the writing of my first book (Shy, 1996) has taught me that textbooks must be written by the author, since any attempt to merely "copy" papers published in the scientific journals and use them as chapters in a book just yields messy chapters. The reason for this lies in the fact that scientific papers are written mainly for the scientific community and are, therefore, written in a "different language" that does not fit into textbooks (or anything else).

For this reason, I took the task of simplifying the literature by building completely new models that are not based on calculus (derivatives, integrals, etc.). As the reader will find out, this task is not easy, since discrete price-competition models with heterogeneous consumers generally do *not* have a Nash-Bertrand equilibrium (see Proposition C.1 on page 308 for example). This is perhaps the major reason why economics journals are flooded with calculus-based models utilizing tedious algebra.

Because of that, I also limited the references to this literature made at the end of each chapter only to those which had some influence on the precise method of presentation that suits the potential readers of this book. Thus, the choice of which papers to cite and which not to cite *does not reflect the degree of importance* of the papers. Therefore, I beg the forgiveness of all those large number of researchers whose works are not cited, and ask them to understand that the sole goal of this book is to bring the economics of networks to a wider audience, which includes undergraduate students as well as researchers and graduate students who have a limited technical ability. However, I do wish to refer the interested reader to a large number of survey articles listed at the end of this chapter, and the Internet site `http://raven.stern.nyu.edu/networks`, which provides a complete list of related literature.

Finally, this is perhaps the right place to criticize the scientific literature (including my own) for the language it uses in published papers. After writing two books in the field of Industrial Organization it is clear to me that economists unnecessarily write models using tedious derivations with an unnecessarily large amount of algebra. The prevailing *myth* in the academic economics profession is that *complicated algebra implies that the argument made is **robust***. Obviously, this widespread myth is rather silly and reflects the hypocrisy of our profession. I have two arguments against this prevailing myth: First, there is no such a thing called a robust model. Every model has its assumptions, which limit the applicability of the model. Second, more importantly, I claim that models that rely more on logic and less on algebra are more robust (more general in plain English) than models utilizing long equations with long derivatives exceeding in size the width of the paper they are printed on.

Thus, the arguments made in this book are simple, but they are not less general than the models published in the scientific literature.

1.4   Notation

Notation is classified into two groups: *parameters*, which are numbers that are treated as exogenous by the agents described in the model, and *variables*, which are endogenously determined. Thus, the purpose of every theoretical model is to define an equilibrium concept that yields a unique solution for these variables for given values of the model's parameters.

For example, production costs and consumers' valuations of products are typically described by parameters (constants), which are estimated in the market by econometricians and are taken exogenously by the theoretical economist. In contrast, quantity produced and quantity consumed are classical examples of variables that are endogenously determined meaning that they are solved within the model itself.

We now set the rule for assigning notation to parameters and variables. *Parameters are denoted by **Greek** letters, whereas variables are denoted by **English** letters.*

After setting this rule, we adhere to the famous statement that *all rules are meant to be broken* and state a few exceptions. For example, π will denote a firm's profit level, despite the fact that profit levels are variables that are endogenously-solved for within a specified model. After breaking all rules, Table 1.1 on page 12 provides some indication of the notation used throughout this book.

1.5   Selected References

Besen, S., and J. Farrell. 1994. "Choosing How to Compete: Strategies and Tactics in Standardization." *Journal of Economic Perspectives* 2: 117–131.

David, P., and S. Greenstein. 1990. "The Economics of Compatibility Standards: An Introduction to Recent Research." *Economics of Innovation and New Technology* 1: 3–41.

Economides, N. 1996. "The Economics of Networks." *International Journal of Industrial Organization* 14: 673–699.

Farrell, J., and G. Saloner. 1987. "The Economics of Horses, Penguins, and Lemmings." In *Production Standardization and Competitive Strategies*, edited by L. G. Gable. Amsterdam: North-Holland.

Gilbert, R. 1992. "Symposium on Compatibility." *Journal of Industrial Economics* 40: 1–8.

Katz, M., and C. Shapiro. 1994. "Systems Competition and Network Effects." *Journal of Economic Perspectives* 2: 93–115.

Kindleberger, C. 1983. "Standards as Public, Collective and Private Goods." *KYKLOS* 36: 377–396.

Leibowitz, S., and S. Margolis. 1994. "Network Externality: An Uncommon Tragedy." *Journal of Economic Perspectives* 2: 133–150.

Shapiro, C., and H. Varian. 1999. *Information Rules: A Strategic Guide to the Network Economy.* Boston: Harvard Business School Press.

Shy, O. 1996. *Industrial Organization: Theory and Applications.* Cambridge, Mass.: MIT Press.

Parameters

Notation	Greek	Interpretation
λ	lambda	number of firms in an industry
ϕ	phi	fixed or sunk production cost
μ	mu	unit production cost
ψ	psi	productivity parameter
ρ	rho	revenue per customer
η	eta	a given population size
β	beta	basic utility derived from a product
α	alpha	intensity of the network externality
ω	omega	a consumer's income (wage)
τ	tau	a particular time period (e.g., $t = \tau$)
ϵ	epsilon	probability or a small number
δ	delta	differentiation (or switching) cost

Variables

t		time period (e.g., $t = 1, 2, \ldots$)
U		utility level of a single consumer
e		a consumer's expenditure
π_i	pi	profit level of firm i
p_i/f_i		price/fee charged by firm i
q_i		quantity produced by a firm i
Q		aggregate industry output
W		social welfare

Symbols

$=$		equals by derivation
$\overset{\text{def}}{=}$		equals by definition
$\approx$		approximately equal
$\neg$		not (negation)
$\Longrightarrow$		implies that
$\Longleftrightarrow$		if and only if
Δ	Delta	a change in a variable/parameter
∂		partial derivative
$\longrightarrow$		approaches (converges) to
$\in$		is an element of the set
$\blacksquare$		end-of-proof (QED)

Table 1.1: General notation for parameters, variables, and symbols.

Chapter 2

The Hardware Industry

A computer is an electrical machine that can both process and store information. The information may consist of numbers, words, or both. Thus, the computer performs a wide variety of services controlled by inputting commands initiated by the users. The most commonly used inputting methods are keyboard and pointing device (e.g., a mouse).

The computer system is composed of hardware and software. Hardware consists of printed circuits, CPU (Central Processing Unit), memory chips, storage devices, connection ports, keyboards, printers, scanners, and monitors. Software consists of digital bits downloaded onto the storage devices. All pieces of hardware connected to the main unit, which houses the CPU, are called *peripherals*.

Software is sold in packages that are designed to perform different tasks commanded by the user(s) of the computer. One piece of software is called the *operating system*. This piece of software is crucial to the operation of the computer, as it acts as an interpreter between the machine (actually the machine language) and the wide variety of software that are designed to perform specific tasks.

Computers first began to be commercially used in the early 1950s. Computers first began to be widely used at home (therefore were given the name *personal computers*, or *PC*s) in the late 1970s with the introduction of the Apple II by Apple Computers. Earlier brands existed before the Apple II, but were not adopted on a large scale. The Apple II was the first personal computer to be supported by over 500 software packages written specifically for its operating system. The market for personal computers was further expanded with the introduction of the IBM PC in 1981 operated by Microsoft's Disk Operating System (DOS) and later on, in 1984, by the Apple Macintosh operated by its own GUI (Graphical User Interface) operating system, which was incompatible with all other operating systems. By the mid 1990s 40 percent of the households in developed countries owned at least one personal computer. Gabel (1991) provides an extended economic history of the personal-computer industry.

Our analysis of the computer industry utilizes three approaches: the network externalities approach (Section 2.2, see also Sections 4.1 and 4.2 in Chapter 4), the components approach (Section 2.3), and the software approach (see Chapter 3). In each approach we will investigate how compatibility affects prices, profits, consumers' utilities, and social welfare.

Each investigation will be carried out separately under monopoly and duopoly market structures in the market for hardware. It is, therefore, important to understand how consumers function under these two market structures. Under monopoly, only one brand is produced. Therefore, when we want to analyze heterogeneous consumers we will assume that consumers place different values on compatibility features. In contrast, when we analyze a duopoly market, we will assume that heterogeneous consumers are those who have different preferences for the different brands. Obviously, this makes the analysis of a duopoly market structure much more realistic. However, the monopoly analysis is still needed mainly in order to introduce the reader to the main definitions and methodology used throughout this book. Thus, under duopoly we assume that each consumer has her "ideal" brand that she likes, so when she is provided with her less preferred brand her utility is reduced by a parameter which we call δ. This parameter can be interpreted in various ways. However, the most widely used interpretation is that δ measures the *switching cost* associated with switching from one operating system to another (Klemperer, 1987). The very existence of switching costs is what gives brand-producing firms some monopoly power, which prevents prices from falling to the unit production cost. For example, users of the Apple Macintosh operating system will find it hard to handle the Windows operating system. The time and effort it takes to train a worker to use a new operating system constitutes the major part of consumer switching costs in the market for computers. In this case, we say that consumers are *locked-in*. Switching costs are not unique to computers. Music lovers found themselves in a dilemma: what to do with the old LP records when the CD digital players were introduced in the late 1980s? The cost of switching from one music system to another is significant for record collectors. The same kind of switching costs applies to the currently shifting standards in home video equipment where the DVD technology competes with the older VHS cassette recording/playing equipment. Chapter 8 will introduce the reader to switching costs associated with switching from one bank to another.

2.1 Hardware Compatibility

The computer industry is called a network industry precisely because the issue of compatibility is most important for the marketing and operations of computer brands in this market. We first need to define what do we mean by compatibility.

DEFINITION 2.1
We say that two machines are **compatible** *if they can work together. Otherwise, we say that the machines are* **incompatible**.

Definition 2.1 is probably too general to be useful reflecting the fact that there is a wide variety of reasons why two machines may or may not be able to work together. In other words, we must be clear in what we mean by stating that machines can "work together." Do we mean that the machines are (perfect) substitutes, and/or do we mean that they can interact with complementary products such as software and the Internet?

The following list demonstrates the complexity of achieving compatibility (or incompatibility) in the computer industry.

- Two pieces of computer hardware may be called compatible if they run the same software. More precisely, compatibility means that every software package written for one machine can be run on a machine with a different brand name, and vice versa. This definition is rather strong since it generally requires that the two machines are running on the same operating system.

- A somewhat weaker definition of compatibility would be to say that two machines are compatible if the *files* generated by the software running one machine can be read and processed by software running on a machine with a different brand name.

- Another weak definition of compatibility would be to say that two machines are compatible if they can be linked to the same storage devices, same printers, etc.

This list demonstrates that the main difficulty of defining compatibility lies in the fact that there can be different degrees of compatibility. For example, one computer brand may run only a fraction of the software designed for the competing brand. In addition, with the introduction of the Internet, most machines are capable of connecting to the same Internet sites (running languages such as HTML, Acrobat, and Java) which makes them somewhat compatible even if they are running on different operating systems.

We therefore need some more precise definitions for the various types of compatibility.

DEFINITION 2.2
(a) *Computer hardware brands are said to be* **strongly compatible** *if they use the same operating system. In this case, we say that the brands operate on the same* **standard***.*

(b) *Brands are said to be* **downward compatible** *if a newer model is compatible with an older model, but not necessarily the other way around.*

(c) *Brands are* **one-way compatible** *if one machine can read the files generated by a competing machine, but not the other way around.*

2.2   The Network Externalities Approach

All computer users find compatibility to be a highly desirable property. Compatibility constitutes the second major factor (after the price) in determining which type of PC to buy. For example, by the mid 1990s, 90 percent of the PCs in the world were operated by the Windows operating system. The dominance of one operating system has no parallel in other industries, reflecting perhaps the fact that consumers value compatibility in the PC market much more than in other industries, such as the automobile market where no car producer maintains such a high (near monopoly) market share.

One way to model consumers' desire for compatibility of the PCs they purchase is to assume that their preferences exhibit network externalities.

DEFINITION 2.3
Consumers' preferences are said to exhibit **network externalities** *if the utility of each consumer increases with an increase in the total number of consumers purchasing the same or a compatible brand.*

The assumption of network externalities *approximates* consumers' desire for compatibility in the sense that instead of defining consumers' utility directly on the degree of compatibility of the machines they purchase and the compatibility of the machines used by other people they tend to associate with (or work with), the utility of consumers is simply defined by the *number of consumers* using the same or compatible brands.

There is a substantial amount of literature on network externalities, see for example Katz and Shapiro (1985, 1986, 1992, 1994), and Farrell and Saloner (1985, 1986). Before we begin with the analytical analysis, we need to discuss what are the major issues and questions that we expect to explain and for which we expect to find answers. In the following subsections we would like to develop artificial environments where the preferences of computer users exhibit network externalities that would assist in finding answers for the following questions:

Q1. How does an increase in brand compatibility affect prices and profit levels of brand-producing firms?

Q2. How does an increase in brand compatibility affect the utility of users and social welfare?

Q3. How does varying the market structure affect the degree of compatibility and the pricing of differentiated brands? More precisely, will an increase in the number of brand-producing firms increase brand compatibility, and/or prices?

The following subsections attempt to provide answers for these questions in monopoly and duopoly market structures.

2.2.1 Monopoly selling a single brand to identical consumers

Monopoly pricing strategy in the presence of network externalities has been examined in Cabral, Salant, and Woroch (1999). We begin our analysis by looking at a market with a single producer of computers, selling to identical computer users who all value compatibility.

A natural question to ask now is why compatibility has a value in a market with only one brand? It is true that if there is only one brand in the market, then all computers run on the same operating system, and are therefore considered to be compatible. However, even if all machines run on the same operating system, compatibility can be achieved only if the machines can be linked either via cables linked to communication ports (directly or via the Internet), or linked via the transfer of storage media such as diskettes and movable hard drives. In order to be more general, we will refer to such devices as *adapters*. Thus, in the monopoly case we interpret the compatibility feature of a computer as the installation of an adapter that will enable any two machines to communicate and work together. Clearly, the installation of adapters increases the production cost of computers, so computer producers often find adapters unprofitable to install.

Computer buyers

There are η identical potential computer users who all value compatibility. Each consumer buys at most one computer. Thus, denoting by $q \geq 0$ the quantity sold by the monopoly, q also denotes the actual number of computer buyers. Let p denote the price of a computer. The utility function of each consumer is given by

$$U \stackrel{\text{def}}{=} \begin{cases} \beta - p + \alpha q & \text{adapter installed} \\ \beta - p & \text{adapter not installed} \\ 0 & \text{does not purchase a computer,} \end{cases} \tag{2.1}$$

where $\beta > 0$ is interpreted as the "basic" utility each consumer derives from using a computer regardless of compatibility. The parameter α (multiplying the total number of computer users, q) measures the degree of importance of compatibility. Thus, the product αq (the utility from network externalities) measures the total utility gain from having a machine with an adapter that can communicate with the total of q machines sold in this market.

Technology

We make the following assumption.

ASSUMPTION 2.1
The monopoly computer producer can produce only one type of computer, i.e., either with or without an adapter, but not both types.

Assumption 2.1 reflects a situation where machines are produced on a single assembly line so production cannot be decomposed into two types of machines. Obviously, in reality this assumption is often violated as manufacturers offer different packages with different storage devices (such as CD-ROM and DVD drives) and communication ports (such as RS-232, SCSI, and Universal). However, it should be pointed out that the provision of compatibility requires much more than just attaching an adapter. We will therefore assume that the cost of redesigning a machine is prohibitive. That is, converting a machine from incompatibility to compatibility is impossible.

In our analysis we ignore sunk and fixed costs that may be associated with the development of the machine. Instead, we will focus on unit production cost of a machine. We therefore denote by μ_c the unit production cost of a machine equipped with all the adapters needed to make it compatible with all other machines. We also denote by μ_n the unit cost of a machine with *no compatibility features*. Then, we assume that $\mu_c \geq \mu_n \geq 0$, meaning that the production of an adapter is costly. Altogether, Assumption 2.1 implies that if the monopoly produces q units, its total production cost is given by

$$TC(q) \stackrel{\text{def}}{=} \begin{cases} \mu_c q & \text{if producing compatible machines} \\ \mu_n q & \text{if producing incompatible machines.} \end{cases} \tag{2.2}$$

Timing of decisions

We assume that the producer makes decisions in a sequential manner divided into three stages.

Stage I (Design): when the computer is designed, the manufacturer decides whether to make the machine compatible or incompatible with other machines by deciding whether or not to install the adapter at an additional cost of $\mu_c - \mu_n$ per machine.

Stage II (Pricing): the machine's design is taken as given and the manufacturer chooses a uniform price which we denote by p.

Stage III (Consumers): each consumer decides whether to purchase one machine or not to purchase at all. In making this decision, each consumer treats the total number of computer users, q as given. After consumers' purchase decisions are made, the monopoly collects its revenue from consumers and profit is realized.

Thus, we have just defined a three-stage extensive-form game where the monopoly gets to move in the first and second stages, whereas the consumers move in the third stage only. We look for a Subgame-Perfect Equilibrium, see Definition B.4 on page 303. As explained in Appendix B, we solve this game *backward* by solving stage III, then stage II, and lastly stage I.

Expectations and coordination issues

Our assumption that each consumer observes how many consumers purchase a computer must be formalized.

DEFINITION 2.4
We say that consumers have a **perfect foresight** *if, at the time of purchase, they can correctly anticipate how many consumers will buy a computer (in the present monopoly case), and how many will buy each brand (in an oligopoly case).*

Definition 2.4 raises two issues that must be discussed. First, in the literature the assumption of perfect foresight is often associated with *coordination* where perfect foresight is viewed as having all consumers agreeing whether to buy or not, say following a supporting review of the product in consumers' magazines. Second, the assumption of perfect foresight often generates multiple equilibria in the sense that there may exist two equilibria: one in which no consumer buys a machine $(q = 0)$, and another in which some consumers buy a machine $(q > 0)$. We, therefore, must formalize this issue of coordination.

DEFINITION 2.5
Suppose that the following conditions are satisfied:

(a) *there exists more than one perfect foresight equilibrium, and*

(b) *in the equilibrium where a group of consumers buys the product* $(q > 0)$, *the utility of each buyer exceeds the utility each consumer gains in the equilibrium when no one buys the product* $(q = 0)$.

Then, we say that the equilibrium where $q = 0$ *is characterized by a* **coordination failure**.

Unless assumed otherwise, the analyses in this book will rely on the following assumption.

ASSUMPTION 2.2
(a) *Consumers have perfect foresight (Definition 2.4).*

(b) *There is no coordination failure (Definition 2.5).*

Stage III: Consumers' purchasing decisions

At this stage, each consumer observes three variables: (1) whether or not the manufacturer has installed adapters (hence, whether the machines sold in the market are compatible with other machines); (2) the price, p; and (3) the total number of consumers buying a computer, q.

Suppose first that the computer is produced with no compatibility features. Then, (2.1) implies that the total number of buyers is

$$q = \begin{cases} \eta & \text{if } p \le \beta \\ 0 & \text{if } p > \beta. \end{cases} \tag{2.3}$$

The reader may wonder why consumers bother to purchase the computer at all as (2.3) implies that when $p = \beta$ consumers gain zero utility, regardless whether they purchase or not. However, the reader will soon realize that this is not really a problem, since if consumers choose not to purchase the machine, the monopoly can lower its price to $p = \beta - \epsilon$, where $\epsilon > 0$ is a small number (could be the smallest currency denomination, e.g., 1¢), thereby inducing all consumers to purchase the machine with a strict utility gain. Since this issue will repeat itself throughout the book, we introduce the following assumption:

ASSUMPTION 2.3
If a consumer is indifferent between buying or not buying, then he will buy the machine.

Now, suppose that the monopoly producer installs adapters in each machine, thereby making all machines *compatible*. Then, (2.1) implies that total number of buyers is

$$q = \begin{cases} \eta & \text{if } p \le \beta + \alpha\eta \\ 0 & \text{if } p > \beta + \alpha\eta. \end{cases} \tag{2.4}$$

Equation (2.4) constitutes a unique consumer equilibrium only under Assumptions 2.2 and 2.3. To see this, suppose that Assumption 2.2 is violated. Then, with lack of coordination it is possible that consumers expect nobody to purchase computers, that is $q = 0$. In this case, (2.4) is exactly (2.3) since compatibility does not play a role.

Stage II: Monopoly selects a price

In this stage, the monopoly selects a profit-maximizing price subject to consumers' demand functions, (2.3) if the machines are incompatible, and subject to (2.4) if the machines are compatible.

If the machines are incompatible, (2.3) applies and the monopoly's profit maximizing price is $p = \beta$, yielding a total profit of

$$\pi_n = (\beta - \mu_n)\eta. \tag{2.5}$$

If the machines are compatible, (2.4) applies and the total profit of the monopoly as a function of price is

$$\pi_c = (\beta + \alpha\eta - \mu_c)\eta. \tag{2.6}$$

Stage I: Monopoly compatibility decision

In the first stage, the monopoly decides how to design its machine, knowing that installing compatibility adapters would raise the production cost by $\Delta\mu = \mu_c - \mu_n$, but would enable raising the price by $\alpha\eta$.

For making the compatibility decision, the monopoly needs only to compare (2.5) with (2.6). Therefore, the monopoly will produce compatible machines if

$$(\beta + \alpha\eta - \mu_c)\eta \geq (\beta - \mu_n)\eta. \qquad (2.7)$$

Equation (2.7) reveals that an increase in the network externality parameter α, or a increase in the number of consumers will increase the parameter range where the monopoly will choose to design a compatible machine. Finally, (2.7) can be simplified to

$$\Delta\mu = \mu_c - \mu_n \leq \alpha\eta. \qquad (2.8)$$

The simple interpretation for (2.8) is that producing compatible machines is profitable if the cost difference does not exceed the gain from compatibility.

Is there a market failure?

A natural question to ask at this point is whether a monopoly reduces social welfare by either not providing compatibility adapters, or by providing them when it is not socially optimal to do so. More precisely, any student in introductory economics is well aware of the fact that monopoly is welfare reducing, since it charges a high price thereby selling fewer than optimal units. However, this fact does *not* necessarily imply that a monopoly distorts social welfare by failing to install adapters or installing adapters when their social cost exceeds social benefit.

We first define the society's social welfare by summing up consumers' utilities and the monopoly's profit. Thus, in the present case, $W = \eta U + \pi$.

Suppose that the social planner decides on making *incompatible* machines. Then, social welfare is given by

$$W_n = \eta U + \pi = \eta(\beta - p) + \eta(p - \mu_n) = \eta(\beta - \mu_n). \qquad (2.9)$$

Notice that prices canceled out in the welfare function (2.9). This is not a coincidence and should always happen when one calculates the welfare level of an economy. The reason for it is that firms' revenues must always equal total consumer expenditure, and, since the firms are owned by consumers, prices reflect only a transfer from consumers to firms (and then from firms to consumers via profit distribution). Hence, the first term in (2.9) measures consumers' aggregate utility and the last term measures aggregate economy production costs.

Now suppose that the social planner designs the machines to be *compatible* machines. Then, social welfare is given by

$$W_c = \eta U + \pi = \eta(\beta + \alpha\eta - p) + \eta(p - \mu_c) = \eta(\beta + \alpha\eta - \mu_c). \qquad (2.10)$$

Comparing (2.9) with (2.10) yields that compatibility is socially preferred if

$$\Delta\mu \stackrel{\text{def}}{=} \mu_c - \mu_n \le \alpha\eta. \tag{2.11}$$

Hence,

Proposition 2.1
A monopoly selling computers to identical consumers will install compatibility adapters if and only if it is socially optimal to do so.

This result is not surprising as it resembles a finding in Swan (1970) which demonstrates that a monopoly lightbulb producer would not have the incentive to shorten the durability of lightbulbs below the socially optimal level even if durability is costly to produce. The reason is that a monopoly uses the price mechanism to extract extra rent, but regarding the choice of technology the monopoly solves the same technology choice problem as the social planner. In what follows, we demonstrate that this result does not hold if consumers have different preferences for compatibility and if the monopoly cannot price discriminate between the different types of consumers.

2.2.2 Monopoly selling a single brand to heterogeneous consumers

We proceed by analyzing a market with a single producer of computers, selling to heterogeneous computer users who differ only with respect to how much they value compatibility.

There are 2η potential computer users who are divided into two groups: those who value compatibility and those who "work alone" and therefore do not use the compatibility features even if the adapter is preinstalled. Thus, the potential consumers are composed of η (type c) consumers who value compatibility, and η (type n) consumers who do not value compatibility.

Each consumer buys at most one computer. Thus, denoting by $q \ge 0$ the quantity sold by the monopoly, q also denotes the actual number of computer buyers. The utility function of each consumer type is given by

$$U_c \stackrel{\text{def}}{=} \begin{cases} \beta - p + \alpha q & \text{adapter installed} \\ \beta - p & \text{adapter not installed} \\ 0 & \text{does not purchase a computer,} \end{cases} \tag{2.12}$$

and

$$U_n \stackrel{\text{def}}{=} \begin{cases} \beta - p & \text{purchase any machine} \\ 0 & \text{does not purchase a computer,} \end{cases}$$

where $\beta > 0$ is interpreted as the "basic" utility each consumer derives from using a computer regardless of compatibility. The parameter α (multiplying the total number of computer users, q) measures the degree of importance of compatibility to type c consumers. Thus, the product αq is the total utility gain from having a machine with an adapter that can communicate with q machines sold in this market. Finally, unit costs are the same as in (2.2), and the timing of decisions is also the same as before.

Stage III: Consumers' purchase decisions

Suppose first that the computer is produced with no compatibility features. Then, (2.12) implies that total number of buyers is

$$q = \begin{cases} 2\eta & \text{if } p \le \beta \\ 0 & \text{if } p > \beta. \end{cases} \tag{2.13}$$

Now, suppose that the monopoly producer installs adapters in each machine, thereby making all machines *compatible*. Then, (2.12) implies that total number of buyers is

$$q = \begin{cases} 2\eta & \text{if } p \le \beta \\ \eta & \text{if } \beta < p \le \beta + \alpha\eta \\ 0 & \text{if } p > \beta + \alpha\eta. \end{cases} \tag{2.14}$$

Stage II: Monopoly selects a price

In this stage, the monopoly selects a profit-maximizing price subject to consumers' demand functions, (2.13) if the machines are incompatible, and (2.4) if the machines are compatible.

If the machine are incompatible, (2.3) applies and the monopoly's profit maximizing price is $p = \beta$, yielding a profit of

$$\pi_n = (\beta - \mu_n)2\eta. \tag{2.15}$$

If the machines are compatible, (2.14) applies and the profit of the monopoly as a function of price is

$$\pi_c = \begin{cases} (\beta + \alpha\eta - \mu_c)\eta & \text{if } p = \beta + \alpha\eta \\ (\beta - \mu_c)2\eta & \text{if } p = \beta. \end{cases} \tag{2.16}$$

Stage I: Monopoly compatibility decision

In the first stage, the monopoly decides how to design its machine, knowing that installing compatibility adapters would raise the production cost by $\Delta\mu \overset{\text{def}}{=} \mu_c - \mu_n$.

Comparing (2.15) with the second part of (2.16) reveals that the monopoly will never design the machine to be compatible and charge only $p = \beta$, as there is no point in investing in compatibility if consumers are not required to pay for it. Hence, in making its compatibility decision, the monopoly need only compare (2.15) with the first part of (2.16). Therefore, the monopoly will produce compatible machines if

$$(\beta + \alpha\eta - \mu_c)\eta \geq (\beta - \mu_n)2\eta. \tag{2.17}$$

Equation (2.17) reveals that an increase in the network externality parameter α will increase the parameter range where the monopoly will choose to design a compatible machine. Finally, (2.17) can be simplified to

$$\mu_c \leq \alpha\eta - \beta + 2\mu_n. \tag{2.18}$$

which has the interpretation that compatibility is profitable if the cost of making one compatible machine does not exceed the gain in revenue by increasing the price for the consumers seeking compatibility, $\alpha\eta$, minus the loss from giving up on the other consumers, β plus the "saving" made by not producing twice as many incompatible machines.

Is there a market failure?

A natural question to ask at this point is whether a monopoly reduces social welfare by over- or under-provision of compatibility adapters. Again, we define the society's social welfare by summing up consumers' utilities and the monopoly's profit.

Suppose that the social planner decides on making *incompatible* machines. Then, social welfare is given by

$$
\begin{aligned}
W_n &= \eta U_c + \eta U_n + \pi \tag{2.19}\\
&= \eta(\beta - p) + \eta(\beta - p) + 2\eta(p - \mu_n) = 2\eta(\beta - \mu_n).
\end{aligned}
$$

Now, suppose that the social planner decides on making *compatible* machines, and selling them to *all* consumers! Then, social welfare is given by

$$
\begin{aligned}
W_c &= \eta U_c + \eta U_n + \pi \tag{2.20}\\
&= \eta[\beta + \alpha(\eta + \eta) - p] + \eta(\beta - p) + 2\eta(p - \mu_c) = 2\eta(\beta + \alpha\eta - \mu_c).
\end{aligned}
$$

Comparing (2.19) with (2.20) yields that compatibility is socially preferred if

$$\mu_c \leq \alpha\eta + \mu_n. \tag{2.21}$$

The conditions given in (2.18) and (2.21) are drawn in Figure 2.1, which

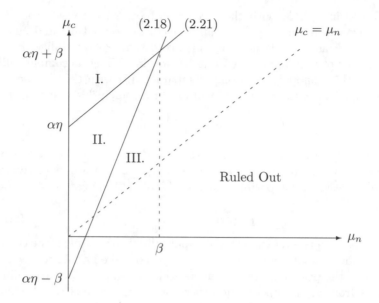

Figure 2.1: Possible market failure due to underprovision of compatibility.

divides the μ_n—μ_c space into three regions: In region I, the unit cost of producing compatible machines is very high comparing to incompatible machines, hence both the social planner and the monopoly will choose incompatibility. Region III reflects the exact opposite extreme, where the cost of producing compatible machines is not very high, in which case both the social planner and the monopoly will choose compatibility. In contrast, region II illustrates a parameter range where a market failure occurs since the monopoly will choose to produce incompatible machines, but compatibility is socially optimal. Hence,

Proposition 2.2
When consumers are not identical, a market failure may occur when a monopoly producer does not provide compatibility but compatibility is socially preferred to incompatibility.

The reason for this failure is that the monopoly cannot price discriminate between the two groups of consumers, hence it fails to induce the compatibility independent consumer to buy the machine and enhance the utility of the compatibility-oriented consumers. More precisely, the monopoly cannot charge a price of β to the consumers who do not value compatibility and a price of $\beta + \alpha 2\eta$ to consumers who value compatibility since the monopoly cannot identify the precise type of each consumer.

2.2.3   Duopoly selling differentiated brands to heterogeneous consumers

Consider a duopoly (two-firm) computer industry producing two brands named *Artichoke* (Brand A), and *Banana* (Brand B). Assume zero production cost for each brand producing firm, and let p_A denote the price charged by Artichoke, and p_B the price charged by Banana.

We model *heterogeneous consumers* who have different orientation (utility) towards the different brands. Notice that consumer heterogeneity here is different from the consumer heterogeneity assumed in the monopoly case analyzed in Section 2.2.2. In the monopoly case, consumers were able to purchase only a single brand, so heterogeneity was assumed to be in different preferences toward compatibility.

In contrast, in this section we assume that all consumers value compatibility in the same way, however consumers have different preferences toward using the different computer brands. Suppose that the 2η potential consumers are divided into two types: η consumers are called brand A-oriented consumers, whereas the remaining η consumers are called brand B-oriented consumers. Formally, the utility of A-oriented and B-oriented consumers are given by

$$
U_A \stackrel{\text{def}}{=}
\begin{cases}
\alpha q_A - p_A & \text{buys } A \text{ ; } A \text{ is incompatible} \\
\alpha q_B - p_B - \delta & \text{buys } B \text{ ; } B \text{ is incompatible} \\
\alpha(q_A + q_B) - p_A & \text{buys } A \text{ ; } A \text{ is } B\text{-compatible} \\
\alpha(q_A + q_B) - p_B - \delta & \text{buys } B \text{ ; } B \text{ is } A\text{-compatible,}
\end{cases}
\tag{2.22}
$$

and

$$
U_B \stackrel{\text{def}}{=}
\begin{cases}
\alpha q_A - p_A - \delta & \text{buys } A \text{ ; } A \text{ is incompatible} \\
\alpha q_B - p_B & \text{buys } B \text{ ; } B \text{ is incompatible} \\
\alpha(q_A + q_B) - p_A - \delta & \text{buys } A \text{ ; } A \text{ is } B\text{-compatible} \\
\alpha(q_A + q_B) - p_B & \text{buys } B \text{ ; } B \text{ is } A\text{-compatible.}
\end{cases}
$$

Thus, a consumer who is oriented toward brand i has a disutility of δ if she is buying her less preferred brand, brand j, where $i, j = A, B$, $i \neq j$. The exogenously-given parameter δ is referred to as the *tastes' disutility parameter*, or the *transportation-cost parameter* (since these types of models are also used to describe consumers' choice among stores with different locations).

A natural question to ask is why computer users have different preferences toward the different brands even if the machines may be compatible? There are several answers to this question.

(a) Some users, such as the author of this book, prefer to use portable machines (laptops) rather than full-size machines (desktops). This distinction depends on whether users tend to travel a lot on business. But the point we are making here is that brands can still be differentiated in the eyes of consumers despite the fact that the brands may operate on the same operating system. Thus, the issue of compatibility (which is related to operating systems) is independent of whether users have preferences for laptops or desktops.

(b) Consumers who are engaged in number crunching prefer to use fast processors, whereas consumers who use computers mainly for word processing can settle for slower processors. This distinction was visible in the late 1980s and early 1990s where manufacturers offered for sale computers with or without math co-processors for the different consumer groups.

(c) Some consumers may prefer to use graphic-oriented computers whereas others prefer to use text-based operating systems. This distinction was highly visible during the 1980s with the introduction of the Apple Macintosh computer based on GUI (Graphical User Interface), which was very different from the DOS-based machines running on the Intel chip. In the late 1990s, this difference was diminished to a minimum, and is expected to become insignificant.

The parameter $\alpha > 0$ which multiplies the relevant network size in (2.22) retains its original interpretation which is the degree of importance of compatibility to consumers. Thus, a computer i user enjoys a network utility of αq_i if machine i is incompatible with machine j, and $\alpha(q_A + q_B)$ if machine i is compatible with j.

Finally, in order to be able to solve for an equilibrium where some consumers buy computer brand A and others buy brand B, we need to make the machines sufficiently differentiated from each other in the eyes of users. Formally,

ASSUMPTION 2.4
The brand differentiation effects in consumers' preferences has a stronger influence on utility than the network sizes. Formally, $\delta > \alpha\eta$.

Assumption 2.4 implies that although the network effects imply that all users are better off when all other users use the same brand, users' preferences for a specific brand still dominate these network effects. Note that if Assumption 2.4 is reversed, in equilibrium all consumers will end up buying the same brand since in that case the network effects dominate consumers' desire for differentiation.

Before we proceed, we would like to avoid modeling a situation where each consumer has market power in the sense that a shift of *one and only one* consumer from consuming one brand to another will affect the relative utilities gained by *other* consumers.

ASSUMPTION 2.5
Let there be q_A Artichoke buyers, and q_B Banana buyers. Then, each consumer treats q_A and q_B as constants which are invariant with respect to her own choice of which brand to purchase.

Assumption 2.5 is justified by the fact that the markets we analyze have a large number of consumers.

Equilibrium when both machines are incompatible

We look for a Nash-Bertrand equilibrium defined in Definition A.4 on page 292. *Unfortunately,* Proposition C.1 on page 308 in Appendix C demonstrates that a Nash-Bertrand equilibrium does not exist in this type of environment.

We therefore look for a pair of prices constituting an *Undercut-Proof equilibrium (UPE)*, see Appendix C. However, before we proceed we need to slightly modify our definition of undercutting (Definition C.1 on page 309) in order to take into account how consumers are affected by the change in the relative network sizes once undercutting takes place.

DEFINITION 2.6
Suppose that initially, η users use computer brand i and η users use computer brand j, where $i, j = A, B$, $i \neq j$. Let p_A and p_B denote brands' prices. Then, brand i producer **undercuts** *brand j producer, if $p_i < p_j - \delta + \alpha\eta$.*

Thus, in order to attract brand j users, brand i producer must reduce its price below its competitor so that the transportation cost δ is subsidized. However, the price can be raised by $\alpha\eta$ since brand j users are joining a network of 2η users compared to a network of only η users.

Definition C.2 on page 309 states that a pair of prices $\langle p_A^U, p_B^U \rangle$ constitutes an UPE if the following conditions are simultaneously satisfied:

(a) For given p_B^U, firm A chooses the highest price p_A^U subject to

$$\pi_B^U = p_B^U \eta \geq (p_A - \delta + \alpha\eta)2\eta.$$

(b) For given p_A^U, firm B chooses the highest price p_B^U subject to

$$\pi_A^U = p_A^U \eta \geq (p_B - \delta + \alpha\eta)2\eta.$$

Hence, equilibrium prices and profit levels given by

$$p_A^U = p_B^U = 2(\delta - \alpha\eta) \quad \text{and} \quad \pi_A^U = \pi_B^U = 2\eta(\delta - \alpha\eta). \qquad (2.23)$$

Therefore,

Proposition 2.3
When users' preferences exhibit network externalities, and if computer brands are differentiated and incompatible, then

(a) *prices and profit levels decline with an increase in consumers' preference toward the network size, i.e. an increase in α;*

(b) *prices and profit levels increase with the degree of differentiation between the machines.*

Thus, when machines are incompatible, an increase in users' desire for compatibility *intensifies* competition and therefore results in reduced prices and profits. Proposition 2.3 is very important since it highlights the effects consumers' desire for compatibility has on price competition when brands are incompatible. As α increases, consumers' choice of which brand to buy becomes more sensitive to the expected network of buyers of each brand. This increases firms' incentives to undercut the rival firm. Hence, firms must reduce prices in order to avoid being undercut. As a result, an increase in consumers' desire for compatibility improves consumer welfare at the expense of firms' reduction in profits. This can be seen by computing users' utility under incompatibility. Thus,

$$U_A = U_B = \alpha\eta - 2(\delta - \alpha\eta) = 3\alpha\eta - 2\delta, \qquad (2.24)$$

which indeed increases with α.

Equilibrium when both machines are compatible

When both machines are compatible, all computer users are exposed to a network of size 2η *regardless* which computer they purchase. That is, under compatibility each consumer gains network utility of $\alpha 2\eta$ regardless of how consumers are allocated between the brands. Hence, their purchase decision is *unaffected* by the network effects. Thus, a pair of prices $\langle p_A^U, p_B^U \rangle$ constitutes an UPE if the following conditions are simultaneously satisfied:

$$\pi_B^U = p_B^U \eta \geq (p_A^U - \delta)2\eta$$
$$\pi_A^U = p_A^U \eta \geq (p_B^U - \delta)2\eta.$$

Hence, equilibrium prices and profit levels given by

$$p_A^U = p_B^U = 2\delta \quad \text{and} \quad \pi_A^U = \pi_B^U = 2\eta\delta. \qquad (2.25)$$

Notice that (2.25) is the limit of (2.23) as when $\alpha \to 0$, i.e., if consumers do not care about network sizes, the same equilibria emerge under compatibility and incompatibility.

Finally, we wish to compute users' utility under compatibility. Thus,

$$U_A = U_B = \alpha 2\eta - 2\delta. \tag{2.26}$$

Comparing (2.23) with (2.25) and (2.24) with (2.26) yields the main result of this section.

Proposition 2.4
When users' preferences exhibit network externalities,

(a) computer producers charge higher prices and earn higher profits when they make their machines compatible;

(b) consumers are worse off when firms sell compatible machines.

Proposition 2.4(a) demonstrates that compatibility reduces price competition when users' preferences exhibit network externalities. In other words, *compatibility is anticompetitive!* The explanation for this is that when the machines are incompatible, the relative utility users gain from each machine depends on the relative network size of each machine *in addition* to the price difference between the two brands. Hence, under incompatibility, each computer brand-producing firm attempts to attract as many customers by reducing its price. In contrast, price competition is relaxed when the machines are compatible, since under compatibility firms' network size becomes irrelevant to consumers' choice of which brand to buy.

Proposition 2.4(b) highlights that despite the fact that consumers' utility is enhanced with compatibility (higher gross utility), consumers end up being worse off under compatibility since equilibrium prices under compatibility are much higher than under incompatibility, where firms manage to extract all the surplus that consumers gain from using compatible machines.

Equilibrium with one-way compatibility

We consider the following asymmetric situation where the producer of brand A makes its machine compatible with machine B, whereas machine B is incompatible with A. Such a situation occurred in the late 1980s when Apple Computers, Inc. installed what they called an "Hyper Drive" diskette drive, which was able to read DOS-formatted 1.44 MB diskettes which were used on the Intel-based personal computers. Thus, files that were produced on Intel-based personal computers were read by

Macintosh users, however, files placed on Macintosh-formatted diskettes were not readable on DOS-machines. This provides a classic example for *one-way compatibility*. One-way compatibility raises the following questions:

(a) Does the firm that makes its machine compatible earn a higher (or lower) profit than the firm that makes its machine incompatible?

(b) Do A-users benefit having their machine compatible with the B machine even if the B machine is incompatible with A machine?

In order to answer these questions, we now solve for the UPE prices. Before we proceed with solving for the UPE prices, we look at how undercutting can take place in this asymmetric environment. Suppose that the total consumer population is evenly divided between the two brands, so η consumers buy each machine. Then, each A-user gains a network utility of $\alpha 2\eta$, whereas each B-user gains only a network utility of $\alpha\eta$. This means that if firm A undercuts B, it increases the network size of B-users by η. Therefore, A can undercut B's price by setting $p_A = p_B - \delta + \alpha\eta$. In contrast, if B undercuts A it does *not* increase the network size for A-users, since A machines are B compatible thereby maintaining the maximal network size of 2η. Hence, in order to undercut A, B must set $p_B = p_A - \delta$.

A pair of prices $\langle p_A^U, p_B^U \rangle$ constitutes an UPE if the following two conditions are simultaneously satisfied:

$$\pi_B^U = p_B^U \eta \;\geq\; (p_A^U - \delta)2\eta$$
$$\pi_A^U = p_A^U \eta \;\geq\; (p_B^U - \delta + \alpha\eta)2\eta,$$

yielding equilibrium prices and profit levels given by

$$p_A^U = 2\delta - \frac{2\alpha\eta}{3}, \quad \text{and} \quad p_B^U = 2\delta - \frac{4\alpha\eta}{3}, \tag{2.27}$$

Hence,

$$\pi_A^U = 2\eta\left(\delta - \frac{\alpha\eta}{3}\right), \quad \text{and} \quad \pi_B^U = 2\eta\left(\delta - \frac{2\alpha\eta}{3}\right). \tag{2.28}$$

Equations (2.27) and (2.28) yield the following proposition which summarizes our results concerning one-way compatibility.

Proposition 2.5
When one machine is made to be compatible with the competing machine, but the other machine is made incompatible,

(a) *the producer of the compatible machine charges a higher price than the producer of the incompatible machine, hence*

(b) *it earns a higher profit;*

As we demonstrate in Chapter 3, Proposition 2.5 is not robust to other types of computer industries. Chapter 3 demonstrates that when each computer brand is supported by brand-specific software, the firm that makes its machine compatible with the other incompatible machine may actually end up reducing its profit.

Finally, we conclude the analysis of one-way compatibility with the calculation of consumers' welfare levels. Substituting the equilibrium prices given in (2.27) into consumers' utility functions (2.22) yield

$$U_A = \frac{8\alpha\eta}{3} - 2\delta \quad \text{and} \quad U_B = \frac{7\alpha\eta}{3} - 2\delta. \tag{2.29}$$

The complete game: the choice of compatibility

We conclude our analysis of compatibility with heterogeneous users by analyzing the profit-maximizing choice of (in)compatibility by computer producers, and the welfare consequences of such choices. From a modeling point of view, it would be "nice" if we could design a two-stage game where in stage I each firm decides whether to make its machine compatible or incompatible with the competing machine; and in stage II determines its price. However, such a game will not have a Subgame-Perfect equilibrium for the very simple reason that the subgames (price stage) do not have a Nash equilibrium (for this very reason we used the UPE to solve for prices). For this reason, the reader should consider the following analysis as a *one-shot game* for predetermined profit levels given in Table 2.1, which summarizes the profit levels of computer brand-producing firms under all possible choices of compatibility by both firms as calculated in (2.23), (2.25), and (2.28).

		Firm 2			
		INCOMPATIBLE		COMPATIBLE	
1	INCOMP	$2\eta(\delta - \alpha\eta)$	$2\eta(\delta - \alpha\eta)$	$2\eta\left(\delta - \frac{2\alpha\eta}{3}\right)$	$2\eta\left(\delta - \frac{\alpha\eta}{3}\right)$
	COMP	$2\eta\left(\delta - \frac{\alpha\eta}{3}\right)$	$2\eta\left(\delta - \frac{2\alpha\eta}{3}\right)$	$2\eta\delta$	$2\eta\delta$

Table 2.1: Profit levels for all choices of compatibility.

Consider the following scenario. While still at the designing stage (i.e., before sales begin) each computer brand-producing firm decides whether or not to make its machine compatible with the competing machine. In order to make this decision each firm calculates the profitability of its machine given the (in)compatibility decision of the competing firm, where all these profits are displayed in Table 2.1.

Formally, we let each firm action set be $S_i \stackrel{\text{def}}{=} \{C, I\}$, where C stands for compatible and I stands for incompatible, $i = A, B$. We now search for a Nash equilibrium for this game (see Definition A.4 on page 292). Comparing the profit levels in Table 2.1 reveal the following results.

Proposition 2.6
(a) *Both firms designing their machine to be compatible,* $\langle C, C \rangle$*, constitutes a unique Nash equilibrium. In fact, the outcome* $\langle C, C \rangle$ *constitutes an equilibrium in dominant actions.*

(b) *This equilibrium also maximizes industry profit.*

The second part of the proposition reveals the finding that there is no "industry failure" in the sense that the noncooperative (Nash) outcome coincides with the collusive (cooperative) outcome. In other words, compatibility will also be chosen by a cartel as well as a noncooperative industry, so coordination is not required in this case.

We conclude this analysis by looking at consumer welfare under all possible compatibility decision outcomes. The utility levels (2.24), (2.26), and (2.29) are compared in Table 2.2.

		Firm 2			
		INCOMPATIBLE		COMPATIBLE	
1	INCOMP	$3\alpha\eta - 2\delta$	$3\alpha\eta - 2\delta$	$\frac{7\alpha\eta}{3} - 2\delta$	$\frac{8\alpha\eta}{3} - 2\delta$
	COMP	$\frac{8\alpha\eta}{3} - 2\delta$	$\frac{7\alpha\eta}{3} - 2\delta$	$2\alpha\eta - 2\delta$	$2\alpha\eta - 2\delta$

Table 2.2: Utility levels of A- and B-users under all choices of compatibility.

Table 2.2 reveals the following result, which some readers may find to be rather surprising.

Proposition 2.7
(a) *Consumers are better off when the machines are incompatible.*

(b) *However, social welfare is maximized when both machines are compatible.*

The first part of Proposition 2.7 is rather surprising since it implies that despite the increase in the network size enjoyed by each user under compatibility, the corresponding increase in price dominates the utility gains from compatibility. Thus, firms manage to extract more surplus under compatibility thereby making compatibility "bad" for consumers.

The second part of the proposition needs to be proven. We define a social welfare function, by

$$W \stackrel{\text{def}}{=} \eta U_A + \eta U_B + \pi_A + \pi_B = \begin{cases} 4\alpha\eta^2 & \text{under } \langle C, C \rangle \\ 2\alpha\eta^2 & \text{under } \langle I, I \rangle \\ 3\alpha\eta^2 & \text{under } \langle C, I \rangle, \langle I, C \rangle. \end{cases}$$

which is clearly maximized under the outcome $\langle C, C \rangle$. The intuition behind it is as follows. Since the firms are owned by consumers, and since prices are merely transfers from consumers to firms and therefore cancel out in the welfare function just defined, the only net effect on social welfare is the utility gain from the network sizes.

2.2.4 Summary of the network externalities approach

The basic questions needed to be answered in analyzing markets affected by network externalities are:

(a) Do firms gain by producing compatible machines or incompatible machines?

(b) Do consumers gain when firms sell compatible machines?

(c) From a social welfare view point, can a market failure occur where firms do not produce compatible machines even though compatibility is socially preferred to incompatibility?

Our analyses have shown that if compatibility is not too costly to produce, firms gain by producing compatible machines. As a result, firms managed to extract a much higher surplus from consumers, thereby making consumers worse off under compatibility despite the fact that compatibility enhances consumers' gross utility. Finally, as it turns out, the answer to our third question is: "it depends," which is a common answer by economists. However, we indeed made some progress as now we understand that it depends on whether consumers are identical, or have different preferences for compatibility. More precisely, our analyses have shown that *as long as all consumers treat the benefits from compatibility in the same way*, no market failure occurs so that firms choose compatibility only when it is beneficial from a social point of view. This result holds both for the case that consumers buy a single brand (our monopoly case), and when consumers have different preferences for the different brand (our duopoly case).

Mkt. Structure	Consumers	Possibility for Market Failure
Monopoly	Identical	No (Proposition 2.1)
Monopoly	H-C	Yes (Proposition 2.2)
Duopoly	H-B	No (Propositions 2.6(a) & 2.7(b))
Duopoly	H-C	Yes (Not analyzed)

Table 2.3: Summary of welfare results under the network externalities approach. (H-C stands for heterogeneous with respect to compatibility; H-B for heterogeneous with respect to brands only.)

Table 2.3 summarizes our welfare results. Table 2.3 implies that neither the market structure nor the existence of network effects are sufficient for generating market failure stemming from a lack of machine compatibility. What is needed to generate such a market failure is consumers who are heterogeneous with respect to how much they value compatibility. Thus, market failure can only occur whenever firms are unable to price discriminate by charging higher prices from consumers with higher preference for compatibility. From this we conclude that government intervention is not needed as the market generally tends to provide compatibility whenever it is socially optimal.

Finally, in order to simplify the exposition we have neglected to solve for asymmetric equilibria. More precisely, suppose that $\eta_A > \eta_B$ meaning that there are more A-oriented consumers than B-oriented consumers. Without going to the formal analysis solving for the UPE prices, firm A will charge a lower price but will earn a higher profit than firm B. However, the general result showing that aggregate-industry profit is higher under compatibility remains the same as in the symmetric case. In the components' approach section below, we do solve for some asymmetric equilibria, so the reader is referred to Proposition 2.9 on page 42, which states which firm gains and which firm loses under from compatibility.

2.3   The Components Approach

In the previous section we introduced the network-externality approach, where a consumer's valuation of a certain brand is affected by the number of consumers purchasing a similar or an identical brand.

The components approach discussed in this section differs from the network-externality in that it does not assume that consumers' preferences exhibit a consumption externality. Instead, it assumes complementarity, in the sense that the basic computer component does not yield utility without a complementary monitor component. That is, a computer system is composed of two products: a computer and a monitor where the two components are perfect complements, in the sense that without having the two components installed the consumer cannot operate the system and will therefore not gain any utility. The components models were first introduced in Matutes and Regibeau (1988) and Economides (1989). We now have a much-simplified components' model.

Computer systems

Consider a system that can be decomposed into two (perfect complements) components. For example, a computer system can be decomposed into a basic unit and a monitor. The basic unit and the monitor are perfect complements since a consumer cannot use one component without using the other. Another example is a stereo system, which is generally decomposed into an amplifier and speakers (and some other components as well). We denote the first component (the basic unit) by X and the second component (the monitor) by Y.

Firms and Compatibility

There are two firms, indexed by A and B, capable of producing both components, which can be assembled into systems. We denote by X_A the first component produced by firm A, and by Y_A the second component produced by firm A. Similarly, firm B produces components X_B and Y_B. With no loss of generality, we simplify by assuming that production is costless.

Turning to compatibility, we can readily see that since the components are perfect complements, each consumer must purchase one unit of X with one unit of Y. The question of compatibility here is whether a consumer can combine components from different manufacturers when he or she purchases and assembles the system. Formally,

DEFINITION 2.7

(a) *The components are said to be **incompatible** if the components produced by different manufacturers cannot be assembled into systems. That is, systems X_AY_B and X_BY_A do not exist in the market.*

(b) *The components are said to be **compatible** if components produced by different manufacturers can be assembled into systems. That is, X_AY_B and X_BY_A are available in the market.*

Consumers

There are three consumers, denoted by AA, AB, and BB, with heterogeneous preferences toward systems. We denote by p_i^X and p_i^Y the price of component X and component Y produced by firm i, respectively, $i = A, B$.

Each consumer has an ideal combination of components. That is, if $p_A^X = p_B^X$ and $p_A^Y = p_B^Y$, then consumer AA would always choose system $X_A Y_A$ over $X_B Y_B$, consumer BB would choose system $X_B Y_B$ over $X_A Y_A$, and if the systems are compatible (see Definition 2.7), then consumer AB would choose system $X_A Y_B$.

A consumer who purchases system $X_i Y_j$ would pay a total price of $p_i^X + p_j^Y$ for this system, $i, j = A, B$. We denote by U_{ij} the utility level of consumer ij, whose ideal system is $X_i Y_j$, $ij \in \{AA, AB, BB\}$, and assume that for $\delta > 0$

$$
U_{ij} \equiv \begin{cases}
\beta - (p_i^X + p_j^Y) & \text{if purchasing system } X_i Y_j \\
\beta - (p_j^X + p_j^Y) - \delta & \text{if purchasing system } X_j Y_j \\
\beta - (p_i^X + p_i^Y) - \delta & \text{if purchasing system } X_i Y_i \\
\beta - (p_j^X + p_i^Y) - 2\delta & \text{if purchasing system } X_j Y_i.
\end{cases} \tag{2.30}
$$

Thus, in this simple model each consumer has a different ideal system (under equal prices). The utility function (2.30) shows that a consumer purchasing his ideal system gains a gross utility level of β. If the system he buys has one component from his ideal system and one component from his less preferred system, his gross utility level is reduced by δ. A consumer who purchases a system in which both components are produced by his less preferred manufacturer has a gross utility level of $\beta - 2\delta$. Finally, we assume that the basic utility gained from any system, as reflected in the parameter β, is sufficiently high, so in equilibrium each consumer will purchase a system. Formally, we let $\beta \geq 4\delta$.

2.3.1   Incompatible systems

Suppose that the components produced by different manufacturers are incompatible (see Definition 2.7), so that only two systems are sold in the market: system $X_A Y_A$ and system $X_B Y_B$. Since each firm sells a complete system, there is no demand for individual components. Therefore, we define the price of system $X_A Y_A$ manufactured by firm A by $p_{AA} \stackrel{\text{def}}{=} p_A^X + p_A^Y$. Similarly, we define the price of system $X_B Y_B$ by $p_{BB} \stackrel{\text{def}}{=} p_B^X + p_B^Y$. Since only systems $X_A Y_A$ and $X_B Y_B$ are available, consumer AB will have to "compromise" and purchase one of these systems, since his "ideal" system $X_A Y_B$ is not available due to incompatibility of the components. Hence, we look for an "asymmetric" equilibrium where consumers AA and AB buy system $X_A Y_A$, whereas only consumer BB buys system $X_B Y_B$. (Obviously, if such an equilibrium exists, then there must exist another equilibrium where only consumer AA buys $X_A Y_A$ and consumers AB and BB buy system $X_B Y_B$.) Figure 2.2 illustrates the trade between firms in consumers for the case of incompatible systems.

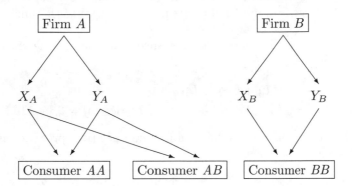

Figure 2.2: Trade with incompatible systems.

Since a Nash equilibrium in prices does not exist for this model, we will use the Undercut-Proof equilibrium described in Appendix C. A pair of prices $\langle p_A^U, p_B^U \rangle$ constitutes an Undercut-Proof equilibrium (UPE), see Definition C.2 on page 309, where firm A sells to consumers AA and AB and firm B sells to consumer BB, if both conditions are simultaneously satisfied:

$$\pi_B^U = p_{BB}^U \times 1 \geq \max\left\{ (p_{AA}^U - \delta) \times 2; (p_{AA}^U - 2\delta) \times 3 \right\}$$
$$\pi_A^U = p_{AA}^U \times 2 \geq (p_{BB}^U - 2\delta) \times 3.$$

The first condition implies that there are two ways in which firm B can undercut firm A. A "mild" undercutting would involve reducing the price below A's price so that consumer AB would switch from buying system AA to buying system BB. For this to happen B has to set $p_{BB} \leq p_{AA} - \delta$. A "strong" undercutting would involve grabbing consumers AA and AB to buy system BB, in which case firm B has to set $p_{BB} \leq p_{AA} - 2\delta$. However, "mild" undercutting yields a higher profit to firm B than "strong" undercutting, that is $(p_{AA}^U - \delta)2 \geq (p_{AA}^U - 2\delta)3$ if and only if $p_{AA}^U \leq 4\delta$ which turns out to be the case. Hence, in calculating the UPE we consider only the case of "mild" undercutting. Therefore, equilibrium prices and profit levels given by

$$p_{AA}^I = 3\delta, \quad p_{BB}^I = 4\delta, \quad \text{and} \quad \pi_A^I = 6\delta, \quad \pi_B^I = 4\delta, \tag{2.31}$$

where superscript I stands for "incompatibility." Equation (2.31) reveals an important property of the UPE, where the firm that has the larger number of consumers (firm A) charges a lower price, but earns a higher profit. The reason is that the firm with the larger market share is always a prey to be undercut by the small firm, since undercutting can significantly increase the small firm's market share. Thus, to avoid being such a prey, the large firm must reduce its price compared to the small firm's price.

We define the aggregate consumer surplus as the sum of consumers' utilities. Hence,

$$
\begin{aligned}
CS^I &\stackrel{\text{def}}{=} U_{AA} + U_{BB} + U_{AB} \qquad\qquad (2.32)\\
&= (\beta - 3\delta) + (\beta - 4\delta) + (\beta - 3\delta - \delta) = 3\beta - 11\delta.
\end{aligned}
$$

We define the economy's welfare as the sum of firms' profit levels and consumer surplus. Thus,

$$
W^I \equiv \pi_A + \pi_B + CS^I = 6\delta + 4\delta + 3\beta - 11\delta = 3\beta - \delta. \qquad (2.33)
$$

The equilibrium social-welfare level given in (2.33) is simply the sum of the gross utility levels of all the consumers.

2.3.2   Compatible systems

When firms design their components to be compatible with components produced by the rival firm, two more systems become available to consumers: system $X_A Y_B$ and system $X_B Y_A$. We look for an equilibrium where each consumer buys (assembles) his ideal system. In this equilibrium, firm A sells two X_A components and one Y_A component whereas firm B sells two Y_B components and only one X_B component. Figure 2.3 illustrates the trade between firms in consumers for the case of incompatible systems.

Since each component is sold separately we treat the market for X as independent of the market for Y. Thus, a pair of prices $\langle p_A^X, p_B^X \rangle$ constitutes an Undercut-proof equilibrium (UPE), see Definition C.2 on page 309, where firm A sells component X to consumers AA and AB, and firm B sells component X to consumer BB only, if

$$
\begin{aligned}
p_B^X \times 1 &\geq (p_A^X - \delta) \times 3\\
p_A^X \times 2 &\geq (p_B^X - \delta) \times 3.
\end{aligned}
$$

For the Y-component market, UPE prices satisfy

$$
\begin{aligned}
p_B^Y \times 2 &\geq (p_A^Y - \delta) \times 3\\
p_A^Y \times 1 &\geq (p_B^Y - \delta) \times 3.
\end{aligned}
$$

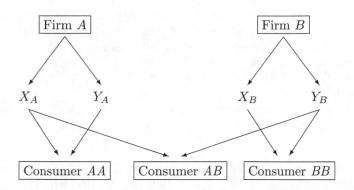

Figure 2.3: Trade with compatible systems.

Therefore, equilibrium prices and profit levels given by

$$p_A^X = p_B^Y = \frac{12\delta}{7}, \; p_B^X = p_A^Y = \frac{15\delta}{7}, \; \pi_A^C = \pi_B^C = 2\frac{12\delta}{7} + \frac{15\delta}{7} = \frac{39\delta}{7},$$
(2.34)

where superscript C stands for "compatibility."

Since each consumer gets his "ideal" brand, consumer surplus is given by

$$
\begin{aligned}
CS^C \; &\stackrel{\text{def}}{=} \; U_{AA} + U_{BB} + U_{AB} \tag{2.35}\\
&= \; \beta - \frac{12\delta}{7} - \frac{15\delta}{7} + \beta - \frac{15\delta}{7} - \frac{12\delta}{7} + \beta - \frac{12\delta}{7} - \frac{12\delta}{7}\\
&= \; 3\beta - \frac{78\delta}{7}.
\end{aligned}
$$

Social welfare is then

$$W^C \equiv \pi_A + \pi_B + CS^C = \frac{39\delta}{7} + \frac{39\delta}{7} + 3\beta - \frac{78\delta}{7} = 3\beta, \qquad (2.36)$$

which equals exactly the sum of gross utilities when each consumer buys his ideal system.

2.3.3 Compatibility versus incompatibility

We now wish to examine the effects of components' compatibility on firms' profits, consumers' utility levels, aggregate consumers' surplus, and social welfare. Comparing (2.32) with (2.35) yields

Proposition 2.8
Consumers are better off when the firms produce incompatible components than when firms produce compatible components.

Thus, despite the fact that under compatibility each consumer gets his ideal system, consumers are worse off since firms charge higher prices under compatibility, thereby absorbing all consumers' gain from compatibility. To see this, comparing (2.31) with (2.34) yields

Proposition 2.9
(a) *Aggregate industry profit is higher when firms produce compatible components than when they produce incompatible components. Formally, $\pi_A^C + \pi_B^C > \pi_A^I + \pi_B^I$.*

(b) *The firm with the higher market share under incompatibility earns a higher profit under incompatibility whereas the firm with the smaller market share under incompatibility earns a higher profit under compatibility. Formally, $\pi_A^I > \pi_A^C$ and $\pi_B^I < \pi_B^C$.*

Also, comparing (2.33) with (2.36) yields

Proposition 2.10
Social welfare is higher when firms produce compatible components.

Thus, the welfare gains derived from having firms increase their profits by making their components compatible exceeds the utility loss of consumers from the high component prices under compatibility. This result is expected considering the fact that the firms are owned by the consumers.

2.3.4   Summary of the components approach

We summarize the components approach by comparing it to the results obtained in the network externalities approach under duopoly. Surprisingly, both approaches ended up yielding identical results.

Comparing propositions 2.6 and 2.9 reveals that industry profit is always higher when firms choose compatibility over incompatibility. Also, comparing propositions 2.7 and 2.8 reveals that consumers are worse off under compatibility, since under both approaches firms manage to extract much higher rents under compatibility, and these high rents far exceed consumers' rise in utility resulting from compatibility. Therefore, since this result is confirmed for both, the network externalities approach and the components approach, we can regard these basic results as robust. Finally, comparing propositions 2.7 and 2.10 the unique socially-optimal outcome is to have compatible machines and compatible components (as long as the costs of designing compatible machines is not too high). Despite this result, one should *not* conclude that governments must impose mandatory standards on computer firms, since as often happens, governments may choose standards that are not valued by the consumers. Hence, despite this result, government intervention is not called to fix this type of a market failure.

2.4 Empirical Findings on Network Externalities

Most empirical research confirming network-externality behavior focused on the software market is analyzed in the next chapter. We therefore refer the reader to Section 3.7, where network behavior is confirmed via consumers' choice of compatible software. In this section we focus only on empirical findings concerning direct network externalities (i.e., we do not discuss empirical findings in markets with network effects generated by complementary services such as computer-specific software).

2.4.1 Keyboard compatibility and network externalities

David (1985) provides a classic example of *path dependent* sequence of failing to replace the currently used inefficient typing keyboard as a result of network externalities. The currently-used QWERTY keyboard has been used since the mid-1890s. Despite the inconvenience of this keyboard this standard has not been replaced even with the introduction of the Dvorak Simplified Keyboard (DSK) which was patented in 1932. Table 2.4 illustrates the two keyboard layouts.

Q	W	E	R	T	Y	U	I	O	P
	A	S	D	F	G	H	J	K	L	;
		Z	X	C	V	B	N	M	,	.
'	,	.	P	Y	F	G	C	R	L
A	O	E	U	I	D	H	T	N	S
;	Q	J	K	X	B	M	W	V	Z

Table 2.4: *Top:* The commonly-used QWERTY keyboard layout. *Bottom:* The Dvorak keyboard layout. Notice that only the letters "A" and "M" appear at the same location.

During the 1940s U.S. Navy experiments have shown that the increased efficiency obtained with the DSK would amortize the cost of retraining a group of typists within the first ten days of the subsequent full-time employment.

As David indicates, the perfection of the first typewriters from 1867 to 1873 led to a change from alphabetical key ordering to the currently used QWERTY in order to *reduce* the frequency of typebar clashes. Since by now, with the introduction of computers, mechanical typewriters are no longer in use, one would expect the Dvorak keyboard to replace the QWERTY keyboard. But as it turns out, the industry continues to be locked in to the de facto QWERTY standard. Interestingly, Cowan (1990) provides a similar story about resistance to technology change in nuclear reactors.

Leibowitz and Margolis (1990) raise doubt concerning the claims of the inefficiency of the QWERTY keyboard. They argue that the QWERTY keyboard was not designed to slow down typing and that the Navy study was poorly documented and designed. As it turned out this study was carried out by Navy Lieutenant Commander August Dvorak, the creator and patent holder of the keyboard bearing his name. More recent studies indicate that practically there is no difference in typing speeds between the keyboard designs, so the Dvorak keyboard story may provide a rather poor empirical base upon which to support a theory.

2.4.2   Mainframe computers

Greenstein (1993) analyzes a federal agency acquisitions of commercial general-purpose mainframes and investigates the empirical relationship between incumbent computer vendors and the government. The analysis finds that even when controlling for factors influencing the vendor-buyer match, an agency is likely to acquire a system from an incumbent vendor. More interestingly, Greenstein provides evidence that indicates that the incompatibility in IBM's product line generated a counter effect to the incumbency status, since former IBM users tended to switch to other vendors most often when they possessed very old IBM equipment (e.g., IBM 1400 series) where the compatible upgrades were limited. Federal IBM users who could upgrade from one compatible system to another (e.g., IBM 360/370) tended to choose IBM much more often.

2.4.3   Network externalities in the market for spreadsheet programs

Although the software industry is analyzed in the next chapter, authors often find it easier to demonstrate the existence of network externalities in a market for a particular software. The spreadsheet market provides a good environment to test for the presence of network externalities since in the 1980s a de facto standard existed where IBM PCs and compatibles were dominated by Lotus. When it was introduced in 1983, Lotus 1-2-3 became the best seller. The Lotus compatibility feature offered by some competing spreadsheet programs indicated the importance of network externalities, since compatible spreadsheet programs could greatly enhance the ability of consumers to share information.

Gandal (1994) estimates hedonic (quality-adjusted) price equations for spreadsheet programs and then used the analysis to test whether network externalities exist. Gandal compiled yearly reports issued by

Data-Pro Research Group from 1986 to 1991 focusing on stand-alone spreadsheet programs (i.e., ignoring programs that integrate spreadsheets with word-processing and database software). The results from his study are that consumers are willing to pay a significant premium for spreadsheets that are compatible with the Lotus platform and for spreadsheets that offer links to external databases, and a smaller premium for spreadsheets that offer local area network compatibility. These results support the hypothesis that consumers' preferences for computer spreadsheet programs exhibit network externalities.

Brynjolfsson and Kemerer (1996) complements Gandal's (1994) research by researching data of unit sales and market prices. They use a sample of spreadsheet programs during the 1987 to 1992 time period where the price of software i in each period t was assumed to be influenced by four sets of variables: $p_i^t = f(N_i^t, S_i^t, F_i^t, T_t)$, where N_i^t summarizes the network externalities defined as the installed base, which is the sum of sales of software i up to period t; S_i^t is standard attributes of software i referring to the use of Lotus 1-2-3 menu tree (implying greater ease of use for the installed base of users who are familiar with Lotus' menu); F_i^t is i specific features as defined by the National Software Testing Laboratories; and T_t is time trend of all software packages in period t.

Brynjolfsson and Kemerer obtain the following three main results: First, network externalities, as measured by the size of a program's installed base, significantly increased the price of the corresponding spreadsheet programs; more precisely, a 1 percent increase in a program's installed base was associated with a 0.75 percent increase in its price. Second, programs that adhered to the dominant standard of the Lotus menu tree interface commanded prices that were higher by an average of 46 percent. Third, similar to Gandal's findings, quality-adjusted prices fell by an average of 16 percent per year.

An article by Gandal (1995) tests for network externalities by looking at *file-transfer compatibility standards* rather than by just checking for the Lotus compatibility feature. His dummy variables for measuring file-transfer compatibility included the ASCII format, DBF (Asthon-Tate's dBase software), LOTUS, and SYLK (Microsoft's Multiplan's file format used mostly on Macintosh machines). The results are that only the LOTUS file compatibility standard is significant in explaining price variations and it is significant in both the spreadsheet *and* database management system (DBMS) markets. This result could be viewed as surprising since this research did not find a premium for the DBF compatibility in the DBMS market, which suggests that there are not significant direct network externalities in this market. This supports the hypothesis that the software market exhibits complementary network externalities.

Finally, for more empirical support of the network externalities hypothesis the reader is referred to Hartman and Teece (1990), Baseman, Warren-Boulton, and Woroch (1995), Bresnahan and Greenstein (1997), Bresnahan and Greenstein (1999).

2.5   Exercises

1. Consider the duopoly computer industry problem with heterogeneous consumers analyzed in Section 2.2.3, but suppose that each computer-producing firm bears a positive production cost. More precisely, assume that each hardware unit costs exactly $c > 0$ to produce. Answer the following questions.

   (a) Calculate the UPE prices and profit level assuming that the brands are incompatible (i.e., how equation (2.23) is modified in the presence of production costs).

   (b) Calculate the UPE prices and profit level assuming that the brands are compatible (i.e., how equation (2.25) is modified in the presence of production costs).

   (c) Conclude whether Proposition 2.4 on page 31 still holds in the presence of production costs.

2. Consider the duopoly computer industry problem with heterogeneous consumers analyzed in Section 2.2.3. Suppose that the computer brands are incompatible and that there are η A-oriented consumers and η B-oriented consumers, with utility functions given by

$$U_A \stackrel{\text{def}}{=} \begin{cases} 2q_A - p_A & \text{buy } A \\ 2q_B - p_B - \delta & \text{buy } B, \end{cases} \quad U_B \stackrel{\text{def}}{=} \begin{cases} 3q_A - p_A - \delta & \text{buy } A \\ 3q_B - p_B & \text{buy } B. \end{cases}$$

   That is, the two types of consumers have different utility gains from their network size. Calculate the UPE prices and profit levels assuming that in equilibrium both brands are sold in the market and that the brands are incompatible.

3. Consider the duopoly computer industry with consumer preferences exhibiting network externalities. Suppose that the computer brands are initially *incompatible* and that there are 100 A-oriented consumers and 200 B-oriented consumers, with utility functions (of each consumer type) given by

$$U_A \stackrel{\text{def}}{=} \begin{cases} q_A - p_A & \text{buy } A \\ q_B - p_B - \delta & \text{buy } B, \end{cases} \quad U_B \stackrel{\text{def}}{=} \begin{cases} q_A - p_A - \delta & \text{buy } A \\ q_B - p_B & \text{buy } B, \end{cases}$$

   where δ is the differentiation (switching cost) parameter. Assume that $\delta > 300$.

   (a) Calculate the UPE prices and profit levels assuming that in equilibrium both brands are sold in the market and the that brands are *incompatible*.

(b) Conclude which firm charges a higher price under incompatibility and which firm earns a higher profit. Explain in words the intuition behind your result.

(c) Calculate the UPE prices and profit levels assuming that in equilibrium both brands are sold in the market and that the brands are *compatible*.

(d) Conclude whether firms are better off when computers are incompatible than when they are compatible.

4. Consider a situation where network effects are very strong, so that Assumption 2.4 on page 28 is violated. More precisely, let there be 60 A-oriented consumers and 60 B-oriented consumers, where

$$U_A \stackrel{\text{def}}{=} \begin{cases} 2q_A - p_A & \text{buy } A \\ 2q_B - p_B - 100 & \text{buy } B, \end{cases} \qquad U_B \stackrel{\text{def}}{=} \begin{cases} 2q_A - p_A - 100 & \text{buy } A \\ 2q_B - p_B & \text{buy } B. \end{cases}$$

Answer the following questions.

(a) Prove that there does not exist an UPE where 60 consumers buy brand A and 60 consumers buy brand B.

(b) Find the price charged by each firm in an equilibrium where all the 120 consumers buy brand A only.

5. You are given the following information about a market with two hardware brands labeled A and B:

- The systems are incompatible.

- There are 100 A-oriented consumers, and 100 B-oriented consumers.

- Each consumer type has a utility function given in Section 2.2.3.

- In an undercut-proof equilibrium, brands' prices are $p_A = p_B = 50$.

Calculate the differentiation (switching-cost) parameter δ.

6. Consider the components model of Section 2.3 but suppose now that there is a fourth consumer named BA whose "ideal" system is $X_B Y_A$. Answer the following questions.

(a) Calculate the UPE prices and profit levels assuming that the systems are incompatible. *Hint:* Consider an equilibrium where firm A sells to consumers AA, AB, and BA, whereas firm B sells to consumer BB only.

(b) Calculate the UPE prices and profit levels assuming that the systems are compatible.

2.6   Selected References

Baseman, K., F. Warren-Boulton, and G. Woroch. 1995. "Microsoft Plays Hardball: The Use of Exclusionary Pricing and Technological Incompatibility to Maintain Monopoly Power in Markets for Operating systems." *Antitrust Bulletin* 40: 265–315.

Bresnahan, T., and S. Greenstein. 1997. "Technical Progress and Co-Invention in the Computing and in the Use of Computers." *Brookings Papers on Economics Activity: Microeconomics* 1–78.

Bresnahan, T., and S. Greenstein. 1999. "Technological Competition and the Structure of the Computing Industry." *Journal of Industrial Economics* 47: 1–40.

Brynjolfsson, E., and C. Kemerer. 1996. "Network Externalities in the Microcomputer Software: An Econometric Analysis of the Spreadsheet Market." *Management Science* 42, 1627–1647.

Cabral, L., D. Salant, and G. Woroch. 1999. "Monopoly Pricing with Network Externalities." *International Journal of Industrial Organization* 17: 199–214.

Choi, J. 1996. "Do Converters Facilitate the Transition to a New Incompatible Technology?: A Dynamic Analysis of Converters." *International Journal of Industrial Organization* 14: 825–835.

Choi, J., and M. Thum. 1998. "Market Structure and the Timing of Technology Adoption with Network Externalities." *European Economic Review* 42: 225–244.

Cowan, R. 1990. "Nuclear Power Reactors: A Study in Technological Lock-in." *Journal of Economic History* 50: 541–567.

David, P. 1985. "Clio and the Economics of QWERTY." *American Economic Review* 75: 332–336.

Economides, N., 1989, "Desirability of compatibility in the absence of network externalities." *American Economic Review* 79: 1165–1181.

Farrell, J., and G. Saloner. 1985. "Standardization, Compatibility, and Innovation." *Rand Journal of Economics* 16: 70–83.

Farrell, J., and G. Saloner. 1986. "Installed Base and Compatibility: Innovation, Product Preannouncements, and Predation." *American Economic Review* 76: 940–955.

Gabel, L. 1991. *Competitive Strategies for Product Standards.* London: McGraw-Hill.

Gandal, N. 1994. "Hedonic Price Indexes for Spreadsheets and an Empirical Test of the Network Externalities Hypothesis." *Rand Journal of Economics* 25: 160–170.

Gandal, N. 1995. "Competing Compatibility Standards and Network Externalities in the PC Software Market." *Review of Economics and Statistics* 599–608.

Greenstein, S. 1993. "Did Installed Base Give an Incumbent any (Measurable) Advantages in Federal Computer Procurement ?" *Rand Journal of Economics* 24: 19–39.

Hartman, R., and D. Teece. 1990. "Product Emulation Strategies in the Presence of Reputation Effects and Network Externalities: Some Evidence from the Minicomputer Industry." *Economics of Innovation and New Technology* 1: 157–182.

Katz, M., and C. Shapiro. 1985. "Network Externalities, Competition and Compatibility." *American Economic Review* 75: 424–440.

Katz, M., and C. Shapiro. 1986. "Product Compatibility choice in a Market with Technological Progress." *Oxford Economics Papers* 38: 146–169.

Katz, M., and C. Shapiro. 1992. "Product Introduction with Network Externalities." *Journal of Industrial Economics* 40: 55–84.

Katz, M., and C. Shapiro. 1994. "Systems Competition and Network Effects." *Journal of Economic Perspectives* 8: 93–115.

Klemperer, P. 1987. "Markets with Consumer Switching Costs." *Quarterly Journal of Economics* 102: 375–394.

Leibowitz, S., and S. Margolis. 1990. "The Fable of the Keys." *Journal of Law & Economics* 33: 1–26.

Matutes, C., and P. Regibeau. 1988. "Mix and match: product compatibility without network externalities." *Rand Journal of Economics* 19: 221–234.

Swan, P. 1970. "Durability of Consumer Goods." *American Economic Review* 60: 884–894.

Chapter 3

The Software Industry

Software consists of digital bits that are downloaded onto the storage devices of a computer. Software is also a general name for audio and video disks that can be inserted into audio or video players connected to stereo systems or television sets. Software consists of software packages, music, or movie titles that are designed to perform different tasks (different themes) commanded by the user(s) of the computer (or player).

Computer software "issues" commands to the hardware devices of the computer instructing these devices how to perform specific tasks instructed by the user. Audio and video software contain all the information for the hardware to be able to play certain music or to show certain movies. All types of software can be modified, replaced, or upgraded. Software packages are generally produced by a large number of software firms that generally are independent of the hardware producers. For this reason software packages are regarded as *supporting services* for the hardware. Thus, a larger variety of software supporting a certain hardware increases the value of this specific hardware machine. Therefore, the approach taken in this chapter is sometimes referred to in the literature as the *supporting services approach.*

The novelty of the analysis presented in this chapter is that consumers are assumed to derive utility directly from the *variety* of supporting services supporting the specific hardware or the operating system they use. That is, instead of assuming network externalities, which would imply that consumers derive utility directly from the total number of consumers buying the same or a compatible hardware (see Definition 2.3 on page 17), here we assume that there are no externalities and consumers determine the value of the hardware machine they buy by the variety of software supporting the machine they buy, in addition to hardware's price. However, since most often there is a positive correlation between the variety of software packages written for a specific machine and the number of users of this machine, some authors refer to the supporting services approach as the *indirect network externalities* approach.

The literature utilizing the supporting services approach includes Chou and Shy (1990, 1993, and 1996), and Church and Gandal (1992a,b, 1993, 1995, and 1996). In many instances, supporting services are incompatible across brands. For example, most software packages are designed to operate on one operating system (such as UNIX, DOS, Macintosh, Windows, etc.) and do not operate on other operating systems. Videotapes recorded on the NTSC television system (used in North America and Japan) cannot be played in Asia, Europe, and in the Middle East, where the dominant television standard is PAL. For a discussion of the newly emerging high-definition television standards see Farrell and Shapiro (1992) and the references therein. For this reason, just like in the previous chapter, we conduct our analysis by comparing the equilibrium prices, profits, and welfare under compatibility and incompatibility.

For the purposes of this chapter, we will slightly revise the definition of compatibility (Definitions 2.1 and 2.2) of the previous chapter.

DEFINITION 3.1
Hardware machines are said to be compatible if they can run the same software. In this case, we can say that the machines are **software compatible***.*

3.1   Principles of Software Production

Like all forms of digitally distributed information products, the production of software requires a large investment in development (see also Section 7.4). This development cost outweighs any other production and in particular it outweighs the cost of distributing the software to consumers. This means that the production of software exhibits sharp economies of scale.

To demonstrate this, we look at the following example. Let q denote the number of buyers and let ϕ denote the cost of developing, testing, and debugging software. The development cost includes mostly total wages paid for thousands of programmers' hours, office and equipment rental, and other types of sunk costs associated with establishing a company. Let μ denote the cost of shipping one piece of software to a consumer. This cost includes the cost of a diskette or a CD in case the software is shipped using this media, or the time it takes to ship this software over the Internet. It could also include the cost of printing the manual attached to this software, and the mailing cost.

We define the average cost as the total production cost per unit of production. Formally, if $TC(q)$ denotes the total cost function (the production cost at each output level), then

$$AC(q) \stackrel{\text{def}}{=} \frac{TC(q)}{q}.$$

We define the marginal cost as the change in production cost associated with a "small" increase in the output level. Formally,

$$MC(q) \stackrel{\text{def}}{=} \frac{\Delta TC(q)}{\Delta q}.$$

We now consider the following example which seems an appropriate presentation of software production cost where $TC(q) \stackrel{\text{def}}{=} \phi + \mu q$. In this case,

$$AC(q) = \frac{\phi}{q} + \mu \quad \text{and} \quad MC(q) = \mu. \tag{3.1}$$

Figure 3.1 (left) illustrates the total cost (3.1) and Figure 3.1 (right) illustrates the derived average and marginal cost functions. The dashed lines on Figure 3.1(left) demonstrate how the average and marginal cost curves can be graphically derived from the total cost function. The slope of the ray from the origin to the total cost function is precisely the average cost at this particular output level. The slope of the cost function itself is the marginal cost which is constant and equals μ for the cost function defined in (3.1). Since the slope of the ray from the

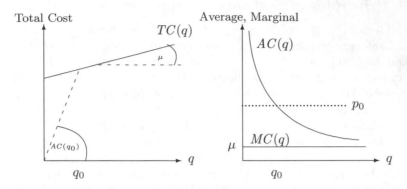

Figure 3.1: Total, average, and marginal software production cost functions.

origin exceeds the slope of the total cost function, we have it that the average cost of producing software exceeds the marginal cost at every output level, and that the two converge at high output levels. Formally, $AC(q) \longrightarrow \mu = MC(q)$ as $q \longrightarrow \infty$.

What are the implications of the total software cost function (3.1) for software pricing? Consider an arbitrary price at the level of $p = p_0$ which is plotted on Figure 3.1(right).

Proposition 3.1
For the software production cost given in (3.1),

(a) *At every price, p_0, there exists a minimum level of sales, q_0, for which any level of sales $q > q_0$ result in strictly positive profit and any sales level $q < q_0$ results in a loss to the software company.*

(b) *Cost-based pricing is not appropriate for software.*

The second part of the proposition highlights the difficulty in predicting software prices as it implies that marginal-cost pricing associated with competitive markets cannot prevail in markets for software simply because marginal-cost pricing implies a loss to the software developer.

3.2   The Determination of Software Variety

Our earlier discussion concluded with the crucial importance of software variety to computer users, music lovers, and video watchers. In this section we develop a model explaining how software variety is determined in an environment where consumers place value on the variety of software.

Suppose that there are η consumers who purchase a certain computer brand. Let ω (for wage) denote the total income of each consumer which is allocated to be spent on one computer and all the available variety of software. Thus, in order to be able to use software, the consumer must pay a price of p to purchase the hardware. Then, the remaining amount is used to purchase software. Therefore, we denote by e (for expenditure) a consumer's total amount of money spent on software, thus $e = \omega - p$.

Let s denote the number of software packages written for this machine (or each operating system). The purpose of this section is to offer a model which calculates the variety of software, s. For this purpose, we need to model the software industry. The software industry consists of many software writers (or software firms), each concentrating on writing one or a few packages for a certain operating system. Instead of going over a long and tedious derivation for how a variety of software is determined in a monopolistically competitive industry (as in Chou and Shy 1990), we simplify the analysis by introducing the following assumption. Let ϕ denote the fixed cost of developing one software package. That is, the cost it takes a software company to write and debug (payments to programmers) and to sell (cost of marketing activities, packing, mailing, and advertising) a package of software.

ASSUMPTION 3.1
The variety (number) of software packages equals total consumer expenditure on this software divided by the software development cost. Formally,

$$s \stackrel{\text{def}}{=} \frac{\eta e}{\phi}. \tag{3.2}$$

Assumption 3.1 merely states a well known result in monopolistically competitive industries where the equilibrium total number of brands in an industry is proportional to total consumer expenditure on the brand divided by fixed software development cost. Here, instead of performing these derivations, we turn this result into an assumption. Substituting $e = \omega - p$ into (3.2) yields

$$s = \frac{\eta(\omega - p)}{\phi}. \tag{3.3}$$

Thus, a reduction in hardware price increases the amount consumers spend on software, thereby increasing the variety of software available for the machine.

Each consumer has a utility function of using computers that is influenced by two variables: s, the number of software packages supporting the machine, and p, the price of one piece of hardware. Software prices are ignored in this presentation. Formally,

$$U \stackrel{\text{def}}{=} \begin{cases} \alpha s - p & \text{Buys the computer and entire variety of software} \\ 0 & \text{Buys none.} \end{cases}$$

(3.4)

Thus, each consumer has a reservation utility of zero, and if he buys the computer and the entire variety of software his utility increases with the available variety and decreases with the hardware's price, p. The parameter α measures the degree of importance of software variety to computer users. A high value of α means that consumers highly regard software variety, whereas a low value of α means that consumers are satisfied with a low variety of software or merely the software that is built into the operating system (say, allowing only word processing).

Consider now a monopoly hardware producer who sets its price, p, to maximize profit. In view of (3.4), the monopoly observes s and sets the maximal price each consumer is willing to pay, which is $p^m = \alpha s$. Substituting into (3.3) yields,

$$p^m = \frac{\alpha \eta (\omega - p^m)}{\phi}, \quad \text{hence} \quad p^m = \frac{\alpha \eta \omega}{\alpha \eta + \phi}. \tag{3.5}$$

Hence,

Proposition 3.2
The price charged by a monopoly hardware firm

(a) *increases with consumers' love for software variety parameter, α; consumers' income, ω; and the number of consumers buying this machine, η;*

(b) *decreases with the software development cost, ϕ.*

The first part of Proposition 3.2 shows that an increase in consumers' love for software variety, α, increases the monopoly hardware price. The reason for this is that a higher utility from software variety enhances the value of the hardware machine, thereby enabling the hardware seller to raise its price. Also, an increase in income, ω, results in a higher demand and therefore a higher monopoly price. Regarding the increase in consumer population, η, the logic goes as follows. When more people buy the machine, more software packages are produced, hence increasing the utility of each consumer, thereby enabling the monopoly to raise its price. The second part of Proposition 3.2 has the following explanation.

An increase in the software development cost reduces the variety of software written for this hardware, hence reduces the value of the hardware, thereby reduces the maximal price a monopoly hardware producer can charge.

Substituting (3.5) into (3.3) and using $e = \omega - p$ yields the equilibrium software variety and a consumer's expenditure on software.

$$s = \frac{\eta \omega}{\alpha \eta + \phi} \quad \text{and} \quad e = \frac{\phi \omega}{\alpha \eta + \phi}. \tag{3.6}$$

Equation (3.6) reveals the following.

Proposition 3.3

(a) *Equilibrium software variety, s, increases with the number of consumers, η; consumers' income, ω; and decreases with consumers' love-for-software variety parameter, α; and with the software development cost, ϕ.*

(b) *A consumer's software expenditure, e, increases with consumers' income, ω; and with the software development cost, ϕ; but declines with an increase in consumers' love-for-software variety parameter, α, and the number of consumers, η.*

Thus, under a monopoly hardware seller, if consumers appreciate more software variety Proposition 3.2 shows that the monopoly hardware firm increases its price thereby lowering consumers' expenditure on software, hence reducing software variety. This shows that a higher appreciation for software variety increases the surplus the hardware monopoly can extract from consumers.

3.3 Software Variety Under Hardware Competition

The previous section computed software variety under the assumption that there is only one hardware producer and therefore all consumers must purchase one brand of hardware. We now extend the analysis to a duopoly computer hardware industry competing for consumers whose utility increases with the variety of software available for each brand.

There are two hardware producers, A (Artichoke) and B (Banana) producing computers at no cost. Let s_A denote amount of software available for brand A, and let s_B denote the available software variety for brand B. Let q_A denote the number of A-users, and q_B the number of B-users. Then, applying Assumption 3.1 for how software variety is determined, we have

$$s_i \stackrel{\text{def}}{=} \frac{q_i e_i}{\phi} = \frac{q_i(\omega - p_i)}{\phi}, \tag{3.7}$$

where $e_i = \omega - p_i$ measures a consumer's total expenditure on software (wage minus the price of the hardware). However, although the model can be worked out completely under the software determination rule (3.7), we choose to further simplify the model with the following assumption.

ASSUMPTION 3.2
The variety (number) of software packages supporting each brand equals total number of consumers using the hardware brand divided by the software development cost. Formally,

$$s_i \stackrel{\text{def}}{=} \frac{q_i}{\phi}, \quad i = A, B. \tag{3.8}$$

There are η consumers whom we call computer brand A oriented, and η consumers who are brand B oriented. The utility function of each type i consumer is given by

$$U_i = \begin{cases} \alpha s_i - p_i & \text{buys brand } i; \ i \text{ is incompatible with } j \\ \alpha s_j - p_j - \delta & \text{buys brand } j; \ j \text{ is incompatible with } i \\ \alpha(s_A + s_B) - p_i & \text{buys brand } i; \ i \text{ is compatible with } j \\ \alpha(s_A + s_B) - p_j - \delta & \text{buys brand } j; \ j \text{ is compatible with } i, \end{cases}$$
(3.9)

where $i, j = A, B$, $i \neq j$. Thus, type i has brand i as his "ideal" brand. If type i consumer buys brand j, his utility is reduced by δ. As before, the parameter δ can also have the interpretation of the *switching costs* associated with having consumer type i learning to operate computer brand j. In addition, for given prices the utility of each consumer is always enhanced when the machine he buys is compatible with (can read the software written for) the rival machine, since this consumer would be able to use the entire variety of software available for *both* machines instead of just using the machine-specific software.

Finally, in order to obtain interior equilibria, that is, an equilibrium where both brands are purchased, we need to make the brands sufficiently differentiated.

ASSUMPTION 3.3
Consumers' software-variety desirability parameter is bounded (or, the two hardware brands are sufficiently differentiated). Formally,

$$\alpha < \frac{\phi \delta}{\eta}, \quad \text{or} \quad \delta > \frac{\alpha \eta}{\phi}.$$

If Assumption 3.3 is reversed, variety of software becomes so important that under incompatible systems only one brand will be sold in the market. In this case, variety of software is maximized as all software is written for one machine only. Thus, Assumption 3.3 is essential for having a multisystem equilibrium.

3.3.1 Incompatible systems

Before calculating equilibrium prices when the two machines are incompatible, we need to modify Definition 2.6 on page 29 for the case where consumers' preferences exhibit love for software variety instead of network externalities. Using the utility function (3.9) and the software variety determination rule of Assumption 3.2, we now define undercutting.

DEFINITION 3.2
*Suppose that initially, η users use computer brand i and η users use computer brand j, where $i, j = A, B, i \neq j$. Let p_A and p_B denote brands' prices and let s_A and s_B be the corresponding software varieties as determined in (3.8). Brand i producer **undercuts** brand j producer, by setting p'_i sufficiently low to satisfy*

$$p'_i \leq p_j - \delta + \alpha(s'_i - s_j) = p_j - \delta + \alpha\left(\frac{2\eta}{\phi} - \frac{\eta}{\phi}\right) = p_j - \delta + \frac{\alpha\eta}{\phi}. \quad (3.10)$$

Thus, in order to attract brand j users, brand i producer must reduce its price below its competitor's so that the transportation cost δ is subsidized. However, the price can be raised by $\alpha(s'_i - s_j)$ since brand j users would also be buying i-software thereby increasing their software variety from s_j to s'_i, where s'_i is the amount of software written for the i machine after firm i undercuts firm j (hence, higher variety due to twice the number of consumers as well as lower hardware prices).

A pair of hardware prices $\langle p^U_A, p^U_B \rangle$ constitutes an Undercut-Proof equilibrium (UPE), see Definition C.2 on page 309, if

$$\pi_B = p^U_B \eta \geq \left(p_A - \delta + \frac{\alpha\eta}{\phi}\right) 2\eta \quad (3.11)$$

$$\pi_A = p^U_A \eta \geq \left(p_B - \delta + \frac{\alpha\eta}{\phi}\right) 2\eta.$$

Solving (3.11) yields the UPE prices and profit levels.

$$p^I_A = p^I_B = \frac{2(\phi\delta - \alpha\eta)}{\phi}, \quad \text{and} \quad \pi^I_A = \pi^I_B = \frac{2\eta(\phi\delta - \alpha\eta)}{\phi}, \quad (3.12)$$

where superscript I stands for "incompatible systems." Hence,

Proposition 3.4
An increase in consumers' preference for variety of software reduces both hardware prices and profits. Formally, as α increases, p_A, p_B, π_A, and π_B all decrease.

Thus, the parameter α is procompetitive meaning that placing more value on the variety of software supporting each hardware brand intensifies competition between the hardware firms. The reason is that if software variety becomes more important, hardware firms intensify their price competition in order to attract more consumers thereby increasing the variety of software written for their machines. Obviously, this result relies on Assumption 3.2 in which the variety of software depends on the number of users of the particular hardware.

Recall that under monopoly Proposition 3.2 showed that an increase in the importance of software variety (an increase in α) increases the price of the hardware since the monopoly manages to extract more surplus when α increases.

To learn about the effect of an increase in the number of users on firms' profit levels, differentiating (3.12) with respect to the number of each type of users yield

$$\frac{\partial \pi_i^I}{\partial \eta} = \frac{2(\phi\delta - 2\alpha\eta)}{\phi} \geq (<)\, 0 \quad \text{if} \quad \alpha \leq (>)\frac{\phi\delta}{2\eta},$$

where either condition is consistent with Assumption 3.3. Therefore,

Proposition 3.5
When the machines are incompatible,

(a) *an increase in consumer population decreases firms' profits when consumers place a sufficient value on software variety.*

(b) *Both, prices and profits increase with the differentiation parameter, δ, and decrease with the software development cost, ϕ.*

The first result is perhaps the most important result of this section and requires an explanation. When consumers place a high value on software variety, competition between the hardware firms intensifies with an increase in consumer population simply because undercutting becomes more profitable as undercutting increases the software variety of the "winning" brand. Intense competition results in lower prices. In fact, under strong desire for software variety, profit declines *despite the fact that the number of each firm's customers increases*. In contrast, when α is low, software variety does not matter much to consumers and hence an increase in consumer population does not affect competition but increases profit due to an increase in the number of customers. The second part of Proposition 3.5 is rather straightforward. An increase in degree of brands' differentiation weakens competition and hence increases profits.

3.3.2   Compatible systems

Suppose that the two hardware producers make their brands compatible, which by Definition 3.1 means that both hardware users are enjoying the entire variety of software written for any machine, $s_A + s_B$. We now need to modify the "undercutting" price (3.10). Brand i producer undercuts brand j producer, by setting p_i' sufficiently low to satisfy

$$p_i' \le p_j - \delta + \alpha(s_A' + s_B' - s_A - s_B) = p_j - \delta. \qquad (3.13)$$

The difference between the undercutting price (3.10) under incompatibility and the undercutting price (3.13) under compatibility is that under compatibility undercutting does not increase the variety of software available to the customers of the undercutting firms simply because under the compatibility case all consumers use all software.

The UPE prices must satisfy $\eta p_i^U \ge 2\eta(p_j - \delta)$ for $i, j = A, B$. Hence, using symmetry (i.e., $p \stackrel{def}{=} p_A^U = p_B^U$),

$$\eta p = 2\eta(p - \delta) \quad \text{or} \quad p^C = 2\delta, \qquad (3.14)$$

where superscript C stands for compatibility.

We can now compare the prices (and therefore profit levels) under compatibility with the case of incompatibility. Comparing (3.14) with (3.12) yields that $p^C \ge p^I$. Therefore,

Proposition 3.6
Equilibrium duopoly hardware prices and profits are higher when the machines are compatible than when they are incompatible.

Altogether, Proposition 3.6 provides a nice ending for our analysis of software variety and its effects on duopoly hardware competition by demonstrating that compatibility weakens price competition compared with incompatibility as it makes the difference in software variety less significant. Note that the same result was found in a completely different setup, where Table 2.3 on page 36 showed that if consumers' preferences exhibit network externalities, compatibility also weakens price competition and results in a higher industry profit. With two different approaches leading to the same conclusion, we can now generalize this result to almost any industry exhibiting some kinds of network effects. In fact, in Chapter 8 we indeed show that banks can only increase their profits by making their automatic-teller machines (ATMs) compatible with the ATMs of the rival banks.

3.4   Software Variety and Partial Compatibility

It is my opinion that compatibility can never be *fully* achieved and that
100 percent compatibility is never really observed. From a technical
point of view, every two different models of machines that are even
made by the same manufacturers cannot always read exactly the same
software packages. As you have probably already noticed, sometimes you
fail to transmit a fax to a remote fax machine because the other machine
does not fully respond to all standards. You have also probably noticed
that audio and video players sometime tend to play at different speeds,
thereby making different sounds. Following Chou and Shy (1993), we
make the following definition.

DEFINITION 3.3
A computer brand i is said to be **partially compatible** *with a ρ_i degree
of compatibility ($0 \leq \rho_i \leq 1$) with computer brand j, if a fraction ρ_i
of the total software written specifically for brand j can also be run on
computer brand i.*

It should be pointed out that Definition 3.3 does not imply that compatibility is a symmetric relation. In other words, it is possible that
a computer of a certain brand is designed to be able to read software
developed for rival machines, but the rival machines are not designed to
read software not specifically designed for them. In the extreme case,
in which $\rho_i = 1$ but $\rho_j = 0$ (machine i can read j software, but machine j cannot read i software), we say that the machines are *one-way
compatible*.

The number of software packages written specifically for machine i
is denoted by s_i, $i = A, B$. The main feature of this model is that the
machines can be partially compatible in the sense that in addition to its
own software, each machine can also run a selected number of software
packages written for its rival machine. That is, ρ_i measures the proportion of machine j software that can be run on an i machine, $i, j = A, B$
and $i \neq j$. Therefore, the total number of software packages actually
available to each i-machine user is given in the following definition.

DEFINITION 3.4
*Let s_A and s_B be the number of software packages written specifically
for A and B machines (operating system), respectively. Then, the* **effective number of software packages** *available to A- and B-users,
respectively are*

$$S_A \stackrel{\text{def}}{=} s_A + \rho_A s_B \quad \text{and} \quad S_B \stackrel{\text{def}}{=} s_B + \rho_B s_A. \tag{3.15}$$

In order to focus on the issue of partial compatibility only, in this section we completely disregard hardware prices and assume that consumers choose which brand to purchase based on the *effective* software variety available for each machine. Formally, let all computer users have the same utility function given by

$$U \stackrel{\text{def}}{=} \begin{cases} S_A & \text{buy computer brand } A \\ S_B & \text{buy computer brand } B, \end{cases} \tag{3.16}$$

where S_A and S_B are given in (3.15).

Finally, on the software production side suppose that there are η_p programmers who can each produce γ ($\gamma > 0$) software packages either for machine A or machine B but not both. Therefore, assuming that all programmers are fully employed implies that the total number of packages produced is

$$s_A + s_B = \gamma \eta_p. \tag{3.17}$$

3.4.1 Determination of brand-specific software variety

Suppose that the software industry produces a positive variety of both types of software. That is, $s_A > 0$ and $s_B > 0$. Consumer adoption equilibrium implies that the utility of buying brand A must be equal to the utility of buying brand B. Otherwise all consumers would switch to using a single brand. Hence, from (3.16) we have

$$S_A = s_A + \rho_A s_B = s_B + \rho_B s_A = S_B, \quad \text{or} \quad \frac{s_A}{s_B} = \frac{1 - \rho_A}{1 - \rho_B}. \tag{3.18}$$

Substituting (3.18) into the full-employment condition (3.17), we can solve for the equilibrium number of software packages written specifically for each machine.

$$s_A = \frac{\gamma \eta_p (1 - \rho_A)}{2 - \rho_A - \rho_B}, \quad \text{and} \quad s_B = \frac{\gamma \eta_p (1 - \rho_B)}{2 - \rho_A - \rho_B}. \tag{3.19}$$

To graphically illustrate how brand-specific software variety is determined, substitute the full-employment condition (3.17) into (3.15) to obtain the effective software varieties as a function of the degrees of compatibility.

$$
\begin{aligned}
S_A(\rho_A) &= s_A + \rho_A(\gamma \eta_p - s_A) = \rho_A \gamma \eta_p + (1 - \rho_A)s_A \tag{3.20} \\
S_B(\rho_B) &= s_B + \rho_A(\gamma \eta_p - s_B) = \rho_B \gamma \eta_p + (1 - \rho_B)s_B.
\end{aligned}
$$

Equations (3.20) are drawn in Figure 3.2.

The horizontal axis in Figure 3.2 measures A's *specific* software (to the right), and B specific software (to the left). The curve which is upward sloping to the right measures A's *effective* software variety whereas

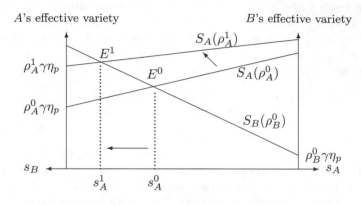

Figure 3.2: Determination of software varieties, $\langle s_A, s_B \rangle$.

the curve which is upward sloping to the left measures B's effective software variety. Both curves are functions of the brands' degrees of compatibility, ρ_A and ρ_B, as defined in (3.20). Note that (3.20) implies that the degree of compatibility parameters, ρ_A and ρ_B affect both the intercept and the slope of the curves measuring the effective software varieties.

Let the degrees of compatibility be ρ_A^0 and ρ_B^0. In view of (3.18), equilibrium software varieties occurs when $S_A = S_B$ (equal effective software variety) hence at the point marked as E^0 in Figure 3.2. Software variety s_A^0 is measured from the left origin and s_B^0 from the right origin.

3.4.2 The effects of changing the degree of compatibility on the variety of brand-specific software

Now, suppose that the producer of computer A makes its machine more compatible with B software (i.e., ρ_A increases from ρ_A^0 to ρ_A^1, so $\rho_A^1 > \rho_A^0$ whereas ρ_B^0 does not change). Clearly the curve $S_B(\rho_B^0)$ in Figure 3.2 does not change. In contrast, the curve S_A shifts upward and its slope declines with the increase from ρ_A^0 to ρ_A^1. The resulting effects on the brand specific software varieties, s_A and s_B are clearly readable in Figure 3.2 (and also from (3.18)). We summarize them with perhaps the most interesting proposition of this book (well, at least according to the author's taste).

Proposition 3.7
When there are two software industries, each producing brand-specific software, an increase in the degree of compatibility of the A-machine with the software written for the B-machine,

(a) will reduce the variety of software specifically written for the A-machine (s_A decreases);

(b) will increase the variety of software specifically written for the B-machine (s_B increases).

Proof. The results are straightforward from Figure 3.2. However, the reader who would like to see a formal proof can verify that (3.19) implies that

$$\frac{ds_A}{d\rho_A} = \frac{-\gamma\eta(1-\rho_B)}{(2-\rho_A-\rho_B)^2} < 0, \quad \text{and} \quad \frac{ds_B}{d\rho_A} = \frac{\gamma\eta(1-\rho_B)}{(2-\rho_A-\rho_B)^2} > 0.$$

∎

The significance of Proposition 3.7 (which was actually known to many computer makers a long time before it was known to economists) is that it shows that a computer manufacturer may refrain from making its machine more compatible with the software supporting the rival machine because compatibility with the rival machine's software will induce software writers to write more software for the rival machine (since part of it is usable for both machines), thereby making the rival machine more attractive to consumers. This result explains why some computer manufacturers may choose different operating systems for their machines.

3.5 Software Piracy

Since the widespread introduction of personal computers in the early 1980s, software firms began gradually removing protection against copying. There were at least two reasons for this policy change on the part of firms.

(a) firms realized that consumers were annoyed by the consequences protective devices had on the effectiveness of their products. For example, see announcements made by MicroPro International Corp. to drop the copy protection from *WordStar 2000* in order to eliminate hardware incompatibility problems and simplify the installation procedure (*PC Week*, February 19, 1985); and by Ashton-Tate to immediately end copy protection on its most popular dBase program (*Computerworld*, August 25, 1986).

(b) When the market expands and competition intensifies, due to large network effects, firms have strategic incentives to remove protection in order to increase the number of consumers using their packages.

In this section we explicitly address the issue of price competition in a differentiated software industry in which firms can choose whether to make their software easy to be copied, or prohibitively costly to be copied. We then study the strategic incentives for firms whether or not to protect their software against piracy.

Our model rests on the assumption that the value of using a specific software package increases with the number of people who legally and illegally use the same package.

As observed by Conner and Rumelt (1991), piracy has two economic impacts on software firms. First, piracy leads to a fall in direct sales. However, by increasing the size of the installed base, it may also boost the demand for the particular software.

In what follows we focus on the software industry only and assume that hardware is purchased without considering software variety. Section 3.7 at the end of this chapter discusses some empirical findings regarding piracy.

Consider a single monopoly software firm which supplies one piece of software to the entire economy. Consumers are heterogeneous in the following way. Some consumers gain an extra utility from the services and support provided by the software firms to those customers who pay for the software, whereas other consumers are "support-independent" and do not gain from the support provided by the software firms. Note that this distinction is similar to the distinction in the copying literature between the relative value of copies and originals to different consumers, see Chapter 7. For example, support-oriented consumers could also be those who are strongly risk-averse vis-à-vis the perspective of being prosecuted for using software illegally.

Formally, consumers are divided according to

Support-oriented consumers (type O): who gain an extra utility from services and support provided by software firms to their legal customers. We assume that there are η support-oriented potential consumers.

Support-independent consumers (type I): who do not derive utility from the services and support provided by the software firms to their legal customers. We assume that there are η support-independent potential consumers.

Altogether, the total population in the economy is 2η.

Each consumer in the economy has *three* options: the consumer can buy software, pirate software, or not use any software. In case of pirating, the consumer does not pay for the software and does not receive any support from software firm.

ASSUMPTION 3.4
(a) The software firm bundles the support with purchase.

(b) *Illegal software users cannot obtain support from an independent supplier.*

The first part of Assumption 3.4 implies that the software producer cannot price discriminate between support-oriented consumers and support-independent consumers. The second part of Assumption 3.4 implies that software support (customers' service) is monopolized by the software writer, hence support-oriented consumers cannot steal the software and buy service from a third-party provider.

Let q denote the number of *users* of this software, that is the total number of consumers who *legally and illegally* use this software. We assume that consumers' utility is enhanced with an increase in the number of other consumers who (legally or illegally) use the same software package. The assumption of a network externality (see Definition 2.3 on page 17) here means that consumers benefit from exchanging files generated by the same software package, which means interacting via the same software increases individuals' utility because these individuals are more productive when they interact with more software users.

Thus, the utility of a support-oriented consumer is given by

$$U^O \stackrel{\text{def}}{=} \begin{cases} (1+\sigma)q - p & \text{buys the software} \\ q & \text{pirates (steals) the software} \\ 0 & \text{does not use this software,} \end{cases} \quad (3.21)$$

where p is the price set by the software monopoly producer, and $\sigma > 0$ measures the value of service to a type O consumer. This means that if a support-oriented consumer buys the software she gains a gross utility of q, plus utility of from the service provided by the firm σq, minus the price.

In contrast, the utility of a support-independent consumer is

$$U^I \stackrel{\text{def}}{=} \begin{cases} q - p & \text{buys the software} \\ q & \text{pirates (steals) the software} \\ 0 & \text{does not use this software.} \end{cases} \quad (3.22)$$

The difference between a support-oriented consumer (3.21) and a support-independent consumer (3.22) is now clear, as the support-independent consumer does not gain any utility from service provided by the software firm to its legal users. Hence, (3.21) and (3.22) yield the following proposition.

Proposition 3.8
(a) *Support-oriented consumers would prefer buying software over pirating software if $p \leq \sigma q$; i.e., if the price of the software package*

does not exceed the value of service provided by the software firm to its legal users.

(b) *If software is not copy protected, support-independent consumers never buy software; i.e., they either pirate it or do not use it at all.*

Whether or not some of the users are pirating depends on the software firm's protection policy as described in Assumption 3.5.

ASSUMPTION 3.5
In addition to price, the monopoly software firm has two options in choosing its protection policy:

Nonprotection policy (n): Any consumer can costlessly pirate the software, but cannot obtain any service from the software firm.

Protection policy (p): Installing devices and/or implementing an enforcement policy in order to make software piracy practically impossible.

Assumption 3.5 means that the software firm can costlessly protect its software and that this protection is absolute. Such a protection is feasible with the help of special devices, such as the installation of plugs attached to the printer's port, or chips that recognize the using machine. Clearly, protection could be costly for the software firm. However, our conclusions become even stronger by assuming costless protection. The main purpose of the present analysis is to investigate which protection policy is profitable for the software firm.

No copy protection

Suppose now that the software is *not* copy-protected, which means that all software users can potentially use the software without having to pay for it, and of course give up on service, if they find it beneficial to do so. Under no protection, Proposition 3.8(b) has shown that support-independent consumers never buy software. Hence, Proposition 3.8(a) implies that the highest price the software monopoly can set and the resulting profit level are

$$p^n = \sigma 2\eta, \quad \text{and} \quad \pi^n = p^n\eta = 2\sigma\eta^2, \tag{3.23}$$

where superscript n stands for nonprotection policy. In this equilibrium each support-oriented consumer buys the software and gains a utility of $U^O = (1 + \sigma)2\eta - p = 2\eta$, and each support-independent consumer pirates the software and gains $U^I = 2\eta$. To see why the price given in

(3.23) is a monopoly equilibrium, note that at this price the support-oriented consumers are indifferent between buying and pirating the software. Hence, raising the price would result in no buyers. In addition, since the support-independent consumers always pirate the software, the monopoly cannot increase profit by lowering the price.

Copy protection

Now, suppose that the software manufacturer protects its software, so piracy is practically *impossible*. In this case, if $\sigma > 1$, there are two candidate equilibria: One, we call a "high-price" equilibrium, where at this price only the η support-oriented consumers buy the software (and since no one pirates the software $q = \eta$). In this case the maximal price that a support-oriented consumer is willing to pay and the resulting profit level are

$$p^{p,H} = (1+\sigma)\eta \quad \text{and} \quad \pi^{p,H} = (1+\sigma)\eta^2, \qquad (3.24)$$

where superscript p stands for a copy protection policy. Notice that since $\sigma > 1$, support-independent consumers will not buy the software (and will therefore not use it), since if they buy they gain a utility of $U^I = 2\eta - (1+\sigma)\eta < 0$.

The second candidate equilibrium is a "low-price" equilibrium where *all* consumers (support-oriented and support-independent consumers) buy this software. In this case, there are 2η buyers so the maximum price the monopoly can charge and the resulting profit level are

$$p^{p,L} = 2\eta \quad \text{and} \quad \pi^{p,L} = 4\eta^2. \qquad (3.25)$$

Comparing the profit levels in (3.24) and (3.25) implies that

$$\pi^{p,H} \geq \pi^{p,L} \quad \text{if and only if} \quad \sigma \geq 3.$$

Note that the above condition applies to the case where $\sigma < 1$ since $\sigma < 1$ implies that $p^{p,L} > p^{p,H}$ so the monopoly's profit maximizing price is $p^{p,L}$. Therefore, if software is protected, the monopoly's price and profit levels are

$$p^p = \begin{cases} (1+\sigma)\eta & \text{if } \sigma \geq 3 \\ 2\eta & \text{if } \sigma < 3, \end{cases} \quad \text{and} \quad \pi^p = \begin{cases} (1+\sigma)\eta^2 & \text{if } \sigma \geq 3 \\ 4\eta^2 & \text{if } \sigma < 3. \end{cases} \qquad (3.26)$$

Should the software firm choose to protect its software?

We now approach our main question. What is the profit maximizing protection strategy for a monopoly software producer? In order to answer this question we need to compare the profit under no copy protection given in (3.23) with the profit levels under copy protection given in (3.26).

Simple calculations show that when $\sigma \geq 3$, $\pi^n \geq \pi^p$, so in this case the monopoly will choose not to protect. However, when $\sigma < 3$, $\pi^n \geq \pi^p$ if $\sigma \geq 2$ so in this case the monopoly will choose not to protect if $2 \leq \sigma < 3$ and to protect if $\sigma < 2$. We now state our main result.

Proposition 3.9
When software users' preferences exhibit network externalities,

(a) *no copy protection yields a higher profit than copy protection if support-oriented consumers place a high value on service offered by the software firm to its legal users, i.e., when $\sigma \geq 2$;*

(b) *copy protection yields a higher profit than no copy protection when support-oriented consumers place a low value for service, $\sigma < 2$.*

Proposition 3.9 demonstrates that if service is very important to support-oriented consumers, nonprotection yields a higher profit than protection. In contrast, if service is not valuable, the firm must protect as the two types of consumers become similar. Figure 3.3 summarizes our main results.

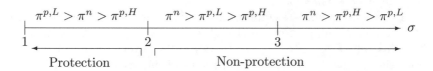

Figure 3.3: Protection policy as a function of support benefits.

Proposition 3.9 (a) was first demonstrated in Conner and Rumelt (1991). In their formulation, the number of support-oriented consumers increases with the aggregate network size and hence software piracy increases the legal demand for software. In present case, the number of support-oriented consumers remains constant at η, however the utility functions (3.21) and (3.22) imply that an increase in the network size from η to 2η increases all consumers' willingness to pay. Hence, there is not much difference between the two demonstrations of this result, except that the present approach does not require the use of calculus.

3.6 Software Pricing and Market Segmentation

Price discrimination according to quality is common in the software industry. The most widely used quality differentiation involves the *removal* of key features from the program and selling the reduced version to consumers with low-willingness to pay. In many instances, the reduced version is released as shareware or freeware via the Internet in order to get the consumers with low-willingness to pay to establish an installed base of users which would then increase the demand from consumers with high-willingness to pay.

Quality discrimination via reduced features is also common in other industries. In the computer hardware industry, Intel introduced its 80386 chip for a high price in 1985. After initial purchases, the 80386SX was introduced at a lower price despite the extra per-unit cost of having to physically disconnect the math coprocessor from the processor itself. Thus, the removal of the math coprocessor made the 386SX chip more costly to produce than the 386 chip itself. However, the 386SX was targeted for the low end of the market. All these examples have something in common.

Proposition 3.10
For the purpose of price discrimination, it may become profitable to increase the unit production cost in order to create a market for low-willingness to pay consumers. As a result, it is commonly observed that the version that is more costly to produce is sold at a lower price than the version that is less costly to produce.

A student of microeconomics may find this observation to be very interesting since classical textbooks teach us that in competitive markets prices fall to unit cost. However, this is not the case in noncompetitive markets in which the manufacturers often need to invest more in order to produce the "cheaper" version. In the Intel example, the 386SX was produced at a higher cost as disabling the math coprocessor was a costly process. The extra afternoon trip Federal Express makes adds cost for the purpose of creating an inferior service. Indeed, Deneckere and McAfee (1994) show that the use of product degradation can, under some circumstances, make all parties to the transaction strictly better off.

Let θ ($\theta > 1$) denote the exogenously-given number of *extra* features embedded in this software. There are two types of consumers, those who are professional and use all the features embedded into the software, and those who are light users that need only the main programs without the fancy features. If we take word processors as an example, professional users are typesetters, authors of books, and people in the academic world. These people have their jobs depending on the output of their word processing. In contrast, light users are often households who need only to type a few letters each month or a shopping list before visiting a shopping mall.

We assume that there are η professional users with a utility function given by

$$U^p \stackrel{\text{def}}{=} \begin{cases} (1+\theta)q - p & \text{if buys the software with } \theta \text{ extra features} \\ q - p & \text{if buys the software with no extra features} \\ 0 & \text{if does not buy the software.} \end{cases}$$
(3.27)

In addition, there are η light users whose utility function is given by

$$U^\ell \stackrel{\text{def}}{=} \begin{cases} q - p & \text{if buys the software with or without the extra features} \\ 0 & \text{if does not buy the software.} \end{cases}$$
(3.28)

Assume that the full version has already been developed so all development costs are considered as sunk. Assume that the software duplication and distribution of each copy is zero (i.e., zero marginal cost). However, let ϕ_r be the cost of developing a *reduced* version of the software, that is, a version that does not have the extra features imbedded in the original complete version.

Selling the complete version only

Suppose that only the complete version is offered for sale at a price denoted by p. Facing the types of consumers defined in (3.27) and (3.28), the profit maximizing prices to consider are either a low price, $p_L = 2\eta$, in which case both types of consumers purchase the software; or setting a high price, $p_H = (1+\theta)\eta$, in which case only the professional users buy this software. Thus, equations (3.27) and (3.28) imply that the number of software buyers and the corresponding profit levels as functions of these two prices are

$$q = \begin{cases} \eta & \text{if } p = (1+\theta)\eta \\ 2\eta & \text{if } p = 2\eta, \end{cases} \quad \text{and} \quad \pi = \begin{cases} \eta^2(1+\theta) & \text{if } p = (1+\theta)\eta \\ 4\eta^2 & \text{if } p = 2\eta. \end{cases}$$
(3.29)

Our assumption that $\theta > 1$ implies the following proposition.

Proposition 3.11
When only the complete version is sold, the monopoly software firm will charge a high price, $p = p_H = (1+\theta)2\eta$ if $\theta > 3$, in which case only professional users buy this software; and a low price $p = p_L = 2\eta$, if $\theta \leq 3$, in which case the entire market is served.

Selling two versions

Now suppose that the software firm sinks ϕ_r into creating a reduced version of this software that does not include the extra θ features. Let

p_r denote the price of the reduced version and p denote the price of the complete version. Clearly, if $p > p_r$, light-users will not purchase the complete version since the extra features do not enhance their utility. Hence, if the seller would like to sell both versions (the complete version to professional users and the reduced version to light users), prices must be set so that

$$(1 + \theta)2\eta - p \geq 2\eta - p_r, \quad \text{or} \quad p - p_r \leq 2\eta\theta \qquad (3.30)$$

meaning that prices should be set so that the utility of a professional user when buying the complete version exceeds the utility from buying the reduced version despite the fact that the price of the reduced version is lower. Another interpretation, prices should be set so that the price differential does not exceed a professional user's utility derived from the extra features.

The method of finding the profit maximizing prices satisfying the condition given in (3.30) is to set the lower price equal to the light users' reservation price, and then add $2\eta\theta$ which is the extra amount professional users are willing to pay for the extra features. Thus, $p_r = 2\eta$ and $p = 2\eta(1 + \theta)$, yielding a profit level given by

$$\pi = \eta p + \eta p_r - \phi_r = 2\eta^2(1 + \theta) + 2\eta^2 - \phi_r. \qquad (3.31)$$

Comparing the profit generated from selling two versions (3.31) with the profit generated from selling only the complete version given in (3.29) yields our main proposition.

Proposition 3.12
If $\phi_r < 2\eta^2\theta$,

(a) *the software firm makes a higher profit by selling two versions of software;*

(b) *and by selling the version that is more costly to develop at a lower price.*

Proposition 3.12 demonstrates that firms should be ready to invest in order to segment the market between heavy and light users. In addition, a profitable segmentation may imply that the firms may have to incur extra cost in order to create a version that is sold in the market prior to its attempt to segment the market.

3.7   Empirical Findings

In this section we provide some justifications for the assumptions made in this chapter concerning the value of software variety to computer users. The reader is also referred to Section 2.4 in Chapter 2 where we discussed empirical studies confirming the existence of software-specific network effects.

3.7.1 Operating systems and software variety

Gandal, Greenstein, and Salant (1999) statistically analyze the transition from the CP/M operating system for microcomputers which was widely used by 1980 to the DOS (Disk Operating System) introduced by Microsoft for the early IBM-PC 16-bit models. The use the term *orphaning* comes out of competition between competing standards. Orphaning occurs when late adopters of a system choose a technology that is incompatible with the technology adopted by early users and suppliers of supporting services who cease to provide their products for the old technology.

By 1984 there were about 11,000 software programs available for the MS-DOS operating system, so by 1986 the CP/M operating system (and even its 16-bit version) effectively was dead. The interesting part of this history is that there is no evidence that the MS-DOS was superior to the CP/M operating system, which makes the question why there was a change in the operating system more interesting. Of course, one answer would be that consumers and software developers simply followed IBM's choice of its operating system. Gandal, Greenstein, and Salant (1999) used quarterly data on the number of pages of advertisements on microcomputers in Byte magazine as proxies for sales, which approximate the demand for operating systems. They track the sales of CP/M from 1978 to October 1986, and the DOS from 1981, running VARs (vector-auto-regressions) on operating system and software/peripheral availability. They found two-way effects: one in which an increase in CP/M or DOS software lead to an increase in advertising for microcomputers running the particular operating system; and the other way around where an increase in advertising for microcomputers running a particular operating system also increases machine-specific software. Thus, Gandal, Greenstein, and Salant (1999) explain the change in the operating system by their finding that the feedback from hardware to software differs significantly between CP/M and DOS.

3.7.2 Compact-disc players and variety of CD titles

The interaction between hardware and the variety of supporting software is *not* limited to the computer industry. The compact-disc technology was developed by Philips in 1979, and introduced in the United States only in 1983. Gandal, Kende, and Rob (2000), estimate a structural model of the CD industry, where the CD player is the hardware and CD titles are the software. Their research aims to investigate the extent to which the diffusion of CD players depends on the variety of software (in addition to price), and the extent to which the provision of CD titles depends on the installed base of the hardware (in addition to the cost of pressing CDs).

Using quarterly data from 1985 to 1992, they demonstrate a positive relationship between the sales of CD-players and changes in the availability of CD titles. In a regression of CD-player sales on changes in software variety, price, and quarterly dummies; and a regression of changes in variety on CD sales, fixed costs, and quarterly dummies; they were able to find a positive feedback between CD-player sales and changes in the availability of CD titles.

3.7.3   Software piracy

Givon, Mahajan, and Muller (1995) suggest a modeling approach to track legal and illegal diffusion of software in order to estimate the pirated adoptions over time and the percentage of legal adoptions due to the influence of pirates. Their study focused on two popular types of software (spreadsheets and word processors) in England. The major difficulty of such a study is that even if one has data on the number of microcomputers and the legal adoption of software, still one cannot assume that all microcomputer owners will either buy the two types of software or use pirated copies. For this reason, building a diffusion model was necessary.

A monthly data of sales of PCs, legal sales of spreadsheets and word processors in England from 1987 to 1992 reveals that the ratio of pirates to buyers increased to six pirates for every buyer who has purchased the software. However, they demonstrate that during the same time the percentage of unit sales of buyers due to the influence of pirates has also grown. In fact, from 1988 on, more than 80 percent of the software purchased by buyers was probably the result of the the influence of the pirates. Thus, through word-of-mouth interactions, pirates may influence the potential users to adopt software, and some of these adopters may eventually purchase the software.

They also found that the percentage of pirated unit adoptions due to the influence of buyers decreased over time stabilizing at around 15 percent in 1987. As expected, all pirated adoptions in the beginning of the diffusion process were due to the influence of buyers because there were not too many pirates.

3.7.4   The future of software

The desire for software compatibility has led to the emergence of a software leader called Microsoft which supplies its Windows operating system and its Office software to more than 90 percent of the personal computers in the world. However, in recent years with the increase in accessibility and the speed of the Internet there is a tendency to disconnect the operating system from office software by developing software that could be supplied on the Internet.

Sun Microsystems, Inc., has been the most visible advocate for removing software from crammed hard drives of computers and placing software on the Internet. The advantages of Internet-based software are:

Compatibility: Users need not worry about compatibility of software with operating systems and CPUs. Users need only acquire machines that can access the Internet via machine-specific browsers. The software itself would run the servers of the Internet-service providers thereby eliminating the need for hardware compatibility.

Accessibility: Traveling users can access this software from any machine in their hotels, airports, offices they tend visit, and even airplanes, thereby eliminating the need to carry their personal bulky machines loaded with their desired software. Today, there are several sites providing e-mail services and calendars with personal storage capability (e.g., `www.hotmail.com`, `www.calendar.com`, `www.calendar.yahoo.com`, and `www.anyday.com`). Soon, it is expected that sites will provide word-processing and spread-sheet services.

Installation and upgrading: Most users are unable to install software themselves. Network computers require no installation as the software resides on the servers of the service providers. Consumers can save effort reinstalling the software each time upgrades appear on the market which makes old versions obsolete.

Flexible payments: Network software will be rented rather than sold. This will allow users with different needs to pay according to the actual usage rather than a lump sum for acquiring the software. Payments according to needs increase economic efficiency, light users pay less than heavy users.

3.8   Exercises

1. Consider the model of software variety determination under a monopoly hardware firm analyzed in Section 3.2. Calculate the software variety

when the monopoly sets its price at the level $p = w/4$, then $p = w/2$, and lastly $p = w$. Conclude how an increase in the hardware price affects the variety of software available for this machine. Explain!

2. Consider the model of software variety determination under a monopoly hardware firm analyzed in Section 3.2. Suppose that the utility function (3.4) is now modified to capture a lower utility from paying the hardware price p. Thus, assume that

$$U \stackrel{\text{def}}{=} \begin{cases} \alpha s - \gamma p & \text{Buys the computer and entire variety of software} \\ 0 & \text{Buys none.} \end{cases}$$

(a) Calculate the price charged by the monopoly hardware firm and the resulting equilibrium software variety.

(b) How would an increase in the parameter γ affect the hardware price and the equilibrium variety of software. Explain!

3. Consider a simplified version of the duopoly hardware industry of Section 3.3. Instead of assuming that machine-specific software variety is determined by the number of users of each software, we now modify (3.8) and assume that the variety of software is *fixed* at the levels of $s_A = 400$ A-specific packages, and $s_B = 600$ B-specific packages. Answer the following questions.

(a) Suppose that each firm sells to its η oriented consumers, and let p_B be given. Which price does firm A have to set in order to undercut firm B if the machines are incompatible? Prove your answer. *Hint:* Since software variety is fixed, undercutting does not enhance the software variety available for the machine produced by the undercutting firm. That is, the variety of A-specific software remains 400 packages and the variety of B-specific software remains 600 packages regardless of the number of users.

(b) Now, let p_A be given. Which price does firm B have to set in order to undercut firm A if the machines are incompatible? Prove your answer.

(c) Calculate the UPE prices and firms' profit levels assuming that the systems are incompatible. Conclude which firm makes a higher profit and explain.

(d) Suppose again that each firm sells to its η oriented consumers. Which price does firm A have to set in order to undercut firm B if the machines are compatible? Prove your answer.

(e) Calculate the UPE prices and firms' profit levels assuming that the systems are compatible. Conclude which firm makes a higher profit and explain.

(f) Compare the profit each firm makes under the incompatibility and compatibility regimes. Explain your result.

4. Consider a market for a popular software DOORS^{TM}. There are 100 support-oriented (type-O) consumers, and 200 support-independent (type-I) consumers, with utility functions given by

$$U^O \overset{\text{def}}{=} \begin{cases} 3q - p & \text{buys the software} \\ q & \text{pirates (steals) the software} \\ 0 & \text{does not use this software,} \end{cases}$$

and

$$U^I \overset{\text{def}}{=} \begin{cases} q - p & \text{buys the software} \\ q & \text{pirates (steals) the software} \\ 0 & \text{does not use this software,} \end{cases}$$

where q denotes the number of users of this software (which includes the number of buyers and the number of pirates, if piracy takes place). Suppose that the software is costless to produce and costless to protect. Also, assume that DOORS^{TM} provides support only to those consumers who buy the software.

(a) Suppose that DOORS^{TM} is *not* protected, so piracy is an option for every consumer. Calculate the software seller's profit-maximizing price. Prove your answer.

(b) Suppose that DOORS^{TM} is protected, so piracy is impossible. Calculate the software seller's profit-maximizing price. Prove your answer.

(c) Suppose that the producer of DOORS^{TM} has the option to protect or not to protect the software. Which option yields a higher profit. Prove your answer.

3.9   Selected References

Chou, C., and O. Shy. 1990. "Network Effects without Network Externalities." *International Journal of Industrial Organization* 8: 259–270.

Chou, C., and O. Shy. 1993. "Partial Compatibility and Supporting Services." *Economics Letters* 41: 193–197.

Chou, C., and O. Shy. 1996. "Do Consumers Gain or Lose When More People Buy the Same Brand?" *European Journal of Political Economy* 12: 309–330.

Church, J., and N. Gandal. 1992a. "Integration, Complementary Products and Variety." *Journal of Economics and Management Strategy* 1: 651–676.

Church, J., and N. Gandal. 1992b. "Network Effects, Software Provision, and Standardization." *Journal of Industrial Economics* 40: 85–104.

Church, J., and N. Gandal. 1993. "Complementary Network Externalities and Technological Adoption." *International Journal of Industrial Organization* 11: 239–260.

Church, J., and N. Gandal. 1996. "Strategic Entry Deterrence: Complementary Products as Installed Base. *European Journal of Political Economy* 12: 331–354.

Conner, K. and R. Rumelt. 1991. "Software Piracy: An Analysis of Protection Strategies." *Management Science* 37: 125–139.

Deneckere, R., and P. McAfee. 1996. "Damaged Goods." *Journal of Economics and Management Strategy* 5: 149–174.

Farrell, J. and C. Shapiro. 1992. "Standard Setting in High-Definition Television." *Brookings Papers: Microeconomics* 1–93.

Gandal, N. 1995. "A Selective Survey of the Literature on Indirect Network Externalities." *Research in Law and Economics* 17: 23–31.

Gandal, N., S. Greenstein, and D. Salant. 1999. "Adoptions and Orphans in the Early Microcomputer Market," *Journal of Industrial Economics* XLVII: 87–105.

Gandal, N., M. Kende, and R. Rob. 2000. "The Dynamics of Technological Adoption in Hardware/Software Systems: The Case of Compact Disc Players," *Rand Journal of Economics* 31: 43–61.

Givon, M., V. Mahajan, and E. Muller. 1995. "Software Piracy: Estimation of Lost Sales and the Impact on Software Diffusion." *Journal of Marketing* 59: 29–37.

Shy, O., and J. Thisse. 1999. "A Strategic Approach to Software Protection." *Journal of Economics & Management Strategy* 8: 163–190.

Chapter 4

Technology Advance and Standardization

Chapter 2 taught us how to compute the network sizes when brand-producing firms compete in prices and consumer preferences exhibit network externalities. Our main assumptions in Chapter 2 were that the technologies were given to the firms (i.e., the firms could not choose or update their technologies), and that governments did not intervene.

In this chapter we depart from these assumptions. Section 4.1 analyzes how firms choose their technologies. Section 4.2 departs from the static nature of our modeling and analyzes the frequency of new-technology adoption in an environment when innovation is constantly undertaken. Section 4.3 analyzes the world market, where we ask whether governments benefit from recognizing the standards used in the production and design of products produced abroad.

4.1   New Technology Adoption: A Static Approach

It is widely acknowledged that a radical technology change requires (or, actually is defined by) a complete redesign of the product, its features, and even its function. When facing a technological revolution, the first question that comes to mind is whether the new technology will be adopted given the large installed base of the existing inferior technology, see Farrell and Saloner (1985, 1986), and Katz and Shapiro (1992, 1986), Cabral (1990), Choi (1996), and Choi and Thum (1998).

Consumers and producers face constant technology changes in every part of their lives. LP (long-play) records have been replaced by a digital CD (compact-disk) technology. Video cassettes are replaced by DVDs (digital video disks). Cellular phones replace the wire technology in Scandinavian countries. Internet services replace some stores and libraries.

Consider a technology-adoption game played by two users (or firms) displayed in Table 4.1.

User _B_

		NEW TECHNOLOGY	OLD TECHNOLOGY
User _A_	NEW	α $\qquad$ α	γ $\qquad$ δ
	OLD	δ $\qquad$ γ	β $\qquad$ β

Table 4.1: The static new technology adoption game

We make the following assumption.

ASSUMPTION 4.1
Both users exhibit network externalities for both technologies. Formally, in terms of Table 4.1, we assume that $\alpha > \delta$ and $\beta > \gamma$.

That is, using the same technology as the other user yields a higher utility (or profit) than using any technology alone. The reader who has read Appendix A can easily prove the following proposition.

Proposition 4.1
Under Assumption 4.1, if users exhibit network externalities then there exist two Nash equilibrium (Definition A.4 on page 292) for the static technology adoption game displayed in Table 4.1 given by (NEW, NEW) and (OLD, OLD).

The existence of multiple equilibria in this game raises the question how the two firms coordinate their actions. Recalling the Pareto ranking of outcomes given in Definition A.6 on page 296, Farrell and Saloner (1985) provided the following terminology for two commonly observed market failures.

DEFINITION 4.1

(a) If (OLD, OLD) is the played Nash equilibrium outcome, and if the outcome (NEW, NEW) Pareto dominates the outcome (OLD, OLD), then we call this situation **excess inertia**.

(b) If (NEW, NEW) is the played Nash equilibrium outcome, and if the outcome (OLD, OLD) Pareto dominates the outcome (NEW, NEW), then we call this situation **excess momentum**.

Thus, *excess momentum* occurs when a new technology replaces an old technology, but the old technology yields a higher utility (or profit) to both users than the new technology. In contrast, *excess inertia* occurs when a new technology yields a higher utility (profit) to both users, however, in equilibrium all users stay with the old technology. Using the example displayed in Table 4.1, if $\beta > \alpha$ and if (NEW, NEW) is played, then we have excess momentum. In contrast, if $\beta < \alpha$ and if (OLD, OLD) is played, then we have excess inertia.

The reader will probably have no problem in finding a large number of real-life examples reflecting a situation of excess inertia. For example, most users of the most popular operating system are fully aware that the system is far from being trouble free (think of how many times you have to reboot your machine each day). However, excess inertia keeps us all from unilaterally shifting to better available operating systems. The reader probably finds it harder to find examples of excess momentum. One example would be the switch to less rigid car bumpers which took place since 1982 when President Reagan relaxed the standards on the effectiveness of bumpers during a crash. Clearly, the switch to plastic-made bumpers is a cost-reducing innovation that car producers were eager to adopt. The method used to have consumers accepting the change from strong bumpers to plastic-made bumper was to change the fashion so that car bumpers will have the same color as the body of the car. Most consumer organizations have managed to prove that rational consumers should be willing to pay an extra \$400 to have a stronger bumper (that could reduce the repair cost after light crush by thousands of dollars). However, the change in the fashion, which now requires bumpers to have the same color as the body of the car, finalized the transition from the old technology to the new (inferior) technology. Thus, car bumpers present a nice example of excess momentum.

4.2   Technology Revolutions: A Dynamic Approach

The purpose of this section is to identify several major factors affecting the pace at which technological progress occurs. Whereas the literature on technological progress focused on the supply side of new technology providers (e.g., firms' incentives to finance R&D and the effect of the patent system), the present analysis isolates a major demand side factor affecting the frequency of new technology adoption, which is the structure of consumer preferences over technological advance and network sizes supporting of each generation of technologies. The advantage of using the demand side approach analyzed in this section is that it provides an explanation why some technologies are replaced more often than others.

Our analysis below identifies several important factors affecting the timing and frequency of new technology adoption, including

(a) consumers' degree of substitution between getting a more advanced technology, and the network size (number of consumers purchasing products belonging to the same generation of technologies);

(b) the technology growth rate and consumer population size;

(c) the degree in which a new technology is compatible with the old technology to be replaced.

The first item on this list is the primary focus of this analysis which attempts to answer the following questions: (a) why technology is replaced more often in some industries than in others, or alternatively, (b) what type of consumers tend to adopt the new technology based products, and what type of consumers do not switch to the new technology product.

The second item on the above list is important since the technology growth rate and population size affect the benefits new consumers derive from adopting a new technology. The third item on this list is the effect of downward compatibility (see Definition 2.2 on page 16). This is important since in most cases technological breakthroughs require redesigning the product, and therefore need not be 100 percent downward compatible with the existing technologies. In many cases, the new technology will be completely incompatible with old technologies, whereas some will be only partially compatible.

More precisely, we demonstrate that new technologies are adopted more frequently when consumers treat quality and network size as more substitutable. The reason is that under high substitution, an increase in quality of the technology causes a significant utility increase even if the network size does not change. In contrast, when the degree of substitution is low, an increase in quality does not enhance utility unless the increase in quality is accompanied by an increase in the network size.

Following Shy (1996), consider a technology or a product which improves over time. For example, in the computer industry, new and faster chips are introduced very often, however, not every improvement is adopted and marketed. Suppose that the utility of consumers is enhanced by the quality of the technology embodied in the product they purchase and by the number of old and new consumers using the same technology. Then, the newest available technology in each period may not be adopted since new consumers may prefer to use a lower quality product but benefit from a larger network of users (composed of old and young consumers). Using this environment, we analyze the frequency of new technology adoption, and focus on how consumer preferences, consumer population, and technology growth rate affect the frequency of new technology adoption.

Consider a discrete time overlapping generations (OLG) economy, where in each period t, $t = 1, 2, \ldots$, the consumer population of the economy consists of two groups of individuals: η_t young consumers and η_{t-1} old consumers. We use the term "generation of consumers" merely for the sake of illustrating a situation where in each period the market consists of entering consumers who have not purchased the product before and a number of consumers who already own this durable product.

4.2.1 Technology improvements

We denote by T_t, $(T_t > 0, \ t = 1, 2, 3, \ldots)$ the period t quality of the potential state-of-the-art technology, and assume that T_t is *exogenously* given and is strictly increasing over time, (i.e., $T_t > T_{t-1}$ for every t). Thus, T_t reflects the ongoing output of an innovation processes which is not modeled here. Since a new technology is not necessarily adopted each period, we denote by V_t the *actual* quality level (stand-alone value) of the period t technology, embodied into the product, to a period t young who purchases this product. Hence, $V_t \leq T_t$ for all t.

Altogether, the actual technological quality consumed by the young consumers in period t is given by

$$V_t = \begin{cases} T_t & \text{if the young at } t \text{ adopt the new technology} \\ V_{t-1} & \text{otherwise.} \end{cases} \tag{4.1}$$

Thus, the quality-law-of-motion (4.1) implies that although technologies (e.g., faster chips) are continuously developed, if no adoption occurs at t, then the quality of the technology does not change compared with period $t - 1$, i.e., $V_t = V_{t-1}$. Investment in the context of our analysis means spending resources on converting the state-of-the-art technology into actual production. Therefore, as frequently observed, some newly developed chips are not adopted (skipping over technologies is commonly observed).

To each newly adopted technology we attach a "serial" number denoted by g, $g = 1, 2, \ldots$. Figure 1 illustrates the path of state-of-the-art technology improvements (T_t), the adoption dates of generations g and $g + 1$ technologies $(t_g$ and $t_{g+1})$, and the path of actually adopted technologies (V_t).

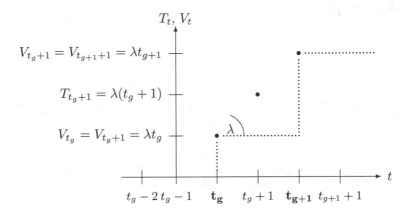

Figure 4.1: Exogenous technology development path (T_t), and the actually adopted technology path (V_t).

The thick dots in Figure 4.1 is the path of T_t which is the value of the state-of-the-art technology available for adoption at each date t. The dotted line illustrates the path of V_t, which is the actual technology available to the young consumers at each date t. t_g and t_{g+1} are two technology adoption dates when innovation brings the actual technology (quality) level available to consumers to the state-of-the-art level given by T_t. At these dates V_t "jumps" to the level of T_t. Note that it is assumed that if adoption does not occur for several periods, once adoption is undertaken, the actual technology catches up with the state-of-the-art level. Thus, some technology levels are not utilized since they are never adopted.

We now make a simplifying assumption that will generate stationary technology-replacement dates.

ASSUMPTION 4.2
The potential state-of-the-art technology follows a linear growth pattern. Formally, $T_t \overset{\text{def}}{=} \lambda t$.

Thus the quality of the state of the art technology, if adopted, is a constant λ multiplied by the adoption *date* as displayed in Figure 4.1. The interpretation of this multiplication is simple, as it merely reflects the fact that the state-of-the-art technology available for adoption at t is improving with t.

4.2.2 Consumers and changing technologies

Consumers adopt the product only when they are young, and are assumed to gain utility from first period consumption only. We further assume that the utility of each young consumer exhibits network externalities in the sense that utility increases with the number of (old and young) consumers using the same technology.

We assume that new generation products are incompatible with old generation products. Therefore, if consumers adopt the state-of-the-art technology, they cannot benefit from the expanded network gains since the old-generation consumers have already purchased the old technology. Thus, if all young consumers buy an old technology product, then the (effective) period t number of users of this technology is $\eta_{t-1} + \eta_t$. However, if all the young consumers buy a new technology product, then since the new technology is incompatible with the old technology, the number of new technology users is equal to η_t. Hence, we assume that the utility of a young consumer of generation τ is given by

$$
U^\tau = \begin{cases} u(T_\tau, \eta_\tau) & \text{young consumers adopt state-of-the-art} \\ u(V_{\tau-1}, \eta_{\tau-1} + \eta_\tau) & \text{young consumers adopt old technology.} \end{cases}
$$
(4.2)

We assume that the function $u(,)$ is monotonically increasing in both arguments (the quality of the technology available at τ, and the effective network size).

The problem of each young consumer of generation τ is to choose whether to purchase the product based on the old technology or whether to purchase the product based on the new technology. Notice that we disregard a potential coordination problem associated with how all young consumers manage to choose the same technology. Recall that this issue has already been dealt with in Assumption 2.2 on page 20.

Generation $t = \tau$ young consumers would choose to purchase the new technology product if and only if

$$
u(T_\tau, \eta_\tau) \geq u(V_{\tau-1}, \eta_{\tau-1} + \eta_\tau). \tag{4.3}
$$

That is, generation τ adopts the new technology product if the utility from the higher quality product ($T_\tau > V_{\tau-1}$) combined with a lower network size ($\eta_\tau \leq \eta_{\tau-1} + \eta_\tau$) overtakes the utility from the old technology product.

4.2.3   New technology adoption

We now turn to investigating how the degree of substitution between the advance of technology and the network size affects the adoption of new technologies. We focus on two extreme cases: The two components are either perfect complements or perfect substitutes. These extreme cases highlight all the intuition behind the adoption of new technologies while keeping the analysis very simple and mainly graphical.

An example for the case of complements

Consider the preferences for *perfect complements* given by

$$
U^\tau = \begin{cases} \min\{T_\tau; \eta_\tau\} & \text{if state-of-the-art is adopted} \\[2ex] \min\{V_{\tau-1}; \eta_{\tau-1} + \eta_\tau\} & \text{if old technology is adopted.} \end{cases} \tag{4.4}
$$

Figure 4.2 illustrates the indifference curves generated by the utility function (4.4), in the network-quality (η, T) space.

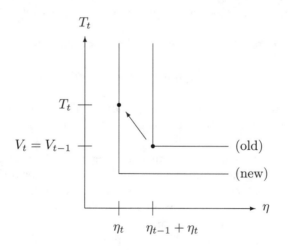

Figure 4.2: Indifference curves exhibiting perfect complements: New incompatible technologies are never adopted.

Figure 4.2 illustrates that new technologies will never be adopted even if the exogenously-given technology growth rate is very high. This happens when the network and technology levels are perfect complements, technology growth cannot be "enjoyed" by young consumers because the adoption of a new technology is associated with a drop in the network size from $\eta_{t-1} + \eta_t$ to η_{t-1} only. Therefore, a market with this type of consumers is likely to be stuck on the original technology with no possibility that a newer and improved technology will ever replace it. We call this a *stagnation equilibrium*.

An example for the case of substitutes

Consider the widely used linear preferences given by

$$
U^\tau = \begin{cases} T_\tau + \eta_\tau & \text{if state-of-the-art is adopted} \\ V_{\tau-1} + \eta_{\tau-1} + \eta_\tau & \text{if old technology is adopted.} \end{cases} \tag{4.5}
$$

Figure 4.3 illustrates the indifference curves generated by the utility function (4.5), in the network-quality (η, T) space.

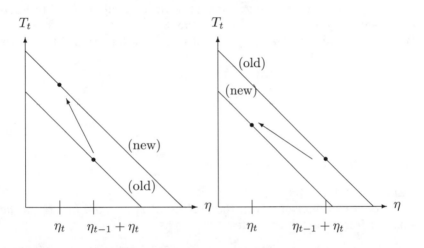

Figure 4.3: Indifference curves exhibiting perfect substitutes: New incompatible technologies are adopted (Left); not adopted (Right).

In contrast to Figure 4.2, Figure 4.3 (left) illustrates how under perfect substitution consumers may benefit from adopting new technologies even if the new technologies are incompatible. Figure 4.3 (right) illustrates that even under perfect substitution, a new technology is not adopted since the quality improvement is not sufficiently high.

Altogether, when consumer preferences exhibit perfect substitution, the dynamic process proceeds as follows. Since technology grows exogenously over time, a new technology is not adopted for several periods as the period t quality of the state-of-the-art technology T_t is not sufficiently high to offset a reduction in the network size, as displayed in Figure 4.3 (right). However, over time T_t continues to grow and in a certain period the gains from adopting the new incompatible technology outweighs the loss of utility associated with adopting a technology which is incompatible with the technology already adopted by the existing older generation, as displayed in Figure 4.3 (left).

4.2.4 Calculating the duration of technologies

Assume that each generation is composed of exactly η consumers, that is $\eta_t = \eta$ for every $t = 1, 2, \ldots$. Also, suppose that all new generations have the utility function given in (4.5) meaning that they treat technological quality and network size as perfect substitutes.

Following Assumption 4.2, the quality of the state-of-the-art technology available for adoption at t is $T_t = \lambda t$. Let g be the latest technology already adopted in period $t = t_g$ (hence, bears a quality level of $T = T_{t_g}$). We now ask the following question: At what date will a newer technology, technology $g + 1$, be adopted? Formally, we seek to calculate t_{g+1}. By the *adoption condition* given in (4.3), the new adoption date, t_{g+1} is found from

$$u\left(\lambda t_{g+1}, \eta\right) \geq u\left(\lambda t_g, 2\eta\right),$$

or, in view of the specific utility function (4.5)

$$\lambda t_{g+1} + \eta \geq \lambda t_g + 2\eta, \quad \text{or} \quad t_{g+1} \geq t_g + \frac{\eta}{\lambda}. \tag{4.6}$$

We need the following mathematical definition.

DEFINITION 4.2
*Let x be a real number. Then the **ceiling** of x, denoted by $\lceil x \rceil$, is the smallest integer which is greater or equal to x.*

For example, $\lceil 3.72 \rceil = 4$, $\lceil 3.001 \rceil = 4$, and $\lceil 3 \rceil = 3$. Therefore, we can now write the exact date in which a state-of-the-art technology will replace the current one.

$$t_{g+1} = \left\lceil t_g + \frac{\eta}{\lambda} \right\rceil. \tag{4.7}$$

We enrich our terminology by the following definition.

DEFINITION 4.3
(a) *The **duration** of technology g, denoted by Δg, is the time difference between the date when generation g technology was first adopted and the date in which generation $g + 1$ replaced it. Formally, $\Delta g \overset{\text{def}}{=} t_{g+1} - t_g$.*

(b) *Suppose that all technologies have the same duration. That is, suppose that $\Delta \overset{\text{def}}{=} \Delta(g + 1) = \Delta g$ for all $g = 1, 2, \ldots$. Then, the*

> ***frequency of technology revolutions*** *(or new-technology adoption), denoted by* f *is* $f \overset{\text{def}}{=} 1/\Delta$.

Equation (4.7) and Definition 4.3 imply that

$$\Delta_g = \left\lceil \frac{\eta}{\lambda} \right\rceil \quad \text{and} \quad f = \frac{1}{\Delta_g} = \frac{1}{\left\lceil \frac{\eta}{\lambda} \right\rceil}.$$

Therefore,

Proposition 4.2

(a) *The duration of each technology,* Δ, *increases with the population size of each generation,* η, *and decreases with the technology-growth parameter,* λ.

(b) *The frequency of new technology adoption,* f, *decreases with the population size of each generation and increases with the technology-growth parameter.*

The positive correlation between the duration of each technology and the population size of each generation of consumers constitutes a particular network effect which we now define.

DEFINITION 4.4
If an increase in population increases the duration of technologies (decreases the frequency of new technology adoption), then we say that a ***lock-in*** *effect prevails.*

Thus, the lock-in effect occurs when a large network of old users makes the new technology adoption less desirable whenever the new technology is incompatible with the old technology. Lock-in effects have been analyzed in Arthur (1989), Farrell and Saloner (1985, 1986), and Katz and Shapiro (1986).

4.3   International Standardization

The trade policy literature focuses mainly on the strategic effects and welfare consequences of "traditional" trade barriers such as tariffs, quotas, and VERs. The success of GATT in reducing these trade restrictions has been accompanied by an increase in less visible trade restrictions or nontariff barriers (NTBs) in which standardization policy is often used as a key instrument. The Uruguay Round of GATT left countries with the option of setting standards on safety and health grounds. Our goal in this section is to examine strategic aspects of governmental standardization policy and the welfare implications when products and standards are horizontally differentiated.

We analyze governments' incentives to recognize foreign standards when there are international network effects. That is, the utility of each consumer rises with an increase in the number of consumers who use the same brand regardless of whether they live in their own country or abroad.

4.3.1 General background about international standardization

The International Electrotechnical Commission (IEC) was founded in 1906 and the International Organization for Standardization (ISO) was founded in 1946. Membership in international standards organizations is open to all countries of the world. The main task is to elaborate and publish standards and to harmonize standards of their members. The bulk of work carried out by the ISO and IEC leads to international standards. However, ISO/IEC members are not obliged to implement international standards as national standards. Every member can freely decide whether it wishes to recognize the international standard directly, that is, to accept it as a national standard, or to develop its own national standard.

There is some concern that while the European Community is committed to ISO/IEC standards, the United States relies heavily on domestic standards. For example, in 1989 the United States recognized approximately 89,000 standards, however, only seventeen were adopted directly from the ISO and none were adopted from the IEC. It should be pointed out that regarding telecommunication the U.S. Federal Communications Commission (FCC) adopted the policy where the standard for terminal equipment is limited only to "no harm to the network" in the very early stage of the industry's deregulation process. This means that no certification is needed, and all consumers can hook in their own phones and fax machines as long as they do not harm the system.

In the European Community, Article 30 of the 1957 Treaty of Rome prohibited not only quantitative restrictions on imports but also *all* measures having *equivalent* effects. Article 36 of the Treaty permits prohibition or restrictions on the movement of goods based on health and safety concerns. Up until 1985, the Community (using the so called "old approach") removed technical barriers by harmonizing technical product specifications. This policy was hard to implement since it fixed technical specifications without taking account of the diversity of production methods and consumers' preferences for variety. In 1985, the Commission adopted a *new approach* to technical harmonization and standards. Under the new policy the manufacturer may freely choose how to meet the essential requirements (EC directives). To assist in the process, the

Commission issued mandates to European Standardization bodies to develop voluntary standards which meet the essential requirements. The European Community has also taken up a number of initiatives in order to reduce technical barriers to trade outside the legislative framework, by supporting close cooperation between the European standard setting bodies and International Standards bodies like the ISO/IEC.

4.3.2 A model with international network externalities

Consider a world with two countries indexed by k, $k = A, B$. In each country there is one firm producing a national brand. Let the firm in country A produce brand 1 and the firm in country B produce brand 2. We index brands by i, $i = 1, 2$. For simplicity, assume that production is costless. Brands are assumed to operate on different standards, where we assume that the standard of the locally produced brand is recognized in the country where it is produced. Whether or not governments recognize the foreign standard is the subject of present analysis.

In each country there are 2η consumers. η consumers are called brand 1 oriented, whereas the remaining η consumers are brand 2 oriented. Let q_i denote the world-aggregate consumption of brand i, $i = 1, 2$. Each consumer in each country buys at most one unit of one of the brands only. This means that q_i also measures the world-aggregate number of consumers who buy brand i, $i = 1, 2$. We rule out market segmentation which means that the price of each brand is the same anywhere in the world. Let p_i denote the international price of brand i. We define the utility function of brand i oriented consumer in country k by

$$U_i^k \stackrel{\text{def}}{=} \begin{cases} \alpha q_i - p_i & \text{if he buys brand } i \\ \alpha q_j - \delta - p_j & \text{if he buys brand } j \neq i, \end{cases} \tag{4.8}$$

where $\alpha > 0$ measures the intensity of the network effects, and $i, j = 1, 2$ and $i \neq j$.

Mutual recognition

We first look for an equilibrium where both governments recognize all standards of all products. Therefore, each firm can costlessly export its brand and sell it in the other country. Figure 4.4 illustrates the movement of goods when each country recognizes all standards.

We now solve for an Undercut-proof equilibrium (UPE), see Definition C.2 on page 309, in price competition between the two international firms. Figure 4.4 demonstrates that in this equilibrium each firm sells η units domestically, and η units are exported to its brand-oriented consumers overseas. Thus, $q_1 = q_2 = 2\eta$. If firm i undercuts the price set by firm j, i.e., firm i sets $p_i' \leq p_j - \delta$, then the network sizes become

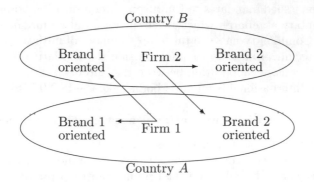

Figure 4.4: Trade under mutual standard recognition.

$q'_i = 4\eta$ and $q'_j = 0$. Therefore, in an UPE, for each firm $i, j = 1, 2$ and $i \neq j$, given p_i, firm j maximizes p_j to solve

$$2\eta p_i \geq 4\eta \left[p_j - \delta + \alpha(4\eta - 2\eta) \right],$$

yielding unique UPE prices and profit levels given by

$$p_1^{\text{MR}} = p_2^{\text{MR}} = 2(\delta - 2\alpha\eta), \quad \text{and} \quad \pi_1^{\text{MR}} = \pi_2^{\text{MR}} = 4\eta(\delta - 2\alpha\eta), \quad (4.9)$$

where the superscript "MR" stands for mutual recognition.

Each consumer buys his ideal brand, hence (4.8) and (4.9) imply that

$$U_i^k = \alpha(2\eta) - p_i^{\text{MR}} = 2\alpha\eta - 2(\delta - 2\alpha\eta) = 2(3\alpha\eta - \delta). \quad (4.10)$$

We therefore state our first proposition.

Proposition 4.3
Let α, δ, and η satisfy

$$\frac{\delta}{3\eta} < \alpha < \frac{\delta}{2\eta}.$$

Then, there exists a unique Undercut-proof equilibrium with strictly-positive prices.

Proof. The first inequality is needed to ensure that the utility from buying exceeds the utility from not buying, that is (4.10) is strictly positive. The second inequality ensures strictly-positive prices, that is (4.9) is strictly positive. ∎

We define the social welfare function of country k, $k = A, B$, as the sum of the residents' utility levels and the profit of the domestic firm. This, of course, assumes that the domestic firm is owned solely by domestic residents. Therefore, the welfare of country A is

$$W_A^{\text{MR}} \overset{\text{def}}{=} \eta(U_1^A + U_2^A) + \pi_1 = 2\eta \times 2(3\alpha\eta - \delta) + 4\eta(\delta - 2\alpha\eta) = 4\alpha\eta^2. \quad (4.11)$$

Clearly, due to symmetry, we can state that $W^B = W^A$.

Mutual nonrecognition

Suppose now that the government of each country prohibits the sale of the product operating on the standard used in the other country. Practically, such regulation simply restricts the import of the good produced in the other country. Figure 4.5 illustrates the movement of goods when each country recognizes only the domestic standard. Figure 4.5 demon-

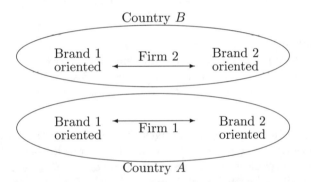

Figure 4.5: Trade under mutual nonrecognition.

strates that each firm is a monopoly in its own country and sells to two groups of consumers, the η brand 1 oriented consumers and the η brand 2 oriented consumers.

Since both countries are similar, it is sufficient to calculate the welfare level of country A only. Notice that firm 1 sells units to brand 1 oriented consumers, and could also, by setting a sufficiently low price, sell to brand 2 oriented consumers in country A.

Suppose first that firm 1 sets $p_1^{\text{NR}} = 2\alpha\eta - \delta$, where superscript "NR" stands for nonrecognition. Therefore, in view of (4.8), it sells to both groups of consumers. Hence, the profit of firm 1 is $\pi_1^{\text{NR}} = 2\eta p_1 = 2\eta(2\alpha\eta - \delta)$. The utility function (4.8) implies that each brand 1 oriented consumer gains a utility of $U_1^A = 2\alpha\eta - p_1 = \delta$, and each brand 2 oriented gains a utility of $U_2^A = 0$. Therefore, the welfare level of country A (similarly, of country B) is given by

$$W_A^{\text{NR}} \overset{\text{def}}{=} \eta U_1^A + \eta U_2^A + \pi_1 = \eta\delta + \eta 0 + 2\eta(2\alpha\eta - \delta) = 4\alpha\eta^2 - \eta\delta. \quad (4.12)$$

Next, suppose that firm 1 sets $p_1^{\text{NR}} = \alpha\eta$ thereby, in view of (4.8), it sells to brand 1 oriented consumers only. Therefore, the profit of firm 1 is $\pi_1^{\text{NR}} = \eta p_1 = \alpha\eta^2$. The utility function (4.8) implies that each brand 1 oriented consumer gains a utility of $U_1^A = \alpha\eta - p_1 = 0$, and each brand 2 oriented gains a utility of $U_2^A = 0$ (since they are not served). Therefore, the welfare level of country A (similarly, of country B) is given by

$$W_A^{\text{NR}} = \pi_1^{\text{NR}} = \alpha\eta^2. \quad (4.13)$$

Comparing mutual recognition with nonrecognition

Comparing the welfare levels (4.11) with (4.12) and (4.13) yields our main proposition.

Proposition 4.4
When consumer preferences exhibit international network externalties, both countries are better off when both countries mutually recognize foreign standards than when both countries do not recognize foreign standards.

Mutual recognition has two advantages over nonrecognition. First, under recognition each consumer buys his ideal brand. Second, under international network externalities, mutual recognition does not reduce the network size of each brand (compared with nonrecognition) since the increase in the number foreign customers offsets the reduction in domestic customers of each brand. This explains Proposition 4.4.

Casella (1996) and Gandal and Shy (2001) formally analyze international standardization. The latter paper demonstrates that mutual recognition Pareto dominates mutual nonrecognition even when preferences exhibit only national network externalities, that is, when utility is enhanced only with the number of domestic residents who buy the same brand. This paper also demonstrates that in a world with three countries, two countries may gain by forming a standardization union that recognizes the standard of the member countries and does not recognize the standard used in the nonmember country.

Finally, there are additional reasons why governments should not intervene in standard setting. First, governments are composed of politicians whose objective is to stay in power. Therefore, politicians are always pressured (via campaign contributions) to protect the standard of the firms that contribute to their campaign. Crane (1979) describes the politics behind the choice of three separate color-TV standards, NTSC in the United States and Japan, PAL in Europe and Asia, and SECAM in France in the 1950s and 1960s. Second, if standards are of different qualities, it is more likely that the market selects the "better" standard than the government.

4.4 Exercises

1. Consider a technology-adoption game played by two users (or firms) displayed in following table.

		User B	
		NEW TECHNOLOGY	OLD TECHNOLOGY
User A	NEW	3 3	1 0
	OLD	0 1	2 2

   (a) Which technology will be adopted by each user in Nash equilibrium. That is, find the Nash equilibrium(ia) for this game (if they exist). Prove your answer!

   (b) Does the outcome (New, New) constitute a case of *excess momentum*? Explain using Definition 4.1 on page 82.

2. Consider the technology revolutions model of Section 4.2, and in particular the method of calculating the frequency of technology revolutions explained in Section 4.2.4. Suppose now that consumer population is no longer constant over time and is growing with time so that $\eta_t = t\eta$ for every $t = 1, 2, \ldots$. Suppose that technology was last replaced in period t_g, and that technology $g + 1$ is about to replace technology g in period t_{g+1}. Answer the following questions.

   (a) Write down the technology $g + 1$ adoption condition similar to (4.6), taking into consideration that population grows with time.

   (b) Calculate the date t_{g+1} of the adoption of technology $g + 1$ as a function of adoption date of technology g (t_g).

   (c) Let $\lambda = 2$, $\eta = 1$, and assume that technology $g = 1$ was adopted in period $t = 2$. Calculate the adoption date of technology $g = 2$ (t_2), the adoption date of technology $g = 3$ (t_3), and the adoption date of technology $g = 4$ (t_4).

3. Consider a simplified version of the model of international standardization described in Section 4.3.2. Suppose that η brand 1 oriented consumers reside only in country B, whereas η brand 2 oriented consumers live only in country A. Thus, the population of each country is η and they prefer the product operating on the standard produced in the other country. Answer the following questions.

   (a) Suppose that both countries recognize all standards. Calculate the UPE prices in an equilibrium where firm 1 (located in country A)

sells to brand 1 oriented consumers who reside in country B; and where firm 2 (located in country B) sells to brand 2 oriented consumers who reside in country A.

(b) Calculate the profit level of each firm and the utility level of each consumer in this equilibrium.

(c) Calculate the social welfare of each country under mutual recognition.

(d) Suppose that that both countries do not recognize foreign standards. Calculate the price charged by each firm and the resulting profit level.

(e) Calculate the utility gained by each consumer and the social welfare on mutual nonrecognition.

(f) Conclude whether countries are better off by recognizing or not recognizing foreign standards. Explain your result.

4.5   Selected References

Arthur, B. 1989. "Competing Technologies, Increasing Returns, and Lock-in by Historical Events." *Economic Journal* 99: 116–131.

Cabral, L. 1990. "On the Adoption of Innovations with 'Network' Externalities." *Mathematical Social Sciences* 19: 229–308.

Casella, A. 1996. "On Standards and Trade: A Review of Simple Results." in: J. Bhagwati and R. Hudec (eds.), *Fair Trade & Harmonization.* Cambridge, Mass.: The MIT Press.

Crane, R. 1979. *The Politics of International Standards.* Norwood, NJ: Ablex Publishing.

Choi, J. 1996. "Do Converters Facilitate the Transition to a New Incompatible Technology?: A Dynamic Analysis of Converters." *International Journal of Industrial Organization* 14: 825–835.

Choi, J., and M. Thum. 1998. "Market Structure and the Timing of Technology Adoption with Network Externalities." *European Economic Review* 42: 225–244.

Farrell, J., and G. Saloner. 1985. "Standardization, Compatibility, and Innovation." *Rand Journal of Economics* 16: 70–83.

Farrell, J., and G. Saloner. 1986. "Installed Base and Compatibility: Innovation, Product Preannouncements, and Predation." *American Economic Review* 76: 940–955.

Gandal, N., and O. Shy. 2001. "Standardization Policy and International Trade." *Journal of International Economics* 53: 363–383.

Katz, M., and C. Shapiro. 1986. "Product Compatibility choice in a Market with Technological Progress." *Oxford Economics Papers* 38: 146–169.

Katz, M., and C. Shapiro. 1992. "Product Introduction with Network Externalities." *Journal of Industrial Economics* 40: 55–84.

Shy, O. 1996. "Technology revolutions in the presence of network externalities." *International Journal of Industrial Economics* 14: 785–800.

Sykes, A. 1995. *Product Standards for Internationally Integrated Good Markets.* Washington, D.C.: Brookings Institution.

Chapter 5

Telecommunication

The telecommunication industry is the fastest growing industry in almost every country. Both, technology advance in the telephony industry in general, and in the wireless technology in particular, as well as technology advance of the Internet contributed the most for the fast growth of this industry. Telecommunication services constitute the most natural example of network externalities, since by definition, the nature of these services involves communicating with a large number of people. For this reason, we devote Sections 5.1 and 5.2 to the construction of the demand for telecommunication services. This type of demand is heavily influenced by network externalities since the decision to buy a particular service is heavily affected by the number of other consumers connected to the same service. Section 5.3 demonstrates how modern regulators manage to maintain competition in industries where service providers must invest a large sum of money to develop the infrastructure for their services. We demonstrate that using access pricing, service providers can utilize each other's infrastructure thereby avoiding the inefficiency associated with multiple investment in the same infrastructure. Thus, this section demonstrates why regulators do not rely any more on the "natural monopoly" argument for licensing only a single provider (see a discussion on "natural monopolies" in Section 1.2.2).

5.1 Telecommunication Services

The demand for telecommunication services in general and telephony, facsimile, and e-mail services in particular exhibits perhaps the highest degree of network externalities. To see this, the reader should ask himself whether he is willing to subscribe to a phone (or an e-mail) service or buy a facsimile machine knowing that nobody else does. The answer to this question is definitely no! Note that this need not be the case in the market for computers where some consumers will be buying a computer even if no one else does, despite the fact that utility rises with the total number of consumers buying computers on the same operating system.

Given the crucial importance of network externalities in telecommunication services, we construct a theory of demand taking into account that network externalities play a major role consumers' demand for phone and e-mail services.

Before we proceed, we must clarify what we mean by demand for telecommunication services. Taking the telephone as an example, there are two services that are provided by telephone companies: First, the telephone company provides a *connection* of consumers to the company's switchboard, which enables the customers to receive and place ongoing phone calls. Second, after connection is completed, the phone company sells ongoing phone calls to consumers using various pricing packages which may or may not include volume discounts.

In this section, we wish to focus only on the first type of service provided by suppliers which is the market for *connecting* customers to the telecommunication network (switchboards in the telephone case). Therefore we assume that each potential customer has a demand for *one* connection. In the telephone example, we assume that each customer has a demand for one "line" to be connected to his house.

5.1.1 The demand for telecommunication services

Consider an economy with two types of consumers who wish to connect to a certain telecommunication service (e.g., obtaining a phone service). There are η type H consumers who place high value on connecting to this service, and η type L consumers who place a lower value for this connection.

Let p denote the connection fee to this service, and q the actual number of consumers connecting to this service. Then, the utility function of each type is given by

$$U_H \stackrel{\text{def}}{=} \left\{ \begin{array}{ll} \alpha q - p & \text{connected} \\ 0 & \text{disconnected} \end{array} \right. \quad \text{and} \quad U_L \stackrel{\text{def}}{=} \left\{ \begin{array}{ll} q - p & \text{connected} \\ 0 & \text{disconnected,} \end{array} \right.$$

$$(5.1)$$

where α measures the degree of importance of this service to a type H consumer. We assume that $\alpha > 4$ which implies that type H consumers highly value this service

We now wish to construct the demand function for connecting to telecommunication services in this economy. Before doing so, the reader is urged to recall Assumption 2.2 on page 20 where we assumed that *there is no coordination failure* meaning that if each consumer in a group of identical consumers benefits from subscribing to the service, given that all other consumers subscribe to this service, then all consumers will indeed subscribe to the service. Figure 5.1 illustrates quantity demanded at each connection fee.

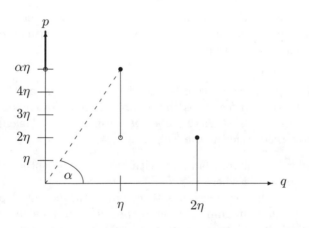

Figure 5.1: Construction of the demand for telecommunication. Dashed line illustrates the critical mass.

The methodology for constructing the demand is as follows. Start decreasing the price from an infinite level and, using (5.1), keep asking yourself whether at a given price p

(a) type H consumers are willing to connect given that only η connect to this service;

(b) type L consumers are willing to connect given that all the 2η consumers connect to this service.

Using this procedure, we now verify that Figure 5.1 is indeed the demand derived from the utility functions (5.1). We look at the following price ranges:

Low-price range $(0 \leq p < 2\eta)$: At this range, the quantity demanded is unique at the level of 2η consumers. To see this we need to show that both types of consumers gain a nonnegative utility. That is, $U_H = \alpha(2\eta) - p > 0$ and that $U_L = 2\eta - p > 0$, which follow directly from (5.1).

Medium-price range $(2\eta < p \leq \alpha\eta)$: At this range the consumer equilibrium involves only the type H consumers, whereas the type L are better off not buying. Suppose that $q = \eta$; then $U_H = \alpha\eta - p > 0$. However, even if all type L consumers also subscribe, $U_L = 2\eta - p < 0$, hence $q = \eta$ constitutes a consumer equilibrium at this price range.

High-price range $(p > \alpha\eta)$: In this range no one subscribes since $U_H = \alpha\eta - p < 0$ and $U_L = 2\eta - p < 0$.

After constructing the demand curve we wish to define a concept which telecommunication firms find very useful when marketing a new telecommunication service.

DEFINITION 5.1
Let p_0 be a given connection fee for this service. The **critical mass** *at a price (connection fee) p_0 is the minimal number of customers needed to ensure that at least this number of consumers will benefit from subscribing to the service at the fee p_0.*

The reader is probably familiar with the concept of the critical mass from his social life where in order to organize a party or a trip during the weekend, the organizer has to convince the potential participants that a certain minimum number of people would indeed attend this party, which would then imply that even a greater number will join due to the increasing network effects. In telecommunication the *critical mass is always a function of the market price*, meaning that a rise in price would imply an increase in the critical mass, and a decrease in the market price will decrease the critical mass since at a lower price customers would be "satisfied" with a reduced network size.

In order to calculate the critical mass, note that if in a consumer equilibrium only one type of consumer connects to this service, this type must be type H. Loosely speaking, consumers who highly value the service are the first to acquire it. Type H's utility function (5.1) implies that a type H consumer will connect to this service if the connection fee is in the range $p \le \alpha q$. Hence, the critical mass at a given connection fee p_0 is

$$q^{\text{cm}}(p_0) = \frac{p_0}{\alpha},$$

which is drawn in Figure 5.1 as the dashed ray from the origin. Clearly, if the connection fee is $p = 0$ then the critical mass is $q^{\text{cm}} = 0$. In the other extreme, if $p = \alpha\eta$, then $q^{\text{cm}} = \eta$ (all type H consumers).

From a marketing point of view, knowing the critical mass is important, since it gives an indication of how much advertising is needed to market a new telecommunication service. Once q^{cm} consumers buy the service, more consumers will connect to this service even after advertising expenditure is reduced.

5.1.2 Monopoly telecommunication service provider

Before the 1980s, most countries had a monopoly market structure in the telecommunication industry, where the monopoly firm commonly was called PTT (Public Telephone and Telegraph). In some countries (for example, Israel in the 1950s and 1960s) the PTT also provided postal services and enjoyed a full-monopoly power over the entire country.

Consider a single firm supplying connections to the market described by aggregate demand function illustrated in Figure 5.1. Figure 5.1 implies that the demand facing this monopoly is given by

$$q = \begin{cases} 2\eta & \text{if } 0 \le p \le 2\eta \\ \eta & \text{if } 2\eta < p \le \alpha\eta \\ 0 & \text{if } p > \alpha\eta. \end{cases} \tag{5.2}$$

On the technology side of the monopoly telecommunication service provider we assume the following.

ASSUMPTION 5.1
In order to connect each consumer to the network of services, the monopoly has to spend μ units of money, where $\mu < \eta$. In addition, the monopoly bears a fixed (connection independent) cost of ϕ, where $\phi < \min\{\eta(\alpha\eta - \mu), 2\eta(2\eta - \mu)\}$.

The restrictions on the parameters μ and ϕ imply that the monopoly will not make a loss even if it sells only to the η type L consumers. Note that if the fixed cost parameter ϕ is large, a monopoly provider may not find it profitable to operate.

From (5.2) and Assumption 5.1, the monopoly's profit as a function of its connection fee is

$$\pi(p) = \begin{cases} 2\eta(p - \mu) - \phi & \text{if } 0 \leq p \leq 2\eta \\ \eta(p - \mu) - \phi & \text{if } 2\eta < p \leq \alpha\eta \\ 0 & \text{if } p > \alpha\eta. \end{cases} \tag{5.3}$$

Now, our assumption that $\alpha > 4$ implies that $\eta(\alpha\eta - \mu) > 2\eta(2\eta - \mu)$, hence, the monopoly's profit-maximizing price and profit level are

$$p = \alpha\eta, \quad \text{and} \quad \pi = \eta(\alpha\eta - \mu) - \phi, \tag{5.4}$$

which implies that all the η type L consumers are not served. We next check whether such an allocation is socially optimal.

5.1.3   Socially optimal provision of telecommunication services

We define social welfare as the sum of consumers' utilities and the firm's profit. Therefore,

$$W \overset{\text{def}}{=} \eta U_H + \eta U_L + \pi \tag{5.5}$$
$$= \begin{cases} \eta(\alpha\eta - p) + \eta 0 + \eta(p - \mu) - \phi & H \text{ connect} \\ \eta(\alpha 2\eta - p) + \eta(2\eta - p) + 2\eta(p - \mu) - \phi & \text{All connect} \end{cases}$$
$$= \begin{cases} \alpha\eta^2 - \eta\mu - \phi & \text{Only } H \text{ connect} \\ 2\eta^2(\alpha + 1) - 2\eta\mu - \phi & \text{All connect.} \end{cases}$$

A simple comparison of the social welfare levels given in (5.5) reveals that social welfare is maximized when all customers are connected. Hence, the monopoly telecommunication service provider generates the familiar monopoly distortion by charging a high price, thereby providing service only to those who highly value this service.

5.1.4   Entry of new firms into the telecommunication industry

During the 1980s, governments began to realize that the monopoly PTTs which were operating under the misconception of what economists used to call "a natural monopoly" distorted the telecommunication markets. The major event that has led a worldwide introduction of competition into this industry was the 1982 AT&T breakup into seven regional phone companies and the introduction of MCI and SPRINT as major competitors in the long-distance and international markets.

The main questions that were debated by regulators in the 1980s were: (a) Given that many users were already connected to the established monopoly telecommunication service provider, can social welfare be improved by allowing a second operator to connect those consumers who were left out of the system during the monopoly era? (b) In the same vein, can an entrant into this market make a profit? A third question that regulators had to deal with is that if the entry of new providers is socially desirable, then how can the incumbent monopoly firm be prevented from engaging in predatory pricing to attract more customers, thereby shrinking the potential market of the entrant.

In 1997 the market for international phone calls was deregulated in Israel, when two new entrants entered at the same time. In order to prevent the Bezeq Company, which was the incumbent monopoly from engaging in unfair price cutting practices, the Ministry of Communication issued a restriction on the Bezeq Company that prohibited price reductions until after its market share fell below 70 percent.

In what follows, we will adopt the strategy used by the Israeli Ministry of Communication so,

ASSUMPTION 5.2
The regulator instructs the incumbent monopoly not to reduce its connection prices (fees) after entry of a competing provider is completed.

This means that the incumbent firm serves only the η type H consumers, and the entrant may serve all type L consumers provided that it reduces the connection fee below that of the incumbent's fee.

Consider a new telecommunication provider entering the industry after the η type H consumers have already purchased connection from the incumbent firm. In this case, the demand facing the entrant is not the aggregate demand facing the industry (5.2) since η consumers are already connected. Thus, we wish to construct the *residual demand* which is facing the entrant. Let q^e denote the (residual) demand facing the entrant, and p^e the connection fee set by the entrant. From (5.1), the residual demand is given by

$$q^e = \begin{cases} \eta & \text{if } p \leq 2\eta \\ 0 & \text{if } p > 2\eta. \end{cases} \tag{5.6}$$

Hence, the entrant's profit-maximizing connection fee and profit level are

$$p^e = 2\eta, \quad \text{and} \quad \pi^e = \eta(2\eta - \mu) - \phi > 0 \tag{5.7}$$

by Assumption 5.1.

Finally, we wish to tackle the question of who benefits from entry into the telecommunication industry? The utility of a type H consumer was $U_H = \alpha\eta - \alpha\eta = 0$ before the entry, and $U_H = \alpha 2\eta - \alpha\eta = \alpha\eta > 0$ after entry. The utility of a type L consumer was $U_L = 0$ before entry (not served), and $U_L = 2\eta - 2\eta = 0$ after entry. The profit of the entrant rises from zero to the level given in (5.7), and that of the incumbent remains unchanged, since the incumbent has already collected all revenue from its customers before entry occurred. Altogether,

Proposition 5.1
Entry into the telecommunication industry increases the utility of the already connected consumers whereas the utility of newly connected consumers remains unchanged. The profit of the entering firm increases.

The reader should bear in mind that we are analyzing the market for "connecting" consumers to the telecommunication network and not the market for the flow of services provided after consumers are connected. Therefore, in the market of service provision (more precisely, the market for phone calls) which we do not analyze here, the incumbent will suffer a reduction in profits. However, we know from Intermediate Microeconomics courses that a price reduction improves social welfare despite the reduction in the incumbent's profit. Thus, entry increases social welfare both in the market for connections and in the markets for telecommunication service provision.

5.1.5   Extension to three consumer types

Consider the discrete-demand model of the market for telecommunication of Section 5.1.1, but suppose now that there are three (instead of two) types of consumers, indexed by i, $i = 1, 2, 3$. There are η consumers of each type. Let q denote total the number of people connecting to this telecommunication service, and by p the connection fee. The utility of each type i consumer is given by

$$U_i \stackrel{\text{def}}{=} \begin{cases} i \times q - p & \text{if connected} \\ 0 & \text{otherwise,} \end{cases} \quad \text{for every type } i = 1, 2, 3.$$

That is, type 1 consumer has the lowest valuation for connecting to this service, whereas type 3 has the highest valuation.

Constructing the aggregate demand curve

If only η consumers connect, the maximum connection fee type 3 consumers are willing to pay is $p = 3\eta$. If only 2η consumers are connected, the maximum fee type 2 consumers are willing to pay is $p = 4\eta$. Finally, if all the 3η consumers are connected, the maximum fee type 1 consumers are willing to pay is $p = 3\eta$. The aggregate demand is depicted in Figure 5.2.

Figure 5.2 reveals an interesting fact, where at the connection fee levels $0 \leq p \leq 3\eta$ there are no intermediate demand levels. The reason is that, at this fee range even if only η consumers are connected the

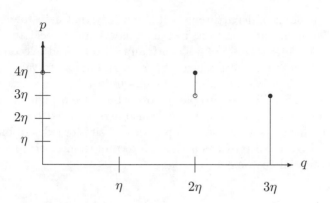

Figure 5.2: Aggregate demand with three consumer types.

utility of type 2 consumer is $U_2 = 4\eta - p \geq 0$, and hence all type 2 consumers will also connect. Given a network size of $q = 3\eta$, type 1 consumers will also connect since $U_1 = 3\eta - p \geq 0$ thereby making the entire population of 3η consumers connecting to this service.

Monopoly service provider and social optimum

Suppose that the monopoly does not bear any production cost associated with connecting consumers to this service. Observing Figure 5.2, the monopoly maximizes profit by choosing among the two "kinks" of the aggregate demand curve. Thus, if the monopoly sets $p = 4\eta$ its profit is $\pi = 4\eta \times 2\eta = 8\eta^2$. If the monopoly sets $p = 3\eta$, $\pi = 3\eta \times 3\eta = 9\eta^2$, which constitutes the monopoly equilibrium.

Finally, since firms do not bear any connection costs, it is clear that social welfare is maximized when the entire market is served. Hence, in this example the monopoly does not distort social welfare as it serves the entire market.

5.2   Telecommunication: A Calculus Analysis

The more advanced student who has some experience in solving elementary optimization problems will find the calculus analysis much more elegant. Our analysis follows the pioneering approach of Rohlfs (1974).

5.2.1   The demand for telecommunication services

Again, our point of departure is that the utility that a customer derives from a communication service increases as others connect to the same service. Consider a group of a η continuum of potential telecommunication customers uniformly indexed by x on the unit interval $[0,1]$ (with density $\eta > 0$). We interpret customers indexed by a low x as those who have high willingness to pay (those who place a high valuation on their ability to communicate), and consumers indexed by a high x as those who have low willingness to pay (less desire for subscribing to this service). Figure 5.3 provides a visual interpretation to the distribution of the potential customers.

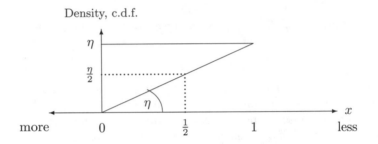

Figure 5.3: Distribution of potential customers for telecommunication services. *Horizontal line* is consumer density; *Ray from origin* is
customers' c.d.f.

The horizontal axis of Figure 5.3 is the potential customers' index number (or their names indexed by a real number between zero and one). Customers indexed on the right find the service less desirable whereas potential customers indexed on the left are in greater need for this service. The horizontal curve at the level of η is called customers' *density function*, which shows that there are η consumers of each type x. The ray from the origin with the slope η is subscribers' *cumulative distribution function (c.d.f.)* which shows for each type x how many customers are there with index types between zero and x. For example, as the figure demonstrates, there are $\eta/2$ customers (half of the total population) who are types indexed on $[0, 1/2]$.

We denote by q, $0 \leq q \leq 1$ the total number of consumers who actually subscribe to this service, and by p the connection fee (or the price) of subscribing to this service We define the utility of a consumer type x, $0 \leq x \leq 1$, as

$$U_x = \begin{cases} (1-x)q^e - p & \text{if she subscribes} \\ 0 & \text{if she does not subscribe,} \end{cases} \tag{5.8}$$

where q^e is consumers' *expected* number of customers subscribing to this telecommunication network. Thus, the utility of each customer exhibits network externalities since it increases with q^e which is the expected total number of customers.

We now derive the consumers' aggregate demand for phone services. We first look at a particular consumer denoted by $\hat{x}$ who is, at a given connection fee p, *indifferent* between subscribing and not subscribing to this service.

For a connection fee $p \le q^e$, (5.8) implies that this "indifferent" consumer is found from

$$0 = (1 - \hat{x})q^e - p, \quad \text{or} \quad \hat{x} = \frac{q^e - p}{q^e} \tag{5.9}$$

Thus, all consumers indexed by $x > \hat{x}$ will *not* subscribe to this service, whereas all consumers indexed by $x \le \hat{x}$ will subscribe. Hence, the actual number of customers is $q = \eta\hat{x}$. Notice that $\hat{x}$ increases whenever q^e increases reflecting the fact that under network externalities more people subscribe to a communication service with a higher expected number of customers.

A natural question to ask is how the expected number of customers is determined. There are many things that may affect consumers' expectation of how many people will actually subscribe to this service, such as the advertising campaigns of the suppliers. However, in economics it is common to avoid speculations and to assume that consumers will attempt to obtain the correct information. We, therefore, make the following assumption.

ASSUMPTION 5.3
Consumers have a perfect foresight (Definition 2.4 on page 20). Formally, $q^e = q = \eta\hat{x}$.

Substituting $q^e = \eta\hat{x}$ into (5.9) yields the inverse demand function for telecommunication services.

$$p = (1 - \hat{x})\eta\hat{x} \tag{5.10}$$

which is drawn in Figure 5.4.

As the reader can easily notice, the inverse aggregate demand function for telecommunication services in Figure 5.4 is upward sloping at small demand levels and becomes downward sloping at high demand levels. The reason is that at small demand levels, customers' willingness to pay rises with the total demand, since the network effect dominates the price effect at a small network size. Once the network size reaches half the population, the negative price effect dominates so the inverse

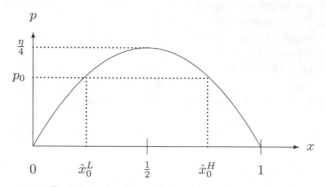

Figure 5.4: Deriving the demand for telecommunication services.

demand function becomes a conventional downward sloping aggregate demand function.

Figure 5.4 also reveals the effect of a uniform increase in the population of all types of potential customers in this economy, as reflected by the increase in the density parameter η. An increase in η raises the peak of the curve, meaning that customers increase their willingness to pay. For example, if η doubles, customers are willing to pay double the connection fee, since they benefit from twice the network size (twice the number of people to make phone calls or to communicate via e-mail or a fax).

The connection fee p_0 in Figure 5.4 intersects twice the inverse demand curve (at points $\hat{x}_0^L$ and $\hat{x}_0^H$). The reader who is interested in the exact value of these points can solve the quadratic equation $p_0 = (1 - x)\eta x$ to obtain

$$\hat{x}_0^L = \frac{\eta - \sqrt{\eta(\eta - 4p_0)}}{2\eta} \quad \text{and} \quad \hat{x}_0^H = \frac{\eta + \sqrt{\eta(\eta - 4p_0)}}{2\eta}. \qquad (5.11)$$

The interpretation for the two intersection points is that for a given connection fee p_0 there can be two levels of demand: a low level, measured by $q = \eta\hat{x}_0^L$, that is associated with a small number of customers, hence, by (5.8) only high-valuation consumers subscribe to the network. In addition, at the same connection fee p_0 there can be a high demand measured by $q = \eta\hat{x}_0^H$, implying that lower-valuation consumers also subscribe. However, only point $\hat{x}_0^H$ is a stable demand equilibrium, since at the intersection point $\hat{x}_0^L$, a small increase in the number of customers would make the phone subscription more desirable, thereby causing all the consumers indexed on $[\hat{x}_0^L, \hat{x}_0^H]$ to subscribe. Finally, the "low demand" point $\hat{x}_0^L$ has a special characteristic defined earlier

(Definition 5.1). Figure 5.4 shows that at p_0 the critical mass is $\eta \hat{x}_0^L$ customers.

5.2.2 Monopoly provider: The zero-connection cost case

Suppose now that there is only one firm providing telecommunication services. For now we assume that this monopoly does not have fixed and sunk costs and that the marginal cost of adding a customer is negligible. Formally, in this section we assume that connection costs are zero for this monopolist. We now ask which connection fee maximizes the monopolist's profit. To solve this problem, we formulate the monopoly's profit-maximization problem, which is to choose $\hat{x}$ that solves

$$\max_{\hat{x}} \pi(\hat{x}) \stackrel{\text{def}}{=} p\eta\hat{x} = (1 - \hat{x})(\eta\hat{x})^2. \qquad (5.12)$$

The profit function (5.12) is drawn in Figure 5.5. The first- and second-

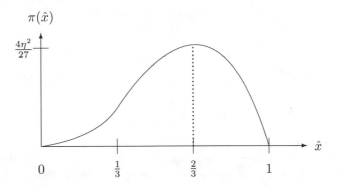

Figure 5.5: The telecommunication monopoly's profit function.

order conditions for (5.12) are

$$0 = \frac{\mathrm{d}\pi}{\mathrm{d}x} = (2x - 3x^2)\eta^2 \quad \text{and} \quad \frac{\mathrm{d}^2\pi}{\mathrm{d}x^2} = (2 - 6x)\eta^2. \qquad (5.13)$$

Now, equation (5.13) and Figure 5.5 completely describe how the profit level is affected by changing the number of customers. Clearly, the profit is zero when there are no customers ($\hat{x} = 0$). The profit is also zero when the entire population is connected to this service, since in order to have the entire population subscribing, the monopoly should reduce the connection fee to zero.

The first-order condition shows that $\hat{x} = 0$ and $\hat{x} = 2/3$ are extremum points. In addition, the second-order condition shows that the second derivative is negative for $\hat{x} > 1/3$, implying that $\hat{x} = 2/3$ is a local maximum point. Since the first-order condition is positive for all $0 < \hat{x} < 2/3$, it must be that $\hat{x} = 2/3$ is a global maximum point. To find the connection fee charged by the monopoly and the profit level, substitute $\hat{x} = 2/3$ into (5.10) and into (5.12) to obtain

$$p = (1 - \hat{x})\eta\hat{x} = \frac{2\eta}{9}, \quad \text{and} \quad \pi = (1 - \hat{x})(\eta\hat{x})^2 = \frac{4\eta^2}{27}. \qquad (5.14)$$

Hence,

Proposition 5.2
A monopoly phone company maximizes its profit by setting its connection fee so that the number of customers exceeds half of the consumer population but is less than the entire population.

Finally, we wish to investigate the effect of a uniform increase in the potential consumer population on the monopoly's connection fee, profit, and welfare of connected consumers. Substituting $\hat{x} = 2/3$ and then into (5.14) and then into (5.8) implies that the utility of a connected consumer is

$$U_x = \frac{2\eta(2 - 3x)}{9}, \quad \text{for consumer types} \quad x \in [0, 2/3]. \qquad (5.15)$$

Equations (5.14) and (5.15) imply the following proposition.

Proposition 5.3
A uniform increase in the consumer population, η, will increase the connection fee and the monopoly's profit. Further, despite the increase in the price, consumers' utility increases as well.

Proposition 5.3 demonstrates that despite the increase in connection fee, the increase in consumer population increases consumers' utility, which means that the monopoly cannot capture the entire surplus from its customers.

5.2.3   Monopoly provider: Connection-cost case

The more advanced student may be bothered by the fact that all costs borne by the monopoly telecommunication provider were assumed to be equal to zero. As it turned out, introducing connection costs has some quantity effects, but qualitatively it does not alter the intuition developed in the model with the absence of these costs.

Thus, for the sake of completion only, we now introduce production costs into the model and reinstitute Assumption 5.1 where the marginal connection cost (cost of connecting one additional customer) is μ, and a fixed cost of ϕ. Under Assumption 5.1, the profit-maximization problem (5.12) now becomes

$$\max_{\hat{x}} \pi(\hat{x}) \stackrel{\text{def}}{=} (p - \mu)\eta\hat{x} - \phi = [(1 - \hat{x})(\eta\hat{x}) - \mu]\,\eta\hat{x} - \phi, \qquad (5.16)$$

yielding first- and second-order conditions given by

$$0 = \frac{\mathrm{d}\pi}{\mathrm{d}\hat{x}} = 2\eta^2\hat{x} - 3\eta^2\hat{x}^2 - \eta\mu, \quad \text{and} \quad 0 > \frac{\mathrm{d}^2\pi}{\mathrm{d}\hat{x}^2} = 2\eta^2 - 6\eta^2\hat{x}.$$

The second order condition is fulfilled only for $x > 2/3$, which implies that we need only to solve for the larger root of the first-order condition to obtain

$$\hat{x} = \frac{\eta + \sqrt{\eta(\eta - 3\mu)}}{3\eta}. \qquad (5.17)$$

The reader can easily verify that (5.17) converges to $\hat{x} = 2/3$ as $\mu \to 0$.

5.2.4 Entry of new firms into the telecommunication industry

Under Assumption 5.2 the entrant can potentially hook all those $(1 - 2/3)\eta$ potential users who are not connected to the system via the incumbent firm. Figure 5.6 demonstrates how the residual demand facing the entrant is constructed by subtracting the $2/3$ of the consumer population who have already connected via the incumbent firm.

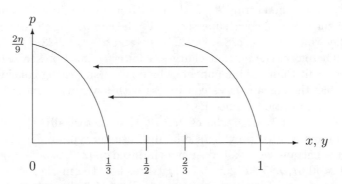

Figure 5.6: Residual demand for telecommunication connection facing the entrant.

Whereas Figure 5.6 shows that a graphical construction of the residual demand is very easy, the algebraic formulation is somewhat more tedious. In order to calculate the residual demand that would resemble

(5.11), we must invert the inverse-demand curve to obtain the "indifferent" type as a function of the connection fee, and only then subtract the 2/3 consumers who are already connected. Thus, in view of (5.11),

$$\hat{y} \overset{\text{def}}{=} \hat{x} - \frac{2}{3} = \frac{\eta + \sqrt{\eta(\eta - 4p_0)}}{2\eta} - \frac{2}{3}. \qquad (5.18)$$

Inverting (5.18), we obtain the residual inverse demand facing the entrant, and the implied profit function of the entrant. Hence,

$$p = \frac{\eta(2 - 3\hat{y} - 9\hat{y}^2)}{9}, \quad \text{hence} \quad \pi = \frac{\eta(2 - 3\hat{y} - 9\hat{y}^2)}{9}\eta\hat{y}. \qquad (5.19)$$

The first- and second-order condition for profit maximization are

$$0 = \frac{\mathrm{d}\pi}{\mathrm{d}\hat{y}} = \frac{\eta^2(2 - 6\hat{y} - 27\hat{y}^2)}{9}, \quad \text{and} \quad 0 > -\frac{2\eta^2(9\hat{y} + 1)}{3},$$

which holds for all nonnegative values of $\hat{y}$. Extracting the positive root of the first-order condition, we obtain the consumer type who is indifferent between connecting to the entrant's services, or staying disconnected. Then, substituting into (5.19) we obtain the entrant's connection fee and profit level. Altogether, we have that

$$\hat{y} = \frac{\sqrt{7} - 1}{9} \approx 0.182, \quad p = \frac{\eta(23 - \sqrt{7})}{81} \approx 0.128, \quad \pi = \eta^2 \frac{14\sqrt{7} - 20}{729}. \qquad (5.20)$$

Labeling the entrant's variables with a superscript "E" and the incumbent's variable by a superscript "I" and comparing (5.20) with (5.14) implies that $p^E \approx 0.128 < 0.222 \approx p^I$ and $\pi^E \approx 0.023\eta^2 < 0.148\eta^2 \approx \pi^I$. Therefore, the entrant charges a lower connection fee and earns a lower profit than the incumbent, which is not surprising considering the fact that the entrant faces consumers with lower willingness to pay for telecommunication connection.

Looking at market shares, recall that historically the incumbent telecommunication provider serves all consumer types indexed on $[0, 2/3]$ and the entrant serves all consumers indexed on $[2/3, 2/3 + \hat{y}] = [2/3, (\sqrt{7} + 5)/9] \approx [0.67, 0.85]$. Figure 5.7 illustrates how the market is divided between the incumbent and the entrant. Figure 5.7 shows that despite the 67 percent market share captured by the incumbent during the monopoly era, the entrant can capture about 18 percent of the market. Clearly, we can now allow for a third entrant, which will further reduce the connection fee. Such sequential entry was practiced in Israel where in 1987 the Ministry of Communication granted a monopoly license to Pelephone

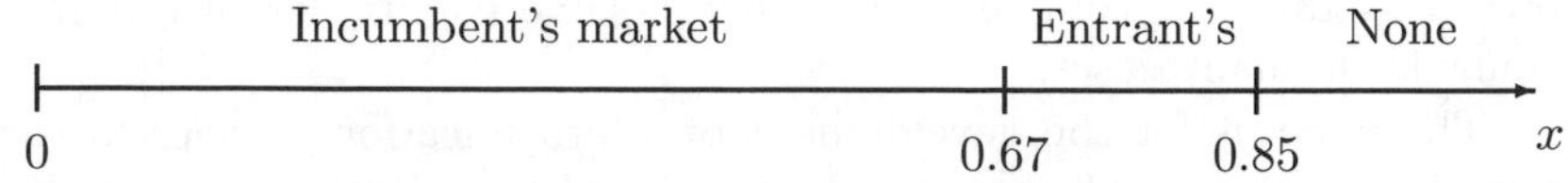

Incumbent's market   Entrant's   None

0   0.67   0.85 x

Figure 5.7: Division of market shares after entry into the telecommunication market.

to operate a cellular phone service. Then in 1995, the Ministry auctioned a license for a second operator, that was won by the "Cellcom" company. In 1999, the Ministry granted a license to a third operator called "Orange-Partner," and is now looking for the possibility of allowing a fourth operator. Each time a new operator entered into this market, prices and connection fees dropped significantly, just like the model predicts.

Finally, we wish to tackle the question of who benefits from entry into the telecommunication industry?

Proposition 5.4
Entry into the telecommunication industry increases the utility of old and newly connected consumers, as well as the profit of the entering firm.

The proposition follows from the fact that old users gain because of the increase in the network size; new users gain because they are connected to this service; and the entering firm makes above normal profit.

5.3   Interconnections

Interconnection is defined as having one carrier using the infrastructure owned by another carrier in the same industry. Interconnections prevail in a wide variety of service industries including the telephone, cable TV, mail, Internet, trains, buses, and the airline industries.

Interconnections are mostly observed in these industries since the fixed and sunk costs invested in the infrastructure are significant relative to the cost of carrying or transmitting one unit of output over these types of infrastructure. For example, wiring and wire maintenance constitute a major part of the infrastructure spending of telephone companies. Thus, the cost of one phone call is negligible compared to the cost of infrastructure. Interconnection means that a phone call originated in a local loop is carried over the network of other carriers both nationally and internationally. For railroad companies, laying down tracks and track maintenance constitute the major expense on infrastructure. Interconnection means that trains belonging to one company use the tracks owned by different companies within the same country or in different countries in many cases.

The impetus for the development of interconnection policies in the telecommunication industry was the opening the telecommunication markets to competition. New entrants (for example, Mercury in England, SPRINT and MCI in the United States, and Barak and Golden Lines in Israel) needed to access the dominant local-network operators (for example, British Telecom in England, AT&T in the United States, and Bezeq in Israel) to reach the customers. The local operators holding the basic infrastructures are sometime referred to as the *essential facility* or the *bottleneck*.

At this point, we do not wish to address the question why essential facilities or bottlenecks exist, except to acknowledge the fact that these bottlenecks exist because the regulating authorities, believe (falsely, according to the author's opinion) that telecommunication service providers are *natural monopolies*. We will go back to this question in Section 6.3 where we demonstrate how digital convergence and the U.S. 1996 Telecommunication Act can bring about the elimination of these bottlenecks. For the purpose of this section we take the common view that the essential facility is monopolized because of large economies of scale, or first-mover advantages, or of technological superiority. In fact, one bottleneck that will continue to stay with us for a long time is the essential facility created by many countries for providing access to foreign providers that transmit international phone calls from the country that a phone call originates to the country of destination.

Given the assumption that bottlenecks are here to stay, the regulating authority (for example, the U.S. Federal Communications Commission) must intervene in order to induce an efficient allocation of resources. This involves creating proper conditions for entry into the competitive segment of the service while avoiding inefficient bypasses. Again, the reader must bear in mind that the existence of bottlenecks generates the welfare distortion, and that promoting entry in connecting services means searching for what we call in welfare economics *second best* policies. From the unwritten "law of the second best" we know that there are no second-best policies, which means that promoting competition in connected services (complementary services) need not always increase social welfare. Thus, I feel that regulators and academic theorists devote too much time to access-pricing regulations instead of dealing with the source of the problem, which is how to eliminate bottlenecks so competition can prevail at all levels of services.

Finally, before going to the analytical analysis, it is instructive to look at some real-life data of access pricing. Figure 5.8 demonstrates how the price of long-distance calls is affected by access fees in the mid-

1990s in the United States. The figure shows how the FCC has been

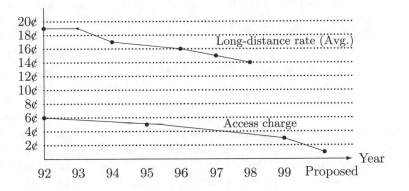

Figure 5.8: Falling long-distance charges and the drop in access charges.

cutting the access charge long-distance carriers pay to regional phone companies to carry their calls. This charge fell from a level of 5.8¢ a minute in 1992 to about 3.3¢ in 1999, and is expected to fall to 1.1¢ by 2004.

5.3.1 Access pricing: Basic methods

In recent years, there have been a variety of practices concerning access pricing, see Laffont and Tirole (1996) and Mitchell and Vogelsang (1991). We illustrate two of these practices with the following one-way access model.

Suppose that initially there is one monopoly telephone service provider (the traditional PTT), which provides both long-distance (LD) and local (LC) phone services. The incumbent's local and long-distance services are illustrated in Figure 5.9.

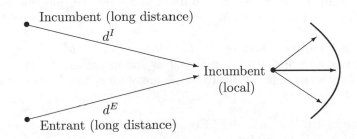

Figure 5.9: "One-way" access of a new long-distance carrier.

Figure 5.9 shows that long-distance calls must access the local carrier in order to be carried to destination customers. Whereas local phone calls are provided solely by the incumbent carrier, d^I long-distance calls can be initiated by the local carrier's customers and d^E by the entering (long-distance) carrier.

Let ϕ^I denote the fixed (sunk) cost invested in the infrastructure for local services, for example, wiring individual homes and business and the cost of acquiring local switches. Let μ_L^I denote the marginal cost associated with one phone call carried from the *local switch to a local consumer*, that is, the cost of executing a local phone call. Let μ^I denote the unit cost of a long-distance call carried by the incumbent and μ^E the unit cost of a long-distance call carried by the entrant. Finally, let q_L denote the number of local phone calls made. Then the local and long-distance incumbent's total cost and the long-distance entrant's total cost are

$$
\begin{aligned}
TC_L^I &= \mu_L^I(q_L + d^I + d^E) + \phi^I, \quad TC^I = \mu^I d^I, \\
TC^E &= (\mu^E + a)d^E,
\end{aligned}
\tag{5.21}
$$

where a is the access fee that the entrant pays the incumbent for accessing the incumbent's local switch, as determined by the regulating authority.

We now describe two common methods used by regulating authorities for setting up the access fee to be paid by the entrant for every long-distance phone call reaching the incumbent's local switch. Let p^I denote the price of a long-distance phone call made via the incumbent, and let p^E denote the price of a long-distance phone call made via the entrant.

Fully distributed costs: $a = \mu_L^I + \phi^I/Q$, where $Q \stackrel{\text{def}}{=} q_L + d^I + d^E$. That is, the entrant pays for the marginal cost generated by having the incumbent carry the call to its final destination, plus its share of the fixed cost according to its relative use of the local switch.

Efficient component pricing rule (ECPR): $a = p^I - \mu^I$. The entrant's access price simply "compensates" the incumbent for the incumbent's loss of profit due to transition of long-distance customers to the entrant.

The ECPR is a rather sophisticated rule and therefore needs further discussion. The main idea is to devise an access-pricing mechanism that prevents inefficient carriers from entering the long-distance market.

Proposition 5.5

Suppose that the incumbent and the entrant in the long-distance phone-call market compete in prices (rates). Then, under the ECPR, only entrants with unit cost $\mu^E \leq \mu^I$ will enter the long-distance phone-call industry.

Proof. In order to get customers to switch from the incumbent and to place long-distance calls with the entrant, the entrant must set its price so that $p^E \leq p^I$. Hence, the maximum profit the entrant can make is $\pi^E = (p^I - \mu^E - a)d^E$. Since under the ECPR $a = p^I - \mu^I$, $\pi^E = [p^I - \mu_E - (p^I - \mu^I)]d^E = \mu^I - \mu^E$. Therefore, $\pi^E \geq 0$ if and only if $\mu^I \geq \mu^E$, i.e., if the entrant is more efficient than the incumbent. ∎

The ECPR has another advantage over the fully distributed cost access price mechanism in that it does not require the regulator to know the production cost of the incumbent phone company. Mechanisms that rely on regulators' knowledge of production costs tend to fail simply because incumbent phone carriers tend to overstate their production costs in order to win a greater compensation from entering carriers.

5.3.2 "Two-way" access pricing under regional monopolies

Two-way access pricing is analyzed in Armstrong (1998), Laffont and Tirole (1994), and Laffont, Rey, and Tirole (1998). Consider a duopoly telephone industry with two regional telephone companies A and B. There are 2η customers subscribed to company A and 2η to company B. Each phone company provides local (LC) and long-distance (LD) phone services as displayed in Figure 5.10. However, for a start we will simplify

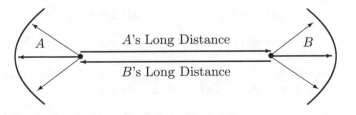

Figure 5.10: Long-distance access pricing between two regional service providers.

our analysis and ignore the local service, focusing only on the pricing of long-distance service and access fees. Each phone company i carries LC calls within its local loop (not modeled), and LD calls which are carried to the switchboard of the competing company and then carried by the competing company using its local loop. For now, we assume that the two phone companies are licensed to operate as *regional monopo-*

lies. The allocation of regions to phone companies is a common practice throughout the world including in the United States prior to the 1996 Telecommunication Act that allows regional competition. The practice is even more common in the cable TV industry. Section 6.3 demonstrates how a change in technology would bring about *digital convergence,* which could eliminate regional monopoly providers, thereby also eliminating the need to regulate access charges.

On the demand side, each company serves customers who are "stuck" with a preassigned company, which is the local monopoly in their area. Further, assume that in each region there are η high-income potential customers who are willing to pay a maximum of β_H for making a long-distance phone call; and η low-income potential customers who are willing to pay a maximum of β_L. Let p_i be the price of a long-distance call initiated from region i. The utility of each consumer type subscribed to the regional monopoly i, $i = A, B$ is

$$U_H \overset{\text{def}}{=} \max\{\beta_H - p_i, 0\} \tag{5.22}$$
$$U_L \overset{\text{def}}{=} \max\{\beta_L - p_i, 0\},$$

where we assume that $\beta_L < \beta_H < 2\beta_L$, meaning that high-income consumers are willing to pay more for a long-distance phone call than low-income consumers, but not more than twice as much.

Let $a_{\vec{AB}}$ denote the access charge levied by company B on company A for every long-distance phone call carried on its local loop. Similarly, let $a_{\vec{BA}}$ be the access charge levied by company A on each long-distance call initiated by company B. The profit of each firm is given by

$$\pi_A = q_A(p_A - a_{\vec{AB}}) + q_B a_{\vec{BA}} \text{ and } \pi_B = q_B(p_B - a_{\vec{BA}}) + q_A a_{\vec{AB}}, \tag{5.23}$$

where q_i is the number of long-distance phone calls placed from company i.

The interaction between the two phone companies takes place in a two-stage extensive-form game (see Appendix B).

Stage I: Both phone companies simultaneously set their access prices, $a_{\vec{AB}}$ by company A and $a_{\vec{BA}}$ by company B.

Stage II: Both phone companies take access prices as given and simultaneously set their long-distance tariffs, p_A and p_B.

We look for a Subgame-Perfect equilibrium (SPE) (Definition B.4 on page 303).

In stage II, since each phone company is a local monopoly (customers cannot choose their phone company), the choice of tariff set by company A does not affect the choice of tariff set by company B, again for the simple reason that consumers cannot switch phone companies. Thus, each company i is affected only by the access charge set by its rival firm.

The consumers' utility functions (5.22) imply that

$$q_i = \begin{cases} 2\eta & \text{if } p_i \le \beta_L \\ \eta & \text{if } \beta_L < p_i \le \beta_H \\ 0 & \text{if } p_i > \beta_H. \end{cases} \qquad i = A, B. \qquad (5.24)$$

Equations (5.23) and (5.24) yield

$$\pi_i = \begin{cases} 2\eta\left(\beta_L - a_{\overrightarrow{ij}}\right) + q_j a_{\overrightarrow{ji}} & \text{if } p_i = \beta_L \\ \eta\left(\beta_H - a_{\overrightarrow{ij}}\right) + q_j a_{\overrightarrow{ji}} & \text{if } p_i = \beta_H \\ q_j a_{\overrightarrow{ji}} & \text{if } p_i > \beta_H. \end{cases} \qquad (5.25)$$

In stage II each phone carrier i takes all access charges *as given* and chooses its phone call price p_i to maximize π_i given in (5.25). Therefore,

$$p_i = \begin{cases} \beta_L & \text{if } a_{\overrightarrow{ij}} \le 2\beta_L - \beta_H \\ \beta_H & \text{if } 2\beta_L - \beta_H \le a_{\overrightarrow{ij}} \le \beta_H \\ a_{\overrightarrow{ij}} & \text{if } a_{\overrightarrow{ij}} > \beta_H. \end{cases} \qquad (5.26)$$

To see why (5.26) constitutes the profit-maximizing pricing strategy for carrier i observe that a direct comparison of profit levels given in (5.25) implies that setting $p_i = \beta_L$ yields a higher profit level than setting $p_i = \beta_H$ if $2\eta(\beta_L - a_{\overrightarrow{ij}}) \ge \eta(\beta_H - a_{\overrightarrow{ij}})$, hence if $a_{\overrightarrow{ij}} \le 2\beta_L - \beta_H$.

In stage I of this game, each carrier i sets the access fee $a_{\overrightarrow{ji}}$ to be paid by carrier j for each phone call originating at j and terminating at i's loop, by taking into consideration how its access price affects the price set by carrier j given in (5.26) and hence the number of phone calls originating from j which is given in (5.24). Let π_i' denote the profit carrier i makes from collecting access charges from carrier j. Formally, $\pi_i' \stackrel{\text{def}}{=} a_{\overrightarrow{ji}} q_j$, $i, j = A, B$, $i \ne j$. Then, (5.24) implies that

$$\pi_i' = \begin{cases} 2\eta(2\beta_L - \beta_H) & \text{if } a_{\overrightarrow{ji}} \le 2\beta_L - \beta_H \\ \eta\beta_H & \text{if } 2\beta_L - \beta_H < a_{\overrightarrow{ji}} \le \beta_H. \end{cases} \qquad (5.27)$$

Hence, carrier i will choose a "low" access charge, $a_{\overrightarrow{ji}} = 2\beta_L - \beta_H$, rather than a "high" access charge, $a_{\overrightarrow{ji}} = \beta_H$, if

$$2\eta(2\beta_L - \beta_H) \ge \eta\beta_H, \quad \text{hence if} \quad \beta_H \le \frac{4}{3}\beta_L.$$

Therefore,

Proposition 5.6
In a SPE, the access charge set by carrier i on a long-distance call originated in j is

$$a_{\vec{ji}} = \begin{cases} 2\beta_L - \beta_H & \text{if } \beta_H \leq 4\beta_L/3 \\ \beta_H & \text{if } \beta_H > 4\beta_L/3. \end{cases} \tag{5.28}$$

Next, we wish to calculate the profit of each carrier under the equilibrium access pricing strategy (5.28), by substituting the revenue collected from access charges levied on the competing carrier given in (5.27) and the equilibrium price (5.26) into (5.25).

If $\beta_H \leq 4\beta_L/3$, then by (5.28) $a_{\vec{ji}} = 2\beta_L - \beta_H$. Hence, by (5.26), $p_i = \beta_L$ and by (5.24) $q_i = 2\eta$, yielding revenue of $2\eta\beta_L$ from customers. Also, by (5.27), the revenue generated from access charges to the competing carrier is $\pi'_i = 2\eta(2\beta_L - \beta_H)$. However, since in this symmetric equilibrium access charges paid out are equal to access charges received, total profit is $\pi_i = 2\eta\beta_L$. In contrast, if $\beta_H > 4\beta_L/3$, then by (5.28) $a_{\vec{ji}} = \beta_H$. Hence, by (5.26), $p_i = \beta_H$ and by (5.24) $q_i = \eta$, yielding revenue of $\eta\beta_H$ from customers. Also, by (5.27), the revenue generated from access charges to the competing carrier is $\pi'_i = \eta\beta_H$. Since access charges paid out are equal to access charges received, $\pi_i = \eta\beta_H$.

Summing up, the equilibrium profit level of each firm is

$$\pi_i = \begin{cases} 2\eta\beta_L & \text{if } \beta_H \leq 4\beta_L/3 \\ \eta\beta_H & \text{if } \beta_H > 4\beta_L/3. \end{cases} \tag{5.29}$$

Finally, we wish to calculate social welfare, which is defined as the sum of consumers' utilities and carriers' profit levels; formally,

$$W \stackrel{\text{def}}{=} 2\eta U_H + 2\eta U_L + \pi_A + \pi_B.$$

To calculate consumers' utilities consider the following two cases: If $\beta_H \leq 4\beta_L/3$, (5.28) implies that $a_{\vec{ji}} = 2\beta_L - \beta_H$, hence by (5.26) $p_A = p_B = \beta_L$, therefore $U_L = 0$ and $U_H = \beta_H - \beta_L$. In contrast, if $\beta_H > 4\beta_L/3$, (5.28) implies that $a_{\vec{ji}} = \beta_H$, hence by (5.26) $p_A = p_B = \beta_H$, therefore $U_H = U_L = 0$. Using (5.29), social welfare is given by

$$W = \begin{cases} 2\eta(\beta_H - \beta_L) + 2\eta \times 0 + 4\beta_L = 2\eta(\beta_H + \beta_L) & \text{if } \beta_H \leq 4\beta_L/3 \\ 4\eta \times 0 + 2\beta_H\eta = 2\beta_H\eta. & \text{if } \beta_H > 4\beta_L/3. \end{cases} \tag{5.30}$$

To verify that (5.30) "makes sense" ask yourself what are the net gain in this economy, considering the fact that firms are owned by consumers, so total consumer expenditure equals total revenue of the two carriers. Since there are no production costs, and since access charges are merely transfers between the two carriers, social welfare must equal total gross consumer utility, that is, utility before reducing prices. This is indeed the result obtained in (5.30), which should come as no surprise once the reader understands the logic behind this argument.

Our assumption that $\beta_H < 2\beta_L$, (5.28), and (5.30) yield our *main* proposition.

Proposition 5.7

(a) *"Low" access pricing, i.e., $a_{\vec{ji}} = 2\beta_L - \beta_H$, yields a higher social welfare than higher access pricing. Hence,*

(b) *a market failure occurs when the valuation parameters satisfy $\beta_H > 4\beta_L/3$ (very high valuation by high-income consumers) as in this range access charges exceed the socially optimal levels. Hence,*

(c) *if $\beta_H > 4\beta_L/3$, socially-optimal policy calls for the regulator to impose a ceiling on access charges at the level $\bar{a} = 2\beta_L - \beta_H$.*

Proof. (a) The assumption that $\beta_H < 2\beta_L$ and (5.30) imply that serving the entire market yields a higher social welfare than serving the high-income consumers only. In order to induce firms to charge $p_i = \beta_L$ instead of $p_i = \beta_H$, (5.26) implies that access charges should not exceed $a_{\vec{ji}} = 2\beta_L - \beta_H$. (b) When $\beta_H > 4\beta_L/3$ (5.28) implies that carriers set high access charges, which are not socially optimal by part (a). Part (c) then follows. ∎

Proposition 5.7 highlights the major problem associated with *partial regulation* where carriers overcharge each other with access prices, thereby artificially increasing each others' cost, which induces carriers to raise consumer prices thereby excluding low-income customers from making phone calls. The situation described here may occur also if the two carriers collude in access prices (rather than setting it competitively) in an attempt to "artificially" raise each other's cost.

Finally, note that in this environment, since there are no externalities the First Welfare Theorem applies in the sense that perfect competition (had it existed) is optimal. Hence, the socially optimal access charges are zero. In our simple discrete model, any low access prices satisfying $0 \le a_{\vec{ij}} \le 2\beta_L - \beta_H$ will not affect market prices and hence will not distort. However, high access charges, $a_{\vec{ij}} > 2\beta_L - \beta_H$, will raise prices and reduce consumption leading to the familiar distortion.

5.3.3 International phone calls settlement rates

In practice, the revenue generated from a call is collected by the telephone company in the country where the call is originated and this revenue can differ across countries with different demand levels (say, because of differences in per-capita incomes). This suggests that carriers ought to have some way of compensating each other in the case there is an imbalance of calls between them. The method of compensating payments is generally a negotiated fixed rate per minute, commonly referred to as the *settlement rate*. These types of arrangements can be traced back to 1865, when 20 European nations formed a union, now known as the International Telecommunications Union (ITU).

Wright (1999) provides a test for the U.S. FCC's claim that the current arrangements cost U.S. consumers billions of dollars annually, largely to subsidize foreign carriers in low-income countries. In 1996, U.S. carriers paid out on the order of \$5.5 billion more in such settlements than they received. The FCC claims that artificially high settlement rates are preventing the prices of international phone calls from falling to competitive rates. For example, in 1997 U.S. customers spent 495 million minutes on calls to Brazil, but Brazilians make only 159 million minutes' worth of calls to the United States. To pay for the deficit of 336 million minutes, U.S. carriers transferred \$154.7 million to Brazil.

In what follows, we provide simple models to analyze the effect of instituting settlement rates under two market structures: (1) each country is served by a local monopoly carrier (PTT) and (2) phone companies are fully competitive in each country.

Monopoly carrier in each country

Consider a world with two countries labeled N (for North) and S (for South). Country N has η_N consumers who wish to place at most one international phone call to country S. Country S has η_S consumers who wish to place at most one phone call to country N. We may think of country N as the country with a higher per-capita income; hence we assume that it has a *larger* number of consumers wishing to place a phone call compared with country S. Formally, let $\eta_N > \eta_S$.

Let p_k denote the price of a phone call from country k as charged by the country k's carrier, $k = N, S$. Each potential consumer has a valuation of $\beta > 0$ for placing this phone call, meaning that the utility function of a consumer in country k is given by

$$U_k \stackrel{\text{def}}{=} \begin{cases} \beta - p_k & \text{if makes an international call} \\ 0 & \text{if does not make an international call.} \end{cases} \tag{5.31}$$

Let a denote the international access charge (settlement rate), which is the payment each carrier makes to the foreign carrier for carrying the phone call to its final destination in the foreign country. At this point, we do not discuss how the settlement rate is determined. Later on, we introduce some rule for how countries mutually agree to a world wide settlement rate. Then the profit of each national phone company is composed of profit generated from sales of international phone calls and the collection of access fees from incoming international phone calls. Thus,

$$\pi_N \stackrel{\text{def}}{=} (p_N - a)\eta_N + a\eta_S, \quad \text{and} \quad \pi_S \stackrel{\text{def}}{=} (p_S - a)\eta_S + a\eta_N. \quad (5.32)$$

Our assumption that $\eta_N > \eta_S$ implies that

Proposition 5.8
An increase in the international settlement rate, a, decreases the profit of phone company N and increases the profit of phone company S.

Proof. The profit of company N is proportional to $a(\eta_S - \eta_N) < 0$ whereas the profit of company S is proportional to $a(\eta_N - \eta_S) > 0$. ∎

The timing of this model is as follows. There are two stages: In the first stage, representatives of the two companies agree on a mutual settlement rate, a. In the second stage, the two companies take the settlement rate as given and set p_N and p_S separately to maximize their profits.

In the second stage, for a given value of a, the monopoly price of a phone call in country k and the implied volume of international phone calls placed from country k, q_k, are

$$p_k = \left\{ \begin{array}{ll} \beta & \text{if } a \leq \beta \\ a & \text{if } a > \beta, \end{array} \right. \quad \text{and} \quad q_k = \left\{ \begin{array}{ll} \eta_k & \text{if } a \leq \beta \\ 0 & \text{if } a > \beta. \end{array} \right. \quad (5.33)$$

Thus, each company collects a profit of $p_k - a$ on each phone call placed in country k, and this profit is strictly positive as long as the access charge does not exceed consumers' valuation, i.e., $a \leq \beta$.

In the first stage countries *bargain* over the international settlement rate, a. In order to simplify the exposition, we assume the following bargaining solution.

ASSUMPTION 5.4
Let a_N be the access charge which maximizes π_N given (5.32), and let a_S be the access charge maximizing π_S given (5.32). Then, in the bargaining process the companies agree to a mutual access charge that is the average of the two profit-maximizing charges, that is

$$\hat{a} \stackrel{\text{def}}{=} \frac{a_N + a_S}{2}.$$

The reader is *warned* that this bargaining solution need not be efficient, and is, therefore, uncommon in economic theory. The reader who is interested in studying efficient bargaining solutions (e.g., Nash 1950) is referred to books on bargaining and cooperative game theory.

Assumption 5.4 and Proposition 5.8 imply that the mutually agreed upon access charge is $\hat{a} = \beta/2$. Then, by (5.33), $p_N = p_S = \beta$, implying that the profit levels (5.32) are now given by

$$\pi_N = \pi_S = \frac{\beta}{2}(\eta_N + \eta_S) > 0. \tag{5.34}$$

Let $T_{\vec{NS}}$ denote the *net* transfer of money from company N to company S, then

$$T_{\vec{NS}} = -T_{\vec{SN}} = a(\eta_N - \eta_S) = \frac{\beta}{2}(\eta_N - \eta_S) > 0. \tag{5.35}$$

Equations (5.34) and (5.35) imply the following proposition.

Proposition 5.9
When phone companies exercise full-monopoly power in their own country over international phone calls, under the bargaining rule of Assumption 5.4:

(a) *the Northern phone company's total access charges paid to the Southern company exceed the total access charges it receives from the Southern company;*

(b) *despite the excessive payment, the Northern company makes a positive profit.*

Part (b) of the proposition is important since it explains why Northern phone companies are willing to sign agreements with Southern companies despite the fact that they end up paying net transfers to Southern firms. In other words, abolishing any agreements would worsen the Northern companies' situation as their profit from international service would drop to zero. Thus, high-income countries agree to such a settlement rate since, with a higher demand, they stand to lose more if they do not reach any agreement.

Competition in each country.

Suppose now that the phone industry in each country is deregulated and therefore becomes competitive so both phone companies charge prices equal to their marginal costs. Since the only cost of placing an international phone call is the international settlement fee (access price to the foreign company's local loop), competitive pricing means that both companies set the price of an international call to $p_N = p_S = a$.

Under competitive pricing, substituting $p_N = p_S = a$ into the profit functions (5.32) yields

$$\pi_N = a\eta_S, \quad \text{and} \quad \pi_S = a\eta_N. \tag{5.36}$$

Equation (5.36) shows that when the phone industry in each country is competitive, the sole source of profit of each carrier comes from the access charges. Therefore,

Proposition 5.10
When phone companies are competitive, an increase in the international settlement rate, a, increases the profit of each phone company.

Comparing Proposition 5.10 with Proposition 5.8 reveals that whereas under monopoly one company must lose from an increase in access pricing, under competition *all* companies gain from an increase in access pricing. This implies that $a_N = a_S = \beta$; hence by Assumption 5.4 the negotiated settlement rate is $\hat{a} = \beta$. The following proposition describes the major concern expressed by many regulating authorities on the effect competition may have on international settlement rates.

Proposition 5.11
When phone companies face competition from other carriers in their own countries, they negotiate higher international settlement rates compared with the case where each company maintains a monopoly position in its country. This means that high settlement rates serve as a means of collusion across carriers in different continents.

In other words, companies *artificially* raise their access rates, knowing that these payments cancel out. However, this artificial fees are rolled over onto the consumers who end up paying the monopoly price, β, even though perfect competition prevails in the domestic market. The reader should not conclude from Proposition 5.11 that introducing competition at the national level is welfare reducing. On the contrary, the distortion created by competition at the national level can be fixed by introducing further competition in international service. More precisely, if carriers in each country can negotiate settlement rates with competing foreign carriers, this form of international collusion will be eliminated. This can be achieved only after the relevant countries introduce full competition among their own carriers.

5.3.4   The future of international telephony

As a result of deregulation in the industry, international phone call rates have dropped between 25 percent to 80 percent in many countries in the past three years, and are expected to keep falling to the level of long-distance rates in the first decade of the third millennium. The sharp fall in rates that has no precedent in the history of international telephone and the reasons leading to this fall go beyond the simple explanation that competition has been introduced in most countries.

Avoiding local monopolies: Today, U.S. carriers that send calls to European countries do not have to go through dominant carriers and can connect to hundreds of local companies that offer much lower prices.

Callback: In the early 1990s, a method emerged to get around high rates. Because overseas calls from the deregulated United States were cheaper than calls into the United States, startup companies took advantage of the gap, offering "callback services." A customer outside the United States would dial a special U.S. number and hang up after a few rings, avoiding the charge for a call. Then, the U.S. number would call back and supply a dial tone to the foreign customer. From there, the caller could dial anywhere in the world at low U.S. prices. Coincidently, in the late 1990s the price of international phone calls from Israel fell to about one-fourth of the U.S. rates. As a result Israeli startups began offering call-back services to U.S. consumers.

International resale: Owners of privately leased phone lines between countries resell unused capacity on their lines to local phone companies. Calls carried on these lines are not subject to settlement fees.

Internet telephony: Early Internet telephone calls required a PC at both ends of the line, but now thanks to gateways that link the Internet to the phone system a PC is not required. Savings result from the fact that no settlement fees are paid.

5.4   Exercises

1. Consider the discrete-demand model of the market for telecommunication of Section 5.1.1. Suppose that there are two types of consumers who wish to connect to a certain telecommunication service (for example, obtaining a phone service). There are 20 type H consumers who place high value on connecting to this service, and 60 type L consumers who place a lower value for this connection.

Let p denote the connection fee to this service, and q the actual number of consumers connecting to this service. Then, the utility function of each type

$$U_H \stackrel{\text{def}}{=} \begin{cases} 2q - p & \text{connected} \\ 0 & \text{disconnected} \end{cases} \quad \text{and } U_L \stackrel{\text{def}}{=} \begin{cases} q - p & \text{connected} \\ 0 & \text{disconnected.} \end{cases}$$

Draw the demand function for connecting to this telecommunication service. Label the axes and prove and explain the graph.

2. Consider the discrete-demand model of the market for telecommunication of Section 5.1.5, with three types of consumers, indexed by i, $i = 1, 2, 3$. There are η consumers of each type. Let q denote the number of people connecting to this telecommunication service, and let p denote the connection fee. The utility of each type i consumer is given by

$$U_i \stackrel{\text{def}}{=} \begin{cases} (i+1)q - p & \text{if connected} \\ 0 & \text{otherwise,} \end{cases} \quad \text{for every type } i = 1, 2, 3.$$

That is, type 1 consumer has the lowest valuation for connecting to this service, whereas type 3 has the highest valuation.

Answer the following questions.

(a) Draw the aggregate demand for telecommunication services. Explain your result!

(b) Suppose that the connection fee is $p = 2\eta$. Find the critical mass (Definition 5.1) associated with this level of connection fee.

(c) Suppose that this market is serviced by a single monopoly firm who has no production costs for connecting people to this service. Find the monopoly's profit-maximizing connection fee and its profit level.

3. This question requires the use of calculus. Consider the model of the monopoly telecommunication service provider described in Section 5.2, but suppose that consumer types are indexed by x on the interval $[0, 2]$ (instead of $[0, 1]$). In order to simplify the calculation, suppose that the density of consumers is $\eta = 1$, meaning that there is only one consumer per type (instead of η consumers per type). Assume that the utility function of each consumer x, $x \in [0, 2]$ is given by

$$U_x = \begin{cases} (1-x)q^e - p & \text{if she subscribes} \\ 0 & \text{if she does not subscribe.} \end{cases}$$

Answer the following questions.

(a) Formulate the inverse demand function facing the monopoly telecommunication service provider.

(b) Formulate monopoly's profit maximization problem. Calculate the first- and second-order condition for profit maximization.

(c) Solve for the monopoly's price, size of the served market and profit level.

4. Consider a simplified version of the "two-way" access pricing model studied in Section 5.3.2. Company D is a long-distance carrier which must access the local loop of a local carrier called company C. Company D is facing demand for its long-distance service from two groups of potential customers (where each consumer makes at most one phone call): A group of η_H high-income consumers who are willing to pay a maximum of 80¢ for a long-distance call; and a group of η_L low-income consumers who are willing to pay a maximum of 20¢ for each long-distance call.

Let $a_{\overrightarrow{DC}}$ denote the access charge carrier C levies on carrier D for each of D's phone calls it carries on its local loop. Let p_D denote the price of each long-distance call D charges it customers. Answer the following questions:

(a) Suppose that $a_{\overrightarrow{DC}} = 0$. Calculate the price of a long-distance phone call which maximizes the profit of carrier D. Your answer should depend on the relative values of η_H and η_L.

(b) Answer the previous question for all possible given access charges satisfying $0 < a_{\overrightarrow{DC}} \leq 80$, assuming that $\eta_H < \eta_L/3$.

(c) Suppose that $\eta_H = 100$ and $\eta_L = 500$. Calculate the access charge which maximizes the profit of carrier C.

(d) Is the outcome found in the previous question socially optimal? *Hint:* Since there is no externality, the First-Welfare Theorem applies, so you can think of marginal-cost pricing. If your answer is negative, is there any policy that the regulator can use to implement the socially-optimal outcome?

5. Consider the model of international settlement rates between the North and the South analyzed in Section 5.3.3. Suppose now that the phone industry in country N is fully competitive, hence the price of an international phone call from N to S is $p_N = a$, where a is the negotiated access charge. Also, suppose that the phone industry in country S remains a monopoly, hence the price of a phone call from country S to N is $p_S = \beta$. Answer the following questions.

(a) Formulate the profit function of each phone company as a function of a, and conclude what level of access charge maximizes the profit of each company.

(b) Using the bargaining rule of Assumption 5.4 on page 127, determine a mutually agreed upon access charge. Compare this access charge to the access charge agreed upon when *both* companies are monopolies. Explain why there is a difference.

(c) Calculate the net flow of money transferred from company N to company S. Compare to the amount transferred when both companies are competitive.

6. Answer the previous question assuming that the phone industry in country N remains a monopoly, whereas the phone industry in country S is competitive. Explain the difference between the two scenarios.

5.5 Selected References

Armstrong, M. 1998. "Network Interconnection in Telecommunications." *Economic Journal* 108: 545–564.

Laffont, J-J., and J. Tirole. 1994. "Access Pricing and Competition." *European Economic Review* 38: 1673–1710.

Laffont, J-J., and J. Tirole. 1996. "Creating Competition Through Interconnection: Theory and Practice." *Journal of Regulatory Economics* 10: 227–256.

Laffont, J-J., P. Rey, and J. Tirole. 1998. "Network Competition: I. Overview and Nondiscriminatory Pricing." *Rand Journal of Economics* 29: 1–37.

Nash, J. 1950. "The Bargaining Problem." *Econometrica* 18: 155-162.

Nilssen, T., and L. Sørgard. 1998. "Time Schedule and Program Profile: TV News in Norway and Denmark." *Journal of Economics & Management Strategy* 7: 209–235.

Rohlfs, J. 1974. "A Theory of Interdependent Demand for Communication Service." *Bell Journal of Economics* 5: 16–37.

Wright, J. 1999. "International Telecommunications, Settlement Rates, and the FCC." *Journal of Regulatory Economics* 15: 267–291.

Chapter 6

Broadcasting

Firms that provide broadcasting services are called networks since they can broadcast the same programs in different geographic locations. As a result of this, regulating authorities fear that large networks may control "too much" information which will enable them to influence the thinking of the citizens and therefore cause damage to pluralism, which strengthens democracies. For this reason, the U.S. Federal Communication Commission (FCC) always sets a limit on how many radio and television stations can be controlled under a single ownership. Section 6.1 of this chapter analyzes the competition among broadcasting networks assuming that the stations use scheduling and program types as strategic means to attract listeners and viewers. Section 6.2 analyzes how the regulating authorities regulate the span of control over the airwaves by allocating limited amount of spectrum to bidders. Finally, Section 6.3 integrates Chapters 5 and 6 by analyzing the market consequences of digital convergence, where digital convergence if defined as the provision of telephony, the Internet, and broadcasting via a single fiber-optic line connected, possibly, to a single provider.

6.1   Broadcasting and Cable Television

Broadcasting differs from cable television in one major respect. Cable services are sold to consumers, whereas broadcasting via the airwaves reaches all consumers who possess the appropriate receiving equipment (e.g., radio, TV set, antenna, etc.). In this respect, cable companies resemble telephone companies who can connect and disconnect unpaying consumers from the network.

Since broadcasting companies cannot collect fees from their viewers and listeners, they resort to generating revenues from advertising only. The revenue from advertising is proportional to the popularity of the broadcasting station, called *rating*, which is the number of viewers watching or listening to a station at a given time period. It should be noted that even cable TV stations resort to some advertising, so cable TV providers generate their revenue from two sources: advertising and fees from viewers. Finally, most countries operate "public" radio and TV stations that are supported by public money and listeners' contributions.

6.1.1   Scheduling competition

Since broadcasters are engaged in nonprice competition among their stations, scheduling of programs becomes the major strategic variable in this industry. Each targeted group of consumers have certain hours during which their major audience turns on their TV sets. For example, soap-opera lovers happen to have time to watch TV in early afternoons, whereas other people tend to watch the news between 6 P.M. to 10 P.M. Clearly, the first group of consumers tend not to be employed in full-time positions, whereas the second group tend to work full time.

Given the limited time period in which particular audiences can be targeted, several stations compete head-to-head on viewers. Therefore, scheduling becomes a major strategic tool, which is as important as the content of the broadcasting itself.

One observation that economists often find puzzling is that many stations tend to broadcast the same types of programs at the same time. For example, the TV morning news tends to be broadcasted between 7 A.M. to 9 A.M., whereas night news tends to be broadcasted at 6:30 P.M. on at least two major TV stations in the United States. The same observation applies to soap operas that tend to be broadcasted at the same time rather then sequentially (on different stations). The reason why economists find this observation puzzling is that in product (brand) differentiation models where firms compete in prices, firms tend to *differentiate* themselves from their competitors by offering slightly different products (more sugar, less fat, less caffeine, etc.). The reason for this is given in Appendix C, which shows that a higher degree of differentiation weakens price competition, hence increasing the monopoly power of brand-producing firms, and hence their profits. In contrast, broadcasters tend to broadcast the same programs exactly at the same time. In this section we seek an explanation for this observation. As we demonstrate below, nonprice competition induces broadcasters to limit differentiation in the timing of their broadcasts.

Figure 6.1 provides an example for how viewers are distributed during prime time.

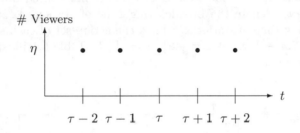

Figure 6.1: Uniform distribution of viewers during prime time.

Figure 6.1 illustrates a prime-time distribution of viewers' ideal watching time, say for an evening news program, where there are η viewers whose ideal (most-preferred) hour is $\tau - 2$, η viewers whose ideal time is $\tau - 1$, and so on. We make the following assumptions on these viewers.

ASSUMPTION 6.1

(a) *The time difference among viewers' ideal watching time is constant.*

(b) *Viewers will choose the channel whose broadcasting time is the closest to their ideal time.*

(c) *If all stations offer their programs at the same time, or if viewers are indifferent between two stations, then the stations equally split the entire viewer population.*

(d) *The profit of a TV station is proportional to the number of viewers. Formally, the profit of station i is $\pi_i \stackrel{\text{def}}{=} \rho \cdot q_i$, where q_i is the number of viewers and $\rho > 0$ is the revenue per viewer generated from advertising.*

Part (a) of Assumption 6.1 follows from the general observation in which people tend to organize their time in certain time frames, either on the hour or on 30 minutes past the hour. The reader should ask himself whether he has ever fixed a meeting at 6:22 P.M.? The answer is probably no, as people tend to round their schedule to either 6 P.M. or 6:30 P.M. As it turns out, TV stations tend to schedule their programs either on the hour or on 30 minutes past the hour. One reason for this is that any deviation from fixed time intervals would make it impossible to print TV guides in a readable format (i.e., columns and rows), which viewers find easier to read.

Two broadcasting stations

Suppose that there are two broadcasting stations labeled station A and station B, competing for viewers of evening news aired during prime time. Let t_A denote the broadcasting time of station A, and t_B the broadcasting time of station B. Thus the action set of each station i is $t_i \in \{\tau - 2, \tau - 1, \tau, \tau + 1, \tau + 2\}$, $i = A, B$. Table 6.1 illustrates this normal-form game.

Station B

	$\tau - 2$		$\tau - 1$		τ		$\tau + 1$		$\tau + 2$	
$\tau - 2$	$5\eta/2$	$5\eta/2$	η	4η	$3\eta/2$	$7\eta/2$	2η	3η	$5\eta/2$	$5\eta/2$
$\tau - 1$	4η	η	$5\eta/2$	$5\eta/2$	2η	3η	$5\eta/2$	$5\eta/2$	3η	2η
A: τ	$7\eta/2$	$3\eta/2$	3η	2η	$5\eta/2$	$5\eta/2$	3η	2η	$7\eta/2$	$3\eta/2$
$\tau + 1$	3η	2η	$5\eta/2$	$5\eta/2$	2η	3η	$5\eta/2$	$5\eta/2$	4η	η
$\tau + 2$	$5\eta/2$	$5\eta/2$	2η	3η	$3\eta/2$	$7\eta/2$	η	4η	$5\eta/2$	$5\eta/2$

Table 6.1: Prime-time scheduling game: Uniform distribution case. *Remark:* All entries (profit levels) should be multiplied by ρ.

We look for a Nash equilibrium (Definition A.4 on page 292) in broadcasting time.

Proposition 6.1

(a) *There exists a time period in which having both stations broadcasting at the same time is an equilibrium. Formally, there exists $\hat{t}$ for which $t_A = t_B = \hat{t}$ is a Nash equilibrium.*

(b) *In the example of Figure 6.1, the equilibrium is unique.*

Proof.

(a) We demonstrate that $t_A = t_B = \tau$ is an equilibrium according to Definition A.4 on page 292. In this equilibrium, $\pi_A(\tau, \tau) = \pi_B(\tau, \tau) = 5\rho\eta/2$ (as the viewers are equally split between the stations). We now check whether any unilateral deviation by station A can be profit enhancing (deviation by B can be similarly examined).

$$\pi_A(\tau - 2) = \rho\frac{3\eta}{2} \quad < \quad \rho\frac{5\eta}{2} = \pi_A(\tau, \tau)$$

$$\pi_A(\tau - 1) = \rho 2\eta \quad < \quad \rho\frac{5\eta}{2} = \pi_A(\tau, \tau)$$

$$\pi_A(\tau + 1) = \rho 2\eta \quad < \quad \rho\frac{5\eta}{2} = \pi_A(\tau, \tau)$$

$$\pi_A(\tau + 2) = \rho\frac{3\eta}{2} \quad < \quad \rho\frac{5\eta}{2} = \pi_A(\tau, \tau).$$

(b) Part (a) showed that in equilibrium $t_A = t_B$. In order to show that the outcome $(t_A, t_B) \neq (\tau, \tau)$ does not constitute Nash equilibria, we need to show that for every such outcome one station will find it profitable to deviate. We leave it to the reader to complete the proof.

∎

In fact, there is an alternative method of proving Proposition 6.1 by constructing the best response function (see Definition A.5 on page 295) of each station, $R_A(t_B)$ and $R_B(t_A)$. Therefore, for every station $i, j = A, B$ and $i \neq j$,

$$t_i = R_i(t_j) = \begin{cases} \tau - 1 & \text{if } t_B = \tau - 2 \\ \tau & \text{if } t_B = \tau - 1 \\ \tau & \text{if } t_B = \tau \\ \tau & \text{if } t_B = \tau + 1 \\ \tau + 1 & \text{if } t_B = \tau + 2, \end{cases} \tag{6.1}$$

which are plotted in Figure 6.2. Figure 6.2 shows that the two best-response functions intersect only once. This proves that there exists a unique Nash equilibrium in broadcasting time.

The reason for why we should be careful about stating uniqueness in scheduling games is revealed in the following example displayed in Figure 6.3, and in Table 6.2 as a normal-form game. In order to find the Nash equilibria for the game defined by Table 6.2, we construct the stations' broadcasting time best-response functions. Therefore

$$t_i = R_i(t_j) = \begin{cases} \tau - 1 & \text{if } t_B = \tau - 2 \\ \{\tau - 1, \tau\} & \text{if } t_B = \tau - 1 \\ \{\tau - 1, \tau\} & \text{if } t_B = \tau \\ \tau & \text{if } t_B = \tau + 1, \end{cases} \tag{6.2}$$

which are plotted in Figure 6.4. Figure 6.4 reveals that in this example, there are four Nash equilibria: $\langle t_A, t_B \rangle = \langle \tau - 1, \tau - 1 \rangle$, $\langle t_A, t_B \rangle = \langle \tau, \tau \rangle$,

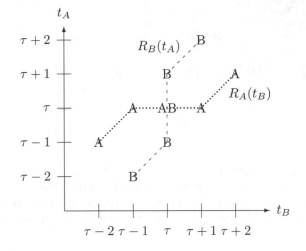

Figure 6.2: Stations' broadcasting time best-response functions: The unique equilibrium case.

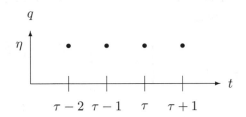

Figure 6.3: Example of multiple Nash equilibria.

and two equilibria with different broadcasting time $\langle t_A, t_B \rangle = \langle \tau - 1, \tau \rangle$, and $\langle t_A, t_B \rangle = \langle \tau, \tau - 1 \rangle$. In all the four equilibria the stations earn a profit of $\pi_A = \pi_B = 2\rho\eta$ as the market is split evenly between the two stations.

We have demonstrated that when there are two broadcasting stations, a Nash equilibrium where two stations broadcast at the same time always exists. The logic behind this result is as follows: If stations are not broadcasting at the same time, then

Step 1: they must be broadcasting in adjacent time periods, since otherwise one station will "move" toward the other and "capture" an additional time-period viewers.

Station B

	$\tau - 2$		$\tau - 1$		τ		$\tau + 1$	
$\tau - 2$	2η	2η	η	3η	$3\eta/2$	$5\eta/2$	2η	2η
$\tau - 1$	3η	η	2η	2η	2η	2η	$5\eta/2$	$3\eta/2$
Station A: τ	$5\eta/2$	$3\eta/2$	2η	2η	2η	2η	3η	η
$\tau + 1$	2η	2η	$3\eta/2$	$5\eta/2$	η	3η	2η	2η

Table 6.2: Multiple equilibria in the prime-time scheduling game. *Remark:* All entries (profit levels) should be multiplied by ρ.

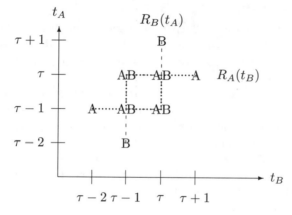

Figure 6.4: Stations' broadcasting time best-response functions: The mutiple equilibria case.

Step 2: In this case, if both stations split the market evenly and broadcast at different time periods, they earn the same as they earn when the broadcast on the same time, hence broadcasting at the same time is a Nash equilibrium.

Step 3: If, however, stations earn different profit levels, then there must be one station that serves more than half of the market and one that serves less than half of the market. Now, the station that serves less than half of the market will deviate and broadcast at the same time as the station with the high profit, thereby raising its market share to serving half of the market. In this case, broadcasting at the same time is again a Nash equilibrium.

Three broadcasting stations

The previous scheduling examples demonstrated that when there are only two stations, there are always Nash equilibria where both stations broadcast at the same time. Suppose now that there are three stations labeled A, B, and C, and consider the viewers' market of Figure 6.1. We again look for a Nash equilibrium in scheduling t_A, t_B and t_C.

Proposition 6.2
Under a uniform distribution of consumers across idea viewing time, there does not exist an equilibrium where all three stations broadcast at the same time.

Proof. If $t_A = t_B = t_C = \tau - 2$, then all stations equally split the viewers so each earns $\pi_A = \pi_B = \pi_C = 5\rho\eta/3$. If station A deviates and sets $t'_A = \tau - 1$, then its profit rises to $\pi'_A = 4\rho\eta$, hence $t_A = t_B = t_C = \tau - 2$ cannot be an equilibrium.

If $t_A = t_B = t_C = \tau - 1$, then all stations equally split the viewers so each earns $\pi_A = \pi_B = \pi_C = 5\rho\eta/3$. If station A deviates and sets $t'_A = \tau$, then its profit rises to $\pi'_A = 3\rho\eta$, hence $t_A = t_B = t_C = \tau - 1$ cannot be an equilibrium.

If $t_A = t_B = t_C = \tau$, then all stations equally split the viewers so each earns $\pi_A = \pi_B = \pi_C = 5\rho\eta/3$. If station A deviates and sets $t'_A = \tau + 1$, then its profit rises to $\pi'_A = 2\rho\eta$, hence $t_A = t_B = t_C = \tau$ cannot be an equilibrium.

Similar deviations are also not profitable at the outcomes $t_A = t_B = t_C = \tau + 1$ and $t_A = t_B = t_C = \tau + 2$. ∎

The prediction of Proposition 6.2 is actually observed in the United States, where NBC, CBS, and ABC compete in the evening news market. Two stations broadcast the news at the same time and the third broadcasts thirty minutes later.

Scheduling and social welfare

In order to calculate social welfare we need first to define viewers' utility function, since so far the only thing that we mentioned about their preferences is that they would prefer to watch television as close as possible to their ideal time. We now define the utility of a viewer whose ideal time is $\hat{t}$ and watches the program at time t by

$$U_{\hat{t}}(t) = \beta - \delta \left| t - \hat{t} \right|, \tag{6.3}$$

where $\beta > 0$ is the viewer's basic utility derived from watching the program, and $\delta > 0$ (differentiation disutility parameter) is the viewer's disutility from having to watch the program one (additional) hour earlier or later than his ideal time.

We generally define a social welfare function as the sum of viewers' utilities plus the stations' profits. However, in this basic model, the entire viewer population is served, hence aggregate industry profit is *always* $\sum_i \pi_i = 5\rho\eta$ for the example displayed in Figure 6.1, and $\sum_i \pi_i = 4\rho\eta$ for the example in Figure 6.3.

Therefore, in these two simple examples, social optimum coincides with scheduling that maximizes aggregate viewers' utility, which in this case is equivalent to scheduling that minimizes aggregate disutility from deviation from viewers' ideal time. The reader is asked to provide the proof for the following proposition.

Proposition 6.3

Suppose that there are two broadcasting stations facing potential viewers whose ideal time distribution is displayed in Figure 6.1. Then,

(a) *Social welfare is maximized when station A broadcasts at $t = \tau - 1$ and station B at $t = \tau + 1$.*

(b) *A market failure always occurs since two stations tend to broadcast at the same time, whereas social welfare is maximized when stations broadcast at different time periods.*

Proposition 6.3 demonstrates an innate market failure in the scheduling of broadcasts, associated with the total conflict between broadcasters' tendency to air the same programs at the same time, and consumers' heterogeneous preferences regarding their ideal viewing time. Indeed, this market failure in scheduling has created an entirely new industry in which cable stations specialize in round-the-clock news, shopping, sports, where each program is repeated every one to two hours.

"One-way" viewers

So far, our viewers could watch their favorite program any time they wished even if their favorite program was aired *earlier* than their ideal time. However, consider a situation where potential viewers come from work every evening at different hours. In this case, those who missed the news will not be able to watch it; they will be able to watch only programs that are aired after they reach home.

Consider again the viewers' market displayed in Figure 6.1, but suppose that no viewer can watch a program which is aired *prior* to his ideal watching time (say, because she spends the time working and arrives home exactly at her ideal watching time). Table 6.3 displays this game in a normal form.

	Station B									
	$\tau-2$		$\tau-1$		τ		$\tau+1$		$\tau+2$	
$\tau-2$	$\eta/2$	$\eta/2$	η		η	2η	η	3η	η	4η
$\tau-1$	η		η		2η	η	2η	2η	2η	3η
A: τ	2η	η	η	2η	$3\eta/2$	$3\eta/2$	3η	η	3η	2η
$\tau+1$	3η	η	2η	2η	η	3η	2η	2η	4η	η
$\tau+2$	4η	η	3η	2η	2η	3η	η	4η	$5\eta/2$	$5\eta/2$

Table 6.3: One-way prime-time scheduling game. *Remark:* All entries (profit levels) should be multiplied by ρ.

Our main result was demonstrated in Cancian, Bills, and Bergstrom (1995).

Proposition 6.4
*With "one-way" viewers, there does **not** exist a Nash equilibrium in broadcasting time.*

Proof. The best response function of each station i, as a function of the broadcasting time of station j can be found to be

$$R_i(i_j) = \begin{cases} \tau+2 & \text{if } \tau-2 \\ \tau+2 & \text{if } \tau-1 \\ \{\tau-1, \tau+2\} & \text{if } \tau \\ \tau & \text{if } \tau+1 \\ \tau+1 & \text{if } \tau+2. \end{cases}$$

Now, we look at the following sequence of responses.

$$t_A = \tau-2 \implies t_B = \tau+2 \implies t_A = \tau+1 \implies t_B = \tau$$

$$\implies t_A = \left\{ \begin{array}{l} \tau-1 \\ \tau+2 \end{array} \right. \implies t_B = \left\{ \begin{array}{l} \tau \\ \tau+1 \end{array} \right. \implies t_A = \left\{ \begin{array}{l} \left\{ \begin{array}{l} \tau-1 \\ \tau+2 \end{array} \right. \\ \tau \end{array} \right. \quad \cdots$$

which means that the sequence of responses never converges and hence a Nash equilibrium does not exist. ∎

The intuition behind Proposition 6.4 is that each station will respond to a given time schedule of the rival by moving its program just ahead of the competitor's broadcast. However, if the rival station schedules its program "very late," the station will respond by scheduling its program as early as possible, i.e., at $t = \tau - 2$, thereby capturing all viewers arriving home early. Nilssen and Sørgard (1998) overcame the nonexistence problem by analyzing a sequential-entry game where, in our case, station A chooses its broadcasting time before station B.

6.1.2 Program-type competition

So far, we have assumed that broadcasting stations compete in one dimension which is scheduling time. However, there is a second dimension of competition among broadcasting stations, which is the type and the nature of broadcasted programs. Steiner (1952), dating back to the age of radio broadcasting, analyzed the program-choice decisions made in monopoly and oligopoly markets, where each station was assumed to maximize its number of listeners. Steiner showed that a monopoly broadcaster typically offers a larger variety of program types than what is offered by an oligopoly industry, since competing stations can gain from concentrating only on popular program types where each station can capture viewers from its rivals. In contrast, a monopoly broadcaster, faces no such business-stealing effect and hence finds it profitable to attract viewers who prefer to watch less profitable programs.

As it turns out, Steiner's result depends heavily on barriers to entry into the broadcasting industry. If there is free entry then eventually all program types will be broadcasted if it is socially optimal to do so. In contrast, barriers to entry imply that the few existing stations concentrate only on the more popular programs and neglect the less popular programs. The duplication of popular programs and the scarcity of less popular programs yield a socially suboptimal allocation.

To see this, suppose that each broadcaster has exactly two channels that can operate at the same time. Suppose further that 81 percent of the potential viewers would like to watch talk shows only, and 19 percent would like to watch only the news. Now, if there is only one broadcaster (monopoly), then it will offer both a talk show on one channel and news on the second channel. In contrast, if there are two broadcasters, each with two channels, then all the four channels will offer only talk shows as each is viewed by $81\%/4 > 19\%$ of the viewers. A similar result is found in Spence and Owen (1977) who showed that, in the advertiser-supported TV industry, there is a bias in favor of program types that generate large number of viewers. Finally, Nilssen and Sørgard (1998) integrated the scheduling strategy model with the program type model and analyze a broadcasting industry competing in two dimensions: scheduling and program profile. We now introduce a simplified version of Steiner (1952).

Program types and viewers

We assume that there are ψ possible program types indexed by $i = 1, 2, \ldots, \psi$. For example, type 1 could be a talk show, type 2 could be the news, type 3 could be a crime show, and so on. Each type of program i is watched by η_i viewers. With no loss of generality, program types are labeled in the order of decreasing number of viewers so that

$$\eta_1 > \eta_2 > \ldots > \eta_\psi.$$

ASSUMPTION 6.2

(a) *Programs are to be aired in prime time only; hence each broadcasting station can air at most one program type.*

(b) *If several stations choose to air the same program type, then the program's viewers are evenly split among the stations.*

Broadcasting stations and the rules of competition

There are three broadcasting stations indexed by $j = A, B, C$. Production is costless. As before, each station earns a profit of ρ on each viewer, so each station attempts to maximize the number of viewers.

We denote by $p_j \in 1, 2, \ldots i, \ldots, \psi$ the action (program type) chosen by station j. We look for a Nash equilibrium (Definition A.4 on page 292) in program-type choices, $\langle p_A, p_B, p_C \rangle$.

Equilibrium program types with three stations

The following proposition states which program types are chosen by each station in a Nash equilibrium.

Proposition 6.5
Let $\eta_1 > \eta_2 > \eta_3$.

(a) *If $\eta_1 > 3\eta_2$, then $\langle p_A, p_B, p_C \rangle = \langle 1, 1, 1 \rangle$ (all stations air only the most popular program) constitutes a unique Nash equilibrium*

(b) *If $2\eta_3 < \eta_1 < 3\eta_2$, there are three Nash equilibria, where exactly two stations air program type 1 and one station airs program type 2: $\langle 1, 1, 2 \rangle$, $\langle 1, 2, 1 \rangle$, and $\langle 2, 1, 1 \rangle$.*

(c) *If $\eta_1 < 2\eta_3$, there are six equilibria where in each equilibrium each station airs a different program type: $\langle 1, 2, 3 \rangle$, $\langle 1, 3, 2 \rangle$, $\langle 2, 1, 3 \rangle$, $\langle 2, 3, 1 \rangle$, $\langle 3, 1, 2 \rangle$, and $\langle 3, 2, 1 \rangle$.*

Proof.

(a) In equilibrium, $\pi_A = \pi_B = \pi_C = \rho\eta_1/3$. If, for example, station A deviates to program type $p'_A = 2$, then $\pi'_A = \rho\eta_2 < \rho\eta_1/3$. Since $\eta_3 < \eta_2$, this station will also not deviate to $p''_A = 3$. For exactly the same reason stations B and C will not deviate.

(b) We construct the best-response function of a representative station i.

$$R_i(p_j, p_k) = \begin{cases} 2 & \text{if } p_j = p_k = 1 \\ 1 & \text{if } p_j = p_k = 2, \text{ or } p_j = p_k = 3 \\ 1 & \text{if } p_j = 1, p_k = 2, \text{ or } p_j = 2, p_k = 1 \\ 1 & \text{if } p_j = 2, p_k = 3, \text{ or } p_j = 3, p_k = 2 \\ 1 & \text{if } p_j = 1, p_k = 3, \text{ or } p_j = 3, p_k = 1. \end{cases}$$

Each of the three equilibria can satisfy simultaneously all the three best-response functions. Also, program type 3 is never a best response, hence these three equilibria are the only equilibria.

Part (c) is left as an exercise at the end of this chapter. ∎

Is there a market failure?

Let each viewer gain a utility of $U_i = \beta$ if the program of her choice is aired, and $U_i = 0$ if the program of her choice is not aired. We define social welfare as the sum of viewers' utilities and stations' profits. Thus, comparing the social welfare levels for representative outcomes for the three parameter ranges analyzed in Proposition 6.5 yields

$$\begin{aligned} W(1,1,1) &= \eta_1\beta + (\eta_1/3 + \eta_1/3 + \eta_1/3)\rho = \eta_1(\beta + \rho), \\ W(1,1,2) &= (\eta_1 + \eta_2)\beta + (\eta_1/2 + \eta_1/2 + \eta_2)\rho = (\eta_1 + \eta_2)(\beta + \rho), \\ W(1,2,3) &= (\eta_1 + \eta_2 + \eta_3)(\beta + \rho). \end{aligned} \tag{6.4}$$

Equation (6.4) and Proposition 6.5 imply the following proposition.

Proposition 6.6
(a) *Social welfare is maximized only when all stations broadcast different types of programs. Formally, the program-type choices $\langle 1, 2, 3 \rangle$, $\langle 1, 3, 2 \rangle$, $\langle 2, 1, 3 \rangle$, $\langle 2, 3, 1 \rangle$, $\langle 3, 1, 2 \rangle$, and $\langle 3, 2, 1 \rangle$, maximize social welfare.*

(b) *When $\eta_1 > 2\eta_3$, a market failure occurs as one program type is not broadcasted by any station.*

6.1.3 Cable TV: The effect of local monopolies

Cable TV became most popular in the early 1980s when extensive wiring of private houses took place in the United States and Europe. Unlike TV stations which broadcasted via the airwaves and earned their profit from advertising and public money, cable TV operators rely on direct fees imposed on subscribers for transmitting a bundle of TV stations to their homes.

The guiding principle of regulators in providing licenses to cable-TV operators was that wiring houses requires an expensive investment and therefore cable-TV operators were considered as natural monopolies. Later on we will criticize this approach. However, it should be pointed out that this view was held by many other regulators who licensed cable-TV operators in the 1980s and early 1990s, which left the industry as a group of operators where each held a monopoly position in a predefined geographical area.

In what follows, we demonstrate why local monopolies are extremely harmful to consumers of cable-TV more than other monopolies in other industries. Since cable-TV operators own the cable itself, they can control the prices of many channels and not only one channel. This, induces the local monopoly cable-TV operator to sell packages of channels for the purpose of extracting more consumer surplus than the surplus extracted by a monopoly selling a single channel only.

Consider a monopoly cable-TV operator providing a service to four types of consumers by transmitting three channels: CNN, BBC, and SHOP(ping). Table 6.4 shows the valuation (maximum willingness to pay) of each consumer type for each channel.

Consumer	CNN	BBC	SHOP
1	10	1	2
2	10	1	5
3	1	10	2
4	1	10	5

Table 6.4: Consumers' valuation of three channels.

We begin our analysis by asking what are the monopoly provider's profit-maximizing prices assuming that the provider must sell each channel separately. When each channel is individually priced, it can be easily verified that the profit-maximizing prices are: $p_C = p_B = 10$, and $p_S = 5$ which yield a profit of $\pi = 20 + 20 + 10 = 50$.

Now, let us consider the exact opposite extreme by assuming that the provider must sell all channels in a single package. The act of selling all channels in a single basket is known as *pure tying*. When all channels are sold as a single package, it can be easily verified that the package's profit-maximizing price is $p_{CBS} = 13$, hence $\pi = 4 \times 13 = 52$. The important thing to realize so far is that tying channels in one package increase the monopoly's profit beyond the profit earned by a conventional nontying monopoly. This result demonstrates our earlier statement in which monopolies in the cable-TV industry enjoy a monopoly power that is greater than the conventional monopoly power studied in Intermediate Microeconomics classes.

Finally, we now demonstrate that there is a pricing structure of this monopoly that can enhance its profit beyond the level obtained by pure tying. Consider now two packages offered for sale by this monopolist: [CNN, BBC] and [SHO]. The sale of channels in baskets where some baskets contain only a single channel is call *mixed tying*. Let the prices of these packages be $p_{CB} = 11$ and $p_S = 5$. Hence, $\pi^{MT} = 4 \times 11 + 2 \times 5 = 54$. Yes, profit goes further up with this mixed tying. Mixed tying is commonly observed in this industry as many operators offer links to individual movie channels that are not included in the packages they offer.

Finally, we wish to discuss whether it is essential to have cable-TV operators operating as local monopolies, thereby capturing large monopoly profits which would pay for their investment in wiring private homes. We can raise three arguments against this conventional view:

(a) Wiring is not unique to the cable-TV industry. Wiring and main-tenance costs are also borne by telephone companies, which have already been exposed to competition in most developed countries. Since regulators found it beneficial to introduce competition in the telecommunication industry, why shouldn't they allow competition in cable-TV?

(b) Similar to the telecommunication industry, avoidance of multiple wiring can be achieved via *access pricing* which was analyzed in Section 5.3.

(c) With the introduction of fiber-optics lines, cable-TV operators can generate more profits by providing other services on the same lines, such as Internet, e-mail, and phone services. This means that the revenue generated by other services can pay for the wiring and main-tenance of lines, whereas TV broadcasts can be sold to viewers at competitive prices.

6.2 Spectrum Allocation

Radio spectrum constitutes a perfect example of an economic good as it is scarce and valuable (profitable) at the same time. The goal of the regulator in allocating spectrum should be to award licenses to the firms best able to turn the spectrum into valuable services for consumers. Licensing spectrum access rights by means other than auctions has been proved to be socially wasteful. Whereas Herzel (1951) and Coase (1959) persuasively argued that the Federal Communications Commission (FCC) should allocate frequencies by auction, not until 1993 did the U.S. Congress grant the FCC authority to assign wireless operating permits via competitive bidding.

Hazlett (1998) describes that from 1927 to 1981, administrative proceedings took place to rank competitive applicants by a "public interest" standard. In 1981, the Congress has adopted legislation permitting the FCC to issue nonbroadcast licenses by lotteries. This procedure went on until 1993 when Congress permitted auctions, which in one year generated over \$20 billion in receivables for the U.S. Treasury. The social cost of allocating spectrum via "awards" not only sacrificed billions of dollars for the Treasury, but the comparative hearings proved to be highly politicized.

6.2.1 Lotteries

The U.S. Congress granted the FCC authority to assign nonbroadcast license rights by lottery in 1981. Lotteries were preferred to comparative hearings since it proved to be a much faster allocation method to release the bureaucratic bottleneck which delayed the introduction of wireless communication (cellular phones), considering the large number of licenses that had to be issued. The value of cellular telephones, allotted 50 MHz of spectrum nationwide, was in the neighborhood of \$90 billion.

The inefficiency of the lottery spectrum allocation method can be seen from the following example. Suppose that there is one frequency bandwidth to be allocated to one and only one firm. The firms we have in mind could be either cellular phone companies, which require some bandwidth to transmit phone calls to mobile phones, or the firms could be radio or TV stations. We assume that there are only two of such firms, labeled as firm A and firm B and that the firms have different technologies (e.g., different standards for mobile phones, such as an analog standard, common in the United States; and the GSM standard which is common in Europe and Asia). With no loss of generality, we let firm A own the more advanced technology. Let ρ_i denote the total revenue firm i can generate if licensed to operate on a certain frequency band. Our model also relies on the following two assumptions.

ASSUMPTION 6.3
(a) *Firm A can raise a higher revenue from its operations than firm B when licensed to operate on the desired frequency band. Formally, assume that $\rho_A > \rho_B > 0$.*

(b) *The government (or the regulating authority) has no way of knowing which firm is more efficient, and what are the profits that each firm can generate if granted the license to use the frequency. In contrast,* firms know both their own and their rival's potential profit in this market.

(c) The government seeks to maximize its revenue from licensing the available frequency bands.

Assignment of frequency bands via a lottery means that each firm can win the frequency band with probability of 50 percent. Let b denote the participation fee each firm must pay in order to participate in the lottery. Then, if both firms participate the expected profit of each firm is $E\pi_i = \rho_i/2 - b$. Hence in order to induce both firms to participate in this lottery, the government must restrict the participation fee to be in the range $0 \le b \le \rho_B/2$. Assuming that the government maximizes its revenue, it would set the participation fee to equal $b = \rho_B/2$, and with two participants, it will collect a revenue of $G = 2b = \rho_B$. Then, the expected profit of each firm is

$$E\pi_A = \frac{\rho_A - \rho_B}{2}, \quad \text{and} \quad E\pi_B = \frac{\rho_B - \rho_B}{2} = 0. \tag{6.5}$$

We define social welfare the sum of the expected profits of the two firms and the government revenue. Formally,

$$W \stackrel{\text{def}}{=} E\pi_A + E\pi_B + G = \frac{\rho_A - \rho_B}{2} + 0 + \rho_B = \frac{\rho_A + \rho_B}{2}. \tag{6.6}$$

However, if we believe that the firm with the highest potential revenue possesses a better technology and can provide a better service, it is clear that the frequency band should be assigned to firm A, in which case the social welfare would be

$$W' = \pi_A + G = \rho_A > \frac{\rho_A + \rho_B}{2}.$$

Hence,

Proposition 6.7
The lottery system for assigning scarce frequency band is inefficient as there is a strictly positive probability that frequency will be assigned to the less efficient firm.

Obviously, one way to turn lotteries into an efficient allocation mechanism is to allow winners to sell their rights for using the scarce frequency to the highest bidder. McMillan (1994) provides an example of a group that was chosen by a lottery in 1989 to run cellular telephones in Cape Cod. The group then sold its license to Southwestern Bell for $41 million. To see this, suppose now that firm B (the less efficient firm) was granted with the sole right to use a certain frequency for broadcasting. Then, its profit is $\pi_B = (\rho_B - \rho_B)/2 = 0$. Firm B can enhance its profit by selling its broadcasting rights to the more efficient firm, firm A. The question now is how much rent firm B can extract from A for selling its broadcasting license? If the license is not sold, then A's profit (loss) is $\pi_A = -b = -\rho_B/2$. If A buys the license from B for b', then its profit becomes $\pi'_A = \rho_A - b - b' = \rho_A - \rho_B/2 - b'$. Clearly, the maximum rent that firm B can extract from A is obtained by selling its right to broadcast for $b' = \rho_A$. In this case, the profit of each firm after B sells its right to A becomes

$$\pi_A = \rho_A - b - b' = -\rho_B/2 \quad \text{and} \quad \pi_B = b' - b = \rho_A - \rho_B/2 > 0. \quad (6.7)$$

Thus, by selling its license to the more efficient firm, firm B can extract the entire rent as it was the efficient firm. Therefore,

Proposition 6.8
If lottery winners are allowed to resell their rights, then the lottery system together with the right to resell constitute a socially efficient spectrum allocation mechanism.

Well, the only reason why governments may not like such a mechanism is that the rents are distributed to the private sector instead of to the public sector. That is, in our example the government collects $G = \rho_B$ and firm B earns $\pi_B = \rho_A - \rho_B/2 > G$. So, most of the rent is extracted by the private sector. If the government knew which firm is more efficient, it could have extracted the entire rent which is $G' = \rho_A$, but this possibility has been ruled out by Assumption 6.3(b). For precisely this reason, governments now use auctions.

6.2.2 Auctions

The spectrum for Personal Communication Services (PCS), the next generation of wireless telephony to be licensed to a cellular competitor having access to 140 MHz of nationwide spectrum was anticipated to be of a substantial value. For this reason the regulator pushed for the change in the spectrum allocation policy. From 1994 to 1996 the FCC held nine spectrum auctions and assigned thousands of licenses to hundreds of firms, see McMillan (1994) and Klemperer (1999).

Consider first an *open bid* auction where each firm openly states how much it is willing to pay (to the government) for obtaining the sole rights to use a certain frequency band. We denote by b_A the bid put by firm A, and by b_B the bid put by firm B. Clearly, no firm would announce a bid which is larger than the maximum revenue it can generate from using the desired frequency. That is, $b_A \leq \rho_A$ and $b_B \leq \rho_B$. We can state the following result now.

Proposition 6.9
Let ϵ be the smallest currency denomination. Under Assumption 6.3,

(a) *there exists a unique open-bid Nash equilibrium given by $\langle b_A, b_B \rangle = \langle \rho_B + \epsilon, \rho_B \rangle$; where firm A wins the bid, and*

(b) *this auction is efficient, however, as with the lottery system, in this equilibrium the government fails to extract all the rents associated with giving away the frequency band to the private sector.*

Proof.

(a) In equilibrium, $\pi_A = \rho_A - \rho_B - \epsilon \approx \rho_A - \rho_B$, and $\pi_B = 0$. If A reduces its bid to $b'_A < \rho_B$ it loses the auction and earns zero profit. If A reduces its bid to $b''_A = \rho_B$ it loses the auction with probability of 50 percent. Finally, if A raises its bid to $b'''_A > \rho_B + \epsilon$ its profit drops, since it continues to win the auction but it pays more for the higher bid.

   If firm B raises its bid to $b'_B > b_A = \rho_B + \epsilon$ it wins the lottery, however it ends up making a loss since $\pi'_B = \rho_B - b'_B < 0$. Finally, lowering the bid would not alter B's profit since at this bidding range firm A wins the auction.

(b) This auction is efficient since the frequency is allocated to the more efficient firm, firm A. However, the government manages to collect only $G = \rho_B$, whereas the remaining surplus goes to firm A in the form of a profit of $\pi_A = \rho_A - \rho_B > 0$.

∎

Can auctions be manipulated?

So far, we have seen that there is no mechanism in which governments can extract full surplus from firms in the private sector that wish to obtain exclusive rights for using the airwaves. The above analysis revealed that auctions are far superior than lotteries since lotteries may assign scarce frequency bands to less efficient firms, which is not the case under open-bid auctions. However, as recently observed, auctions are sometimes manipulated by sophisticated telecommunication firms which happen to collude on submitting very low bids, thereby "fooling" the government to believe that these frequency bands are not very profitable.

To demonstrate why manipulating the auction could become profitable for both firms (even for the more efficient firm, firm A, which can always win this auction), assume that $\rho_A < 2\rho_B$ which means that the revenues firms can generate are not too far apart. Now, suppose that prior to the auction both firms collude by agreeing that each firm would submit an equal bid satisfying $\bar{b} < 2\rho_B - \rho_A$.

We now prove that bid $\bar{b}$ raises expected profit of each firm. Since both firms submit the same bid, there is probability of 50 percent for each firm to win the license for the scarce frequency band. Hence, their expected profits are

$$\mathrm{E}\pi_A = \frac{\rho_A - \bar{b}}{2} > \frac{\rho_A - (2\rho_B - \rho_A)}{2} = \rho_A - \rho_B, \quad \text{and}$$

$$\mathrm{E}\pi_B = \frac{\rho_B - \bar{b}}{2} > \frac{\rho_B - (2\rho_B - \rho_A)}{2} = \frac{\rho_A - \rho_B}{2} > 0.$$

Notice that under the open-bid auction with no collusion $\pi_A = \rho_A - \rho_B$ and $\pi_B = 0$. Hence, collusion raises the expected profit of each firm! Clearly, governments can sometime spot this collusion by observing that the firms' bids are almost the same, in which case the auction must be canceled since, just like the lottery system, it may end up assigning the frequency band to the less efficient firm.

Will auctions be used forever?

Noam (1998) argues that technology advances that eliminated interference problems would make it socially desirable to dispose the auction method for allocating scarce frequency bands. A better alternative not driven by revenue needs of governments, is a license-free spectrum. Users would gain entry to frequency bands on a pay-as-you-go basis, instead of controlling a slice of the spectrum. The users would transmit their content together with access tokens (electronic money). Access prices would vary with congestion, set by automatic clearing houses of spectrum users.

Once technology and economics can solve the interference problem in ways other than exclusivity, competitive bidding of the right to control a certain bandwidth need no longer be socially optimal. Now, new digital technologies make new ways of thinking about spectrum use that were not possible in the analog world. The new paradigm in which many users of various radio-based applications can enter spectrum bands without exclusive license to any slice of spectrum is called *open access*.

6.3   Digital Convergence

The Telecommunication Act of 1996 revolutionized the entire information and entertaining media industries in that it allows cable companies to provide Internet services (hence video and audio communication) and phone companies to provide cable and Internet services. In economic terms, the major consequence of this radical policy change is that phone and cable companies can implicitly or explicitly *tie* the sales of one information service with others, where we define *tying* as a marketing strategy where a firm or a service provider makes the sale of one of its services conditional upon the purchaser also buying some other service from it.

This reform was unavoidable considering the technological advances that have made it possible to transmit digital TV (compressed and uncompressed) via fiber-optic lines. One reason why this radical change occurred relatively late is that the regulating authorities (both the antitrust authorities and the FCC) feared that tying may lead to (1) an increase in dominant positions of dominant firms, and (2) "leveraging" which refers to the use of monopoly power in one market to gain an advantage or reduce competition in another market.

In this section, we construct extremely simple examples in order to examine whether tying of different information services leads to increase in dominance of one (say, phone-service) provider, and whether it is possible to have an extreme situation where one company is foreclosed by another, which ties several services in one bundle sold to all consumers.

The Model

Consider a market with two providers of telephone service, which we denote as A and B, and one provider of Internet service denoted by C. Suppose that consumers desire to purchase a bundle of services consisting of one unit of a phone service and one unit of an Internet service. To simplify our exposition, we assume that production of both, phone and Internet, services is costless.

There are two consumers, one who is phone company A oriented and another who is phone company B oriented. Let β be the gross utility parameter, and δ the disutility from obtaining phone service from the less desired company. Then, consumers' preferences for telephone and Internet services of each consumer are given by

$$U_A \stackrel{\text{def}}{=} \begin{cases} \beta - p_A - p_C & \text{buys } A \text{ and } C \\ \beta - \delta - p_B - p_C & \text{buys } B \text{ and } C \\ 0 & \text{Otherwise,} \end{cases} \tag{6.8}$$

$$U_B \stackrel{\text{def}}{=} \begin{cases} \beta - \delta - p_A - p_C & \text{buys } A \text{ and } C \\ \beta - p_B - p_C & \text{buys } B \text{ and } C \\ 0 & \text{Otherwise.} \end{cases}$$

This utility function is motivated by the observation that some consumers do not switch among phone companies even when there is a change in the relative price of phone services. This behavior occurs when consumers develop loyalty toward one telephone company, or because one telephone company offers a bundling package that suits a particular preference of a particular consumer.

A second assumption imbedded in the utility function (6.8) is that phone and Internet services are perfect complements. There are two justifications for this assumption. First, if we show that foreclosure of one phone company is unlikely to occur when phone and Internet services are complements in the eye of consumers, then this result is even more likely to hold when these services are viewed as independent by consumers. Second, digital convergence indeed changes the characteristics of these services, so it is likely that in the future both services will be treated as complements.

We make the following assumption.

ASSUMPTION 6.4
The two phone companies provide services that are sufficiently differentiated. Formally, $\delta < \beta < 2\delta$.

Assumption 6.4 implies that each customer highly values his/her most preferred phone company compared to the competing company.

Our analysis proceeds as follows. We analyze three regulatory regimes:

Preregulation: phone companies A and B are restricted to phone services; whereas firm C is restricted to Internet services only.

Partial Deregulation: Phone company A is permitted to provide Internet services. Here, we check whether foreclosure is possible and profitable.

Complete deregulation: all phone companies can provide Internet services.

6.3.1   Preregulation

Suppose now that the two telephone companies A, B, and the Internet provider C are independently owned, and suppose that the regulating authority limits the scope of operation of each firm to one type of service. That is, this regulatory regime mandates that a phone company cannot provide Internet services and that an Internet-service provider cannot sell phone services. We look for a Nash-Bertrand equilibrium in prices (see Definition A.4 on page 292). Unfortunately, there is more than one equilibrium corresponding to a high Internet-service price and low phone-service prices or a low Internet price and high telephone service prices. Therefore,

Proposition 6.10
When the industry is decomposed into three independent firms:

(a) *The following prices constitute a Nash-Bertrand equilibrium: $p_A = p_B = \delta$, $p_C = \beta - \delta$. In this equilibrium the telephone-provider A sells one unit to the A-oriented consumer, phone-service provider B sells one unit to the B-oriented consumer, and the Internet provider C sells two units (one unit to each consumer); the firms earn profit levels of $\pi_A = \pi_B = \delta$ and $\pi_C = 2(\beta - \delta)$.*

(b) *The above equilibrium is not unique.*

Proof. If firm C raises its price, no consumer would buy any system. Also, since all consumers already buy a unit of C, firm C cannot increase its profit by lowering its price. In order for phone company A to undercut phone company B it must set $p_A = \delta - \delta = 0$, and hence cannot increase its profit. Therefore, undercutting is not profitable for firms A and B. This establishes part (a).

To establish part (b), observe that the following triplets are also equilibria: $(p_A, p_B, p_C) = (\beta - \delta, \beta - \delta, \delta)$, $(p_A, p_B, p_C) = (0, 0, \beta)$, and $(p_A, p_B, p_C) = (\beta, \beta, 0)$. ∎

Proposition 6.10 shows that there can be two types of price configurations: one with high telephone-service prices and a low Internet price, and one low phone-service prices and a high Internet price. To determine which equilibrium is more likely to observe we need to decide which service existed first. Thus, if phone services existed prior to the Internet service, it is likely that most surplus is extracted by the phone-service provider. In this respect, the equilibrium prices stated in the proposition are more likely to occur.

6.3.2 Partial deregulation

A commonly stated consequence of permitting phone companies to provide other services is a foreclosure of competing firms via a merger or acquisition of firms supplying complementary services. We now demonstrate the possibility how phone company A can drive phone company B out of business when it acquires (or merges with) the Internet supplier C and sells products A and C tied in a single package. Suppose that the newly merged firm, denoted by AC, offers the package containing phone service A with Internet service C for a price of p_{AC}. We now state our main proposition:

Proposition 6.11

The bad news: By setting the package price to $p_{AC} = \beta$ (or lower), the firm selling the package AC drives phone company B out of business. Thus, tying can serve as a tool for foreclosing a competing firm. In this case, the B-oriented consumer is not served, hence, a merger is socially inefficient.

The good news: Foreclosing is not profitable for the tying firm. The profit of the merged firm AC when engaged in foreclosing firm B is lower than the sum of the two premerged firms A and C.

Proof. Suppose that firm B sets the lowest possible price $p_B = 0$. When $p_{AC} = \beta$, the utility of the B-oriented consumer when buying system AC and product B for $p_B = 0$ is $U_B = \beta - p_{AC} - 0 = 0$. Hence, phone company B will not sell, and the B-oriented consumer will not be served. This proves the "bad news" part. Under this foreclosure equilibrium, $\pi_{AC} = \beta$. However, the sum of the profits of firms A and C prior to this merger was $\delta + 2(\beta - \delta) > \beta$ (Assumption 6.4 and Proposition 6.10). ∎

Proposition 6.11 shows that tying for the purpose of foreclosing a horizontally competing firm is too costly to the foreclosing firm and is therefore unlikely to be realized even when it eliminates the independent Internet supplier. The proposition also shows that the act of foreclosing the market reduces aggregate industry profit, since the foreclosure causes one consumer not to be served. Thus, after firm B is foreclosed the industry serves a reduced number of consumers, and hence earns a lower aggregate industry profit. Note that the "bad" news is not so bad considering the fact that the present model makes an extreme assumption that phone and Internet services are perfect complements. The "bad news" part of Proposition 6.11 need not hold when the two services are not complements. Thus, this part of the proposition presents the worst-possible extreme case.

6.3.3 Complete deregulation

Suppose now that the telecommunication industry has reached the maximum degree of deregulation, which means that all phone companies are allowed to tie phone service with Internet service. In this case, the independent Internet service provider goes out of business and

Proposition 6.12

(a) The unique equilibrium prices are $p_{AC} = p_{BC} = \beta$.

(b) Foreclosure (of phone companies) cannot occur.

Proof. In this equilibrium each firm sells to one consumer and earns $\pi_A = \pi_B = \beta$. If firm A attempts to undercut firm B, the utility function (6.8) implies it must set p'_{AC} to satisfy $\beta - \delta - p'_{AC} > \beta - p_{BC}$, hence $p'_{AC} < \beta - \delta + \beta - \beta = \beta - \delta$, thereby earning $\pi'_{AC} \approx 2(\beta - \delta) < \beta$ by Assumption 6.4. Hence, undercutting is not profitable. ∎

The main purpose of this section was to demonstrate that if local phone companies are allowed to provide long-distance services, and if long-distance companies are allowed to enter the local phone markets; and if, more generally, cable companies can provide phone and Internet services, and phone companies provide cable TV and Internet services (in short, all are allowed to provide all digital services on the same fiber-optic line) then: (a) there will *not* be a foreclosure, and (b) there will not be bottlenecks. Thus, in order to ensure that foreclosures will not take place, regulators should allow all service providers to sell the entire variety of telecommunication, broadcasting, and Internet services.

6.4 Exercises

1. Consider the scheduling model of Section 6.1.1 and suppose that there are two broadcasting stations facing 2η potential viewers whose ideal watching time is 5 P.M.; η viewers whose ideal time is 6 P.M.; and η viewers whose ideal time is 7 P.M. Let t_A denote the broadcasting time of station A, and t_B the broadcasting time of station B. Answer the following questions.

   (a) Find all pairs of broadcasting times that constitute Nash equilibria. Prove your result.

   (b) How would your answer change if the number of potential viewers whose ideal time is 5 P.M. went up from 2η to 3η? Prove.

2. Consider the scheduling model of Section 6.1.1 with three broadcasting stations labeled A, B, and C, facing 3η potential viewers whose ideal watching time is 5 P.M.; η viewers whose ideal time is 6 P.M.; and η viewers whose ideal time is 7 P.M.

   (a) Find all Nash equilibria in broadcasting time periods. Prove!

   (b) Conclude whether Proposition 6.2 holds for this case involving a nonuniform distribution of consumers.

3. Consider the broadcasted news scheduling model with three broadcasting stations labeled A, B, and C, facing 600 potential viewers whose ideal watching time is 5 P.M.; 100 viewers whose ideal time is 6 P.M.; and 200 viewers whose ideal time is 7 P.M.

Assume that each station can air its news broadcast at one and only one time period. Also assume that each station earns exactly \$1 per viewers (as determined by rating surveys conducted during the broadcasting hours). Let t_i denote the broadcasting time of station i, $i = A, B, C$.

(a) Find one Nash equilibrium in broadcasting time. Prove your answer!

(b) We now define the utility of a viewer whose ideal time is $\hat{t}$ and watches the program at time t by $U_{\hat{t}}(t) \stackrel{\text{def}}{=} \beta - \delta \left| t - \hat{t} \right|$. Define the social welfare function and determine whether the Nash equilibrium in scheduling time you found in (a) is socially optimal. Prove your answer!

4. Consider the competition among three broadcasting stations on viewers by setting product types, Section 6.1.2.

(a) Is there a condition under which the program-type choices $\langle p_A, p_B, p_C \rangle = \langle 1, 2, 2 \rangle$ constitute a Nash equilibrium? Prove your answer!

(b) Prove that the program-type choices $\langle p_A, p_B, p_C \rangle = \langle 1, 2, 3 \rangle$ constitute a Nash equilibrium under the condition specified in part (c) of Proposition 6.5.

5. Consider a monopoly cable-TV operator providing service to three consumers by transmitting three channels: CNN, BBC, and SHOP(ping). Table 6.5 shows the valuation (maximum willingness to pay) of each consumer type for each channel.

Consumer	CNN	BBC	SHOP
1	5	1	2
2	5	1	5
3	1	5	2

Table 6.5: Consumers' valuation of three channels.

Assuming zero production cost answer the following questions and prove your answers.

(a) Calculate the profit-maximizing prices assuming that the monopoly must sell each channel separately.

(b) Calculate the profit-maximizing price assuming that the monopoly sells all the channels in a single package.

(c) Suppose now that the monopoly can package channels any way it wants to. Which combination of packages maximize the monopoly's profit?

6.5   Selected References

Cancian, M., A. Bills, and T. Bergstrom. 1995. "Hotelling, Location Problems with Directional Constraints: An Application to Television News Scheduling." *Journal of Industrial Economics* 43: 121–124.

Coase, R. 1959. "The Federal Communications Commission." *Journal of Law and Economics* 2: 1–40.

Hazlett, T. 1998. "Assigning Property Rights to Radio Spectrum Users: Why did the FCC License Auctions Take 67 Years?" *Journal of Law and Economics* 41: 529–575.

Herzel, L. 1951. " 'Public Interest' and the Market in Color television Regulation." *University of Chicago Law Review* 18: 802–816.

Klemperer, P. 1999. "Auction Theory: A Guide to the Literature." *Journal of Economic Surveys* 13: 227–286.

McMillan, J. 1994. "Selling Spectrum Rights." *Journal of Economic Perspectives* 8: 145–162.

Mitchell and Vogelsang. 1991. *Telecommunication Pricing: Theory and Practice.* Cambridge: Cambridge University Press.

Nilssen, T., and L. Sørgard. 1998. "Time Schedule and Program Profile: TV News in Norway and Denmark." *Journal of Economics & Management Strategy* 7: 209–235.

Noam, E. 1998. "Spectrum Auctions: Yesterday's Heresy, Today's Orthodoxy, Tomorrow's Anachronism. Taking the Next Step to Open Spectrum Access." *Journal of Law and Economics* 41: 765–790.

Spence, A., and B. Owen. 1997. "Television Programming, Monopolistic Competition, and Welfare." *Quarterly Journal of Economics* 91: 103–126.

Steiner, P. 1952. "Program Patterns and Preferences, and the Workability of Competition in Radio Broadcasting." *Quarterly Journal of Economics* 66: 194-223.

Chapter 7

Markets for Information

Information and know-how constitute perfect examples of what economists call *public goods*. A *public good* is a commodity or a service in which the "consumption" of one agent does not preclude its use by other agents, where the term agents here refers to consumers and firms. See Kindleberger (1983) and Varian (1995) for discussions of public goods in this context.

Further, there are two reasons why we view information industries as network industries. First, since buyers of information can reproduce it at a relatively low cost and then distribute it or sell it to other consumers, information providers must take into account the "networks" at which their information products are distributed. Such networks may include legal and illegal copying, rental stores, and libraries. Second, with the transition from printed to digital information, the transmission of information may result in congestion over the network resulting from overloading of the system by many information seekers.

Section 7.1 characterizes the major networks under which information is diffused. Section 7.2 provides a comprehensive analysis of one particular "network" of information distribution, namely, libraries and rental places. Section 7.3 develops the economics of the Internet, which is likely to dominate all other forms of information distribution networks in the near future. Section 7.4 briefly describes various methods commonly used in determining how to price information products.

7.1 Information Reproduction

Pricing of information depends on how information is reproduced or copied. Therefore, before analyzing how the distribution of rents vary with the various copying technologies, we need to understand how information is diffused.

7.1.1 Classification of information reproduction

We now define three extreme patterns in which information can be reproduced or copied by users who may not acquire permissions to make copies from the original provider. Figure 7.1 illustrates three patterns of information reproduction in a market where η consumers wish to copy information from agent 0 that owns an original copy of this information.

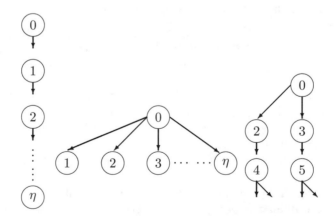

Figure 7.1: *Left:* "Vertical" information reproduction. *Middle:* "Horizontal" information reproduction. *Right:* "Mixed" reproduction. *Note:* Agent 0 is the information provider.

Formally, we say that information is

Vertically reproduced if each agent (the provider and each consumer) makes one copy for the benefit of another consumer.

Horizontally reproduced if each consumer makes copy from the original provider.

Mixed reproduced if information is copied in "horizontal" and then "vertical" layers.

Clearly, in general it is hard to describe exactly how information is copied. However, some types of information cannot be copied vertically for a large number of times. For example, photocopying, and dubbing of audio and video (analog) information are distorted when they are dubbed vertically more than once or twice. Thus, a library photocopying model cannot assume vertical information copying. In fact, only digital-information technologies allow for vertical copying for a large (potentially infinite) number of times.

The horizontal information copying describes how journal photocopying is provided by libraries. Each library subscriber makes one photocopy of a journal article, generally for private use.

The "mixed" information pattern describes how journal article copying is recently done in the academic-education sector. First, photocopying enterprises (e.g., Kinko's) make a photocopy from a nearby university library. Then, they photocopy this photocopy for an entire class in the form of course packs. Further reproduction of these course packs is generally not feasible due to the reduced quality that characterizes the photocopying technology.

As a result of the public-good nature of information, consumers can gain access to information without having to pay for obtaining it, as long as some consumers initially obtain it and then distribute it for free to other consumers. Consequently, information providers have been forced to design information-transmitting media that can, at least partially, exclude nonpaying consumers from easily accessing the information purchased by one agent. Examples for such hardware devices include: decoders for cable TV, plugs connected to computers' parallel ports that limit the use of the software, software-protection algorithms for preventing software duplications, watermarks on paper, and printing with blue ink on a blue paper to prevent photocopying of originals. It is interesting to note that these devices generally produce side effects of reducing the quality of *originals* and therefore their value to consumers.

7.1.2 Copy protection: Digital versus nondigital media

The economic effects of copy protection vary significantly among the different types of information-providing media. Besen and Kirby (1989) argue that the differences in conclusions regarding the effects of private copying on social welfare result from differences in (1) the extent to which the sellers of originals can appropriate the value placed on them by *all* users; (2) the relative market sizes for used and new copies; and (3) the degree of substitution between originals and copies.

A natural question to ask at this point is how copying of digital information (e.g., software piracy, which was analyzed in Section 3.5), differs from journal and book photocopying, or even the reproduction of audio and video cassettes. Digital reproduction differs from journal and book photocopying in several aspects:

(a) In the case of digital reproduction (for example, when software is not protected), any copy and copies of copies would be identical to the original. In contrast, paper and cassette copies are not equal to the originals, and copies of copies tend to become unreadable. Moreover, paper copying always loses information such as fine lines, fine print and color images (even in color copying).

(b) In the case of photocopying (or dubbing of analog media), the number of copies made depends on the number of originals purchased in the market, whereas digital reproduction can theoretically originate from a single source (a diskette for example). However, there is also a limit on the number of copies that can be made from a single diskette because of the rising costs of identifying a large number of additional users.

(c) Journal and book publishers find it difficult and costly to physically protect their rights against illegal photocopying, whereas software developers can install protective devices that make piracy very difficult, and sometimes impossible.

(d) Software users depend on services and documentation provided by developers, whereas copied journal articles and books can be read without reference to the original publishers. Similarly, listening and viewing audio and video cassettes does not require the use of any operating instructions from the manufacturer.

Because of these differences, the law treats photocopying and software piracy in different ways. For example, Section 170 of Copyright Act states: "the fair use of copyrighted work ... for purposes such as criticism, comment, newsreporting, teaching (including multiple copies for classroom use), scholarship, or research, is not an infringement of copyright." In contrast, the Computer Software Copyright Act does not have an equivalent Fair-Use Doctrine as photocopying. In fact, on February 12, 1996 the U.S. Court of Appeals for the Sixth Circuit handed down a landmark ruling (Princeton University v. Michigan Document Service, Inc., 74 F. 3d 1512 [6th Cir. 1996]) that the Copyright Act does not prohibit professors and students who may make copies themselves from using the photoreproduction services of a third party in order to obtain those same copies at less cost. Thus, this ruling allows third parties to produce course packs based on copyrighted material. Note that (a) this ruling has been overturned by the same court, and (b) a different finding was reached under a somewhat different set of facts, in American Geophysical Union v. Texaco Inc., 60 F. 3d 913 (2d Cir. 1995).

Therefore, the law recognizes that photocopying has different market consequences on journal and book publishers compared with the market consequences of software piracy.

7.1.3 The built-in copy protection of printed media

Pure vertical photocopying is technically not feasible in the printed media. Thus, unlike the digital media, publishers of printed matters are protected by the fact that one original is insufficient to produce a large number of copies, unless the copying pattern switches to a horizontal form at one stage of the information-reproduction chain.

Enforcement of copyright laws ensures that reproduction centers do not reproduce originals. Paradoxically it is a fact that quality of photocopying is lower than the quality of originals that motivates agents to purchase originals rather than engage in photocopying reproduction. Thus, even if individual users are engaged in vertical reproduction of printed material, the publishers should be able to appropriate the rents from all the users by charging a higher price for the originals.

To see this, consider the following example. Each information consumer is willing to pay \$1 for an original journal article. However, since quality declines with each photocopy a consumer is willing to pay 50 percent less for a photocopy, and 50 percent of 50 percent for a copy of a copy, and so on. The first consumer buys an original, makes a photocopy, and sells it to the second consumer, who also makes a photocopy and sells it to a third consumer, and so on. Table 7.1 illustrates the willingness to pay of each of five individuals who are engaged in vertical photocopying of printed or digital information.

Table 7.1 shows that if publishers raise the price of originals from \$1 to \$1.93, they can successfully capture the *entire* surplus associated with vertical copying. The only consumer to purchase the original may

Info Format	1	2	3	4	5	Total Surplus
Printed	$1.00	$0.50	$0.25	$0.13	$0.06	$1.93
Digital	$1.00	$1.00	$1.00	$1.00	$1.00	$5.00

Table 7.1: Surplus obtained by individuals from vertical photocopying.

incline to pay the high price. Notice however, that if this information is digital, the entire surplus sums up to five times the valuation of each consumer, so it is unlikely that any consumer will be willing to pay this price. Thus, the point here is to emphasize that printed information providers are more protected, in the sense that they tend to capture a higher percentage of total surplus than digital information providers. Section 7.1.4 below extends Table 7.1 and demonstrates how to calculate the surplus generated from copying for an arbitrary number of information users under vertical and horizontal copying patterns.

The above argument may imply that copy protection is more profitable to digital-information providers than to printed-information providers. However, as the reader may recall from Section 3.5, even when information is digital, software protection is not always profitable to software producers when there are network externalities.

7.1.4 Captured and uncaptured surplus from copying

This section provides a method for how to calculate the total surplus associated with copied information. This surplus can be interpreted as the maximum profit an information-providing firm can extract from each original if it can appropriate the rents from all users.

Calculating total surplus from copying

Without specifying how and if consumers pay for the information, we now calculate how much surplus consumers get from digital and nondigital copied information under the two extreme information-copying patterns illustrated in Figure 7.1.

First, since digitally stored information does not deteriorate during reproduction, each consumer always gains a surplus of $1 no matter who is the provider of this information. Therefore, total surplus is always $\$\eta$, which is the number of consumers times $1. Second, for nondigitally stored and reproduced information, the total surplus gained by consumers depends on how information is transmitted.

Let $0 < \rho < 1$. Under vertical reproduction, the consumer who copies directly from the original gains a surplus of ρ. The consumer who copies directly from the first-reproduced copy gains a surplus of ρ^2, and so on. For example, if $\rho = 1/2$, the surplus of the consumer who copies from the original is 50¢, the consumer who makes a copy from the first copy gets a surplus of 25¢, and so on.

Table 7.2 shows the surplus obtained by each consumer and by the entire group under the two types of information. Table 7.2 also shows

Info Format	1	2	3	$\cdots$	η	Total Surplus
	VERTICAL INFO COPYING					
Printed	ρ	ρ^2	ρ^3	$\cdots$	ρ^η	$\dfrac{\rho(1 - \rho^\eta)}{1 - \rho}$
Digital	1	1	1	$\cdots$	1	η
	HORIZONTAL INFO COPYING					
Printed	ρ	ρ	ρ	$\cdots$	ρ	$\eta \times \rho$
Digital	1	1	1	$\cdots$	1	η

Table 7.2: Surplus obtained by consumers from reproduced information.

that under both, vertical- and horizontal-information reproduction patterns, total surplus generated by transmitted digital information exceeds total surplus generated from photocopying of printed information. From Table 7.2 we can conclude that

Proposition 7.1
Under either vertical or horizontal information reproduction, total surplus enjoyed by the η consumers is higher when information is digital compared with printed information.

This result is not surprising considering the fact that the average quality of digital information exceeds the average quality of nondigitally reproduced information.

"Uncaptured" surplus by information providers

We focus the analysis here on situations where consumers share the information with other consumers without charging them. In this case, the provider can charge \$1 for digital information and $\rho < 1$ for a copy of a printed information. Therefore, the amount of consumer surplus which is *uncaptured* by a digital information provider is UCD $= \eta - 1$. The amount of uncaptured surplus by a provider of printed information is

$$\text{UCP} = \frac{\rho(1 - \rho^n)}{1 - \rho} - \rho = \frac{\rho(\rho - \rho^n)}{1 - \rho}.$$

Since UCD > UCP we have it that

Proposition 7.2
*The amount of uncaptured consumer surplus when information is digital
exceeds the amount of uncaptured surplus when information is printed.*

Thus, despite the fact that consumers prefer digital information over
printed information by all consumers, digital information providers earn
proportionally less relative to the potential surplus captured by the
providers of printed information. Thus, despite the fact that digital
information is priced higher (\$1 compared with ρ), the amount of un-
captured surplus is higher when information is digital.

7.2   The Economics of Libraries

7.2.1   What is a library?

We define a library as a facility designed for renting information. Libraries can operate for profit or operate as nonprofit organizations.
However, since libraries must always fund themselves either from direct fees imposed on the readers, or from donors and taxpayers, the
use of the term *information renting* seems an appropriate description of
what constitute libraries' activities. Libraries provide a wide variety of
information goods such as journals, magazines, music recordings of all
sort (long-play records, CD, and audio tapes and cassettes), computer
software, newspapers, government publications, encyclopedias, and, of
course, books.

Information goods such as books, journals, computer software, and
videos are often rented out at libraries and special rental stores. Since information publishers find it profitable to supply information in this form,
it is worthwhile investigating the circumstances under which sharing information in the form of renting may increase or decrease producers'
profits, as compared with selling it directly to consumers.

Circulating libraries operating for profit were common in England
toward the end of the eighteenth century and the nineteenth century.
These libraries appealed to the popular taste, particularly that of women,
due to the fact that women were interested in fiction and partly due to
the fact that women were not welcomed in other clubs. For-profit libraries continued to be popular well into the twentieth century. These
libraries were often run by booksellers who could not purchase a sufficient number of most recently published books, and, therefore, resorted

to renting in order to be able to match an unsatisfied demand. Today, it is a common practice for academic libraries to share subscription lists and divide up the cost of subscribing to rarely used journals.

In the late 1970s there were about 200,000 VCR (video cassette recorder) owners in the United States, since then cumulated sales exceeded 15 million by 1987, after prices dropped below $1,000 by 1980 and below $400 in 1985. During that period stores began selling and renting prerecorded video cassettes, eventually reaching 28,000 video rental stores in the United States, thereby adding values to VCRs, which originally were designed as a device for "time-shifting" television shows.

7.2.2   How the value of a library is determined

The economics literature on information reproduction from journals, books, and music recordings include Novos and Waldman 1984, Johnson 1985, Liebowitz 1985, Besen 1986, and Besen and Kirby 1989, and more recently Varian 2000b. These papers model the market for legal subscribers and photocopying as the market for durable goods where photocopying is modeled as similar to a secondary market for used-durable goods. This literature shows that publishers may earn higher profits when photocopying of originals is allowed compared with the case where information is protected, and that, as a result, restrictions on photocopying may reduce total welfare. These results were obtained under the assumption that publishers can price discriminate between individual subscribers and libraries (or other types of dealers), thereby charging the libraries higher subscription rates that take into account the number of photocopies normally made from these journals. More precisely, the argument relies on the assumption that a library's willingness to pay for journals should increase when photocopying is done on the premises because the availability of photocopying causes the users of a library to value the library's journal holdings more highly and library funding will increase as a result. Figure 7.2 demonstrates the library model. Figure 7.2 shows that the introduction of copying facilities increases number of library users, which may result in an increase in library funding and therefore an increase in the ability of libraries to pay higher subscription prices.

Recall that Section 3.5 provided an *alternative* approach to this literature by ignoring the issue of appropriability of value generated from copies, and focusing instead on network effects generated from users' compatibility needs in the market for software.

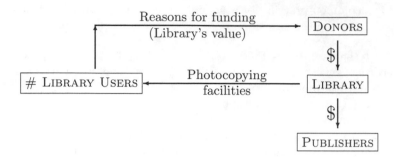

Figure 7.2: The library model: An increase in journal photocopying increases library's value and hence funding, which in turn allows journal publishers to increase subscription fees.

7.2.3 Pricing library services

It is often presumed that the presence of renting facilities reduces the profit of original producers of information. However, as we show below even if the presence of libraries and rental stores may reduce the demand for purchases of books and video prerecorded cassettes, because there are many readers/viewers who benefit from a library's purchase of a book, or an acquisition of a new movie by a video rental store, the willingness to pay of libraries or rental stores may far exceed the willingness to pay of an individual. Thus, renting could be profit enhancing.

Consider the following model. There is one monopoly publisher who offers a single book for sale. Each book costs $\mu > 0$ to produce. The publisher utilizes one and only one marketing strategy: it either sells it to individual readers via bookstores or it sells the book to libraries. Obviously, in reality publishers sell to, both, individual readers and libraries. However, since our purpose here is to demonstrate that the availability of libraries or other facilities that rent information do not necessarily reduce publishers' profits, the extreme assumption that publishers' strategies are confined to either selling to individuals or selling to libraries but not both is helpful for such a demonstration. Thus, the purpose of this model is to answer the following questions:

Q1. Which price maximizes the publisher's profit when it sells to libraries only?

Q2. When selling to libraries only, how does the number of libraries affect the publisher's profit level?

Q3. Under what conditions does the publisher earn a higher profit when it sells only to libraries compared with selling to individual consumers only?

There are λ libraries, indexed by $i = 1, 2, \ldots, \lambda$, and there are η potential readers (consumers) in this market. Let p^b denote the price of the book, and p_i^r the price of renting the book from the library (or renting a movie cassette from a video rental store). Each consumer has the following utility function.

$$U \stackrel{\text{def}}{=} \begin{cases} \beta - p^b & \text{if she buys and owns the book} \\ \beta - p_i^r - \delta & \text{if she borrows (rents) from library } i \\ 0 & \text{does not read the book.} \end{cases} \quad (7.1)$$

The parameter $\beta > 0$ measures a consumer's basic utility from reading the content of this book (or watching the movie from a video cassette). The parameter δ $(\delta < \beta)$ measures the consumer's cost of going to the library to borrow the book, which includes the cost of delay due to the waiting time needed until other borrowers return the book to the library. Alternatively, the parameter δ measures the consumer's loss of utility from not owning the book, which equals the utility loss associated with the inability to repeat the reading without going to the library again. In what follows, we calculate the publisher's profit level when it sells directly to consumers, and then the profit when it sells to libraries only.

Publisher sells directly to consumers

Suppose now that the publisher does not sell the book to libraries. In view of consumers' utility function (7.1), the monopoly maximizes profit by extracting the entire surplus from consumers by setting $p = \beta$. Hence, with direct sales, the publisher's profit level is

$$\pi^b = \eta(p^b - \mu) = \eta(\beta - \mu). \quad (7.2)$$

Publisher sells to λ libraries only

Now suppose that the monopoly does not sell to consumers, but instead it sells one copy to each library (hence, a total of λ copies). We wish to calculate what price charged to each library would maximize the publisher's profit. In order to find this price, the publisher has to calculate the maximum rental price each library can charge each borrower/renter. The borrowers' utility function (7.1) implies that, with the absence of direct sales, each consumer is willing to pay a maximum rental price of $p_i^r = \beta - \delta$.

Next, the publisher observes that with η readers and λ libraries, each library i lends to $q_i = \eta/\lambda$ readers. Altogether, the maximum price in which the publisher can sell the book to library i is

$$p_i = p_i^r q_i = (\beta - \delta)\frac{\eta}{\lambda}.$$

Since there are λ libraries, and since each library buys only one copy, the publisher's profit is given by

$$\pi^r = (p_i - \mu)\lambda = (\beta - \delta)\eta - \mu\lambda. \tag{7.3}$$

A comparison of selling versus renting

Which type of market yields a higher profit to the publisher: the library/rental market or the market with direct consumer sales? In order to answer this question, we need to compare the profit level in (7.3) with (7.2). Hence,

$$\pi^r \geq \pi^b \quad \text{if} \quad \delta \leq \frac{\mu(\eta - \lambda)}{\eta}.$$

With this condition, we can now state our main proposition.

Proposition 7.3
Selling to libraries yields a higher profit to the publisher than selling directly to readers when:

(a) *readers do not place a high value on owning the book (δ is small), or*

(b) *books are costly to produce (μ is high), or*

(c) *there are fewer libraries relative to the number of readers ($\eta - \lambda$ is large).*

The intuition behind Proposition 7.3 is as follows. The main advantage that libraries yield to the publisher is that the publisher can access the same number of readers while producing a smaller number of copies. Therefore, on the supply side, the availability of libraries substantially reduces the publisher's production cost. On the demand side, however, readers are not willing to pay as much for borrowing/renting the information goods as they are willing to pay for acquiring these goods. Hence, on the demand side, the price per reader must be lower once libraries are utilized.

Finally, there is a question whether libraries improve social welfare. The analysis above indicates that libraries are socially optimal whenever the monopoly publisher finds it profitable to sell to libraries rather than to individuals. The reason is that in our model the publisher always manages to extract the entire surplus from consumers whether or not they buy or borrow the book. However, selling to libraries only need not be socially optimal once we introduce the cost of maintaining libraries into the model.

Changing the number of libraries

We now want to investigate how increasing the number of libraries (an increase in λ) affects the profit of a publisher selling only to libraries. The following proposition follows directly from (7.3).

Proposition 7.4
An increase in the number of libraries reduces the publisher's profit.

Proposition 7.4 implies that from the publisher's point of view the profit maximizing number of libraries is one. The reason is as follows. In our model each library serves an equal share of the population. Thus, if there is only one library, it serves the entire population which means that the publisher needs to produce only one copy for the entire economy. Obviously, this result is unrealistic as if all consumers are served by one library, the waiting time to borrow the single copy available will be extremely long, perhaps longer than a lifetime. However, our model can be easily generalized in order to make it more realistic in the following way. Instead of defining the utility of a borrower, see (7.1), as $\beta - p_i^r - \delta$, where δ is a fixed parameter, define δ to be a function of the number subscribing readers, q_i, such that

$$\delta(q_i) \stackrel{\text{def}}{=} \alpha \frac{\eta}{\lambda - 1}, \quad \text{where } \alpha > 0, \ \lambda > 1.$$

Thus, the disutility from borrowing (rather than buying) becomes infinite as the number of libraries, λ, declines to 1. In this case the publisher's profit-maximizing number of libraries exceeds 1.

7.3 The Internet

7.3.1 Historical development of the Internet

The Internet's history can be traced back to ARPANET, which was started in 1969 by the U.S. Department of Defense for research into networking.

ARPAnet was opened to nonmilitary users later in the 1970s, and early takers were the big universities although at that stage it resembled nothing like the Internet we know today. International connections started in 1972, but the Internet was still just a way for computers to talk to each other and for research into networking. There was no World Wide Web and no e-mail as we now know it.

It wasn't until the early to mid 1980s that the services we now use most started appearing on the Internet. The recording of identifiers was provided by the Internet Assigned Numbers Authority (IANA) who has delegated one part of this responsibility to an Internet Registry, which acted as a central repository for Internet information and which provided central allocation of network and autonomous system identifiers, in some cases to subsidiary registries located in various countries. The Internet Registry (IR) also provided central maintenance of the Domain Name System (DNS) root database which points to subsidiary distributed DNS servers replicated throughout the Internet. The DNS distributed database is used, inter alia, to associate host and network names with their Internet addresses and is critical to the operation of the higher level TCP/IP protocols including electronic mail. In 1997 further progress was made when Internet Registry was delegated to the private sector.

The World Wide Web, which is a collection of hyperlinked pages of information distributed over the Internet via a network protocol called HTTP (hyper text transfer protocol), was invented in 1989 at CERN, the European Particle Physics Laboratory. The WWW was initially used for text (ASCII) only. Graphics was introduced in the early 1990s after a browser called Mosaic was developed. Both the most commonly used browsers Microsoft's Internet Explorer and Netscape Navigator are based on Mosaic.

7.3.2 Pricing Internet services: A calculus analysis

The Internet is not owned by any particular agency or firm. The Internet can best be described as a highway system in which some segments are freeways and some are tollways. In order to connect to the Internet, a user must connect to an ISP (Internet Service Provider) whose charges can vary from lump-sum fees to hourly rates. However, after the connection is made, surfing the WWW or sending information (e-mail or files) is free to the user.

From a social-welfare viewpoint, similar to roads, there is no particular reason for charging consumers for using the Internet unless there is congestion. Thus, similar to charging tolls for using the congested parts of the highway system, congestion on the Internet cannot be prevented unless each Internet user is charged for her "contribution" to the overall congestion. Following MacKie-Mason and Varian (1995), we develop some analytics of pricing a congestible resource such as the Internet.

Suppose that there are η potential Internet users, indexed by $i = 1, \ldots, \eta$. Each consumer i transmits q_i packets over the net, so the aggregate number of packets transmitted (in a given time period) is

$Q \overset{\text{def}}{=} \sum_{i=1}^{\eta} q_i$. In the short run, the network has a limited capacity, denoted by $\bar{Q}$, which is measured in terms of the aggregate number of packages that can be transmitted in a given time interval.

Consumers gain utility from the the amount of information (measured by the number of packets) they transmit via the net. They also gain disutility from delays or transmission slow-downs caused by congestion. Let p be the price per packet transmitted over the Internet. Therefore, we assume that the utility function of each consumer i, $i = 1, \ldots, \eta$, is

$$U_i \overset{\text{def}}{=} \sqrt{q_i} - \delta \frac{Q}{\bar{Q}} - pq_i = \sqrt{q_i} - \delta \frac{\sum_{j=1}^{\eta} q_j}{\bar{Q}} - pq_i, \tag{7.4}$$

where $\delta > 0$ measures the intensity of the disutility caused by congestion. The delay itself is measured by $Q/\bar{Q}$ which is the ratio of actual transmission to capacity. If $Q < \bar{Q}$ the network is underutilized. When $Q > \bar{Q}$ the network is overutilized and consumers are subjected to delays in transmitting and receiving information.

Equilibrium usage with no congestion-based pricing

Suppose that each consumer can transmit and receive any amount of information over the Internet without having to pay for it. Each consumer takes the network usage by other consumers, $\sum_{j \neq i} q_j$, as given and chooses her usage q_i to that solves

$$\max_{q_i} U_i = \sqrt{q_i} - \delta \frac{q_i + \sum_{j \neq i} q_i}{\bar{Q}}, \tag{7.5}$$

yielding first- and second-order conditions for a maximum given by

$$0 = \frac{dU_i}{dq_i} = \frac{1}{2\sqrt{q_i}} - \frac{\delta}{\bar{Q}}, \quad \text{and} \quad \frac{d^2 U_i}{d(q_i)^2} = \frac{-1}{4\sqrt{(q_i)^3}} < 0.$$

Hence, the individual and aggregate packet transmission levels are

$$q_i = \left(\frac{\bar{Q}}{2\delta}\right)^2 \quad \text{and} \quad Q = \eta q_i = \eta \left(\frac{\bar{Q}}{2\delta}\right)^2. \tag{7.6}$$

Therefore,

Proposition 7.5
Individual usage of the Internet increases quadratically with the capacity of the network, $\bar{Q}$, and decreases with the disutility of delay parameter, δ.

The first part of the proposition is a well known fact in transportation economics, in which an expansion of highway systems always results in an increase in congestion and traffic jams, since people tend to buy more cars and use less public transportation. Recently, the same thing is observed in traffic on the Internet, where expansion of lines result sometimes with an increase in delay, as more people shift to transmitting graphics, movies, voices and sounds instead of text-based (ASCII) information only. Another way to see that is use our definition of congestion which is the actual number of transmitted packets divided by capacity. Formally, using (7.6) congestion as a function of capacity is given by

$$\text{congestion} = \frac{Q}{\bar{Q}} = \eta \frac{\bar{Q}}{4\delta^2},$$

which demonstrates again the claim made in Proposition 7.5 that congestion increases with capacity.

Socially optimal congestion-based pricing

First, we wish to calculate the socially optimal network usage given the capacity of the network. Second, we choose the price per packet that would implement the socially optimal outcome as an equilibrium.

Since all consumers have identical utility functions, we look for socially optimal usage of the network where all consumers use it at the same level. That is, $q_i = q$ for all $i = 1, 2, \ldots, \eta$. Then, the social planner chooses a common q to maximize social welfare which is defined as the sum of consumers' utilities. Thus,

$$\max_q W \stackrel{\text{def}}{=} \eta \left(\sqrt{q} - \delta \frac{\eta q}{\bar{Q}} \right),$$

yielding first- and second-order conditions given by

$$0 = \frac{dW}{dq} = \frac{\eta}{2\sqrt{q}} - \frac{\delta \eta^2}{\bar{Q}}, \quad \text{and} \quad \frac{d^2 U_i}{d(q_i)^2} = \frac{-\eta}{4\sqrt{(q_i)^3}} < 0.$$

Hence, the socially optimal individual and aggregate usage of the net is

$$q^* = \left(\frac{\bar{Q}}{2\delta\eta} \right)^2 \quad \text{and} \quad Q^* = \eta q^* = \eta \left(\frac{\bar{Q}}{2\delta\eta} \right)^2. \qquad (7.7)$$

Comparing (7.6) with (7.7) yields the following proposition.

Proposition 7.6
When the Internet is provided free of charge, the network is overused by a factor equal to the square of the number of consumers. Formally, $q/q^* = Q/Q^* = \eta^2$.

Notice that there is no distortion if $\eta = 1$ (i.e., if there is only one consumer) since in this case there are no congestion effects.

We now wish to find the price per packet which would implement the socially optimal level of using the Internet. Then, (7.4) implies that each consumer i chooses q_i that solves

$$\max_{q_i} U_i = \sqrt{q_i} - \delta \frac{q_i + \sum_{j \neq i} q_i}{\bar{Q}} - p q_i, \tag{7.8}$$

The first-order condition yields

$$0 = \frac{dU_i}{dq_i} = \frac{1}{2\sqrt{q_i}} - \frac{\delta}{\bar{Q}} - p, \quad \text{or} \quad p^* = \frac{\bar{Q} - 2\delta\sqrt{q_i^*}}{2\bar{Q}\sqrt{q_i^*}}.$$

Substituting (7.7) for q_i^* yields

$$p^* = \frac{\delta(\eta - 1)}{\bar{Q}}. \tag{7.9}$$

Thus, the socially optimal price is zero when there is only one consumer ($\eta = 1$) and increases with η since each user contributes to the congestion of more consumers. This rise in optimal price with η is even faster when δ increases since the disutility from congestion rises faster with the number of consumers. Finally, the socially optimal price also decreases with capacity since a higher capacity level reduces congestion.

7.3.3 Internet commerce

Internet commerce is likely to shift the balance of commercial power from sellers to buyers. There are several reasons for this shift of power:

Instant choice: On the Net, competition is just a click away. If consumers have trouble finding a book at www.amazon.com, they can go to www.barnesandnoble.com.

Comparison shopping: Consumers can easily find a wealth of information on the Internet to compare prices. There are many Internet sites offering detailed information on more than 100,000 consumer products. For example, www.comparenet.com, www.acses.com, www.pricescan.com, www.pricewatch.com, and even a site for comparing bank charges www.bankrate.com.

Monopsony power: The Internet allows consumers and corporate buyers from all over the world to band together, pool their purchasing power, and get volume discounts.

Global reach: The Internet eliminates the geographic protections of local businesses. Car dealers selling online, for example, have drawn buyers from hundreds of miles away.

Surprisingly, at the time of writing this book, world-wide Internet household online sales do not exceed $200 billion a year, and, therefore, constitute a negligible fraction of gross domestic products. However, it is expected to at least double each year. One reason, perhaps, for the slow penetration of Internet commerce is the slow adoption of electronic money devices which would facilitate transactions over the Internet. Because of that, and since consumers are afraid of giving their credit card number over the Internet, consumers use the Internet for "window shopping" and then use the phone to finalize the transaction itself.

7.3.4 Taxing Internet commerce

With the rapid growth in Internet commerce, more and more merchants are able to pass on paying taxes to local authorities. The average sales tax in the United States is about 6.3%. Goolsbee (1999) estimated that in 1999 the value of unpaid tax associated with Internet commerce is about $430 million. Of course, one should not attribute the entire amount to lost taxes, as it is not clear that all of these transactions would have been carried out if they were taxed. Note that a similar claim was made in Section 3.5, where we argued that not all pirated software should be considered as "lost" sales, since some pirates would not buy the software anyway. In fact, the empirical research shows that applying existing sales taxes to the Internet could reduce the number of online buyers by 25 percent and online spending by 30 percent.

Sales tax revenue account for almost 50 percent of all state tax revenue, so it is very likely that in a few years, when Internet commerce will account for a larger fraction of the gross domestic product, new rules and agreements among states and countries will be established. The empirical research shows that Internet sales are highly sensitive to local taxation. People in high-sales tax locations are significantly more likely to make purchases over the Internet, exhibiting purchase decisions similar to consumers who live in geographic border areas with different tax structures.

From the consumers' point of view, the emergence of Internet commerce reduces the importance of the physical location of service-providing firms. More precisely, by using the Internet to purchase services, the consumer generally has no reason for associating the seller with a certain location, since consumers use only the IP address or Internet domain name to transact with the seller. From the sellers' point of view, businesses are easy to relocate, in particular, for those businesses that provide information only, since relocation implies only relocation of computer hardware (servers and storage devices).

The problems faced by tax authorities regarding Internet commerce are:

(a) The location of the business may differ from the location of the service-manager or operator and the computer-server that handles the commerce.

(b) The location of the server is not easily identifiable. That is, in order to fight tax evasion, tax authorities will have to investigate the source of every commercial Internet Protocol (IP) address.

(c) How would the tax authorities enforce the Internet commercial enterprises to pay overdue taxes. Will tax authorities be provided with the right to terminate commercial Internet sites? Or, will it be considered a violation of the free-speech constitutional right?

(d) Even if the seller is identifiable, how would tax authorities determine the value added of an Internet site, Internet servers, and Internet storage devices?

Suppose that an information seller has its Internet server located in Texas, the databases storage devices in Massachusetts, and that its owner/operator living in Connecticut. A paying user, say, living in Minnesota, is charged on her credit card for information services retrieved from Texas and Massachusetts, which is paid to the seller living in Connecticut. Figure 7.3 illustrates this example.

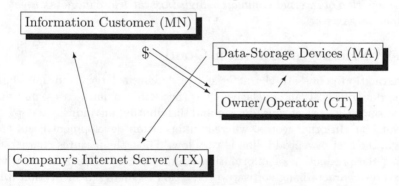

Figure 7.3: The problem of taxing Internet services. Arrows represent information flows. Double arrows represent $ flow.

Suppose that the firm earns a profit of $1. Note that the service is provided by a server located in Texas and storage devices located in Massachusetts. Under the value added approach, the owner of this firm will be asked to submit a statement concerning the value added of the server in Texas and the value added of the storage devices in Massachusetts. Clearly, if the tax rate is 4% in Texas and 5% in Massachusetts, the owner will state that storage devices should account for 1¢ of the $1 production profit (1% of the value added), whereas the server should be accounted for 99¢ of the profit (99% of the value added). In contrast, if the tax rate is 6% in Texas, the owner will state that storage devices are responsible for 99¢ of the $1 profit.

Table 7.3 illustrates how declarations of value added vary with the tax rates. Table 7.3 demonstrates the difficulty in collecting tax in high-

MA tax rate	5%	5%
TX tax rate	4%	6%
Declared value added of storage devices (MA)	1¢	99¢
Declared value added of server (TX)	99¢	1¢

Table 7.3: Declared value added of Internet sites.

tax states. Whereas firms tend to relocate to lower-tax states over time, Internet sites can always be declared to produce low value added in high-tax states/countries. Hence,

Proposition 7.7
Firms declare a lower value added in high-tax states. Hence, with the introduction of Internet commerce, high-tax states lose more tax revenue than low-tax states.

7.4   Pricing Information Goods

Information goods are characterized by having a large fixed and sunk "production" cost, and a relatively low (negligible in many cases) marginal cost since the cost of reproducing and distributing an additional copy is negligible. In other words, whereas information development costs are high, the cost of reproduction is very low. Thus, the features characterizing the production of information goods have a lot in common with features characterizing software production as analyzed in Section 3.1. This implies that cost-based pricing makes little sense and value-based pricing is much more appropriate.

A firm selling a unique type of information that it monopolizes by copyright protection can utilize several strategies to extract large amounts of surplus from consumers of information goods. Shapiro and Varian (1999) and Varian (2000a) call these strategies *versioning infor-*

mation goods. All these strategies have one thing in common, which is causing consumers to sort themselves into different groups according to their willingness to pay. These strategies are highly profitable whenever consumers have radically different values for a particular information good, so techniques for differential pricing become very important. In this section we describe the main strategies that lead to profitable market segmentations.

Information release delay: Selling the information with no delay to those consumers who are willing to pay the most and delaying the sale for consumers with low willingness to pay.

Popular books are sold initially in hard covers; several months later they are reissued in paperbacks editions. Movies are released for the big screens in the first year, and only later they are distributed on prerecorded video cassettes.

Financial network firms that provide access to stock pricing in Wall Street charge a monthly fee of close to $100 for real-time quotes. In contrast, the same firm charges less than $10 a month for providing stock values using 20-minute delayed quotes.

Time-delay market segmentation is not unique to information goods. It is also common to delivery systems. For example, Federal Express commits to next-day delivery of a package for a price of about $12, and for a morning delivery for about $22. What consumers do not know is that both types of deliveries arrive to the destination cities on the same plane and therefore at the same time. In many cases, Federal Express makes a special afternoon trip to the same neighborhood that was visited in the morning solely for the purpose of maintaining the market for consumers with low-willingness to pay.

Quality discrimination: Selling a full-scale version with all the bells-and-whistles bundled with a fast service to consumers with a high willing to pay, and a version with reduced features to consumers with low willingness to pay. For a rigorous analysis of how to segment the market using reduced-quality versions see Section 3.6.

Information publishers often face the problem of deciding how many versions of the same products to offer. Simonson and Tversky (1992) point out that it may be profitable to offer three versions (rather than two) since most consumers attempt to avoid choosing an extreme version (the one with most features and the one with the least features). They call this consumer behavior by *extremum aversion*.

Upgrades and new editions: Periodically, releasing improved versions with more features and selling them to the consumers with high willingness to pay, and selling outdated version to consumers with low willingness to pay.

A major problem faced by information providers in general and textbook publishers in particular is the reduction in demand for their products resulting from the accumulation of used textbooks, stemming from the durability nature of information goods.

One strategy that publishers employ in order to survive is to come up with new editions intended to kill-off the market for their used products. It is often thought that textbook publishers come up with yearly revisions in order to prevent the used-books market from taking sales away from the publishers.

Renting versus selling: Selling to libraries and to video rental stores instead of to individuals (see Section 7.2.3 below).

Bundling: Bundling can work only if consumers have different tastes for different features of the information product. Bundling involves creating information products with features that are highly valuable for one group of consumers and is less valuable for second group *and* features that are highly valuable for the second group of consumers and less valuable for the first group of consumers. Examples of bundling in the TV cable industry were given in Section 6.1.3.

7.5   Exercises

1. Consider the calculations of captured and uncaptured surplus from copying analyzed in Section 7.1.4. Suppose that each consumer values a copy as $3/4$ of the original, $(3/4)^2$ a copy of a copy of the original, and so on. That is, let $\rho = 3/4$.

   Assume that there are 100 consumers who copy vertically printed media from each other without paying for the copies. calculate (a) the aggregate total surplus captured by all consumers, and (b) the amount of surplus which is not captured by the publisher of the original.

   Hint: In order to simplify the calculations, assume that $\rho^{100} \approx 0$.

2. Consider the library-pricing model analyzed in Section 7.2.3. Suppose that there are $\eta = 1200$ potential readers and $\lambda = 50$ libraries. The utility function of each potential reader is given by

$$
U \stackrel{\text{def}}{=}
\begin{cases}
\beta - p^b & \text{if she buys and owns the book} \\
\beta - 2p_i^r & \text{if she borrows (rents) from library } i \\
0 & \text{if she does not read the book.}
\end{cases}
$$

There is one publisher who can sell either to individual readers, or to libraries but not to both. Each copy of the book costs μ to produce. Answer the following questions.

(a) Calculate the publisher's profit-maximizing price and her profit level, assuming that the publisher sells directly to individual readers.

(b) Calculate the publisher's profit-maximizing library price and her profit level assuming that the publisher sells one copy to each library only.

(c) Calculate the minimal value of μ (unit production cost) for which selling to libraries only yields a higher profit level to the publisher than selling only to individual readers.

7.6 Selected References

Benjamin, D., and R. Kormendi. 1974. "The Interrelationship Between Markets for New and Used Durable Goods." *Journal of Law and Economics* 17: 381–402.

Besen, S. 1986. "Private Copying, Reproduction Costs, and the Supply of Intellectual Property." *Information Economics and Policy* 2: 5–22.

Besen, S., and S. Kirby. 1989. "Private copying, Appropriability, and Optimal Copying Royalties." *Journal of Law and Economics* 32: 255–280.

Goolsbee, A. 1999. "A World Without Borders: The Impact of Taxes on Internet Commerce." National Bureau of Economic Research, Working Paper No. 6863, `http://www.nber.org/`.

Johnson, W. 1985. "The Economics of Copying." *Journal of Political Economy* 93: 158–174.

Kindleberger, C. 1983. "Standards as Public, Collective and Private Goods." *KYKLOS* 36: 377–396.

MacKie-Mason, J., and H. Varian. 1994. "Economic FAQs About the Internet." *Journal of Economic Perspectives* 8: 75–96.

MacKie-Mason, J., and H. Varian. 1995. "Pricing the Internet." In B. Kahin and J. Keller (eds.), *Public Access to the Internet*. Cambridge, Mass.: The MIT Press.

Novos, I., and M. Waldman. 1984. "The Effects of Increased Copyright Protection: An Analytical Approach." *Journal of Political Economy* 92: 236–246.

Shapiro, C., and H. Varian. 1999. *Information Rules: A Strategic Guide to the Network Economy*. Boston: Harvard Business School Press.

Simonson, I., and A. Tversky. 1992. "Choice in Context: Tradeoff Contrast, and Extremum Aversion." *Journal of Marketing Research* 29: 281–295.

Varian, H. 1995. "The Information Economy." *Scientific American* September: 161–162.

Varian, H. 2000a. "Versioning Information Goods." In B. Kahin, and H. Varian (eds.), *Internet Publishing and Beyond: The Economics of Digital Information and Intellectual Property.* Cambridge, Mass.: The MIT Press.

Varian, H. 2000b. "Buying, Sharing, and Renting Information Goods." *Journal of Industrial Economics* 48: 473–488.

Chapter 8

Banks and Money

The banking industry displays many characteristics of other network industries. For example,

Network effects: People tend to associate larger banks with more stable ones, that is, banks with a lower probability of realizing bankruptcy.

Network services: Banks perform a wide variety of services involving money transfers and payments among individuals, firms, and the government. From an operational point of view, a money transfer between two accounts belonging to the same bank constitutes an entirely different operation than a money transfer between accounts belonging to different banks.

Switching costs and lock-in: Consumers must bear a significant cost of moving their financial activities from one bank to another. Section 8.1 demonstrates how the presence of these switching costs reduces the competition in the banking industry.

Cash withdrawals: Since cash (currency) is widely used in trade, and since currency is costly to store, individuals resort to frequent cash withdrawals mainly from automatic teller machines (ATMs). If banks share the same network, then customers of one bank can withdraw cash from an ATM owned by a competing bank. Thus, ATMs generate network of users who can withdraw cash from a network of machines. Section 8.2 analyzes how competition among banks is affected by having banks sharing their ATMs.

Panics and bank runs: Most banks maintain less than a 10% reserve ratio. This means that banks can easily be subjected to panics each time a small number of depositors demand their deposits in the form of cash and spread the rumor that the bank has run out of money.

Money is a medium of exchange. Money consists of a wide variety of means of payment upon which individuals commonly agree to exchange for goods and services. The mutual agreement on certain means of payment creates a major network effect among all trading agencies. Thus, media of exchange constitute different networks of mutually agreed trading patterns, which is the subject of Section 8.3.

8.1   Switching Costs and Competition

Customers bear switching costs when shifting their financial activities from one bank to another. Although consumer switching costs are not unique to the banking industry (for example, consumers switching from one computer operating system to another face high learning costs and a significant time loss associated with file conversion), the banking, insurance and health sectors constitute major sectors in the economy in which switching costs seem to be prevalent.

It is widely observed that consumers refrain from switching among banks even when they are fully informed of large differences in bank service fees. The main (perhaps the only) explanation for this consumer behavior is the existence of switching costs that are encountered by consumers each time they terminate services with one bank and switch to a competing bank. Theoretically consumer switching costs confer market power on banks. Thus, banks face a trade off between charging lower fees in early periods in order to attract consumers and placing them in a lock-in positions, thereby increasing market-shares which will be used in subsequent periods to extract supra-normal rents and increase profits.

There are several reasons for the existence of switching costs when customers shift their financial activities from one bank to another:

Electronic deposit: Most earnings, including paychecks, dividends, and tax reimbursement are done electronically to a specific account. Once the consumer opens a new account at a different bank, the consumer must inform all the relevant institutions about this bank change. Switching costs, therefore, include the time it takes to communicate the information about the change, and the expected loss stemming from mistakes occurring due to a miscommunication concerning the exact account routing number and the resulting loss of income due to delays in getting deposits.

Loans and credit: A high-quality borrower (i.e., a borrower with a low probability of defaulting a loan) who switches to a competing bank that is not familiar with the financial record of the borrower may be pooled with low-quality borrowers thereby encountering unfavorable borrowing and service conditions. Once a customer shifts to a new bank, the new bank possesses less information on the consumer and will be willing to extend less credit compared to a fully informed bank. Of course, this argument could be reversed for a risky customers who will benefit from taking credit from a less informed bank.

Payments and automatic deductions: In most countries, payments for utilities such as electricity, gas, water, daycare, schooling, and phone services are done via the assignment of long-term withdrawal rights to the supplier to withdraw the amount of the bill in certain periods. Any consumer who switches to a different bank has a high probability of paying multiple bills (withdrawals from the old and the new account). In this case, switching costs consist of the time it takes to reverse multiple withdrawals.

Surprisingly, the literature neglects both theoretical and empirical analyses of switching costs in the banking industry. The introduction of switching costs into consumer choice is due to von Weizsäcker (1984) and Klemperer (1987a,b, 1995). Application of switching costs to the banking industry are given in Tarkka (1995) and Sharpe (1997).

8.1.1   A model of switching costs and fee competition

We now develop a theory of switching costs in the banking industry when banks are engaged in a *fee competition*. Then, we use the model to estimate switching cost in the banking industry. In this fee competition, a small reduction in fee is not profitable since, due to strictly positive switching costs, a small reduction in fees by one bank is insufficient to attract consumers from other banks. Thus, in this model, banks must substantially lower their fees in order to attract consumers from a competing bank (undercutting in what follows). Obviously, this friction helps banks in maintaining high fees without the fear of being undercut.

Following Shy (2002), consider a banking industry with $\lambda \geq 2$ banks indexed by $i = 1, 2, \ldots, \lambda$. Depositors are distributed between the banks so that initially η_i consumers (type i consumers in what follows) have already opened an account with bank i, $i = 1, 2, \ldots, \lambda$.

Bank charge fees from each account holder. For simplicity, we do not get into the nature of the fees imposed on account holders, which include a fixed monthly fee, check fees, withdrawal fees, and a lot more. Let f_i denote the fee charged by bank i. Also, let $\delta_i > 0$ denote the cost of switching from bank i (where the consumer has an account) to a new account in a different bank.

Let U_i denote the utility of a consumer served by bank i. Thus, the utility of a type i consumer is given by

$$U_i \stackrel{\text{def}}{=} \begin{cases} -f_i & \text{staying with bank } i \\ -f_j - \delta_i & \text{switching from bank } i \text{ to bank } j \neq i. \end{cases} \tag{8.1}$$

Let q_i denote the (endogenously determined) number of consumers holding an account with bank i. We assume that banks do not bear production costs of maintaining accounts. Thus, the profit of bank i, as a function of fee charges and the number of accounts is

$$\pi_i(f_1, \ldots, f_\lambda) = f_i q_i, \quad i = 1, 2, \ldots, \lambda. \tag{8.2}$$

We look for an Undercut-proof equilibrium in banks' fee levels (Definition C.2 on page 309). However, in order to solve for the UPE, we must extend Definition C.2 to more than two firms (banks in our case). The extension from two to λ banks goes as follows. Each bank considers whether to undercut *one and only one* competing bank at a time. Clearly, the bank which is targeted the most by banks is the bank *with the largest number of accounts*. With no loss of generality, we index the banks so that bank 1 has the largest number of accounts, bank 2 has the second-largest number of accounts, and so on. Formally,

$$\eta_1 > \eta_2 > \ldots > \eta_\lambda.$$

Definition C.2 is now extended in the following way:

(a) Each bank $i \neq \lambda$ fears to be undercut by the smallest bank (bank λ), and hence sets its fee, f_i, in reference to f_λ.

(b) The smallest bank (bank λ) fears that it is targeted by bank 1 (the largest bank), and therefore sets its fee, f_λ, in reference to f_1.

Thus, each bank $i \neq \lambda$ takes f_λ as given and sets the largest fee f_i subject to

$$\pi_\lambda = f_\lambda \eta_\lambda \geq (f_i - \delta_i)(\eta_i + \eta_\lambda). \tag{8.3}$$

That is, each bank i, fearing being undercut by bank λ, maximizes its fee, f_i subject to the constraint that bank λ will not find it profitable to undercut.

Since the fees f_is *are observed*, we can now solve for the *unobserved switching costs* of the customers of each bank. From (8.3) we have

$$\delta_i = f_i - \frac{\eta_\lambda}{\eta_i + \eta_\lambda} f_\lambda, \quad i \neq \lambda. \tag{8.4}$$

Equation (8.4) provides the switching cost of a bank i consumer as a function of the fees and market sizes of bank i and bank λ.

Finally, the smallest bank assumes that it is targeted by bank 1, it maximizes f_λ subject to

$$\pi_1 = f_1 \eta_1 \geq (f_\lambda - \delta_\lambda)(\eta_1 + \eta_\lambda).$$

Since f_1 and f_λ are observed, we can solve for the unobserved remaining switching cost δ_λ.

$$\delta_\lambda = f_\lambda - \frac{\eta_1}{\eta_1 + \eta_\lambda} f_1. \tag{8.5}$$

8.1.2 Empirical estimations of switching costs

As far as empirical research may be concerned, the reliance on some a-priori facts regarding the existence of switching costs is not sufficient. According to Kim, Kliger, and Vale (1999), a comprehensive empirical research must answer the following questions:

(a) What are the empirical regularities, if any, associated with switching costs?

(b) What is the magnitude of switching costs necessary for making consumers locked in?

(c) Is switching cost an important empirical phenomenon?

The answers to these questions are probably that in different industries and across different product lines, switching-costs sufficient to render consumers locked-in are different. Thus, the task of empirical research in the area is to develop and embed models of (endogenous) consumer switching costs in some general behavioral model of the bank, and investigate empirically the dependence of conduct in general and the associated firm strategies in particular on the presence and magnitude of switching costs.

Banks provide a wide variety of services. However, most activities with consumers and business firms can be classified into two major activities: (a) Services related to demand deposits which include handling customers' checking accounts, payment services, and automatic teller machines. (b) Making loans to individuals and business firms. We therefore address these two markets separately.

Switching costs in the market for demand deposits

We simulate real-life data taken from the 1997 Finnish banking industry. The data consists of four major banks and includes:

Number of accounts: which tends to overestimate the active number of accounts as some of these accounts are inactive.

Fees: There are various fees charged to account holders. All fees are computed on an annual basis.

Direct fees: are upfront fees levied on each account holder for maintaining the account with the bank.

Transaction fees: are the fees paid for each payment transaction done via the bank.

Foregone interest: is an implicit fee levied on each account holder for maintaining a noninterest bearing balance with the bank. These fees are ignored, but the reader is warned that foregone interest may increase the actual cost to customers by a factor of two.

Table 1 displays the data used later for the calibration of the switching-cost model.

Data	Bank 1	Bank 2	Bank 3	Bank 4
# Accounts (η_i)	6,017,340	4,727,051	4,051,852	952,093
Average Balance	4154	3946	2350	4137
Fees Per Account	21	19	22	18
Over Lifetime (f_i)	525	475	550	450
Switching Costs	463	400	464	−3
SC/Avg.Bal.(%)	11%	10%	20%	0%

Table 8.1: The Finnish banking industry 1997 (four largest banks only). All figures are in \$U.S. Lifetime discounted sum of fees are based on a 4 percent real interest rate.

Since fees are annual flows, when a consumer considers switching between banks the consumer must compare not the annual fees but the discounted sum of life-time fees since switching is generally a one-time operation (due to switching costs). Therefore, the fees f_i in Table 8.1 are calculated by discounting the infinite sum of per-account fees assuming a 4 percent real interest rate.

The switching cost, δ_i, associated with maintaining an account with bank i are found by substituting the relevant number of accounts, η_i, and f_i into (8.4) and (8.5) by taking bank 4 as the smallest bank ($\lambda = 4$). Therefore,

$$\delta_1 = f_1 - \frac{\eta_4 f_4}{\eta_1 + \eta_4} = 525 - \frac{952,093}{6,017,340 + 952,093} \, 450 \approx 463,$$

$$\delta_2 = f_2 - \frac{\eta_4 f_4}{\eta_2 + \eta_4} = 475 - \frac{952,093}{4,727,051 + 952,093} \, 450 \approx 400,$$

$$\delta_3 = f_3 - \frac{\eta_4 f_4}{\eta_3 + \eta_4} = 550 - \frac{952,093}{4,051,852 + 952,093} \, 450 \approx 464,$$

$$\delta_4 = f_4 - \frac{\eta_1 f_1}{\eta_1 + \eta_4} = 450 - \frac{6,017,340}{6,017,340 + 952,093} \, 525 \approx -3.$$

The calculated switching costs are also displayed in Table 8.1. The major finding from this exercise is that large banks in general serve customers with high switching costs, whereas the smallest bank serves customers with no switching costs. Thus, the bank with the lowest fees (bank 4) captures consumers with a low value of time who use this bank because this bank happens to have the lowest fees. That is, for these consumers switching is not costly, so they switch to the bank with the lowest fees. In contrast, banks 1 and 2 which have high fees capture consumers with high value of time in which switching to banks with lower fees is very costly. Bank 3 is somewhat problematic, so we ignore it for this discussion.

The last row in Table 8.1 provides a measure of the magnitude of switching costs in the market for bank deposits by looking at the ratio of switching costs to the average balance held in each bank. Thus, we can conclude that switching costs account for between 0 percent to 11 percent of the average balance a depositor maintains with the bank.

Switching costs in the market for loans

Kim, Kliger, and Vale (1999) construct a model in order to extract information on the magnitude and significance of switching costs as well as on customers' transition probabilities, from conventionally available aggregated data which does not contain customer-specific information. Thus, a switch between banks entails not only the direct costs associated with closing an account with one bank and opening an account with another, but also the unobserved and rather more significant costs associated with the foregone capitalized value of the previously established long-term customer-bank relationship.

A potential difficulty in this research is to isolate a possible *product differentiation* effect from the estimated switching costs. Product differentiation may emanate from two major sources: (a) customers' location (physical distance to branches of the specific bank they use), and (b) the range of loans that are provided by the specific bank. For this reason, the estimation is carried out on subsamples according to branches and different loan sizes.

This study is based on annual observations for Norwegian banks, spanning nine years from 1988 to 1996. Due to mergers, the number of banks declined from 177 in 1988 to 139 in 1996. The banks in the sample significantly vary in size (both in terms of market shares and the number of branches, with correlation 0.88 between the two).

The investigators' major finding is that given that the average prevailing real interest rate in Norway was 12% (with almost zero inflation rate), the average switching cost is 4.1% which equals one-third of the market average interest on loans. More precisely, if a business firm is expected to pay 12% interest on a loan taken from the bank where the business is already "locked-in" then if the same firm attempts to take a loan from a competing bank, it may end up paying 12% *plus* 4.1% interest.

Another important question raised in this research is what is the value of the "lock-in" effect from the *banks viewpoint*. This research shows that banks can attribute 25% of their marginal profit (profit on an additional borrower) to their customers' lock-in effect. In addition, an average of 35% of the average bank's market share is due to its established bank-borrower relationship. The model's estimates imply an average of 13.5 years of bank-customer relationship, which is in line with various surveys taken in the United States and in European countries.

Table 8.2 elaborates on the relationship of switching costs and the size of the bank as measured by the minimum number of branches. Table 8.2(a) clearly indicates that switching costs decline with the size of the bank as measured by the number of branches each bank maintains. For very large banks (those with 60 branches or more) switching cost constitute 2.1% of the loans made out by these banks, and a very high level of 6.9% for a group of banks constituting at least 20 branches. That is, given an average real interest rate of 12%, if a customer of a large bank takes a loan from a competing bank, its actual cost would be the market interest rate plus approximately an additional 1/5 of the interest in terms of switching costs. In contrast, small bank customers who switch to a competing bank would suffer a hefty additional 1/3 of the interest of switching costs.

(a) Subsamples According to Minimum # Branches

# branches:	1	10	20	30	40	60
Switching cost (%):	4.1	6.0	6.9	3.4	2.9	2.1

(b) Subsamples According to Minimum Total Loans

Loans (bil.NOK):	0	2	3	5.5	7.5	12
Switching cost (%):	4.1	8.4	6.3	4.1	5.6	0.21

Table 8.2: Switching costs as a function of banks' size measured by (a) the minimum number of branches and (b) total loan size; given an average market interest rate of 12%.

The decline in switching costs with bank size indicates that larger banks (many branches) serve a higher proportion of large and mobile customers, such as publicly traded firms for which the problem of asymmetric information is less significant. Further, larger customers are better at obtaining information about financial markets, which makes them more mobile (lower switching costs).

Finally, the authors repeat their investigation by looking at subsamples of banks according to total loan sizes, exhibited in Table 8.2(b), which highlights the robustness of this research showing that switching costs decline with the size of loans made by the bank. Of course, the two subsamples are correlated since banks with a larger number of branches happen to give more loans and to have a larger number of borrowers. Finally, Table 8.2(b) shows even more clearly than Table 8.2(a) that for banks with extremely high aggregate loan size switching costs become negligible (less than 2% of the interest cost), and are therefore statistically insignificant.

Deposit accounts versus the market for loans

The empirical analyses conducted for the deposit accounts market and the market for loans have shown that switching costs differ significantly between these two markets. In the deposit-accounts market, switching costs tend to rise with the size of the bank as measured by the number of accounts. In contrast, in the market for loans switching costs tend to decline with the size of the bank as measured either by the number of branches or the total loan size.

The explanation for this difference may be attributed to the fact that in the market for deposit accounts the reason why a bank remains "big" could be attributed to the fact that the bank has managed to capture customers with high switching costs who therefore do not switch to other banks. In contrast, in the market for loans, heavy customers (large firms), which tend to take loans from large banks, do not have significant switching costs since the information on the credit worthiness of large firms is known to all banks, implying that they can switch without facing an interest hike.

8.2 Automatic Teller Machines (ATMs)

8.2.1 Overview of ATMs

Automatic teller machines were introduced in the 1970s. This was the first attempt to automate banking services, which, as we know today, can be efficiently provided via the Internet or via touch-tone telephones. As commonly observed in the banking industry, consumers were slow to adopt the new technology and therefore were slow to accept the fact that money can be safely handled by a machine rather than by a human teller. This resulted in consumers continuing to form long lines inside the branches while leaving the ATMs with no queues. A similar type of consumer behavior is observed today, long after ATMs were fully accepted by consumers, where consumers resist adopting the smart electronic cash cards that replace currency notes, and also resisting giving their credit card numbers over the Internet, thinking that privacy is better preserved over the phone than over the Internet.

Although banks began adopting ATMs in the early 1970s, the large increase in ATMs occurred only in the early 1980s with shipments of new ATMs reaching about 14,000 per year in 1983 in the United States Then after new locations for ATMs became scarce, the sale of new ATMs fell to about 9,000 per year in 1986, reaching a total number of 60,000 ATMs in operation in the United States ATMs are expensive to buy and maintain. An ATM can cost $30,000 to buy, and about $12,000 a year to maintain. This may explain the limited access consumers have to ATMs.

ATMs provide a good example for a market influenced by network effects, since cardholders are better off the larger the number of geographically dispersed ATMs from which they can access their accounts. The convenience of access to one's account wherever one happens to be means that the value of ATM network increases in the number of ATM locations it includes. A bank can increase the value of its network by either adding more ATM locations, and/or by linking its network with the networks of other banks.

8.2.2   A model of bank competition with ATMs

We analyze fee competition between banks serving consumers who wish to withdraw cash from ATMs and, perhaps, perform other transactions using an ATM. Such models are found in Economides and Salop (1992) and Matutes and Padilla (1994).

Consider two banks, indexed by $i = A, B$. Bank A has a_A ATMs and bank B has a_B ATMs. At this moment, we assume that the number of ATMs belonging to each bank is exogenously given. Let f_i denote the fee charged to each bank i account holder, $i = A, B$. Let δ denote the cost to a customer who switches from one bank to another (see Section 8.1 for more details). We make the following assumption.

ASSUMPTION 8.1
Either switching costs are very high, or the numbers of ATMs installed by the banks are not too diverse. Formally, $\delta \geq |a_A - a_B|$.

This assumption is needed in order to have two banks serving in equilibrium. Bank A has η customers and bank B has η customers. We need to define compatibility in the context of ATMs.

DEFINITION 8.1
ATMs are said to be

(a) **incompatible**, *if customers of bank A can withdraw cash only from ATMs belonging to bank A, and customers of bank B can withdraw cash only from ATMs of bank B; and*

(b) **compatible** *if all customers can withdraw cash at any ATM.*

Saloner and Shepard (1995) empirically identified a connection between network effects and banks' adoption of ATMs. Therefore, we assume that the utility of each account holder is enhanced with an increase in the number of ATMs he has access to. Formally, the utility function of each consumer who has an account with bank i, $i = A, B$, is given by

$$
U_i \stackrel{\text{def}}{=}
\begin{cases}
\alpha a_i - f_i & \text{banks with } i \text{ (incompatible ATMs)} \\
\alpha a_j - f_j - \delta & \text{switches to } j \text{ (incompatible ATMs)} \\
\alpha(a_A + a_B) - f_i & \text{banks with } i \text{ (compatible ATMs)} \\
\alpha(a_A + a_B) - f_j - \delta & \text{switches to bank } j \text{ (compatible ATMs).}
\end{cases}
$$
$$(8.6)$$

Let q_i denote the number of accounts (consumers) in bank i. Therefore, assuming no production costs, the profit of bank i is $\pi_i = f_i q_i$, for every bank $i = A, B$.

Incompatible ATMs

Suppose that ATMs from different banks are incompatible. We now define undercutting in the context of the banking industry.

DEFINITION 8.2
Bank i is said to be undercutting the fee set by bank j if bank i reduces its fee so that all the customers of bank j switch to bank i. Formally, given a_A, a_B, and f_j, firm i sets

$$f_i' < f_j - \delta + \alpha(a_i - a_j), \quad i,j = A, B, \ i \neq j.$$

Clearly, in order for bank i to attract the customers of bank j, it has to subsidize the switching costs, δ. However, if $a_i > a_j$ for example, bank i can raise its undercutting fee by $\alpha(a_i - a_j)$ since it provides the switching consumers with additional ATMs. In contrast, if $a_i < a_j$, bank i must further reduce the price by $\alpha(a_j - a_i)$ as it provides the switching customers with less ATMs.

We look for an Undercut-proof equilibrium (UPE) in fees as characterized in Definition C.2 on page 309. Thus, bank A sets the highest f_A subject to the constraint that bank B will not find it profitable to undercut f_A. Formally, f_A is determined by

$$\pi_B = f_B \eta \geq [f_A - \delta + \alpha(a_B - a_A)]2\eta. \tag{8.7}$$

Similarly, f_B is determined by

$$\pi_A = f_A \eta \geq [f_B - \delta + \alpha(a_A - a_B)]2\eta. \tag{8.8}$$

Solving (8.7) and (8.8) simultaneously yields the equilibrium fee charged by each bank. Therefore,

$$f_A^I = 2\delta + \frac{2\alpha(a_A - a_B)}{3} \quad \text{and} \quad f_B^I = 2\delta + \frac{2\alpha(a_B - a_A)}{3}, \tag{8.9}$$

where superscript I stands for incompatibility. Since each bank serves η consumers (η accounts), the profit levels are given by

$$\pi_A^I = 2\delta\eta + \frac{2\eta\alpha(a_A - a_B)}{3}, \quad \text{and} \quad \pi_B^I = 2\delta\eta + \frac{2\eta\alpha(a_B - a_A)}{3}. \tag{8.10}$$

Therefore, industry profit is given by $\Pi^I \stackrel{\text{def}}{=} \pi_A^I + \pi_B^I = 4\delta\eta$. Figure 8.1 illustrates the fee charged by each bank, and banks' profit levels as functions of the difference between the number of ATMs available to each bank. Figure 8.1 implies the following proposition.

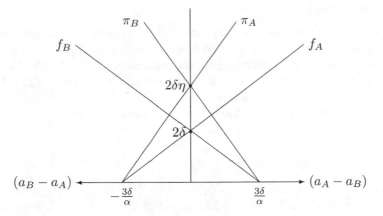

Figure 8.1: Fees and profit levels when ATMs are incompatible.

Proposition 8.1
In an UPE, each bank increases its fee (and therefore its profit) when it increases the number of installed ATMs relative to the competing bank.

Notice that the aggregate industry profit is constant at the level of $4\delta\eta$. Therefore, when a bank increases the number of installed ATMs, it merely transfers rents from the competing bank to itself.

Compatible ATMs

Suppose now that ATMs are compatible according to Definition 8.1. Then, all customers of all banks are served by all ATMs. In this case, undercutting according to Definition 8.2 becomes

$$f'_i < f_j - \delta + \alpha[(a_i + a_j) - (a_i + a_j)] = f_j - \delta, \quad i, j = A, B, \ i \neq j.$$

That is, since all ATMs are available to all consumers regardless of which bank maintains their accounts, undercutting is independent of the number of ATMs installed by each bank. Therefore, the UPE prices are found from

$$\pi_B = f_B\eta \ \geq \ (f_A - \delta)2\eta$$
$$\pi_A = f_A\eta \ \geq \ (f_B - \delta)2\eta,$$

yielding

$$f_A^C = f_B^C = 2\delta, \quad \text{and} \quad \pi_A^C = \pi_B^C = 2\delta\eta, \tag{8.11}$$

where superscript C stands for compatibility. Thus, the aggregate industry profit equals to $\Pi^C \stackrel{\text{def}}{=} \pi_A^C + \pi_B^C = 4\delta\eta$, which is the same as the industry profit under incompatibility.

One-way compatibility

Suppose now that bank A makes its ATMs available to all customers, including the customers of bank B; however bank B installs incompatible ATMs so that only the customers of bank B can access its ATMs. Notice that in this case, customers of bank B have access to more ATMs than the customers of bank A, since they can access the ATMs installed by bank A. Therefore, if bank A attempts to undercut the fee set by bank B and attract B's customers it must set its undercutting fee to

$$f'_A \leq f_B - \delta + \alpha[a_A - (a_A + a_B)] = f_B - \delta - \alpha a_B,$$

where the reduction in fee $(-\alpha a_B)$ is needed for compensating bank B customers for the reduction in the number of accessible ATMs once they transfer to bank A. In contrast, if bank B attempts to undercut f_A, it has to set

$$f'_B \leq f_A - \delta + \alpha(a_A + a_B - a_A) = f_A - \delta + \alpha a_B,$$

since the customers of bank A have access to more ATMs after they switch to bank B. Altogether, the UPE prices are the solution of

$$\pi_B = f_B \eta \;\geq\; (f_A - \delta + \alpha a_B)2\eta$$
$$\pi_A = f_A \eta \;\geq\; (f_B - \delta - \alpha a_B)2\eta,$$

yielding

$$f_A^C = 2\delta - \frac{2\alpha a_B}{3} \quad \text{and} \quad f_B^I = 2\delta + \frac{2\alpha a_B}{3}, \qquad (8.12)$$

where superscript C stands for compatible ATMs, and superscript I stands for incompatible ATMs. Hence, the profit levels are

$$\pi_A^C = 2\delta\eta - \frac{2\alpha a_B \eta}{3} \quad \text{and} \quad \pi_B^I = 2\delta\eta + \frac{2\alpha a_B \eta}{3}. \qquad (8.13)$$

Thus, industry profit under one-way compatibility is $\Pi^{C,I} \overset{\text{def}}{=} \pi_A^C + \pi_B^I = 4\delta\eta$. We now state our main proposition.

Proposition 8.2
The profit level of a bank declines when it makes its ATMs available for the customers of a competing bank.

The intuition behind Proposition 8.2 is as follows. When bank A makes its ATMs compatible with bank B, it makes the customers of bank B better off, whereas the utility of its own customers is not changed as the customers of bank A do not have access to more ATMs. Thus, when bank A makes its ATMs available for use by bank B customers, it lowers its value relative to bank B, and therefore must drop its fees. Recall that a similar result (in an entirely different context) was obtained in Section 3.4, where we showed that the profit of a computer hardware producer decreases when the producer increases the degree of compatibility with the software produced specifically for the competing hardware (see Proposition 3.7 on page 65). Moreover, in case *both* banks agree to make compatible ATMs, the bank with the larger number of ATMs will lose its advantage. Therefore, even a mutual agreement is unlikely to be realized.

The reader may feel uneasy with the result obtained in Proposition 8.2, since it implies that banks will refrain from making their ATMs available for customers of competing banks. However, in reality, we observe that many banks do share their ATMs. How can we reconcile this observation with our finding? Very simple. Proposition 8.2 predicts that banks engaging in intensive fee competitions will refrain from making their ATMs available to customers of competing banks. However, in reality, in most countries that banking industry should be better viewed as a cartel where banks implicitly coordinate their fees. In such an industry, banks can only gain from sharing their ATMs since by doing so they can mutually raise their fees thereby extracting more surplus from consumers who are better off when banks share their ATMs.

8.3 Media of Exchange as Networks

Modern economies use a wide variety of means of payment. The most widely used payment instruments today are currency, payment orders, checks, debit cards, and credit cards. Among these means of payment only currency, which is legal tender, provides for an immediate final settlement of the transaction in which it is used. The others are linked to the payers' bank accounts or credit lines extended by card issuers.

8.3.1 Money and network effects

Perhaps, the most mysterious unsolved question in economics is why people hold money? Most people would "answer" this question by saying that they are willing to receive money (in exchange for goods) because other people, merchants, and the government are also willing to receive money from them in return for goods and services. Obviously, this common statement is far from explaining why money is valuable, but it highlights what consumers think about *fiat money* (i.e., money that does not have a consumption value, for example, paper money).

Figure 8.2 demonstrates a pure-exchange economy consisting of individuals who can gain from trade with other individuals. Alice has

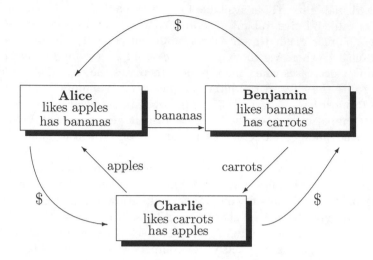

Figure 8.2: Pure exchange economy: the effect of fiat money.

bananas, but likes only apples; Benjamin has carrots, but likes only bananas; and Charlie, has apples, but likes only carrots. Assuming that each consumer gains a utility of $\beta > 0$ when consuming her most desired food item, and zero utility otherwise, without money there is no barter trade pattern that would generate a Pareto-dominated market allocation (see Definition A.6 on page 296). That is, Alice cannot benefit from trading with Benjamin since Benjamin does not have apples. Benjamin cannot benefit from trading with Charlie, since Charlie does not have bananas, and Charlie cannot benefit from trading with Alice since Alice does not have carrots. Thus,

Proposition 8.3
Suppose that there is no money in this economy. Then, any meeting (or a sequence of meetings) between any two people will result in no trade. Hence, a barter economy cannot achieve a Pareto-optimal allocation.

Now, suppose that the government endows each individual with pieces of paper called dollars. Figure 8.2 demonstrates that with fiat money the economy can reach a Pareto-optimal allocation after each individual meets at most twice with other individuals. Thus, Alice meets Benjamin and trades her bananas for dollars. Then, Alice meets Charlie and trades her dollars for apples. Finally, Charlie meets Benjamin and trades his dollars for carrots. Therefore,

Proposition 8.4
An introduction of fiat money into an economy supports trades that result in a Pareto-optimal allocation.

Proposition 8.4 can be interpreted in two ways. First, money reduces *transaction costs* associated with trade. In order to get the parties to trade without money, the parties need to employ experts (say, lawyers) who will write contracts that would guarantee that Charlie transfer apples to Alice conditional on having Benjamin transferring bananas to Charlie. Not only are these contracts hard to phrase, they are extremely hard to enforce via the court system since they involve more than two parties. Thus, we can say that without money, transaction costs are prohibitively costly and trade is less likely to be realized.

A second interpretation of Proposition 8.4 is that money serves as a *medium of exchange* which facilitates the computations during the trade. More precisely, a trade with no money would involve having all parties calculating three exchange ratios: apples for bananas, bananas for carrots, and the implied apples for carrots. In contrast, when money is used, each individual needs to compute only two exchange ratios: the dollar price of her endowed good and the dollar price of her desired good.

The reader should bear in mind that even Proposition 8.4 does not provide an adequate explanation for why money is valued so that individuals are willing to trade their endowed food for useless paper money. To see this, suppose that in the economy described in Figure 8.2 the consumer named Charlie "loses" trust in money and asserts that he refuses to give up his apples for dollars. Then, it is clear that Alice will follow suit and also refuse to accept dollars, as there is no way in which she can later trade dollars for apples, her desired food item. Thus,

Proposition 8.5
It is sufficient that a relatively small number of individuals refuse to trade with money for having all individuals in the economy refusing to accept money in return for goods.

Proposition 8.5 highlights the crucial role network effects play in determining the value of money, and the resulting fragility of the value of money generated by its dependency on rumors and social moods. As a result, for the purpose of reducing the risks of monetary crises where money loses its value, governments support their currency by giving it a legal status called *legal tender*. When currency is declared as a legal tender, the law mandates all commercial enterprises to accept currency as a means of payment. As we demonstrate in Section 8.3.2 below, the choice of currency as the legal tender affects (and in fact distorts) the choice of means of payment in commercial transactions.

Clearly, even if currency serves as the legal tender in the economy so that legally all stores operating for profit must accept currency, past experience shows that this "law" is impossible to enforce during crises when the currency suddenly loses all its value. Hence, the imposition of the legal tender may provide some means for stabilizing the currency, but by no means can protect the currency from losing its value. However, there could be one more factor related to government that further enhances the chances that money will be recognized as a means of payment by all individuals and not only by commercial enterprises. Figure 8.3 illustrates our economy which now has a government that collects taxes in order to provide services thereby paying wages to its employees. Figure 8.3 portrays an economy where Alice and Charlie are government

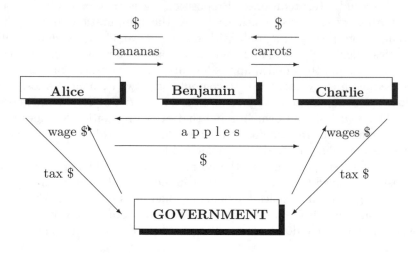

Figure 8.3: Fiat money: the role of taxes and wages.

workers and receive their wages in currency notes. Like most government workers, Alice and Charlie may have other sources of income, such as selling their food items. Finally, Alice and Charlie are good citizens and they pay their taxes in currency notes. In contrast, Benjamin is not a government worker, and whether or not he pays taxes does not matter for the purpose of our argument here. What is important to notice in this economy is that individuals may be willing to receive money during the trade even if other consumers do not. The reason for this is that even if money cannot buy other goods, money can always be used to pay taxes. Hence,

Proposition 8.6
Even in states of public panic concerning the loss of value of the currency,

currency could still serve as the main medium of exchange as long as governments accept tax payments and pay salaries using currency notes.

8.3.2   Coexistence of different payment instruments

The previous section demonstrated how fiat money can generate a Pareto improving allocation when introduced into a barter economy. A natural question to ask now is why there exist more than one means of payments. More precisely, given that money is the declared legal tender, how come other means of payment such as checks, credit cards, and electronic cash cards are also used in various transactions?

There are two different approaches to explain the coexistence of different payment media. The common approach, see for example Santomero and Seater (1996) and their references therein, is to realize that different payment media bear different rates of return, so it may be beneficial for some consumers and merchants to hold more than one medium of exchange. However, we take a different approach based on the observation that all the prevailing means of payment suffer from major weaknesses stemming from their high handling costs. In the case of currency, these costs are generated by the physical handling and storing of notes and coins. In the case of account-linked instruments the costs are generated by the credit verification, bookkeeping and communication with the central operators of the system. Due to the cost structure, currency is still the dominating means of payment in small transactions, whereas the account-based instruments are used mainly for medium-sized and large transactions. We are now facing an era when a new payment instrument is being introduced, namely the electronic cash card, which intends to replace currency for small transactions.

The present model ignores all fees imposed on merchants and buyers by the various card issuers. Shy and Tarkka (2002) focus on fee determination. Consider an economy in which a wide variety of point-of-sale (POS) transactions are made in a given period. The transactions vary in value, that is, some are small in value such as buying a newspaper from a newspaper stand or a machine, and some are larger, say filling up a gas tank, buying an electrical appliance and so forth.

In this economy, there are two types of interacting agents:

Buyers: who wish to buy goods and services from merchants.

Merchants: who can be identified as stores, vending-machine owners, and basically all commercial service providers doing POS business.

In this economy there are three means of payment: electronic-cash cards, currency notes and coins (legal tender), and charge cards. A reader in the United States may wonder why the present model ignores checks, as the data shows that an average person in the United States writes 270 checks per year compared with 7 checks in Scandinavian countries. The reason for this omission is that checks happened to be a highly inefficient means of payment, mainly because of the costly check clearing procedure (mailing, processing, reading, and crediting) and therefore are likely to disappear in a few years. The only reason why checks are still commonly used in the United States is that consumers and banks do not bear the cost of clearing checks as check clearing is subsidized by the Federal Reserve System.

Merchants and buyers

We denote by p, $p > 0$, a particular transaction value that is the price (amount of money) transferred from a buyer to a merchant during the purchase. We assume that each merchant specializes in one size of transaction only. Thus, we refer to a merchant specializing in selling goods valued at p as a type-p merchant.

Merchants are uniformly distributed over the p-axis, which is interpreted as having exactly one merchant performing transactions valued each at p. For example, there is one merchant (or POS) that offers a good/service at a price of $p = 35¢$ (which, for example, could be interpreted as the price of a daily newspaper or a chewing gum). Figure 8.4 illustrates the space of transactions.

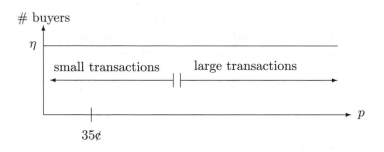

Figure 8.4: Point-of-sales and transaction values.

Merchants

A merchant selling a product valued at p is faced by η identical buyers. The merchant must accept currency if the buyer offers it, since currency is the (only) legal tender in this economy. In addition, each merchant has the option of accepting electronic cash cards and charge cards if they find it profitable to do so.

In what follows, we make some assumptions on the non-fee costs merchants must bear when accepting each medium of payment.

Currency: Accepting currency notes and coins for the trade subjects the merchant to two types of costs:
(1) Loss of time, denoted by τ^M, which is the value of time associated with accepting currency notes and coins, counting it, checking for fraud, and returning change to the customer.
(2) Expected loss with probability $0 \leq \lambda^M \leq 1$ (due to robbery and misplacement).
Altogether, a merchant who is engaged in a transaction size p and receives currency will face an expected per-transaction cost of

$$\tau^M + \lambda^M p. \tag{8.14}$$

Electronic cash cards: We assume that in the absence of fees charged by card issuers, no physical costs are associated with electronic cash card transactions.

Charge cards: We capture the essence of a charge card transaction by assuming that merchants must pay for the customer's credit verification service via a third party. Thus, unlike a transaction paid for with electronic cash card, a merchant accepting a charge card from a consumer is required to get an authorization that verifies that the customers has a sufficient credit to cover for the purchase. Let ϕ denote the merchant's credit verification per-transaction cost.

Figure 8.5 illustrates how merchants rank the different payment media from the least costly medium (first-choice) to the second and the most costly (second- and third-choice) media.

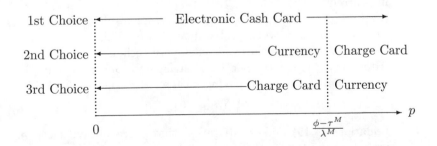

Figure 8.5: Merchants' ranking of payment media.

Clearly, merchants find the electronic cash card to be the most profitable means of payment since transactions do not generate any cost for them. If, for some reason, electronic cash cards are not used, then a currency transaction is less costly than a charge card transaction if $\tau^M + \lambda^M p \leq \phi$, hence for all small transactions satisfying $p \leq (\phi - \tau^M)/\lambda^M$. Obviously, the region where currency is the second most profitable means of payment is non-empty if the credit verification cost is sufficiently large, i.e., if $\phi > \tau^M$.

Buyers

The buyers in our model are shoppers who purchase goods and services from merchants. A buyer can always use currency to pay for the transaction, and may use an electronic cash card or a charge card only if the merchant agrees to accept these cards. The buyers' costs for each means of payment are:

Currency: There are two types of costs borne by consumers:
   (1) The value of lost time, denoted by τ^B, associated with sorting out notes and coins, handing them out at the cashier, lifting fallen coins from the floor, and sorting out the change.
   (2) Loss of money with probability λ^B.
   Altogether, the per-transaction cost facing a buyer who pays with currency notes and coins a transaction of size p is:

$$\tau^B + \lambda^B p. \tag{8.15}$$

Electronic cash card: Electronic cash cards save buyers a substantial amount of time associated with currency transactions. Therefore, we will assume that electronic card transactions are instantaneous. However, buyers using electronic cash cards still face some other costs.
   (1) Loss of the card with probability λ^B (same probability as losing currency).
   (2) Loss of e-cash due to magnetic errors resulting in a loss of reading capability, with probability of γ^B. This cost highlights the limitation of the electronic cash card technology.
   Altogether, the per-transaction cost facing a buyer engaging in a transaction of size p and paying with an electronic cash card is:

$$(\lambda^B + \gamma^B)p. \tag{8.16}$$

Equations (8.15) and (8.16) reveal that currency and electronic cash card share a common loss probability, λ^B, as a person who loses his wallet will lose currency notes as well as the electronic cash card. In addition, electronic cash cards can lose their value in case of magnetic errors, whereas currency cannot be erased even if washed in a washing machine.

Charge cards: We assume that charge cards do not impose any physical costs on buyers. Therefore, from the consumers' point of view, charge cards are the least costly means of payment.

Figure 8.6 illustrates how buyers rank the different payment media from the least costly (first-choice) to the second and the most costly (second- and third-choice) media. Figure 8.6 reveals that consumers al-

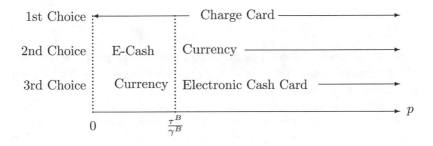

Figure 8.6: Buyers' ranking of payment media.

ways prefer to pay with charge cards. If charge cards are not accepted, buyers prefer to pay with electronic cash cards for small transaction satisfying $(\lambda^B + \gamma^B)p \leq \tau^B + \lambda^B p$, and with currency for large transactions. The reason is that buyers are afraid to load their electronic cash cards with large amounts because of the probability of magnetic errors that could erase the value of the cards.

Equilibrium determination of payment media

We now turn to our main question, which is how can it happen that multiple payment media coexist in a given economy. The key issue in the determination of equilibrium usage of payment media is that *currency is the legal tender*. The implication of this is that merchants and buyers can refuse any means of payment except currency. Thus, any party to the transaction can insist that currency will be used as the means of payment if the party finds it beneficial to do so.

Figure 8.7 combines Figures 8.5 and 8.6 and demonstrates that electronic cash cards and charge cards are refused by one of the parties for transactions in the range of $\tau^B/\gamma^B \leq p \leq (\phi - \tau^M)/\lambda^M$. Therefore, in the middle transaction range, the parties will settle on using currency which is the legal tender. For small transactions, $p < \tau^B/\gamma^B$, merchants refuse to accept charge cards (they can do it since cards are not legal tender). Figure 8.5 reveals that merchants prefer to be paid with electronic-cash cards, and Figure 8.6 shows that electronic-cash

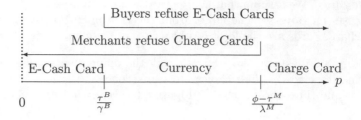

Figure 8.7: Equilibrium usage of payment media.

cards is the buyers' second-best choice after charge cards (which is refused by merchants). Therefore, small transactions will be paid for with
electronic cash cards.

Finally, for large transactions, $p > (\phi - \tau^M)/\lambda^M$, buyers, fearing
magnetic errors, will refuse to pay with electronic cash cards. Figure 8.6
shows that buyers prefer paying with charge cards, and Figure 8.5 reveals that charge cards are the merchants' second-best choice of payment (since buyers refuse to pay with electronic cash cards). Hence,
large transactions are paid for with charge cards.

Proposition 8.7

(a) Let $\tau^B/\gamma^B < (\phi - \tau^M)/\lambda^M$. Then, electronic cash cards, currency
notes (legal tender), and charge cards will coexist as means of pay-
ment.

(b) As illustrated in Figure 8.7, small transactions will be paid for
with electronic cash cards, medium-sized transactions with currency
notes and coins, and large transaction with charge cards.

(c) A reduction in the probability of magnetic errors, γ^B, in electronic
cash cards, or a reduction in merchants' credit verification cost, ϕ,
can bring into the elimination of currency as a means of payment.

The last part of Proposition 8.7 serves as a prediction for the future concerning the widening of the usage of electronic means of payment. At
the time these lines are written (three days before the end of the twentieth century) electronic cash cards have failed to gain the confidence
of buyers and adoption of these cards has been minimal. As the model
suggested, buyers fear trading their currency notes and coins for digital bits stored on cards because magnetic errors can erase their money.
However, as soon as confidence is built around these cards, buyers will
substitute electronic cash cards for notes and coins, which are extremely
hard to handle.

8.4 Exercises

1. Consider the empirical estimation of switching costs in the market for bank deposits, but instead of using the 1997 data exhibited in Table 8.1 let us analyze the 1996 data exhibited in Table 8.3.

Data	Bank 1	Bank 2	Bank 3	Bank 4
# Accounts (η_i)	5,744,741	4,695,078	3,937,119	849,955
Average Balance	4952	4459	2756	4722
Over Lifetime (f_i)	600	425	625	525
Switching Costs				
SC/Avg.Bal.(%)				

Table 8.3: Switching costs in The Finnish banking industry 1996.

Fill in the missing switching costs (both in absolute $U.S. and as a proportion of the average balance held in each bank in 1996). Compare your results to the level of switching costs calculated for 1997 exhibited in Table 8.1.

2. Consider a banking industry with automatic teller machines (ATMs) analyzed in Section 8.2.2. Suppose that bank A has twice as many ATMs as bank B. Thus, if bank B has a ATMs, bank B has $2a$ ATMs. Also, let μ, $\mu > 0$, denote the cost of maintaining one ATM machine. Answer the following questions:

   (a) Assuming that ATMs are incompatible between the banks (i.e., customers of bank A cannot withdraw money from bank B's ATMs, and vice versa), calculate the UPE fees charged by each bank, and the resulting profit levels.

   (b) Explain how an increase in the maintenance cost of each ATM (an increase in the parameter μ) affects (1) equilibrium fees, and (2) equilibrium profit levels.

   (c) Calculate the UPE fees and the resulting profit levels assuming that the ATMs are compatible (i.e., customers of any bank can withdraw money from any ATM).

   (d) Explain how an increase in the maintenance cost of each ATM (an increase in the parameter μ) affects (1) equilibrium fees, and (2) equilibrium profit levels.

3. Consider the U.S. economy where checks are still widely used. Suppose that there exist only two payment media: currency notes (the legal tender) and checks.

   Each merchant accepting a check is subjected to a fixed per-transaction cost of $\tau^{M,ck}$ which reflects the value of time spent on reading the information on the check and going to the bank in order to deposit the check. Each merchant accepting currency notes and coins is subjected to the cost summarized by equation (8.14).

Each buyer who writes a check is subjected to a fixed cost of $\tau^{B,ck}$ associated with the time it takes to write a check. Each buyer who pays with currency notes and coins is subjected to the cost summarized by equation (8.15).

Assuming that $\tau^{M,ck} > \tau^M$, and that $\tau^{B,ck} > \tau^B$, answer the following questions:

(a) Which type of payment medium minimizes merchants' transaction cost at every transaction's value of p, $p > 0$. Plot your result on a graph similar to Figure 8.5.

(b) Which type of payment medium minimizes buyers' transaction cost at every transaction's value of p, $p > 0$. Plot your result on a graph similar to Figure 8.6.

(c) Find the equilibrium usage of payment media for every transaction value p, $p > 0$, and plot your result on a graph similar to Figure 8.7. *Hint:* There can be two cases depending on the parameters of the model.

(d) Suppose that for every transaction value p there is one buyer and one seller. For every transaction value p, determine which payment media minimizes social cost. *Hint:* Social cost is defined as the sum of the buyer's and merchant's transaction costs.

(e) Conclude whether checks are over-used or under-used in this economy. Explain your result.

8.5   Selected References

Economides, N., and S. Salop, 1992, "Competition and Integration Among Complements, and Network Market Structure." *Journal of Industrial Economics* 40: 105–123.

Kim, M., D. Kliger, and B. Vale. 1999. "Estimating Switching costs and Oligopolistic Behavior." Norges Bank, Research Department, Working Paper #1999/4.

Klemperer, P. 1987a. "Markets with Consumer Switching Costs." *Quarterly Journal of Economics* 102: 375–394.

Klemperer, P. 1987b. "The Competitiveness of Markets with Switching Costs." *Rand Journal of Economics* 18: 138–150.

Klemperer, P. 1995. "Competition when Consumers have Switching Costs: An Overview with Applications to Industrial Organization, Macroeconomics, and International Trade." *Review of Economic Studies* 62: 515–539.

Matutes, C., and A. Jorge Padilla. 1994. "Shared ATM networks and Banking Competition." *European Economic Review* 38: 1113–1138.

Saloner, G., and A. Shepard. 1995. "Adoption of Technologies with Network Externalities: An Empirical Examination of the Adoption of Automated Teller Machines. *Rand Journal of Economics* 26: 479– 501.

Santomero, A., and J. Seater. 1996. "Alternative Monies and the Demand for Media of Exchange." *Journal of Money, Credit, and Banking* 28: 942–960.

Sharpe, S. 1997. "The Effect of Consumer Switching Costs on Prices: A Theory and Its Applications to Bank Deposit Market." *Review of Industrial Organization* 12: 79–94.

Shy, O. 2002. "A Quick-and-Easy Method for Estimating Switching Costs." *International Journal of Industrial Organization* 20: 71–87.

Shy, O., and J. Tarkka. 2002. "The Market for Electronic Cash Cards." *Journal of Money, Credit, and Banking* 34: (forthcoming February).

Tarkka, J. 1995. *Approaches to Deposit Pricing: A Study in the Determination of Deposit Interest and Bank Service Charges.* Helsinki: Bank of Finland and Studies E:2.

von Weizsäcker, C. 1984. "The Cost of Substitution." *Econometrica* 52: 1085–1116.

Chapter 9

The Airline Industry

Transportation industries in general, and the airline industry in particular exhibit different types of networks compared to networks analyzed in previous the chapters. Whereas the markets for hardware, software, and information are characterized by having *consumers* whose preferences exhibit network externalities, transportation industries are characterized by having *producers* whose production technologies exhibit economies of networks. These production networks are composed of the large number of routes and alternative routes in which passengers can be transported from cities of origin to cities of destination.

By definition, the service provided by a transport firm is the physical movement of passengers and freight from one point in geographic space to a second point in geographic space. This particular characteristic of transportation services implies that the creation of route structures involves establishing transportation networks on which passengers and cargo are transported. Despite the fact that most types of transportation industries (e.g., airlines, railroad, buses, and marine) exhibit economies of networks, we chose to deal exclusively with the airline industry since both in the United States and in the European Community this industry was exposed to rapid changes due to intensive programs of deregulation which ultimately led to the complete absence of price and entry controls (see Viscusi, Vernon, and Harrington 1995, Ch.17; Doganis 1993).

Section 9.1 starts out with the definition of the physical networks commonly used by airline firms to transport their passengers and the cost implications of using the various route networks. Section 9.2 investigates the impact of the deregulation of the airline industry, on the network structures, and on airfares. Section 9.3 analyzes the market consequences of code-sharing agreements among airline companies, which are widely used since the deregulation of this industry.

9.1   Network Structures and Network Economies

Our major observation of network restructuring comes from the recent deregulation of the U.S. airline industry. Perhaps the most visible outcome of this deregulation is the increased use of the hub-and-spoke (HS) network. That is, the increase in the competition among airline firms has caused airline firms to decrease the relative number of nonstop direct flights and to reroute passengers via a third city which we call a hub. The HS network is also very common in the overnight-package-delivery industry in which small packages are flown to a single city (hub), and from there, planes leave for all destination points.

In this section we analyze a unique feature of transportation firms which is that in addition to the use of airfare as a strategic variable, airline firms also use network structuring as a strategic variable. Figure 9.1 illustrates a tri-city environment, where there are three cities denoted by A, B, and C. Figure 9.1 (Left) illustrates a fully connected network

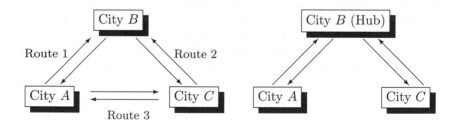

Figure 9.1: *Left:*Fully connected (FC) network. *Right:* Hub-and-spoke (HS) network.

(FC), where all passengers fly nonstop from origin cities to their destinations. Figures 9.1 (Right) illustrates a hub-and-spoke network (HS), where all passengers, except those whose city of origin or destination is city B, fly indirectly and stop at the hub city B.

Several economists claim that due to the topographical (network) structure imbedded in transportation services, airline firms have technologies in which the cost functions are affected not only by the number of passengers, but also by the network structure (see Bittlingmayer 1990). Consider a one-way traveling pattern similar to the two-way pattern illustrated in Figure 9.1 in which η_1 passengers wish to travel from city A to city B, η_2 passengers wish to travel from city B to city C, and η_3 passengers wish to travel from city A to city C. Let the total cost of an airline be a function of the number of passengers transported on each route, and denote it by $TC(\eta_1, \eta_2, \eta_3)$.

DEFINITION 9.1
*An airline technology is said to exhibit **economies of network** if*

$$TC(\eta_1, \eta_2, \eta_3) < TC(\eta_1, 0, 0) + TC(0, \eta_2, 0) + TC(0, 0, \eta_3),$$

that is, if the cost of operating on all the three routes by a single airline firm is lower than the sum of costs of three separate firms, each operating on a single route.

Often, economies of network is referred to in the literature as economies of scope, which generally satisfies a property more general than the one given in Definition 9.1, called "subadditivity," (see Baumol, Panzar, and Willig 1982; and Sharkey 1982).

Now, let us suppose that there is only one airline serving the three cities. Which network of operation will minimize the cost of this airline company?

Let TC be a separable cost function defined by

$$TC(\eta_1, \eta_2, \eta_3) \stackrel{\text{def}}{=} c(\eta_1) + c(\eta_2) + c(\eta_3), \tag{9.1}$$

where

$$c(\eta) \stackrel{\text{def}}{=} \phi + \eta^2.$$

Thus, in this example, the cost of operating on a route is composed of a fixed cost ϕ which is attributed to renting departure and arrival gates at the local airports, hiring local staff, and landing fees; and a variable cost which in this example is rising quadratically with the number of passengers, say due to aircraft capacity limits.

In view of Figure 9.1, under the FC network, the total cost of operation is $TC^{\text{FC}} = 3\phi + (\eta_1)^2 + (\eta_2)^2 + (\eta_3)^2$, where under the HS network $TC^{\text{HS}} = 2\phi + (\eta_1 + \eta_3)^2 + (\eta_2 + \eta_3)^2$. Assuming equal number of passengers on each route ($\eta_1 = \eta_2 = \eta_3 = \eta$), we have it that

$$TC^{\text{HS}} < TC^{\text{FC}} \quad \text{if and only if} \quad \phi > 5\eta^2.$$

That is, if the fixed cost associated with maintaining a route (route 3) is large relative to the number of passengers on each route, then the HS network is the cost-saving network. If the fixed cost of operating a route is small (ϕ is small) then the FC becomes the cost-saving network of operation.

9.2   Deregulation and Entry

Among the many changes that took place in the U.S. airline industry
since its deregulation in 1978, the substantial decline in the number
of major carriers and the intensified use of the hub-and-spoke network,
stand out as the most significant ones. From a height of over forty major
carriers in the period immediately after the deregulation, the number has
steadily declined to a presently low of only six or seven major carriers
(Borenstein, 1989). At the same period, the hub-and-spoke routing has
increased by about 50 percent. In fact, Doganis (1993, Ch.10) reports
that even for the short period following the deregulation, 1978–1984,
the proportion of all passengers making an on-line connection with the
same carrier rose from 25% to 45%. Thus, the post-deregulation U.S.
aviation industry can be characterized as being highly oligopolistic. In
addition, airlines operate a route network, which is essentially a central
hub oriented.

In this section, following Berechman, Poddar, and Shy (1998), we
show that the decline in the number of airlines can (at least in part)
be attributed to successful entry deterrence and entry accommodation
strategies used by incumbent airline firms, where a major strategy is the
transition to a hub-and-spoke network. The theoretical network model
developed below shows that by switching to a hub-and-spoke network
from a fully connected one, under a deregulatory market regime, the
incumbent airline firm can gain a strategic advantage over a potential
entrant, thereby impeding or limiting his entry into the market.

Consider an economy composed of three cities, labeled A, B, and
C, and three possible routes denoted by i, $i = 1, 2, 3$ as depicted in
Figure 9.1. A passenger can be transported by an airline firm either
directly from his city of origin to his city of destination, or indirectly
through a third city called a hub (city B in Figure 9.1). In contrast
to Figure 9.1, we consider only one-way travel, where passeners wish to
travel from A to B, from A to C and from B to C without returning.

Passengers

We assume that on *each* route i, $i = 1, 2, 3$, there are two types of
passengers who are differentiated with respect to their value of time.
The first type involves η passengers with high value of time who are
assumed to lose a utility of δ, ($\delta > 0$), if they fly indirectly through
the hub rather than nonstop from origin to destination. The second
type involves η passengers with sufficiently low value of time who are
indifferent between flying directly or indirectly to their destination. Let
p_i denote the airfare on route i.

The utility of a passenger traveling on route i and having a high value of time is affected by whether the flight is direct or indirect and by the airfare. The utility of a passenger with low value of time on route i is affected by the airfare only. Formally,

$$U_i^H \stackrel{\text{def}}{=} \begin{cases} \beta - p_i & \text{flies directly to destination} \\ \beta - \delta - p_i & \text{flies to destination via a hub} \\ 0 & \text{does not fly,} \end{cases} \qquad (9.2)$$

and

$$U_i^L \stackrel{\text{def}}{=} \begin{cases} \beta - p_i & \text{flies directly or indirectly} \\ 0 & \text{does not fly.} \end{cases}$$

where β ($\beta > 0$) is the basic value a passenger attaches to the service of being transported from city of origin to the city of destination.

The airline firm

Let μ denote the airline's cost per flight on any route i. Notice that this cost is per flight and not per passenger, and therefore sometime is referred to as the *ACM* cost (AirCraft Movement cost).

9.2.1   A single monopoly airline

Consider an airline firm operating under a regulatory regime which permits only one firm to provide services to all cities. This type of regime is observed in a number of countries where only one airline is allowed to provide all domestic flights. We assume that this firm charges monopoly airfares. This analysis will serve as our base case.

Fully Connected service only

A Fully Connected (FC) network is defined here as a network in which travel from any city of origin to any city of destination is a direct flight which does not involve routing via a hub.

Let π_i denote profit from the operation on route i, $i = 1, 2, 3$, and let π denote the monopoly airline's profit from the operation of the entire network. That is, $\pi \stackrel{\text{def}}{=} \pi_1 + \pi_2 + \pi_3$.

Under the FC the monopoly airline can extract maximum surplus by setting $p_i = \beta$ where all passengers are served. Since aircrafts are assumed to have an unlimited capacity, there is one flight on each route. The profit on each route i is $\pi_i = 2\eta\beta - \mu$. Therefore, the profit of this monopoly airline under the FC network is

$$\pi^{\text{FC}} = 3\pi_i = 6\eta\beta - 3\mu. \qquad (9.3)$$

Hub-and-Spoke

Using a HS network, the airline transports route 3 passengers via a hub in city B. In order to determine the airline's monopoly airfares under the HS network, we need to make the following assumption.

ASSUMPTION 9.1
*Passengers purchasing a ticket from city A to city C and are flown via the hub located in city B, are **unable** to get off or get on a plane in city B.*

In other words, passengers whose destination or origin is city B cannot purchase a flight ticket for route 3, and embark or disembark the plane during the intermediate stop at the hub city B. Assumption 9.1 does not rule out an airfare profile where $p_1 > p_3$ or $p_2 > p_3$. In fact, some data shows that airfare for passengers whose destination or origin is a hub city pay higher airfares than passengers whose destination is not a hub city. Formally, it means that the monopoly can price discriminate between route 3 passengers and the passengers on other routes. However, note that the monopoly airline must restrict the airfare on route 3 to satisfy $p_3 \leq p_1 + p_2$ as otherwise route 3 passengers are better off by purchasing two tickets (from A to B, and then from B to C).

   Assumption 9.1 is more realistic than assuming the polar situation where passengers can freely embark or disembark at city B, since airline companies make it difficult for passengers whose destination is city C to disembark in city B by shipping their luggage to city C. Assumption 9.1 is relaxed in Exercise 2 at the end of this chapter.

   Under the HS network the utility functions (9.2) and Assumption 9.1 imply that the monopoly airline sets $p_1 = p_2 = \beta$ thereby extracting maximum surplus from passengers on routes 1 and 2 who fly directly to their destinations. For route 3, two levels of airfares must be considered. First, a high fare of $p_3 = \beta$ thereby "losing" the η route 3 passengers with a high value of time. Second, a low fare of $p_3 = \beta - \delta$ thereby serving all passengers on all routes. Therefore, the profit levels of the monopoly airline under the HS network are

$$\pi^{\mathrm{HS}}\Big|_{p_3=\beta} = 5\eta\beta - 2\mu \quad \text{and} \quad \pi^{\mathrm{HS}}\Big|_{p_3=\beta-\delta} = 6\eta\beta - 2\eta\delta - 2\mu. \quad (9.4)$$

Comparing the profit levels (9.3) with (9.4) yields

$$\pi^{\mathrm{FC}} > \pi^{\mathrm{HS}} \quad \text{if} \quad \mu < \eta\beta \text{ and } \mu < 2\eta\delta. \quad (9.5)$$

Proposition 9.1
For a sufficiently small aircraft movement cost, μ, the FC network is more profitable to operate than the HS network for the monopoly airline.

9.2.2 Partial deregulation and partial entry

Partial deregulation is defined as a policy regime where entry is permitted in one market (route) only. We now analyze the strategic use of the network structure by the incumbent airline when entry is allowed into route 3. The incumbent firm is denoted by I and the potential entrant by E. Under this policy regime, a new entrant firm can enter on one route only. Given that under HS there is no direct service on route 3, this route is a natural candidate for entry. We assume that the potential entrant has the same cost and capacity structure as the incumbent airline firm. This rules out any kind of ex ante asymmetry (for example cost or capacity advantage) between the two airline firms.

We will use the following terminology:

DEFINITION 9.2

An airline industry equilibrium is called an **entry accommodation equilibrium** *if an entrant makes a strictly positive profit. An airline industry equilibrium is called an* **entry deterrence equilibrium** *if no entrant can make a positive profit.*

In what follows, we demonstrate the strategies employed by the incumbent when it deters entry into route 3 and the strategies employed when the incumbent accommodates entry into route 3. We make the following assumption.

ASSUMPTION 9.2

The number of passengers on each route is sufficiently large relative to the cost of operating a flight. Formally, $\mu < 2\eta\delta$ and $\mu < \eta\beta$.

Assumption 9.2 implies that the condition listed in (9.5) holds, which means that in the absence of a threat of entry the FC network is more profitable than the HS network.

Entry Deterrence using a FC network

Suppose for a moment that the incumbent decides to completely deter entry regardless of whether such an action is profitable or not. Suppose first that the incumbent operates a FC network. Under entry deterrence, the incumbent lowers the price to per-passenger cost so $p_3^I = \mu/2\eta$. Clearly, entry is blocked since in order for the entrant to get in it must set $p_3^E < \mu/2\eta$, thereby earning a profit of $\pi^E = 2\eta p_3^E - \mu < 0$. Since there is no threat of entry on routes 1 and 2 the incumbent airline can charge the monopoly airfares $p_1^I = p_2^I = \beta$. Therefore, entry deterrence using the FC network leaves the incumbent with a profit level

$$\pi^I = 4\eta\beta + 2\eta p_3^I - 3\mu = 4\eta\beta - 2\mu. \tag{9.6}$$

Entry Deterrence using a HS network

Now suppose that the incumbent operates a HS network. In order to deter entry on route 3 the incumbent must set $p_3 = \mu/2\eta - \delta$. That is, since an entrant can lower its airfare to a minimum of $p_3^E = \mu/2\eta$, the incumbent must further lower its airfare by δ in order to compensate route 3 passengers with a high value of time for flying them indirectly via a hub. Assumption 9.1 again implies that $p_1^I = p_2^I = \beta$. Therefore, the incumbent earns

$$\pi^I = 4\eta\beta + 2\eta p_3^I - 2\mu = 4\eta\beta - 2\eta\delta - \mu. \tag{9.7}$$

Comparing (9.6) with (9.7) reveals that under Assumption 9.2 entry deterrence via a FC network is more profitable than entry deterrence via a HS network.

Entry Accommodation

Definition 9.2 implies that in an entry accommodation the entrant must make a strictly positive profit. Therefore, an entry accommodation equilibrium does not exist when the incumbent operates a FC network, since under a FC network the incumbent and the entrant provide identical services (direct flights on route 3), which generates an intense airfare competition on route 3, thereby leaving the entrant with zero or negative profit. Therefore, suppose now that the incumbent airline operates a HS network.

There are two ways in which the incumbent can accommodate entry. First, the simplest accommodation involves abandoning of route 3 by the incumbent, in which case the incumbent earns a profit of

$$\pi = \pi_1 + \pi_2 = 4\eta\beta - 2\mu. \tag{9.8}$$

Second, the incumbent airline can further enhance its profit by allowing for a partial entry accommodation. Under entry accommodation, the incumbent serves those route 3 passengers that have low value of time by transporting them via a hub, while the entrant serves only route 3 passengers with a high value of time. We look for an Undercut-proof equilibrium (UPE) (Definition C.2 on page 309), in the airfares p_3^I and p_3^E. Again, Assumption 9.1 implies that $p_1^I = p_2^I = \beta$. Thus, in an UPE, the entrant sets maximal p_3^E subject to

$$\pi^I = 4\eta\beta + \eta p_3^I - 2\mu \geq 4\eta\beta + 2\eta(p_3^E - \delta) - 2\mu. \tag{9.9}$$

That is, subject to the constraint that the incumbent airline serving only $(4 + 1)\eta$ passengers will not find it profitable to undercut the entrant's price by setting $p_i^{I'} = p_3^E - \delta$ thereby serving all the 6η passengers including those with a high value of time. Similarly, the incumbent airline maximizes p_i^I subject to

$$\pi^E = \eta p_3^E - \mu \geq 2\eta p_3^I - \mu. \tag{9.10}$$

That is, the entrant is better off serving only the η passengers with a high value of time compared with undercutting the incumbent's airfare in order to gain the η passengers who have no value of time by setting $p_3^{E'} = p_3^I$. Solving the two constraints with equality yields the unique entry accommodation equilibrium prices. Thus,

$$p_3^I = \frac{2\delta}{3} \quad \text{and} \quad p_3^E = \frac{4\delta}{3}. \tag{9.11}$$

Clearly, $p_3^E > p_3^I$ since the entrant provides a direct nonstop service. Substituting the equilibrium prices into the profit functions (9.9) and (9.10) yields

$$\pi^I = 4\eta\beta + \frac{2\eta\delta}{3} - 2\mu \quad \text{and} \quad \pi^E = \frac{4\eta\delta}{3} - \mu. \tag{9.12}$$

Comparing (9.12) with (9.8) reveals that the incumbent makes a higher profit by not abandoning the entire service on route 3. Instead, it utilizes the infrastructure for routes 1 and 2 to provide service to route 3 passengers who have low value of time.

Comparing (9.6) with (9.12) reveals that under the threat of entry the incumbent finds entry accommodation via a HS network to be more profitable than entry deterrence via a FC network, and this result is general in the sense that it is independent of Assumption 9.2. In addition, comparing (9.7) with (9.12) proves our main proposition.

Proposition 9.2
Suppose that the number of passengers on each route exceeds a certain threshold value (Assumption 9.2). Then,

(a) *Under partial deregulation, the incumbent airline finds entry accommodation more profitable than entry deterrence.*

(b) *Deregulation of the airline industry induces airline companies to abandon the FC network and to utilize the HS network.*

Our analysis demonstrated the strategic use of the network structure in response to a threat of entry of a new airline. Prior to the threat of entry, condition (9.5) implied that the monopoly airline will utilizes a

FC network unless the aircraft moving cost is high. In contrast, Proposition 9.2 shows that the threat of entry is sufficient to induce the incumbent to switch to a HS network. In the case that the incumbent does not abandon route 3 entirely, the use of the HS network under entry accommodation serves the incumbent as a means to differentiate the service provided by the incumbent and the entrant. By shifting to the HS the incumbent can prevent a stiff price competition with the entrant associated with having both airline firms providing a homogeneous service under the FC network.

9.3 Code-Sharing Agreements

As we already pointed out in this chapter, the deregulation of the U.S. airline industry in the late 1970s, and of the European market in 1996 induced airline firms to restructure their entire method of operation. In addition to restructuring their route networks, we recently began observing that airline firms enter into mutual agreements which are referred to as *alliances*. All these agreements attempt to raise passengers' value of traveling with the contracting airline firms. One common method used by contracting airline firms in order to become more attractive to passengers is to merge their computerized reservation systems, a procedure which is commonly called *code sharing*. Under code sharing, each airline can issue tickets on flights operated by all contracted airline companies. Moreover, all flights of each contracting airline bear all the flight numbers of all other contracting airline firms. All this means is that a passenger buying a ticket from one airline using that airline's flight number system, may end up sitting in an aircraft operated by a different airline.

Obviously, since code sharing is widely used, we now want to construct a model for the purpose of explaining the reasons why airline companies find it profitable to engage in code-sharing agreements, and the implications of these agreements for passengers' welfare.

9.3.1 Frequency of flights and airfare competition

One important feature that passengers highly value when choosing among airline companies is the frequency of flights offered by each airline on their desired route. A high frequency of flights allows passengers more flexibility in booking the flight at the desired time, and flexibility in changing the flight if they wish to reschedule their flight. Therefore, we now explicitly introduce frequency of flights into passengers' utility functions.

Consider two countries labeled A and B with two national airlines labeled α and β, respectively. There are 2η passengers who wish to fly between country A and B. The direction of their travel is irrelevant as each airline firm provides flights in both directions.

The 2η passengers are heterogeneous with respect to their preference for the two airline companies. η passengers are airline α oriented, and η passengers are airline β oriented. One way to interpret passengers' orientation toward a particular airline is that passengers wish to accumulate frequent-flier points with a single airline. A second interpretation is to assume that passengers prefer to fly with their national airline because the crew speaks their national language.

Equilibrium airfares with no code sharing

Let f_α, $f_\alpha \geq 1$, denote the frequency of flights (number of flights at a given time period) provided by airline α. Similarly, let f_β be the frequency of flights offered by airline β. Also, let p_i denote the airfare charged by airline i, $i = \alpha, \beta$. The utility function of an airline i oriented passenger is

$$U_\alpha \stackrel{\text{def}}{=} \begin{cases} f_\alpha - p_\alpha & \text{flies } \alpha \\ f_\beta - \delta - p_\beta & \text{flies } \beta, \end{cases} \quad \text{and} \quad U_\beta \stackrel{\text{def}}{=} \begin{cases} f_\alpha - \delta - p_\alpha & \text{flies } \alpha \\ f_\beta - p_\beta & \text{flies } \beta. \end{cases}$$
(9.13)

We are looking for an Undercut-proof equilibrium (UPE) in airfare competition, where η passengers fly α and η passengers fly β. In this equilibrium, if airline α wishes to undercut the airfare set by airline β and grab all its passengers, it has to set its airfare to $p'_\alpha = p_\beta - \delta + f_\alpha - f_\beta$, as it must compensate β's oriented passengers for flying their less-favorite airline. However, it can add $f_\alpha - f_\beta$ (reduce, if negative) to the airfare which is the difference between α's frequency and β's frequency, since (9.13) implies that passengers are sensitive to the difference in frequencies between the two airline firms. Let the flight frequencies, f_α and f_β be given. Definition C.2 on page 309 implies that in an UPE, airline β maximizes p_β subject to

$$\pi_\alpha = \eta p_\alpha \geq 2\eta(p_\beta - \delta + f_\alpha - f_\beta). \tag{9.14}$$

Similarly, in an UPE airline α maximizes p_α subject to

$$\pi_\beta = \eta p_\beta \geq 2\eta(p_\alpha - \delta + f_\beta - f_\alpha). \tag{9.15}$$

Solving (9.14) and (9.15) with equality yields the UPE airfares. Thus,

$$p_\alpha = 2\delta + \frac{2(f_\alpha - f_\beta)}{3} \quad \text{and} \quad p_\beta = 2\delta + \frac{2(f_\beta - f_\alpha)}{3}. \tag{9.16}$$

Equations (9.16) imply the following proposition.

Proposition 9.3
The airline which provides a higher frequency of flights charges a higher airfare. Formally, $p_\alpha \geq p_\beta$ if and only if $f_\alpha \geq f_\beta$.

Proposition 9.3 is rather intuitive. Since passengers' utility is enhanced with the frequency of flights, an airline firm will charge a higher airfare if it provides a higher frequency compared with the competing airline.

Equilibrium airfares under code sharing

Under code sharing all passengers benefit from the flight frequencies provided by both airline firms. Thus, the utility functions given in (9.13) become

$$U_\alpha \stackrel{\text{def}}{=} \begin{cases} f_\alpha + f_\beta - p_\alpha & \text{flies } \alpha \\ f_\alpha + f_\beta - \delta - p_\beta & \text{flies } \beta, \end{cases} \quad U_\beta \stackrel{\text{def}}{=} \begin{cases} f_\alpha + f_\beta - \delta - p_\alpha & \text{flies } \alpha \\ f_\alpha + f_\beta - p_\beta & \text{flies } \beta. \end{cases}$$
$$(9.17)$$

Clearly, under code sharing flight frequencies do not affect passengers' choice of which airline to fly, since code sharing implies that passengers of all airline firms gain utility from the combined frequencies of both airline firms. Thus, undercutting of airline i requires only that it sets $p'_i < p_j - \delta$, $i, j = \alpha, \beta$ and $i \neq j$. In this case the UPE conditions (9.14) and (9.15) become

$$\pi_\alpha = \eta p_\alpha \geq 2\eta(p_\beta - \delta) \tag{9.18}$$
$$\pi_\beta = \eta p_\beta \geq 2\eta(p_\alpha - \delta).$$

Solving (9.18) for the equality case yields the unique UPE airfares under code sharing. Thus,

$$p_\alpha = p_\beta = 2\delta. \tag{9.19}$$

9.3.2 Code sharing and profits

In order to investigate the effect of code sharing on the profits made by the airline firms, we need to introduce the cost functions for the two airline firms. Before doing that, we must define what is a unit of output of an airline firm. There are two possibilities of how to measure a unit of output. The first is to assume that one unit of output of an airline firm equals one passenger. This definition is problematic since the major part of an airline's cost is attributed to the cost of operating one flight which is much higher than the cost of flying a single passenger. Therefore, the second possibility of measuring an airline's unit of output is to use the cost per one flight which we have already termed as Air Craft Movement Cost (ACM). Using this definition, following Berechman and Shy (1996), the total output of an airline firm is the frequency of flights it provides for its passengers, since frequency is defined by the number of flights offered in a given time period.

In order to simplify the exposition, we now assume that each airline company can operate only two levels of flight frequencies: a high frequency, f^H, or a low frequency of flights, f^L. The cost of operating high frequency is μ^H, and the cost of operating low frequency if μ^L, where $\mu^H > \mu^L \geq 0$. Finally, we define the difference between a high frequency and a low frequency by $\Delta f \overset{\text{def}}{=} f^H - f^L$, and the difference in the associated costs by $\Delta\mu \overset{\text{def}}{=} \mu^H - \mu^L$.

Profit without code sharing

The profit of each airline firm i, $i = \alpha, \beta$, is $\pi_i = \eta p_i - \mu_i$, where $\mu_i = \mu^H$ or $\mu_i = \mu^L$, depending the frequency of flights offered by airline i. The UPE airfares (9.16) imply that the profit of each airline firm when choosing either a high or a low frequency of flights is given by Table 9.1

Airline α \ Airline β

	f^L		f^H	
f^L	$2\eta\delta - \mu^L$	$2\eta\delta - \mu^L$	$\frac{2\eta(3\delta - \Delta f)}{3} - \mu^L$	$\frac{2\eta(3\delta + \Delta f)}{3} - \mu^H$
f^H	$\frac{2\eta(3\delta + \Delta f)}{3} - \mu^H$	$\frac{2\eta(3\delta - \Delta f)}{3} - \mu^L$	$2\eta\delta - \mu^H$	$2\eta\delta - \mu^H$

Table 9.1: Profit levels for all frequency choices.

Consider the following game where airline α chooses its frequency $f_\alpha \in \{f^L, f^H\}$, and airline β chooses its frequency $f_\beta \in \{f^L, f^H\}$. We look for a Nash equilibrium (Definition A.4 on page 292) for this game.

Proposition 9.4

(a) If $\Delta f > 3\Delta\mu/2\eta$ then $\langle f^H, f^H \rangle$ is a unique Nash equilibrium.

(b) If $\Delta f < 3\Delta\mu/2\eta$ then $\langle f^L, f^L \rangle$ is a unique Nash equilibrium.

(c) If $\Delta f = 3\Delta\mu/2\eta$, every outcome constitutes a Nash equilibrium.

(d) The $\langle f^L, f^L \rangle$ equilibrium yields a higher profit to each airline firm than the $\langle f^H, f^H \rangle$ equilibrium.

Proof. The proof follows immediately from Table 9.1. (a) If airline α deviates from $\langle f^H, f^H \rangle$ it earns

$$\frac{2\eta(3\delta - \Delta f)}{3} - \mu^L < 2\eta\delta - \mu^H$$

under the condition of part (a). The same proof applies for a deviation of airline β. (b) If airline α deviates from $\langle f^L, f^L \rangle$ it earns

$$\frac{2\eta(3\delta + \Delta f)}{3} - \mu^H < 2\eta\delta - \mu^L$$

under the condition of part (b). The same proof applies for a deviation of airline β. (c) Part (a) and (b) implies that deviation from any symmetric outcome is not profitable. (d) Follows immediately from Table 9.1. ∎

Figure 9.2 interprets the condition of Proposition 9.4.

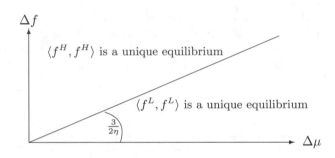

Figure 9.2: Equilibria with high and low flight frequencies.

Figure 9.2 shows that when the difference in costs increases, the equilibrium will result in low frequencies. In contrast, as the difference in cost declines, both airline firms will choose high frequencies. In addition, Figure 9.2 shows that as the number of passengers grow, the dividing ray tilts towards the horizontal axis, meaning that when the passenger population is high, both airline firms will choose high frequencies.

Part (d) of Proposition 9.4 reveals a possiblity for an industry failure, if $\Delta f > 3\Delta\mu/2\eta$ as the equilibrium with high flight frequencies yields a lower profit level to each firm compared with the outcome that both supply low frequency of flights. Thus, under the condition of part (a) airline firms will look for ways to avoid this equilibrium. Since coordination is generally not allowed under Antitrust laws, code sharing succeeds in eliminating the inefficient (from the firms' perspective) frequency competition.

Profit under code sharing

Suppose now that the two airline companies sign a code-sharing agreement, so that each company can issue flight tickets on all flights operated by airline α and airline β. This implies that a passenger's decision which airline to fly with is not affected by the relative frequency of flights, since each passenger is exposed to $f_\alpha + f_\beta$ frequency of flights. Thus, under code sharing the equilibrium airfares (9.19) are independent of flight frequencies. Hence, (9.19) implies that the profit level of each airline firm as a function of flight frequencies is now given by Table 9.2. Clearly, un-

Airline α \ Airline β

	f^L		f^H	
f^L	$2\eta\delta - \mu^L$	$2\eta\delta - \mu^L$	$2\eta\delta - \mu^L$	$2\eta\delta - \mu^H$
f^H	$2\eta\delta - \mu^H$	$2\eta\delta - \mu^L$	$2\eta\delta - \mu^H$	$2\eta\delta - \mu^H$

Table 9.2: Profit levels for all frequency choices under code sharing.

like the frequency game played in Table 9.1 (no code sharing) the unique Nash equilibrium for the frequency game played in Table 9.2 (with code sharing) is that both airline firms supply low frequency of flights. The reason for this is that under code sharing, maintaining a high frequency of flights does not affect the revenue of the firm, but it increases the cost and hence is profit reducing.

We now state our main proposition regarding code-sharing agreements.

Proposition 9.5
If $\Delta f > 3\Delta\mu/2\eta$, a code-sharing agreement is profit enhancing to the contracting airline firms. Under such an agreement, competition is softened and each airline firm cuts its cost by reducing its frequency of flights.

Whether or not passengers suffer from code sharing depends on whether $2f^L \leq f^H$ in which case code sharing reduces the frequency of flights available to passengers, or whether $2f^L \geq f^H$ in which case passengers face a higher flight frequency after the code-sharing agreement is implemented.

9.4   Exercises

1. Consider the model of Section 9.1 and Definition 9.1 where we defined economies of network for the airline industry. Assume that $\eta_1 = \eta_2 = \eta_3 = \eta$, that is, there is an equal number of passengers on each route. Answer the following questions.

   (a) Suppose that $c(\eta) \stackrel{\text{def}}{=} \eta$ for the cost function defined in (9.1). Find the condition on ϕ and η under which the total cost of operating a HS network is lower than the total cost of operating a FC network. Prove your answer.

(b) Answer the previous question assuming that $c(\eta) \stackrel{\text{def}}{=} \sqrt{\eta}$.

2. Consider the partial deregulation model of Section 9.2. Suppose now that Assumption 9.1 is reversed so passengers on route 3 are able to disembark or embark aircraft in the hub city if they find it beneficial to do so. One important consequence of reversing Assumption 9.1 is that the airline firm cannot price discriminate among the routes, which means that the incumbent airline is restricted to setting the airfare on route 3 to satisfy $p_3 \geq \max\{p_1, p_2\}$. That is, we now rule out a situation where the passengers on route 3 traveling via the hub in city B pay a lower airfare than passengers traveling from A to B, or from B to C. Answer the following questions.

(a) Calculate the airfares p_i, $i = 1, 2, 3$, which are charged by a monopoly airline that operates a FC network. Calculate the profit level of this airline company.

(b) Answer the previous question assuming that the airline operates a HS network.

(c) Find the condition on μ, δ, β, and η under which operating a FC network is more profitable that operating a HS network for a monopoly airline.

(d) Calculate the UPE airfares under an entry accommodation of an airline firm that serves only the passengers with high value of time on route 3. Assume that the incumbent airline does not abandon route 3 completely, so that it serves route 3 passengers with a low value of time by transporting them via the hub in city B. State which airline charges a higher airfare on route 3, and explain the intuition behind your answer.

3. Consider a modified version of the code-sharing agreement model given in Section 9.3. Suppose that the frequency of flights provided by airline α and airline β are f_α and f_β, respectively. Suppose that f_α and f_β are given exogeneously and cannot be altered by any airline. Suppose now that passengers' utility functions are given by

$$U_\alpha \stackrel{\text{def}}{=} \begin{cases} 3f_\alpha - p_\alpha & \text{flies } \alpha \\ 3f_\beta - \delta - p_\beta & \text{flies } \beta, \end{cases} \quad \text{and} \quad U_\beta \stackrel{\text{def}}{=} \begin{cases} 3f_\alpha - \delta - p_\alpha & \text{flies } \alpha \\ 3f_\beta - p_\beta & \text{flies } \beta. \end{cases}$$

Assume that the airline firms do not bear any type of cost (i.e., $\mu = 0$). Answer the following questions.

(a) Calculate the UPE airfares and the associated profit levels assuming that there are no agreements between the two airline firms.

(b) Calculate the UPE airfares and the associated profit levels assuming that the two airline firms are engaged in a code-sharing agreement.

(c) Suppose that $f_\alpha > f_\beta$, which means that airline α maintains a higher frequency than airline β on this route. Which airline gains and which airline loses from the code-sharing agreement?

9.5   Selected References

Baumol, W., J. Panzar, and R. Willig. 1982. *Contestable Markets and the Theory of Industry Structure.* New York: Harcourt Brace Jovanovich.

Berechman, J., and O. Shy. 1996. "The Structure of Airline Equilibrium Networks." In J. van den Bergh, P. Nijkamp, and P. Rietveld (eds.:) *Recent Advances in Spatial Equilibrium Modelling: Methodology and Applications.* Amsterdam: Springer.

Berechman, J., S. Poddar, and O. Shy. 1998. "Network Structure and Entry in the Deregulated Airline Industry." *Keio Economic Studies* 35: 71–82.

Bittlingmayer, G. 1990. "Efficiency and Entry in a Simple Airline Network." *International Journal of Industrial Organization* 8: 245–257.

Borenstein, S. 1989. "The Evolution of US Airline Competition." *Journal of Economic Perspectives* 6: 45–73.

Doganis, R. 1993. *Flying off Course: The Economics of International Airlines.* London: Routledge. 2nd Edition.

Sharkey, W. 1982. *The Theory of Natural Monopoly.* Cambridge: Cambridge University Press.

Viscusi, K., J. Vernon, and J. Harrington. 1995. *Economics of Regulation and Antitrust.* Cambridge, Mass.: The MIT Press.

Chapter 10

Social Interaction

Each society is characterized by its collection of social norms, or simply a culture. The fact that consumers live in societies imply that their actions in general, and consumption choice in particular, are affected by what social norms dictate. Ever since Veblen (1899), it is a well-documented fact that consumer choices are not only based upon their own preferences and income; they are also affected by the consumption choices of others. Such influences have proven to be important in many markets where the decision to buy from a particular vendor is positively or negatively affected by the number of consumers purchasing the same brand or patronizing the same store. The corresponding effects are known as bandwagon, congestion, or snob/conformity effects (Leibenstein, 1950). The microeconomic foundations of such effects as well as the market and welfare implications of this type of consumer behavior are explored in this chapter.

Section 10.1 starts out with basic definitions of conformity and status-seeking. This section utilizes elementary calculus so it can be easily skipped by those who do not know any calculus. Section 10.2 introduces price competition among firms producing products or services and compares the market outcomes when consumer preferences exhibit conformity to the case when preferences exhibit vanity. Section 10.3 demonstrates the consequences of network effects in entertainment places. Section 10.4 demonstrates the inefficiency of the practice of gift-giving.

10.1 Status-Seeking vs. Conformism: A Calculus Approach

Social decisions are those decisions that depend on others' decisions and also influence decisions of others. There is a significant difference between social decisions and conventional economic decision-making. Conventional decision-making concerns choosing, for example, among alternative food items in an ordinary supermarket which generally affect only the utility of the buyer. The key difference between social decisions and conventional economic decisions is that social decisions have social consequences whereas economic decisions do not.

One cannot characterize exactly which goods and services require "social decision" as it varies among individuals. However, food items such as potatoes and milk are not related to either status-seeking or conformity. In contrast, at least for some people, the choice of which car to drive is affected by status-seeking. Status-seeking also influences the choices of where to live, where to study, what to wear, whom to marry, where to dine, which entertainment places to go to, hotels, vacations, and many more. Akerlof (1997) offers some utility functions that are consistent with social choices.

10.1.1 A model of status-seeking

Consider an economy with η individuals who each has to choose a real number $x \geq 0$. The variable x can be interpreted as how much to spend on a car, a house, on clothes, and so on. Suppose that each individual j chooses $x_j = \hat{x}$ except, perhaps, individual i. All individuals have identical utility functions. Thus, the utility of individual i when he chooses x_i and all others choose $\hat{x}$ is by

$$U_i\big|_{\substack{x_j = \hat{x} \\ \forall j \neq i}} \stackrel{\text{def}}{=} -\delta(\hat{x} - x_i) - \alpha(x_i)^2 + \beta x_i, \qquad (10.1)$$

where the parameters α, β, δ are strictly positive. The first term in (10.1) reveals that the person loses utility in amount $\delta(\hat{x} - x_i)$ insofar as he falls behind everyone else. In addition, x has an intrinsic value to him of $-\alpha(x_i)^2 + \beta x_i$. The utility function of individual i given in (10.1) is drawn in Figure 10.1.

The problem of each individual i, $i = 1, \ldots, \eta$, is to solve the following maximization problem. Given that all individuals $j \neq i$ choose $x_j = \hat{x}$, individual i has to choose x_i that maximizes (10.1). The first- and

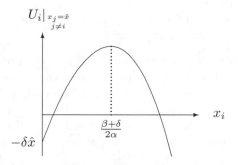

Figure 10.1: The utility function of a status-seeker.

second-order conditions are given by

$$0 = \frac{dU_i}{dx_i} = \beta + \delta - 2\alpha x_i, \quad \text{and} \quad \frac{\partial^2 U_i}{\partial (x_i)^2} = -2\alpha < 0.$$

Since all individuals are identical, they all behave in the same way as individual i. Hence, in a status-seeking equilibrium each individual chooses

$$x_i = \frac{\beta + \delta}{2\alpha}, \quad i = 1, \ldots, \eta. \tag{10.2}$$

A natural question to ask at this point is whether the race for status distorts social welfare. We therefore define the social welfare function as the sum of individuals' utilities. Since all individuals are identical and have strictly concave utility functions given in (10.1), we can conclude that in social optimum all individuals make the same choices, that is $x_i = x$ for all $i = 1, , \ldots, \eta$. Hence, the social planner chooses a common x to solve

$$\max_x W \stackrel{\text{def}}{=} \sum_{i=1,\ldots,\eta} U_i = \eta \left[-\delta(x - x) - \alpha x^2 + \beta x \right] = \eta \left(-\alpha x^2 + \beta x \right).$$

The first- and second-order conditions for a maximum are

$$0 = \frac{dW}{dx} = -\eta(2\alpha x + \beta), \quad \text{and} \quad \frac{d^2 W}{dx^2} = -2\alpha \eta < 0.$$

Therefore, the socially optimal choice is that each individual chooses

$$x_1^* = x_2^* = \cdots = x_\eta^* = \frac{\beta}{2\alpha}. \tag{10.3}$$

Comparing (10.2) with (10.3) implies that $x_i > x_i^*$. Therefore,

Proposition 10.1

A competitive race for status is inefficient, since it induces individuals to choose a higher-than-optimal level of x.

First, notice that the inefficiency is due to the presence of an externality and that this externality is similar to what occurs in any congestion model (see for example Section 7.3). Second, (10.2) reveals that despite the fact that the race for status induces individuals to choose a higher-than-optimal level of x, in equilibrium all individuals choose the same level. This explains why the race for status leads to an inefficient outcome.

10.1.2   A model of conformism

We shall now examine the alternative case—of conformity—in which each individual wants to minimize the social distance between himself and others. As before, suppose that all individuals $j \neq i$ choose $x_j = \hat{x}$. In contrast to (10.1), the utility of a conformist is given by

$$U_i\big|_{\substack{x_j=\hat{x} \\ \forall j \neq i}} \stackrel{\text{def}}{=} -\delta(x_i - \hat{x})^2 - \alpha(x_i)^2 + \beta x_i, \qquad (10.4)$$

The difference between (10.4) and the utility function of a status-seeker (10.1) is that the term $-\delta(x_i - \hat{x})^2$ is squared for a conformist. This means that for a conformist, any deviation in any direction (i.e., $x_i > \hat{x}$ or $x_i < \hat{x}$) is welfare reducing. In contrast, for a status-seeker, only $x_i < \hat{x}$ is welfare reducing whereas $x_i > \hat{x}$ is welfare enhancing.

Each individual i takes $\hat{x}$ as given, and chooses x_i to maximize (10.4). The first- and second-order conditions for a maximum are

$$0 = \frac{\mathrm{d}U_i}{\mathrm{d}x_i} = -2(\alpha + \delta)x_i + \beta + 2\delta\hat{x}, \quad \text{and} \quad \frac{\mathrm{d}^2 U_i}{\mathrm{d}(x_i)^2} = -2(\alpha + \delta) < 0.$$

Since all individuals are identical, in equilibrium $x_i = \hat{x}$ for all $i = 1, \ldots, \eta$. Hence,

$$x_i = \frac{\beta}{2\alpha}. \qquad (10.5)$$

To compute the socially optimal level, the social planner chooses a common x to solve

$$\max_x W \stackrel{\text{def}}{=} \sum_{i=1,\ldots,\eta} U_i = \eta \left[-\delta(x-x)^2 - \alpha x^2 + \beta x \right] = \eta \left(-\alpha x^2 + \beta x \right),$$

yielding the same social optimum as (10.3). That is, the social optimum under conformism is the same as under status-seeking. Therefore, comparing (10.5) with (10.3) we have the following proposition.

Proposition 10.2
There is no market failure when all individuals have identical utility functions that exhibit conformism.

The reason for this efficiency is that each individual equates her choice to the choice of others and this coincides with the maximization problem solved by the social planner. It should be pointed out that the result of Proposition 10.2 need not hold when individuals have different utility functions. Moreover, our analysis was restricted to one homogeneous product/service. However, in a more general setting where products are differentiated, it can happen that conformism leads to a market failure by having all individuals choosing the "wrong" standard (see for example Section 4.1).

10.2 Conformity, Vanity, and Price Competition

Observations justifying the analysis of this section involve stores with a large number of consumers that tend to provide more services to their clients (after-sale service and large parking lots), which makes the stores more attractive. In contrast, crowded stores may deter consumers who refuse to incur the corresponding congestion costs and prefer to shop at other places just because they hate congestion and value quietness, thus exhibiting a behavior consistent with negative network effects.

Following Grilo, Shy, and Thisse (forthcoming) consider consumers who can choose between two products labeled A and B, produced at zero cost by two separate firms labeled in the same way. A and B can also be interpreted as two types of services, social or health clubs, or even two shopping malls. The utility of a product i oriented consumer, $i = A, B$, is given by

$$U_i \stackrel{\text{def}}{=} \begin{cases} \alpha q_i - p_i & \text{if he buys product } i \\ \alpha q_j - \delta - p_j & \text{if he buys product } j \neq i, \end{cases} \qquad (10.6)$$

where $i, j = A, B$ and $i \neq j$, and $\alpha < \delta/\eta$. We assume that there are η A-oriented consumers, and η B-oriented consumers, where $\eta > 0$. The variable q_i denotes the number of consumers buying product i, $i = A, B$, and the parameter α measures how the network of users affects the utility of a buyer.

The reader has seen a utility function like (10.6) several times before, especially in Chapters 2 and 4. What makes the presentation in (10.6) unique is that we allow the parameter α in (10.6) to take negative values. Therefore, we need the following definition.

DEFINITION 10.1
Consumer preferences are said to exhibit

- **conformity,** *or positive network effects if* $\alpha > 0$,

- **vanity,** *or negative network (bandwagon) effects if* $\alpha < 0$.

Thus, when $\alpha > 0$ the utility of each consumer rises with the number of people buying the same product. This case is the familiar one. In contrast, when $\alpha < 0$ people behave like snobs, their utility declines with the number of consumers buying the same product. The case of vanity has not been analyzed so far in this book. This case can be also interpreted as a snob behavior. Examples include those who drive specially designed cars in order to make them look different when driving in the street, shopping at exclusive shopping malls, flying first class and staying at fancy hotels just to feel special, buying memberships at exclusive social or health clubs, and so on. What unifies all these examples is that these people wish to join small groups of consumers with different consumption patterns than the majority of consumers.

We now solve for an Undercut-proof equilibrium (Definition C.2 on page 309) in price competition between the two firms. Firm B maximizes p_B subject to

$$\eta p_A \geq 2\eta \left[p_B - \delta + \alpha(2\eta - \eta) \right].$$

The last two terms measure the effect of increasing the network of B-users when firm A undercuts firm B. Similarly, firm A maximizes p_A subject to

$$\eta p_B \geq 2\eta \left[p_A - \delta + \alpha(2\eta - \eta) \right].$$

Solving these two conditions yields the equilibrium UPE prices and profit levels

$$p_A = p_B = 2(\delta - \alpha\eta) \quad \text{and} \quad \pi_A = \pi_B = 2\eta(\delta - \alpha\eta). \tag{10.7}$$

Figure 10.2 illustrates how prices vary with the population size, η, under conformity ($\alpha > 0$) and vanity ($\alpha < 0$). Figure 10.2 (left) shows that prices decline with a rise in population when preferences exhibit conformity. This result should be familiar from Chapter 2 and stems from the fact that price competition is intensified when firms compete over more consumers who, in the case of conformity, have positive network externalities. Figure 10.2 (right) demonstrates a new result where, in the case of vanity, prices increase with the population size. The reason for this is that a higher network size *reduces* the value of the product or the service and hence consumers' willingness to pay. By raising the

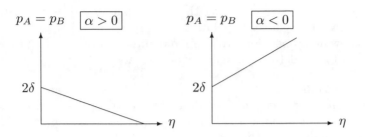

Figure 10.2: Equilibrium price vs. population under conformity and vanity.

price firms attempt to "get rid" of some of the customers in order to increase the value of the product. This means that an increase in consumer population increases equilibrium prices.

Substituting the equilibrium price (10.7) into the utility function (10.6) yields

$$U_A = U_B = 3\alpha\eta - 2\delta. \tag{10.8}$$

Figure 10.3 illustrates how the utility of each consumer varies with an increase in the consumer population size, η, under conformity ($\alpha > 0$) and under vanity ($\alpha < 0$). Figure 10.3 (left) reveals that equilibrium

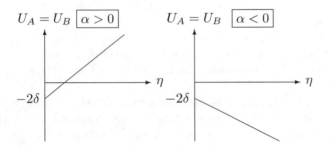

Figure 10.3: Equilibrium utility vs. population under conformity and vanity.

utility rises with population since there are two effects working in the same direction. First, there is a direct effect where, under conformity, a larger network size enhances individuals' utilities. Second, since under conformity a larger consumer population intensifies price competition, consumers also benefit from lower prices.

Figure 10.3 (right) reveals that a larger consumer population reduce equilibrium utility levels. The direct effect implies that consumers' utility declines with the population size due to the vanity effect (which could also be interpreted as the congestion effect). The indirect effect follows from our previous analysis showing that under vanity, prices rise with an increase in the consumer population.

The following proposition, which follows directly from (10.7), (10.8) and Figures 10.2 and 10.3, summarizes our results.

Proposition 10.3
(a) *When consumer preferences exhibit conformity, an increase in the consumer population will (1) decrease equilibrium prices, and (2) increase equilibrium utility levels.*

(b) *In contrast, when consumer preferences exhibit vanity, an increase in the consumer population will (1) increase equilibrium prices, and (2) decrease equilibrium utility levels.*

10.3   The Economics of Entertainment Places

We can observe with some astonishment that popular restaurants, theaters, bars, and dancing places often have people standing in line to get in. What is even more astonishing is that these entertainment places do not raise prices in the presence of queues (excess demand) as predicted by the simple conventional, demand-and-supply theory. That is, simple demand-and-supply theory tells us that in the presence of excess demand, a firm can increase its price without reducing its output level, thereby increasing its profit. So, why do restaurant owners refrain from raising prices when they observe the formation of lines in front of their establishments? Of course, this puzzle is not unique to restaurants. We also observe long lines in football games and performances of rock stars, and the price of tickets sold at box offices do not rise with the formation of long queues.

Becker (1974, 1991) and Karni and Levin (1994) propose a solution for this puzzle along the following line of thinking. As it turns out restaurant economics has a lot in common with the economics of computers analyzed in Chapter 2. The demand for restaurants shares similar characteristics with the demand for computers, since in both industries consumers' choices are affected by "social" conditions that are in turn affected by the choice of other consumers. Hence, the demand for some restaurants, coffeehouses, nightclubs, discotheques, and other entertainment and sports clubs exhibit network externalities.

Consider a monopoly restaurant with 2η potential heterogeneous consumers. Let q denote the number of consumers going to this restaurant, and let p the price of a meal set by the restaurant's owner. Out of the 2η potential consumers, η are called type H (consumers who highly value the restaurant), and the remaining η consumers are called type L consumers (consumers who place a low value on this restaurant). The utility function of each consumer type i, $i = H, L$, is given by

$$U_i \overset{\text{def}}{=} \begin{cases} \alpha_i q - p & \text{if he goes to the restaurant} \\ 0 & \text{if he does not go to the restaurant,} \end{cases} \tag{10.9}$$

where $\alpha_H > 2\alpha_L > 0$. Thus given the number of restaurant goers, q, type H consumers are willing to pay more than twice for a meal than type L consumers are willing to pay. Figure 10.4 illustrates the aggregate demand for this restaurant's meals. The aggregate demand

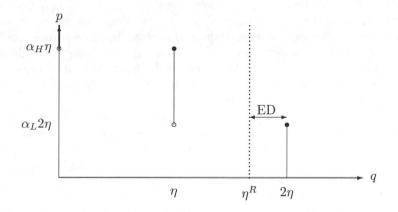

Figure 10.4: Demand and supply for meals at the restaurant. η^R is restaurant's seating capacity; ED measures excess demand.

for meals is constructed as follows. At a very high price no one buys a meal. As the price declines to $p = \alpha_H \eta$, (10.9) reveals that the η type H consumers enter the market and demand each one meal. As the price falls to $\alpha_L 2\eta$, (10.9) reveals that the η type L consumers enter the market and the aggregate demand expands to 2η. Thus, the aggregate demand is downward sloping and has two discontinuities: at $p = \alpha_H \eta$ and at $p = 2\alpha_L \eta$.

The supply side is fixed by the number of tables in the restaurant: the restaurant cannot supply more than η^R meals at a given time (or, in the case of theaters, there is always a limited seating capacity). We assume that $\eta < \eta^R < 2\eta$ which means that the restaurant cannot serve the entire population. This means that at any price $p \leq 2\alpha_L \eta$ there are $\text{ED} = 2\eta - \eta^R$ consumers waiting outside on line to be seated, where ED stands for excess demand. We can therefore state our main proposition.

Proposition 10.4
Suppose that

$$\eta^R > \frac{\alpha_H \eta}{2\alpha_L}.$$

Then, the profit-maximizing price of a meal is $p = 2\alpha_L\eta$, thereby maintaining a steady excess demand for meals at this restaurant.

Proof. The profit at this price equals $(2\alpha_L\eta)\eta^R$. At a higher price, $p = \alpha_H\eta$, there are $\eta < \eta^R$ customers, hence earning a profit of $\alpha_H\eta^2$. The condition of the proposition implies that the profit at full capacity exceeds the profit made at the high price.   ∎

It is important to notice that consumers gain from a network of 2η even if only η^R consumers are actually served, since the consumers consider both those who are eating inside and those who are standing outside on line as part of the network of restaurant goers. Thus, the actual network exceeds the seating capacity of the restaurant. Hence, at full capacity each consumer is willing to pay $p = \alpha_L 2\eta$, although only $\eta^R < 2\eta$ are actually being served. Therefore, this result shows that queues enhance the profit of restaurant owners since they enhance the popularity and the social value of their establishments.

Proposition 10.4 demonstrates that a restaurant may refrain from raising its price even in the presence of excess demand in the form of long queues. This result is not predicted by the simple demand-and-supply theory which is taught in "Principles of Economics" classes. The reason for why the price is not raised is that in the presence of network externalities, even a small rise in price will significantly reduce the network of restaurant goers and will make the restaurant much less popular and hence with fewer customers.

10.4 Gifts

Gift giving is an action taken by an individual who purchases an item for another person for (supposedly) no-trade reason. Gift-giving has been observed in all cultures, countries, at all ages since the biblical time. Participation in gift-giving rituals start in daycare, where kids from the age of three and up are being told by their teachers that they should bring a present to each child who celebrates his or her birthday. In all countries, gifts are given on wedding dates and some other family celebrations. However, all this cannot be compared to the magnitude of presents given on Christmas Day.

There have been several empirical studies investigating whether the gift-giving phenomenon can be justified on an economic basis. These studies found that in general the (money denominated) value to a gift-recipient happened to be lower than the value to the person who is giving the gift (which equals the price paid in the store). Waldfogel (1993) found that holiday gift-giving destroys between 10 percent to a third of the value of gifts. Since holiday expenditures average $40 billion per year, a conservative estimate of the deadweight loss associated with

Christmas gift-giving could range from \$4 billion to \$13 billion per year. Table 10.1 summarizes Waldfogel's data.

Giver	Value (\$)	Price (\$)	Avg.Yield (%)	Cash (%)
Aunt/Uncle	40.5	64.6	64.4	14.3
Brother/Sister	23.5	28.3	86.2	5.8
Parents	133.3	135.6	86.5	9.6
Significant	24.1	25.4	91.7	0.0
Grandparents	56.1	75.9	62.9	42.3
Friend	22.1	25.3	98.8	6.1
All	77.6	84.0	83.9	11.5

Table 10.1: Gifts' yield and tendency to give cash. *Note:* Value is a gift recipient's willingness to pay for the gift. Average yield is the average of all gift recipients' ratios of the value they attach to non-cash gifts to the price paid by the giver." This is why the third column is not exactly equal to the ratio of the first column to the second column.

For the particular data used in Table 10.1, it is clear from the column entitled "Average Yield" that, on average, gift recipients are willing to pay only 83.9% of the price that was actually paid by givers. This finding can be interpreted as having a social welfare loss of 16.1% of the price for every gift given during the holiday season. This column indicates that the yield vary significantly with the type of the giver. Friends happen to give gifts that match recipient's preference by 98.8%. In contrast, grandparents, aunts, and uncles tend to give the least efficient gifts in the sense that recipients undervalue the gift by nearly 40% of the price that was paid. This, obviously, reflects a generation gap in tastes for products.

The column entitled "cash" reveals that grandparents are not so bad after all, as they are smart enough to recognize the generation gap in tastes and to provide more cash gifts than any other type of gift givers. In fact, 42.3% of gifts given by grandparents are in cash rather than gifts in kind. 14.3% of aunts and uncles also seem to recognize this generation gap and to provide cash gifts rather than gifts in kind.

The above-listed observations raise the puzzling question why people want to spend money to buy items for other people knowing that other people will not be willing themselves to spend this amount and buy these items by themselves. In this section we attempt to provide an answer to this paradox by investigating an environment where in equilibrium, selfish consumers end up giving gifts. We then ask whether the equilibrium is optimal from a social viewpoint.

10.4.1   Cash versus gifts-in-kind: A graphical illustration

The most important feature of gift-giving is that the consumption choices are made by someone other than the final consumer. We now demonstrate, using a simple microeconomic model, that a gift may leave the recipient worse off than if he had made his own consumption choice with an amount of cash equal to the price paid for the gift by the giver.

The following is a true story that happened to the author while he was teaching at a certain economics department on the East Coast. One colleague got married, and all the faculty members started collecting money for the purpose of buying an expensive gift. As the department was dominated by relatively old people, there was a consensus among the faculty that the money should be used to buy crystal glasses. Figure 10.5 illustrates the commodity space of this gift recipient assuming that he consumes only two goods: crystal glasses and other goods.

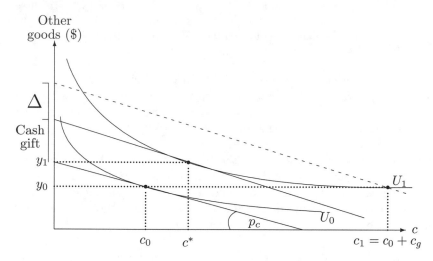

Figure 10.5: Measuring deadweight loss associated with a gift in kind. The variable c measures the consumer's stock of crystal glasses.

In Figure 10.5, the consumption level c_0 represents the consumer's initial purchase (or initial stock) of crystal glasses (before his wedding) The consumption level c_0 is optimal as it maximizes the consumers utility subject to his budget constraint, thereby yielding an initial utility level of U_0. Suppose now that the consumer receives c_g amount of crystal as a gift for his marriage. Given his initial stock of c_0, the new total stock of crystal of $c_1 = c_0 + c_g$, which places him on a higher indifference curve with a utility level of $U_1 > U_0$. Clearly the consumption bundle associated with c_1 is not a utility maximizing bundle. In fact the figure shows that the same utility level, U_1, can be achieved with a smaller expenditure if the givers would give cash rather than crystal glasses. The consumer will end up choosing to own a stock of $c^* < c_1$ of crystals and will spend $y_1 > y_0$ on other goods. Moreover, since the price of other goods is normalized to equal 1, the figure provides an exact measure, given by Δ of how much givers have overpaid in order to provide the recipient with a utility level of U_1. Thus, Δ equals one minus the yield given in Table 10.1 for every \$1 dollar spent.

10.4.2 A general model of gift giving and receiving

Perhaps the most important microeconomic characteristic of gift-giving is that gifts are likely to be mismatched with the recipients' preferences for goods. We now develop a model for an economy where individuals, receiving gifts, feel social pressure to return a gift, perhaps on another occasion. We then compare the welfare level in an economy where gift giving is a social norm to an economy where people do not give gifts.

Consider an economy with λ goods indexed by $j = 1\dots,\lambda$, and η individuals indexed by $i = 1,\dots,\eta$. The utility of each individual is composed of two subutilities, the utility of receiving a gift, denoted by V_i^R, and the utility (disutility, possibly) of giving gifts, denoted by V_i^G. All individuals have identical utility functions.

Among all the λ goods, each individual likes one good more than all the others and attaches to it a value of β. All other goods are also valuable to the individuals but not as much. Thus, each individual attaches a utility of $\beta - \delta$, where $\beta > \delta > 0$ to each of all other goods. Formally, the utility of individual i, whose ideal good is good j, from receiving a gift of good k is assumed to be given by

$$V_i^R(j) \stackrel{\text{def}}{=} \begin{cases} \beta & \text{if he receives good } k = j \\ \beta - \delta & \text{if he receives good } k \neq j. \end{cases} \tag{10.10}$$

Since there are λ goods, the expected utility from receiving a random gift is

$$\text{EV}_i^R = \frac{1}{\lambda}\beta + \frac{\lambda - 1}{\lambda}(\beta - \delta) = \beta - \frac{\lambda - 1}{\lambda}\delta. \tag{10.11}$$

We now turn to the act of giving gifts. Let p denote the price of each good and assume that all the λ goods are equally priced. Therefore, buying a gift confers a disutility of p on the giver. In addition, we capture the *social pressure* to give gifts by the disutility parameter γ which is the extra disutility confered on an individual who receives a gift but does not return a gift to the giver. Formally, we define the utility of giving a gift by

$$V^G \overset{\text{def}}{=} \begin{cases} 0 & \text{if he does not give and does not receive a gift} \\ -p & \text{if he receives a gift and then gives a gift} \\ -\gamma & \text{if he receives a gift but does not return one.} \end{cases}$$

(10.12)

We make the following assumption.

ASSUMPTION 10.1
The social "embarassement" of not returning a gift is higher than the utility loss of paying the price for the gift. Formally, $\gamma > p$.

The utility from giving (10.12) and Assumption 10.1 together imply that

Proposition 10.5
(a) *Any individual who receives a gift will return a gift.*

(b) *Any individual who does not receive a gift will not give a gift.*

Proof. (a) If a gift is received, the utility of giving is $V^G = -p > -\gamma$ which is the utility of not returning a gift. (b) If a gift is not received, the utility of not giving is $V^G = 0 > -p$ which is the utility of giving a gift. ∎

Consider now an economy with η individuals where each person receives a gift from everyone except herself. A natural question to ask now is how many gifts are given in this economy. Table 10.2 demonstrates how the total number of gifts in the economy is calculated. This calcu-

Population Size	1	2	3	4	$\cdots$	η
# gifts received by each	0	1	2	3	$\cdots$	$\eta - 1$
Economy's total # gifts	0	2	6	12	$\cdots$	$\eta(\eta - 1)$

Table 10.2: Calculating the total number of gifts in the economy.

lation goes as follows. Suppose that there are η individuals. Therefore, each individual receives $\eta - 1$ gifts. Since there are η such individuals, the total number of gifts exchanged in this economy is $\eta(\eta - 1)$. We can make the following claim.

Proposition 10.6
Each individual is better off in an economy where gifts are not exchanged than in an economy where everybody exchanges gifts with everybody else.

Proof. Consider an economy with population size η and suppose that gifts are not exchanged. Then, each individual has an option of purchasing $\eta - 1$ gifts for herself, thereby gaining a utility of $(\eta - 1)(\beta - p)$, since each consumer knows which good is her ideal one. In contrast, in an economy where gifts are exchanged by everybody, (10.11) and (10.12) imply that the expected utility of each person is

$$EU = (\eta - 1)\left(EV_i^R + V^G\right) = (\eta - 1)\left(\beta - \frac{\lambda - 1}{\lambda}\delta - p\right), \qquad (10.13)$$

which is lower than $(\eta - 1)(\beta - p)$. ∎

Proposition 10.5 implies that there are two equilibria in this economy: one in which all individuals give (and receive) gifts, and the other in which no one gives gifts (however, each individual has an option of buying $\eta - 1$ gifts for herself). Proposition 10.6 demonstrates that the first equilibrium is inefficient as all individuals are worse off compared with the second equilibrium. It is therefore instructive to construct a measure of social inefficiency associated with the gift-giving equilibrium. Equation (10.13) reveals that the (per-gift) utility loss to each individual from having to participate in the gift-exchange ritual is $(\lambda - 1)\delta/\lambda$ which is precisely the expected utility loss associated with giving a consumer her less-preferred product (compared with her ideal product). Since, each individual receives $\eta - 1$ gifts, and since the population size equals η, we define the social welfare loss function by

$$L(\eta, \lambda, \delta) \stackrel{\text{def}}{=} \eta(\eta - 1)\frac{\lambda - 1}{\lambda}\delta, \quad \text{for} \quad \eta, \lambda > 1. \qquad (10.14)$$

The variation of the social loss with respect to increases in the population size, number of products in the economy, and the mismatch parameter are illustrated in Figure 10.6. Equation (10.14) and Figure 10.6 imply the following proposition.

Proposition 10.7
The social loss associated with gift-giving (a) increases quadratically with the population size, (b) increases at a declining rate with the number of products in the economy, and (c) increases linearly with the tastes' mismatch parameter.

The reason for the quadratic increase in social loss with respect to population growth is that the number of gifts rises quadratically with the population size. The reason for the declining rate of increase with respect to the number of available products is that with a large number of products the gift giver is "most-likely" to give gifts which are not viewed as ideal by recipients. For example, if there are only 100 products to

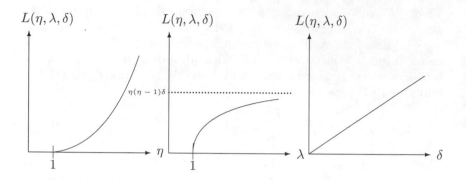

Figure 10.6: Changes in social loss associated changes in population size (η), number of products (λ), and mismatch in tastes parameter (δ).

choose from, the probability of mistmatch is $99/100 = 99\%$, and if there are 1,000 products, $999/1,000 \approx 99.9\%$ so the difference in the probability of mismatch hardly makes a difference for Christmas shoppers.

10.5   Exercises

1. Consider the model of conformity and vanity of Section 10.2. Suppose now that there are 300 product A oriented consumers and only 100 product B oriented consumers. Let p_A denote the price of product A, and p_B the price of product B. The utility function of a product i oriented consumer, $i = A, B$, exhibits vanity and is given by

$$U_i \stackrel{\text{def}}{=} \begin{cases} -q_i/2 - p_i & \text{if he buys product } i \\ -q_j/2 - 100 - p_j & \text{if he buys product } j \neq i, \end{cases}$$

where $i, j = A, B$ and $i \neq j$. Firms do not bear any production cost. Answer the following questions.

(a) Suppose that all the brand A oriented consumers buy brand A and all brand B oriented consumers buy brand B. Given p_B, find the price p'_A in which firm A undercuts the price of firm B and grabs all its 100 consumers. Then, given p_A, find the price p'_B in which firm B undercuts the price of firm A and grabs all its 300 consumers. *Hint:* Notice that in the case of vanity consumers' utility decline with an increase in the number of consumers buying the same product. Therefore, when a firm undercuts the other, it must "compensate" the consumers who switch from the other firm for the increase in the network size.

(b) Solve for the UPE prices. Conclude which firm charges a higher price and explain why.

(c) Calculate the profit level of each firm and conclude which firm makes a higher profit.

2. In a small town called *Lake Gift* all the residents live around a lake as illustrated in Figure 10.7. For over 200 years, the town has the tradition

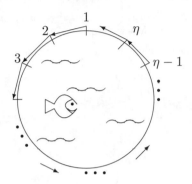

Figure 10.7: Lake Gift.

of giving gifts every Christmas in a counterclockwise pattern. That is, resident 1 gives a gift to resident 2, resident 2 gives a gift to resident 3, and so on. Resident η gives a gift to resident 1. Assume that there are λ products to buy in Lake Gift. Suppose that each resident of Lake Gift has a utility function of receiving a gift given by (10.10), and a utility function of giving a gift given by (10.12). Answer the following questions.

(a) Calculate the total number of gifts exchanged every Christmas in Lake Gift.

(b) Calculate each individual's expected utility from receiving a gift.

(c) Calculate the social loss function of Lake Gift, and demonstrate how the social loss varies with an in increase in the population size (i.e., an increase in η).

10.6   Selected References

Akerlof, G. 1997. "Social Distance and Social Decisions." *Econometrica* 65: 1005–1027.

Becker, G. 1974. "A Theory of Social Interactions." *Journal of Political Economy* 82: 1063–1093.

Becker, G. 1991. "A Note on Restaurant Pricing and Other Examples of Social Influences on Prices." *Journal of Political Economy* 99: 1109–1116.

Grilo, I., O. Shy, and J. Thisse. forthcoming. "Price Competition when Consumer Behavior is Characterized by Conformity or Vanity." *Journal of Public Economics.*

Karni, E. and D. Levin. 1994. "Social Attributes and Strategic Equilibrium: A Restaurant Pricing Game." *Journal of Political Economy* 102: 822–840.

Leibenstein, H. 1950. "Bandwagon, Snob, and Veblen Effects in the Theory of Consumers' Demand." *Quarterly Journal of Economics* 64: 183–207.

Veblen, T. 1899. *The Theory of the Leisure Class. An Economic Study of Institutions.* London: Macmillan.

Waldfogel, J. "The Deadweight Loss of Christmas." *American Economic Review* 83: 1328–1336.

Chapter 11

Other Networks

This final chapter continues in the spirit of Chapter 10 demonstrating that network economics can be applied to the modeling of a wide variety of social phenomena. The analysis of languages carried out in Section 11.1, deals perhaps with individuals' most important network, the language, which is the fundamental input to any production process and technology progress. Section 11.2 models a social phenomenon that has been with us for thousands of years and continues through the third millennium, namely religious affiliation. Section 11.3 explains how it can happen that attorneys' fees rose over the years while during the same period the number of (per-capita) practicing attorneys has been steadily increasing. Section 11.4 verbally describes the way in which international time is coordinated. Section 11.5 verbally discusses the history of the two different driving patterns found in our world.

11.1   Languages as Networks

It is hard to imagine how humans could interact without the use of some kind of a language. Spoken and written communication constitutes the basic activity of each person, and provides the most essential input for human progress.

11.1.1   Major observations

Our major observation is that people speak a wide variety of languages. Different languages are spoken in different countries and within countries. For example, in India there are twenty-four languages each spoken by a million or more persons; and numerous other languages and dialects, for the most part mutually unintelligible. English is the most important language for national, political, and commercial communication, but Hindi is the national language and primary tongue of 30% of the people. Other official languages include Bengali, Telugu, Marathi, Tamil, Urdu, Gujarati, Malayalam, Kannada, Oriya, Punjabi, Assamese, Kashmiri, Sindhi, and Sanskrit. In Finland there are two official languages: Finnish spoken by 93.5% and Swedish spoken by 6.3% of the population. In Canada, both English and French are official languages. Chinese languages include Standard Chinese or Mandarin, Yue (Cantonese), Wu (Shanghaiese), Minbei (Fuzhou), and Minnan (Hokkien-Taiwanese). In Peru, both Spanish and Quechua are official. In Belgium, Flemish 54%, French 45%, and German 1%. In South Africa there are eleven official languages, including Afrikaans, English, Ndebele, Pedi, Sotho, Swazi, Tsonga, Tswana, Venda, Xhosa, and Zulu. In contrast to these examples, we observe countries like Japan and Germany where almost 100% of the people speak a single national language.

A natural question to ask at this point is why people speak different languages? The first attempt to answer this question is given in the Bible. The story of its construction, given in Genesis 11:1-9, appears to be an attempt to explain the existence of diverse human languages. According to Genesis, the Babylonians wanted to make a name for themselves by building a tower "with its top in the heavens." God disrupted the work by so confusing the language of the workers that they could no longer understand one another. The city was never completed, and the people were dispersed over the face of the earth. The similarity in pronunciation of Babel (pronounced *Ba'vel* in Hebrew) and *ba'lal* ("to confuse") led to the play on words in Genesis 11:9: "Therefore its name was called Babel, because there the Lord confused the language of all the earth." This story combines an explanation for the diversity of languages as well as the first recognition that the language provides the most essential input for construction.

11.1.2 A model of diversity of languages

Our point of departure is that people speak different languages. Our purpose is to explain why people do not switch to a single dominant language such as Chinese, English, or Spanish. Following Church and King (1993) consider an environment with η individuals and two languages indexed by $\ell \in \{E, H\}$, English (denoted by E) and Hebrew (denoted by H). Initially, suppose that each individual speaks one and only one language. Let η_E denote the (exogenously given) initial number of English speakers, and η_H the (exogenously given) initial number of Hebrew speakers. Therefore, $\eta_E + \eta_H = \eta$. We will sometime refer to these two groups as native-English speakers and native-Hebrew speakers, respectively. Each individual can invest in learning a new language by investing a fixed sum of ϕ, $\phi > 0$. The fixed cost of learning a new language, ϕ, includes the time, effort, and fees paid to instructors and the school, and for the learning material needed to acquire a new language.

Let n_{EH} denote the number of native English speakers who learn Hebrew, and let n_{HE} the number of native Hebrew speakers who learn English. Clearly, $n_{EH} \leq \eta_E$ and $n_{HE} \leq \eta_H$. Let U_E denote the utility of an English speaker and U_H the utility of a Hebrew speaker. We define,

$$U_E \stackrel{\text{def}}{=} \begin{cases} \alpha(\eta_E + n_{HE}) & \text{if he doesn't learn } H \\ \alpha\eta - \phi & \text{if he learns } H, \end{cases} \tag{11.1}$$

and

$$U_H \stackrel{\text{def}}{=} \begin{cases} \alpha(\eta_H + n_{EH}) & \text{if he doesn't learn } E \\ \alpha\eta - \phi & \text{if he learns } E. \end{cases} \tag{11.2}$$

In the above, the parameter $\alpha > 0$ reflects the degree of importance each individual places on being able to communicate with others. The utility function (11.1) reveals that there are two ways in which the utility of a native-English speaker can be enhanced. First, the cheaper way, is to rely on Hebrew speakers to learn English. In this case, the number of people with whom an English speaker can communicate is increasing with n_{HE} which is the number of native-Hebrew speakers who learn English. Second, the expensive way, is to learn Hebrew, in which case he can communicate with the entire population, η. By symmetry the utility function (11.2) is similarly interpreted.

Our analysis relies on the following assumptions.

ASSUMPTION 11.1

(a) *Each individual treats the number of individuals learning languages n_{EH} and n_{HE} as constants which are invariant with respect to his own choice of whether to learn a different language.*

(b) All individuals have perfect foresight in the sense that they can correctly predict and observe the number and type of people who learn the different languages, n_{EH} and n_{HE}.

Assumptions 11.1(a) and 11.1(b) have been extensively used throughout this book, for example see Assumption 2.5 on page 29, and therefore will not be discussed here.

DEFINITION 11.1
*A **language acquisition equilibrium** is the pair $\langle n_{EH}, n_{HE} \rangle$ (i.e., the number of people who learn the different languages) that satisfy*

$$\text{given } n_{HE}, \text{ E-speakers learns } H \quad \Longleftrightarrow \quad \alpha\eta - \phi \geq \alpha(\eta_E + n_{HE})$$
$$\text{given } n_{EH}, \text{ H-speakers learns } E \quad \Longleftrightarrow \quad \alpha\eta - \phi \geq \alpha(\eta_H + n_{EH}).$$

The first condition in Definition 11.1 means that an English speaker learns Hebrew if and only if his utility from being able to communicate with the entire population, η, after paying the learning cost of ϕ, exceeds the utility he gains from not learning Hebrew, thereby communicating only with native-English speakers and native-Hebrew speakers who learn English. The second condition deals with Hebrew speakers who learn English, which has a similar interpretation as the first.

The two conditions of Definition 11.1 can be written as

$$E\text{-speaker learns } H \quad \Longleftrightarrow \quad \phi \leq \alpha(\eta_H - n_{HE}) \qquad (11.3)$$
$$H\text{-speakers learn } E \quad \Longleftrightarrow \quad \phi \leq \alpha(\eta_E - n_{EH}). \qquad (11.4)$$

Thus, we can now state our first proposition.

Proposition 11.1
If all native-English speakers learn Hebrew, then native-Hebrew speakers will not learn English. Similarly, if all native-Hebrew speakers learn English, then no native-English speaker will learn Hebrew.

Proof. Suppose that all native-English speakers learn Hebrew. Then, $n_{EH} = \eta_E$ implies that condition (11.4) is not satisfied. Hence, native-Hebrew speakers do not learn English. Suppose now that all native-Hebrew speakers learn English. Then, $n_{HE} = \eta_H$ implies that condition (11.3) is not satisfied. Hence, native-English speakers do not learn Hebrew. ∎

Proposition 11.1 highlights the externality imbedded in the acquisition of a new language. When a native-English speaker learns Hebrew, he also increases the utility of the native-Hebrew speakers who then do not have to learn English. Similarly, when a native-Hebrew speaker learns

English he increases the utility gained by an English speaker who does not learn Hebrew. We have encountered this form of externality several times in this book. For example, Section 3.4 demonstrated that a hardware-producing firm enhances the profit of a competing hardware firm when it makes its machine more compatible with the software produced for the competing machine, simply because software users will divert their effort to writing software for the competing firm. Also, Section 8.2 demonstrated a similar type of externality when a bank enables customers of a competing bank to withdraw cash from its automatic-teller machines, thereby increasing the profit of the competing bank.

Proposition 11.1 implies that there does not exist an equilibrium where all native-English speakers learn Hebrew and all native-Hebrew speakers learn English. That is, $\langle n_{EH}, n_{HE} \rangle = \langle \eta_E, \eta_H \rangle$ is not an equilibrium. Since all native-English speakers are identical, in equilibrium they all either learn Hebrew or do not learn Hebrew. Similarly, either all native-Hebrew speakers learn English or none of them. Therefore, there are only three possible language acquisition equilibria given by $\langle n_{EH}, n_{HE} \rangle = \langle \eta_E, 0 \rangle$, $\langle n_{EH}, n_{HE} \rangle = \langle 0, \eta_H \rangle$, and $\langle n_{EH}, n_{HE} \rangle = \langle 0, 0 \rangle$. That is, the three possible equilibria are either that all native-English speakers learn Hebrew, all native-Hebrew speakers learn English, or no one learns any language. We, now state our main proposition.

Proposition 11.2
Suppose that there are more native-English speakers than native-Hebrew speakers, that is, $\eta_E > \eta_H$. Then,

(a) *If $\phi \leq \alpha\eta_H$ there are two language acquisition equilibria given by $\langle n_{EH}, n_{HE} \rangle = \langle \eta_E, 0 \rangle$, and $\langle n_{EH}, n_{HE} \rangle = \langle 0, \eta_H \rangle$. That is, either all native-English speakers learn Hebrew, or all native-Hebrew speakers learn English.*

(b) *If $\alpha\eta_H < \phi \leq \alpha\eta_E$ the unique equilibrium is $\langle n_{EH}, n_{HE} \rangle = \langle 0, \eta_H \rangle$. That is, all native-Hebrew speakers learn English.*

(c) *If $\alpha\eta_E < \phi$ the unique equilibrium is $\langle n_{EH}, n_{HE} \rangle = \langle 0, 0 \rangle$. That is, no individual acquires a new language.*

Proof. (a) For $\langle \eta_E, 0 \rangle$ to be an equilibrium, (11.3) and (11.4) imply that $\phi \leq \alpha(\eta_H - n_{HE})$ and $\phi > \alpha(\eta_E - n_{EH})$ must hold. Substituting $\langle n_{EH}, n_{HE} \rangle = \langle \eta_E, 0 \rangle$ in the above yields

$$\phi \leq \alpha\eta_H \quad \text{and} \quad \phi > 0, \tag{11.5}$$

which is the condition given in (a).

Also, for $\langle 0, \eta_H \rangle$ to be an equilibrium, (11.3) and (11.4) imply that $\phi > \alpha(\eta_H - n_{HE})$ and $\phi \leq \alpha(\eta_E - n_{EH})$ must hold. Substituting $\langle n_{EH}, n_{HE} \rangle = \langle 0, \eta_H \rangle$ in the above yields

$$\phi > 0 \quad \text{and} \quad \phi \leq \alpha \eta_E, \quad\quad\quad (11.6)$$

which holds since $\phi \leq \alpha \eta_H < \alpha \eta_E$.

(b) Since $\phi > \alpha \eta_H$, the conditions (11.5) do not hold, thus $\langle \eta_E, 0 \rangle$ is not an equilibrium. Since $\phi \leq \alpha \eta_E$, the conditions (11.6) hold, thus $\langle 0, \eta_H \rangle$ is an equilibrium.

(c) Since $\phi > \alpha \eta_E$, the conditions given in (11.5) and (11.6) do not hold. By Proposition 11.1, $\langle \eta_E, \eta_H \rangle$ is not an equilibrium. Thus, the unique equilibrium is $\langle 0, 0 \rangle$. ∎

Figure 11.1 illustrates all possible equilibrium configurations in the $\alpha \eta_H$–$\alpha \eta_E$ space. Figure 11.1 (left) corresponds to low learning cost

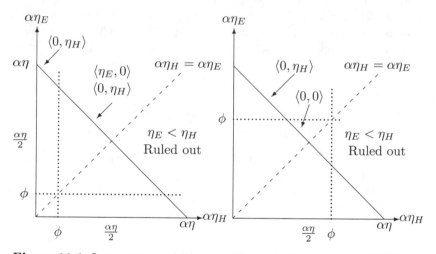

Figure 11.1: Language acquisition equilibria. *Left:* $\phi < \alpha \eta / 2$. *Right:* $\phi > \alpha \eta / 2$.

satisfying $\phi < \alpha \eta / 2$. Figure 11.1 (right) corresponds to high learning cost satisfying $\phi > \alpha \eta / 2$. In both figures, the parameter range corresponding to the area below the 45° ray is ruled out since we assumed that $\eta_E > \eta_H$. The downward sloping line corresponds to the equation $\alpha \eta_E = \alpha \eta - \alpha \eta_H$ which reflects all possible combinations of native speakers since $\eta_H + \eta_E = \eta$.

When ϕ is low, Figure 11.1 (left) demonstrates two possible equilibrium configurations. The upper segment of the downward-sloping line corresponds to Proposition 11.2 (b) where $\langle 0, \eta_H \rangle$ is a unique equilibrium. In this range, all native speakers of the less-popular language (Hebrew) learn English, but no native-English speaker learns Hebrew. The intuition behind the $\langle 0, \eta_H \rangle$ equilibrium is that Hebrew speakers have a lot to gain by learning English since they can communicate with $\eta - \eta_H$ additional individuals, and this gain overweighs the cost of learning, ϕ. In contrast, English speakers do not gain much by learning Hebrew since by learning Hebrew they can increase the number of individuals they can communicate with by $\eta - \eta_E$ which is a very small number that does not justify the spending of ϕ on learning Hebrew.

Figure 11.1 (left) also demonstrates a range of multiple equilibria where either all native-English speakers learn Hebrew, or all native Hebrew speakers learn English (but not both, according to Proposition 11.1). In this range, the learning cost is sufficiently low relative to the increase in the number of people associated with learning a new language.

Figure 11.1 (right) corresponds to a high learning cost, ϕ. In this case, there is no parameter range associated with multiple equilibria. Instead, the middle range where the number of native-English speakers is not much different from the number of native-Hebrew speakers, corresponds to no learning by both groups of speakers.

We conclude our analysis with a welfare analysis. We define the economy's social welfare function as the sum of individuals' utility levels. That is, $W \stackrel{\text{def}}{=} \eta_E U_E + \eta_H U_H$. Therefore, from (11.1) and (11.2) we compute the following.

$$
\begin{aligned}
W(0,0) &= \alpha(\eta_E)^2 + \alpha(\eta_H)^2, \\
W(\eta_E, 0) &= \alpha\eta^2 - \eta_E\phi, \\
W(0, \eta_H) &= \alpha\eta^2 - \eta_H\phi, \\
W(\eta_E, \eta_H) &= \alpha\eta^2 - \eta\phi.
\end{aligned}
\tag{11.7}
$$

Clearly,

$$
W(\eta_E, \eta_H) < W(\eta_E, 0) < W(0, \eta_H).
\tag{11.8}
$$

The first inequality implies that social welfare reaches the lowest level when everybody learns a second language. The second inequality implies that it is never optimal to have the native speakers of the most commonly used language learning the language used by the minority of people, as it should be the other way around. Equation (11.8) implies that the only potentially socially optimal outcomes are $\langle 0, 0 \rangle$ or $\langle 0, \eta_H \rangle$. Thus, no learning is socially inferior to having all Hebrew speakers learning English if and only if

$$
W(0,0) = \alpha(\eta_E)^2 + \alpha(\eta_H)^2 \leq \alpha\eta^2 - \eta_H\phi = W(0, \eta_H),
$$

$$\Longleftrightarrow \quad \alpha(\eta_E)^2 + \alpha(\eta_H)^2 \;\leq\; \alpha(\eta_E + \eta_H)^2 - \eta_H\phi,$$
$$\Longleftrightarrow \quad \alpha(\eta_E)^2 + \alpha(\eta_H)^2 \;\leq\; \alpha\left[(\eta_E)^2 + (\eta_H)^2 + 2\eta_E\eta_H\right] - \eta_H\phi,$$
$$\Longleftrightarrow \quad \frac{\phi}{2} \;\leq\; \alpha\eta_E. \tag{11.9}$$

Figure 11.2 compares condition (11.9) with the equilibrium condition given in Proposition 11.2(b). Figure 11.2 reveals that for a sufficiently

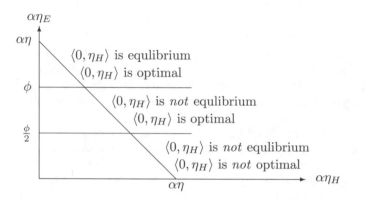

Figure 11.2: Language acquisition equilibria, and the social optimum.

high value of η_E or a sufficiently low value of ϕ, the outcome $\langle 0, \eta_H \rangle$ is an equilibrium if and only if it is socially optimal. However, for intermediate values of ϕ we can state the following proposition.

Proposition 11.3
When $\phi/2 < \alpha\eta_E < \phi$ there exist a market failure where it is socially optimal to have all Hebrew speakers learning English, but such an outcome is not an equilibrium.

Proposition 11.3 demonstrates the condition under which governments of countries with dual (or more) languages should subsidize individuals' learning costs of a second language. This subsidy is needed since native-Hebrew speakers do not take into account the welfare improvement associated with the increase in the utility of native-English speakers when they decide to learn English.

Finally, the reader should bear in mind that our welfare analysis does not take into account two important issues related to the acquisition and maintenance of different languages. First, some researchers argue that progress is established only in pluralistic societies since pluralism generates more intense competition among the different groups in a given society or among societies. Second, learning a second language may have benefits beyond enhancing one's ability to communicate with more people. Learning languages can enrich the logical thinking and teach the student about cultures and behavior, which could improve a person's ability to think and create as well as a person's productivity.

11.2   Religious Affiliations as Networks

So far, all networks studied in this book reflected relatively new industries such as computers, operating systems, software, communication, information, and so on. In this section, we analyze perhaps the oldest network type known to us, namely religious affiliations. Iannaccone (1998) defines religion as any shared set of beliefs, activities, and institutions premised upon faith in supernatural forces.

The endurance of religions seems to be so strong that neither economic efficiency nor scientific rationalism has diluted the overwhelming force of religious beliefs, rituals, and myths. The tendency to become religious is not linked to per capita income or whether there is a separation of church from state, as for example, in the United States 90 percent of the people claim to engage in prayer and over 60 percent attend church on Sundays. In fact, Iannaccone (1998) points out that the American rates of church membership have risen throughout the past two centuries. Religion is not the province of the poor or uninformed. In numerous analyses of cross-sectional survey data, rates of religious belief and religious activity tend not to decline with income, and most rates increase with education. Social scientists have little choice but to take religion into account, because religion shows no sign of dying out.

Thus, we observe that people have a tendency to want to be affiliated with a religion. Obviously, economists are not the right people to investigate why people seek religious or ethnic affiliations. However, network economics may be the right framework needed for calculating the size and distribution of religious networks. Therefore, for our modeling purpose, we will assume that each citizen of the world must be affiliated with one and only one religion of his choice.

In the following, we attempt to suggest some answers for these questions.

Q1. Which factors determine or influence the size and distribution of religious networks? More precisely, why do some religions have a large number of affiliates and some have only a small number of affiliates?

Q2. Why are some religions open to converts and why do some impose restrictions to converts attempting to join in?

Q3. How does the number and distribution of believers affect the administrators of each religion?

11.2.1　A basic model of religious affiliation

Consider a world with two religions indexed by i, $i = \alpha, \beta$. Let n_α denote the endogenously determined number of believers who affiliate themselves with religion α, and n_β the number of believers who affiliate themselves with religion β. The world is divided into two types of believers. There are η^n nonconformist believers whose behavior exhibits vanity (type n), and η^c believers whose behavior exhibits conformity (type c). The utility function of each believer type when affiliated with religion i, $i = \alpha, \beta$ is defined by

$$U_i^n \stackrel{\text{def}}{=} \beta - \gamma^n n_i, \quad \text{and} \quad U_i^c \stackrel{\text{def}}{=} \beta + \gamma^c n_i, \quad \text{where } \gamma^n, \gamma^c > 0. \quad (11.10)$$

Thus, all believers receive a utility of β by affiliating themselves with one religion, however, the utility of type n believers declines with the number of other believers who are affiliated with the same religion. In contrast, the utility of a type c believer is enhanced with an increase in the number of believers who are affiliated with the same religion. Conformity behavior and nonconformity (snob, or vanity) behavior have been analyzed earlier in this book (see Section 10.2) as consumers who like to purchase the same products and services or shop at the same store as others (conformity), or dislike to purchase the same products and services purchased by others (vanity). Here we maintain the same social interpretation but apply it to whether believers would like to affiliate themselves according to what others believe or whether they would like to isolate their religion from other believers, and hence impose obstacles that prevent new converts from joining the religion.

Each religion i, $i = \alpha, \beta$, has an acceptance policy regarding the admission of converts from the other religion. Let a_i denote the acceptance policy of religion i, $i = \alpha, \beta$. Thus, religion i can be open (formally, $a_i =$ OPEN) which means that it does not impose any obstacles for those who want to join in. Alternatively, religion i can be closed (formally, $a_i =$ CLOSED) which means that the religion does not accept converts. At this point we do not analyze how acceptance policies are being formed. Sections 11.2.2 and 11.2.3 below provide a rigorous analysis showing how conversion policies are being determined.

Let n_i^n (n_i^c) denote the endogenously determined number of type n (type c) believers who are affiliated with religion i, respectively. Clearly, $n_i^n + n_i^c = n_i$ which is the total number of believers affiliated with religion i. Our analysis relies on the following assumptions.

ASSUMPTION 11.2

(a) *Let there be n_α and n_β believers affiliated with religion α and β, respectively. Then, each individual believer treats n_α and n_β as constants which are invariant with respect to her own choice of whether to convert to the competing religion.*

(b) *All believers have perfect foresight in the sense that they can correctly predict and observe the allocation of believers between the two religions.*

(c) *Believers do not bear any switching costs by converting from one religion to another.*

Assumptions 11.2 (a),(b) have been extensively used throughout this book, for example see Assumption 2.5 on page 29. The purpose of imposing Assumption 11.2 (c) is to simplify the exposition. Clearly, in reality, converting from one religion to another could be difficult for some believers as conversion may mean disconnecting with family members who may not be willing to accept any departure from their roots.

   We now define an equilibrium allocation of believers between the two religions.

DEFINITION 11.2

For given religious policies, a_α and a_β, we say that an allocation of believers $\langle n_\alpha^n, n_\alpha^c, n_\beta^n, n_\beta^c \rangle$ constitutes a **religion equilibrium** *if the following conditions are satisfied*

(a) *if a_β=OPEN, then $U_\alpha^n(n_\alpha) \geq U_\beta^n(n_\beta)$ and $U_\alpha^c(n_\alpha) \geq U_\beta^c(n_\beta)$;*

(b) *if a_α=OPEN, then $U_\beta^n(n_\beta) \geq U_\alpha^n(n_\alpha)$ and $U_\beta^c(n_\beta) \geq U_\alpha^c(n_\alpha)$.*

Definition 11.2 merely states that in an equilibrium allocation believers must be "happier" being affiliated with their allocated religion than with the competing religion *only if* the competing religion is open. In other words, they will not want to convert. Notice that if both religions are closed, then any allocation of believers between the two religions constitutes a religion equilibrium, since no believer can convert to the competing religion even if the other religion yields a higher utility.

   We make the following definition.

DEFINITION 11.3

A religion allocation of believers is said to be of **equal size** *if*

$$n_\alpha \overset{\text{def}}{=} n_\alpha^n + n_\alpha^c = n_\beta^n + n_\beta^c \overset{\text{def}}{=} n_\beta. \tag{11.11}$$

Otherwise, we say that the allocation is of **unequal size**.

Definitions 11.2, 11.3, and Assumption 11.2 imply the following proposition.

Proposition 11.4
Suppose that both religions are open (i.e., $a_\alpha = a_\beta =$ OPEN). Any equal-size allocation constitutes a religion equilibrium.

Proof. Clearly, (11.11) implies that conditions (a) and (b) of Definition 11.2 are satisfied with equality. ∎

All the equal-size equilibria can be criticized on two grounds. First, these equilibria are unstable in the sense that even if a "small" group of conformists (formally, a group with a strictly positive measure but as small as we want) converts from some religion to another, the latter religion immediately becomes more attractive to all conformists thereby violating either condition (a) or (b) of Definition 11.2. Second, the most popular religions that we observe today in the real world are of very different sizes. For the rest of this chapter we simplify our analysis by focusing *only* on unequal-size equilibria. This is a simplification since it lets us conduct our analysis without having to deal with stability and coordination issues. We now characterize the conditions under which unequal size equilibria exist.

Proposition 11.5
Suppose that both religions are open (i.e., $a_\alpha = a_\beta =$ OPEN).

(a) *If $\eta^n < \eta^c$, there are exactly two unequal-size religion equilibria that are given by*
$\langle n_\alpha^n, n_\alpha^c, n_\beta^n, n_\beta^c \rangle = \langle \eta^n, 0, 0, \eta^c \rangle$, *and* $\langle n_\alpha^n, n_\alpha^c, n_\beta^n, n_\beta^c \rangle = \langle 0, \eta^c, \eta^n, 0 \rangle$.
In both equilibria all the nonconformists are affiliated with one religion whereas all the conformists are affiliated with the competing religion.

(b) *If $\eta^n \geq \eta^c$, there does not exist an unequal-size religion equilibrium.*

Proof. (a) Due to symmetry, it is sufficient to show that $\langle \eta^n, 0, 0, \eta^c \rangle$ is an equilibrium. Since $\eta^n < \eta^c$, if a type n believer converts to religion β, her utility becomes

$$U_\beta^n = \beta - \gamma^n \eta^c < \beta - \gamma^n \eta^n = U_\alpha^n,$$

which is her utility before the conversion. Hence, conversion reduces her utility. If a type c believer converts to religion α,

$$U_\alpha^c = \beta + \gamma^c \eta^n < \beta + \gamma^c \eta^c = U_\beta^c,$$

which is the utility before she converts. Altogether, any unilateral conversion of any believer is welfare reducing.

(b) By a way of contradiction, suppose that an unequal-size equilibrium exists. With no loss of generality suppose that in this equilibrium religion α has more believers than religion β, that is $n_\alpha > n_\beta$. Since both religions are open, it must be that all the η^c conformists are affiliated with religion α (since each conformist seeks to join the religion with the largest number of believers). Similarly, all the η^n type n believers must be affiliated with religion β (the smaller religion). Altogether, in this equilibrium $n_\alpha = \eta^c$ and $n_\beta = \eta^n$. Since $\eta^c \leq \eta^n$ by assumption, we have $n_\alpha \leq n_\beta$. A contradiction.   ■

Propositions 11.4 and 11.5 together demonstrate that in a world with open religions, unequal size religions are likely to be realized only if the total number of conformists exceeds the number of nonconformists. That is, if there are less conformists than nonconformists, religions must be of equal size. Clearly, since equal-size religions are not observed in reality, we can conclude that either conformists constitute the majority of believers, or that some religions are not open, which is the focus of our analysis in what follows.

A natural question to ask now is how decisions regarding the acceptance of converts are determined in each religion. Section 11.2.2 below analyzes religion equilibria under the assumption that the rules governing the acceptance of converts are determined by a simple majority of the believers affiliated with the religion. Section 11.2.3 assumes that acceptance decisions are determined nondemocratically by those who earn their living from administering the religions.

11.2.2 Democratic religions

We now assume that the rules governing the acceptance of converts are determined by a simple voting mechanism where in each religion i, the choice of $a_i \in \{\text{OPEN}, \text{CLOSED}\}$ is determined by the majority rule. Formally,

DEFINITION 11.4
Religion i ($i = \alpha, \beta$) is said to be democratic if

(a) $a_i = \text{OPEN}$ whenever $n_i^c \geq n_i^n$; and

(b) $a_i = \text{CLOSED}$ whenever $n_i^c < n_i^n$.

That is, if the majority of believers affiliated with religion i consists of conformists, this majority will vote to open the religion for converts. In contrast, if the majority consists of nonconformists, the majority will vote to prohibit converts from joining their religion. As it turns out, the religion equilibria are highly sensitive to whether conformists constitute the majority of believers or whether they are a minority among all believers in the world. We, therefore, first conduct the analysis under the assumption that $\eta^c \geq \eta^n$ and then for the case where $\eta^c < \eta^n$.

Conformists constitute the majority of believers

Suppose that $\eta^c \geq \eta^n$. Figure 11.3 illustrates how conversion rules are determined for every possible allocation of believers between the religions. The dimension of the box in Figure 11.3 is $\eta^c \times \eta^n$ which is the

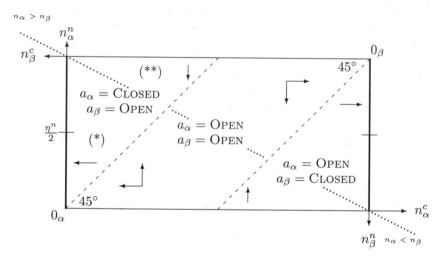

Figure 11.3: Conversion rules and religion equilibria when $\eta^c \geq \eta^n$. Thick side lines represent religion equilibria.

total number of believers in this environment. This rectangle resembles an Edgeworth's box, which is a common tool used in microeconomic theory to analyze resource allocation problems. Here, we utilize this box to illustrate how the η^c conformists and the η^n nonconformists are allocated between religion α and religion β. The horizontal axis stemming from the original marked as 0_α measures the number of conformists affiliated with religion α, n_α^c. The vertical axis stemming from 0_α measures the number of nonconformists affiliated with religion α, n_α^n. The axes stemming from the origin 0_β are similarly defined. Finally, the main (downward-sloping and dotted) diagonal divides the regions where $n_\alpha > n_\beta$ (meaning that religion α has more affiliated believers than religion β), and the region where $n_\alpha < n_\beta$. Therefore, below the diagonal, conformists affiliated with religion α will convert to religion β provided that β is open. Similarly, above the diagonal, conformists affiliated with β will convert to religion α provided that α is open.

In Figure 11.3 the area between the two dashed lines corresponds to believer allocations where $n_\alpha^c > n_\alpha^n$ and $n_\beta^c > n_\beta^n$ so that conformists constitute the majority of believers in both religions. Therefore, in this middle range, both religions will accept converts from the other religion $(a_\alpha = a_\beta = \text{OPEN})$. Clearly, any believer allocation in this range is not a religion equilibrium, since all the conformists will convert to the religion that has the largest number of affiliated believers (see left and right arrows in Figure 11.3). Also, in this region all nonconformists will convert to the religion that has the smaller number of affiliates.

The believer allocations in the upper-left regions of Figure 11.3 (the area above the left $45°$ dashed line) correspond to having a majority of nonconformist affiliated with religion α and a majority of conformists affiliated with religion β. Therefore, in this region religion α prohibits conversion from religion β, but religion β allows conversion from α to β. It follows then that any allocation in the interior of the region marked by a (*) cannot be a religion equilibrium, since conformists will convert from α to β since β is the larger religion. It also follows that in the area marked by (**) all nonconformists affiliated with α will convert to β, since β is the smaller religion. Altogether, in the upper-left region all believer allocations on the left-hand side of the box constitute religion equilibria

The lower-right region in Figure 11.3 is similar to the upper-left region where the roles of religions α and β are reversed. We can now state our main proposition.

Proposition 11.6

In an environment where most believers are conformists $(\eta^c \geq \eta^n)$ there are two types of unequal-size religion equilibria.

(a) *In one equilibrium type all conformists and some nonconformists are affiliated with religion α, whereas the remaining nonconformists are affiliated with religion β. Formally, any allocation satisfying $\langle n_\alpha^n, n_\alpha^c, n_\beta^n, n_\beta^c \rangle = \langle n_\alpha^n, \eta^c, \eta^n - n_\alpha^n, 0 \rangle$ constitutes a religion equilibrium.*

(b) *In an equilibrium of the second type, all conformists and some nonconformists are affiliated with religion β, whereas the remaining nonconformists are affiliated with religion α. Formally, any allocation satisfying $\langle n_\alpha^n, n_\alpha^c, n_\beta^n, n_\beta^c \rangle = \langle n_\alpha^n, 0, \eta^n - n_\alpha^n, \eta^c \rangle$ constitutes a religion equilibrium.*

(c) *In any equilibrium, the religion with which all conformists are affiliated is open to converts from the competing religion, whereas the religion that has only some nonconformists affiliated with it is closed to converts.*

Proposition 11.6 predicts that in a world dominated by conformists we are likely to observe a large religion (having conformists and some nonconformists) that is open to more converts from small religions, and a small religion with only nonconformists that is closed to converts from large religions.

Conformists constitute a minority of believers

We now look at an environment where nonconformists constitute the majority of believers. Suppose that $\eta^n \geq \eta^c$. Figure 11.3 illustrates how conversion rules are determined for every possible allocation of believers between the religions. The origins of the box in Figure 11.4 are the same

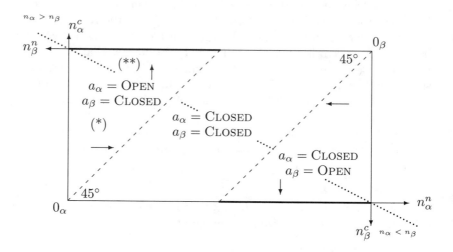

Figure 11.4: Conversion rules and religion equilibria. Thick lines and the middle range are religion equilibria.

as in Figure 11.3 but the axes are flipped so the horizontal axis stemming from 0_α now measures the number of nonconformist believers affiliated with religion α (reflecting the fact that there are more nonconformists than conformists in this economy). The middle part of Figure 11.4 (the area between the two 45° dashed lines) corresponds to believer allocations where nonconformists constitute a majority in each religion. Hence, in the interior of the middle region both religions are closed to converts and every believers' allocation in this range constitutes a religion equilibrium.

The upper-left region of Figure 11.4 (the area above the left-45° dashed line) corresponds to having conformists being a majority in religion α and a minority in religion β. Hence, α is an open religion whereas β is closed to converts. Believer allocations in the area marked by a (*) are not religion equilibria since nonconformists will convert from β to α since α is the smaller religion. In the area marked by (**) religion α is the larger religion, so conformists affiliated with β will convert to α. Thus, the only equilibrium allocations in the upper-left region correspond to the thick upper side of this region. Finally, by symmetry, the lower-right region resembles the upper-left region with religion α replaced by β and vice-versa.

11.2.3 Profit-making religions

We now solve for religion equilibria and conversion policies assuming that each religion is "owned" by an exogenously appointed group of people, which we will call *religion administrators*. Each group of administrators collects fees from each believer affiliated with his religion, which are translated into incomes for the group members. The treatment of religions as profit-making entities is, of course, problematic. However, it is clear that in religion there are administrators who make their living from working for the religion. For example, Iannaccone (1998) presents a graph showing that the fraction of the U.S. population employed as clergy remained around 1.2 per thousand for the past 150 years.

Some readers may wonder whether religions collect fees from their affiliated believers, as assumed in the present chapter. The answer is clearly yes, since it is clear that each religion must rely on some revenue sources (including donations) for supporting the administrators as well as investment in infrastructure. Sources of revenue could come from donations, money collected at the service, and from governments of countries where there is no formal separation of church and state. Iannaccone (1998) argues that total church contributions remained around 1 percent of GNP since at least 1955. Religious giving consistently accounts for about half of all charitable giving in the United States.

However, these examples show that whether the fees are collected directly or indirectly, religions cannot be modeled as fee-setting oligopoly firms since religions generally do not embarrass potential believers by imposing the fee as a precondition for admittance. We therefore assume that the fees collected by religions are exogenously determined. For example, it is a custom in U.S. churches that people donate \$1 during each Sunday service. Most people, would be ashamed to donate less than \$1, so in this case we can assume that church goers in the United States pay a predetermined fee of \$52 per year.

Our analysis will focus on a single religion with n believers. In addition, we assume that there is an unlimited number of believers who wish to join this religion. Suppose that each believer contributes an amount of ϕ dollars which we call the "fee." In what follows, we need to make some assumptions on how religions are administered.

ASSUMPTION 11.3

(a) *Let $\lambda(n)$ be a function satisfying $0 \leq \lambda(n) \leq 1$ for every $n > 1$. In every religion with n affiliated believers, $\lambda(n)$ is the fraction of administrators. That is, $\lambda(n)n$ believers are administrators.*

(b) *Administrators do not pay fees. All administrators equally divide the revenue generated from affiliated believers.*

(c) *The conversion rules (OPEN and CLOSED) are decided by the administrators to maximize the income of each administrator.*

Assumption 11.3 (a) implies that there are $[1 - \lambda(n)]n$ who are not administrators. Hence, out of n believers who are affiliated with the religion, the total revenue from fees collected by the religion is $\pi = [1 - \lambda(n)]n\phi$. Assumption 11.3 (c) goes back to Adam Smith (1965 [1776], pp.740–766), who argued that self-interest motivates clergy just as it does secular producers.

Our results will depend on how the number of administrators varies with the number of believers affiliated with the religion.

DEFINITION 11.5

(a) *A religion is said to be **efficient** if the fraction of administrators out of the number of believers, λ, declines with an increase in the number of believers, n. In this case, we will be using an example where*

$$\lambda = \lambda^e \stackrel{\text{def}}{=} \frac{1}{n}, \tag{11.12}$$

hence $\lambda^e \to 0$ as $n \to \infty$.

(b) *A religion is said to be **inefficient** if the fraction of administrators out of the number of believers, λ, increases with an increase in the number of believers, n. In this case, we will be using an example where*

$$\lambda = \lambda^i \stackrel{\text{def}}{=} 1 - \frac{1}{n} = \frac{n-1}{n}, \tag{11.13}$$

hence $\lambda^i \to 1$ as $n \to \infty$.

Let w denote the wage (salary) paid to an administrator. Then, in a religion with n believers we have

$$w = \frac{\pi}{\lambda(n)n} = \frac{[1 - \lambda(n)]n}{\lambda(n)n}\phi = \frac{1 - \lambda(n)}{\lambda(n)}\phi. \tag{11.14}$$

Thus, the wage is low when λ is close to 1, the case where most affiliated believers happen to be administrators. In contrast, the salary becomes very large when λ declines, which is the case where there are only a very few administrators.

In order to find the actual wage paid to administrators of efficient, w^e, and inefficient religions, w^i, substitute (11.14) into (11.12) and (11.13) to obtain

$$w^e = \frac{1 - \frac{1}{n}}{\frac{1}{n}} = n - 1, \quad \text{and} \quad w^i = \frac{1 - \frac{n-1}{n}}{\frac{n-1}{n}} = \frac{1}{n - 1}, \tag{11.15}$$

respectively. Equation (11.15) clearly reveals that as more believers join an efficient religion the wage paid to administrators increases since the ratio of administrators to believers declines. In contrast, the wage paid to administrators of an inefficient religion declines with the number of affiliated believers. All this proves the our main proposition.

Proposition 11.7
Administrators of efficient religions will leave the religion open for new converts, whereas administrators of inefficient religions will close the religions for new converts.

The reader who happens to be affiliated with a certain religion can use Proposition 11.7 to test whether his religion is efficient or inefficient by just looking at the religion's conversion rules. If the religion imposes many difficulties on people who attempt to join the religion, Proposition 11.7 implies that the religion is inefficient. In contrast, if one observes a religion which is open to new converts, Proposition 11.7 implies that the religion must be an efficient one.

11.3 Lawsuits and Lawyers

Beginning in the 1960s, the legal profession experienced unprecedented expansion, which began to slow down in the 1980s. Major elements in this expansion were the postwar baby boom, the opening of new university law faculties, and the entry of women into the profession in significant numbers for the first time. The growth of the profession has increased competitive pressures for jobs and business.

There are two reasons for the rapid expansion of the legal industry. First, there seems to be a trend toward specialization and bureaucratization in the modern legal profession, stemming from a de facto division of labor between those lawyers who advise clients and those who appear and argue before tribunals as well as increasing specialization in various legal fields, such as tax law, real estate, malpractice, labor disputes and much more. Second, law suits become more profitable to lawyers and the resulting increase in expected amount of legal fees paid to lawyers has attracted more young people to law schools.

In this section we focus our analysis on the second reason. Our analysis will concentrate on identifying the relationship between the number of lawyers and their fees. Our major observation is that the fees collected by lawyers have increased significantly despite the rapid increase in the number of lawyers. This observation is rather puzzling since it seems to contradict the law of demand and supply which predicts that wages (attorney's fees in the present case) should decline with the increase in the number of people in the profession.

The counter-intuitive phenomenon where fees rise with an increase in the supply of service people is not observed in most industries. For example, the increase in the supply of dentists in the 1980s has decreased real fees paid to dentists for the very basic reason that dentists (and the fluoride poured into the water system) did a "perfect" job by curing most dental problems. Good health was quickly translated into a decrease in the demand for dental services, thereby decreasing real fees. In contrast, the increase in the size of the legal industry not only did not decrease the excess demand for legal services, but it significantly increased the excess demand and as a result the real legal fees. To some degree, a similar phenomenon was also observed in the computer industry. Innovation in the computer industry has introduced personal computers in most offices and at homes, however, further developments introduced into the industry (faster chips and high-performance operating systems) have boosted the demand for service personnel specializing in maintaining the machines. Thus, similar to the legal industry, innovation in the computing industry did not reduce the demand for service personnel.

To summarize, the purpose of the analysis of this section is to resolve the puzzle stemming from the observation that for a long period of time lawyers' fees were steadily on the rise while the per-capita number of lawyers was also rising. In order to demonstrate this possibility, we will utilize a network model of attorneys where the increase in the number of practicing lawyers creates a disproportional increase in the demand for lawyers.

11.3.1 The demand for legal services

In our analytical framework we deal with one aspect of attorneys work which is called litigation. In order to construct the demand and supply for attorneys' services, we first must define the unit of output "produced" by attorneys. In what follows we will assume that lawyers deal with *cases*. By a case we refer to a law suit or an action of law, which could be handling the prosecution, the defense, or handling the case for the legal system (e.g., a judge, a clerk, and so on). Thus, we refer to cases as the output generated by attorneys.

In this economy there are η residents. Each resident is considering suing another resident. For simplicity, we assume that each resident does not sue more than once. We make the following assumptions.

ASSUMPTION 11.4
(a) *Both, plaintiffs and defendants increase their chances of winning a lawsuit by hiring an attorney.*

(b) *Every law suit requires three attorneys: one serving on the prosecution, one on the defense, and one judge.*

Assumption 11.4 (a) is motivated by the observation that most people tend to show up in court with their privately hired attorney. Several courts provide a court-appointed attorney to low-income people. However many low-income people still prefer to buy attorney's services outside the court system. It must be mentioned that the law generally does not require people to hire attorneys. However, the legal system definitely encourages people to avoid representing themselves. It is beyond the scope of this book to analyze the reasons why courts do not encourage people to represent themselves, however, one speculative answer would be that the laws governing court procedures are written by politicians and many politicians tend to come from the legal profession, thereby creating a legal system that utilizes people from their own profession.

Assumption 11.4 (b) is the core of our analysis, as it highlights the *externality* imbedded in each law suit. That is, every law suit must involve three lawyers: The suing side must hire an attorney, the defendant, and one must be the arbitrator (or the judge in a formal law suit). The number three was arbitrarily chosen but it does not qualitatively affect our results. For example, wealthy people tend to be represented by more than one attorney (some hire more than twenty attorneys to handle a single case). Also, the legal system itself may assign more than one attorney to a single case (for example, a judge and a clerk). Our analysis is not affected qualitatively by changing the number of attorneys that must be employed by each party to a law suit as long as the number of lawyers demanded by the prosecution does not exceed the sum of the number of lawyers hired by the defendant and the legal system.

Let ϵ ($0 < \epsilon < 1$) be the probability that a plaintiff wins in a law suit. Also, let β ($\beta > 0$) denote the monetary award the defendant must pay the plaintiff if the plaintiff wins the trial. Therefore, the expected reward to the plaintiff is $\epsilon\beta$, which also equals the expected penalty to be paid by the defendant. Let f denote the common fee per case paid to an attorney. More precisely, let f^p be the fee paid to an attorney for handling a prosecution case, and f^d for handling a defense case. Let U^p denote the utility of a resident wishing to sue another fellow resident (the plaintiff), and let U^d denote the utility of the defendant. We define,

$$U^p \stackrel{\text{def}}{=} \begin{cases} \epsilon\beta - f^p & \text{files a law suit against a represented defendant} \\ \beta - f^p & \text{files a law suit against a nonrepresented defendant} \\ 0 & \text{does not file a law suit, or does not hire an attorney,} \end{cases}$$
(11.16)

and

$$U^d \stackrel{\text{def}}{=} \begin{cases} -\epsilon\beta - f^d & \text{hires a defense lawyer} \\ -\beta & \text{does not hire a lawyer.} \end{cases}$$
(11.17)

The utility function (11.16) conforms to Assumption 11.4 (a) which states that without an attorney the plaintiff cannot win a law suit. Hiring an attorney increases the plaintiff's probability of winning from none to ϵ, in which case the plaintiff is awarded β. The defendant's utility function (11.17) demonstrates that the defendant will lose the case for sure unless he hires an attorney. Losing the case implies that the defendant has to pay β to the plaintiff. However, if the defendant hires an attorney and pays him a fee of f^d, he increases the probability of not losing the case from none to $(1 - \epsilon)$.

Equation (11.16) implies that the plaintiff will file a law suit (and hire a lawyer) if and only if $\epsilon\beta - f^p \geq 0$, or $f^p \leq \epsilon\beta$. Equation (11.17) implies that a defendant will hire an attorney if and only if $-\epsilon\beta - f^d \geq -\beta$, or $f^d \leq (1 - \epsilon)\beta$. We make the following assumptions which are crucial for obtaining our results.

ASSUMPTION 11.5

(a) *A plaintiff's probability of winning a lawsuit exceeds the probability of not winning the case. Formally, $\epsilon > 1/2$.*

(b) *Lawyers choose which case to handle based on the potential reward to their clients.*

(c) *Lawyers place the lowest priority on serving as judges or arbitrators.*

Assumption 11.5 (a) implies that the expected gain to a plaintiff from hiring an attorney exceeds the gain to a defendant from hiring an attorney, since $\epsilon\beta > (1-\epsilon)\beta$. This implies that prosecuting lawyers' fees are likely to be higher than defense lawyers' fees (i.e., $f^p > f^d$). Following Assumption 11.5 (b) we can conclude that attorneys will not take defense cases as long as there are some plaintiffs who are not represented. Clearly, $\epsilon > 1/2$ reflects the history of court rulings, where we assume that courts judge for the plaintiff in more than 50 percent of the cases. This assumption, of course, can be easily put to an empirical test.

Assumption 11.5 (c) implicitly implies that government jobs pay less than private practices, hence lawyers will take government jobs only after they find out that all plaintiffs and all defendants are already represented.

In what follows, we construct the demand for attorneys as a function of the number of practicing lawyers in the economy. This demand is composed of two components. First, the demand for prosecutors by plaintiffs. Notice that we assumed that the number of plaintiffs is constant and equals to the population size, η (each individual would like to place one law suit). The second component stems from the legal system which requires a defense attorney and an attorney for the legal system for law suit that is actually being filed. Observe that this additional demand does not exist as long as no law suits are filed.

Let η_L denote the exogenously determined number of lawyers in this economy. Let Q denote the demand for attorneys. Formally, Q is given by

$$Q = \begin{cases} \eta + 2\eta_L & \text{if } \eta_L \leq \eta \\ 3\eta & \text{if } \eta_L > \eta. \end{cases} \tag{11.18}$$

The first component in (11.18) is the η potential plaintiffs (the population size). The second component in (11.18) is a variable component that equals twice the number of practicing attorneys. This follows from the fact that due to fee differentials attorneys first take prosecution cases until all the η individuals hire a prosecutor. Therefore, as long as $\eta_L \leq \eta$ any newly entering attorney increases the demand by two additional attorneys. Thus, the first component always exists and is independent of the number of practicing lawyers. In contrast, the second component represents the externality generated by having lawyers file lawsuits on behalf of plaintiffs, which generates a further increase in demand for one defense lawyer and for one lawyer for the court system (judge, clerk, etc.).

The aggregate demand for lawyers (11.18) cannot exceed 3η, which is the level in which all parties are represented so no more lawyers are required by any party. Finally, the reader should *not* be concerned that (11.18) implies that the demand is satiated only after the number of lawyers reaches three times the population size. This follows from our simplifying assumption that each lawyer can represent no more than one client and cannot handle more than a single case. Section 11.3.3 below demonstrates that this assumption is not really a restriction and that the model can be generalized so that each attorney can handle more than one case.

Figure 11.5 illustrates the demand and supply of lawyers in this economy. Note that the demand for lawyers displayed in Figure 11.5 is

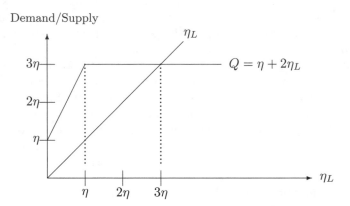

Figure 11.5: Demand for attorneys as a function of the supply of attorney.

very different from ordinary demand functions which connect quantity-demand to prices, and are therefore independent of supply functions. Here, the demand for lawyers is augmented by the increase in the supply of lawyers, since every new lawyer who files a law suit immediately creates the demand for a defense lawyer and a demand by the legal system. Thus, *lawyers create their own demand*.

Subtracting the exogenously given supply of lawyers, η_L from the demand for lawyers given in (11.18) yields the excess demand function for attorneys, which is given by

$$ED = Q - \eta_L = \begin{cases} \eta + \eta_L & \text{as long as } \eta_L \leq \eta \\ 3\eta - \eta_L & \text{for } \eta_L > \eta. \end{cases} \tag{11.19}$$

The excess demand function (11.19) is drawn in Figure 11.6. Thus, Figure 11.6 demonstrates that the excess demand for attorneys reaches a peak when there are η attorneys in the economy. This follows from Assumption 11.4 which implies that these η lawyers are all engaged in filing law suits on behalf of each resident, thereby generating a demand for addition 2η lawyers. When $\eta_L > \eta$, all law suits are filed, so newly

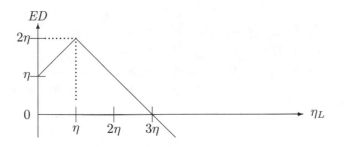

Figure 11.6: Excess demand for attorneys as a function of the supply of attorneys.

entering attorneys act either as defense attorneys, or join the legal system. Finally, when $\eta_L = 3\eta$, all attorney positions are filed, so when $\eta_L > 3\eta$ there is an excess supply of lawyers.

11.3.2 Equilibrium fees

So far, we have demonstrated the possibility that *excess* demand increases with an increase in the supply of lawyers. However, recall that the purpose of our analysis is to explain the fact that in the Western hemisphere attorneys' fees were rising during the 1980s and 1990s despite the sharp increase in the supply of practicing lawyers.

To demonstrate this, we need to specify the rule under which fees adjust to changes in the excess demand function. In other words, our analysis here is more complicated than the elementary price determination analysis, which generally involves a simple intersection of demand and supply curves, since the market for lawyers is generally characterized by a steady excess demand situation, which we call *disequilibrium*. We define $f^{\max} \stackrel{\text{def}}{=} \min\{\epsilon\beta, (1-\epsilon)\beta\}$ to be the maximum fee attorney can charge so that both, the plaintiffs and the defendants, will each find it beneficial to hire an attorney. Also, denote by $f^{\min}$ the minimum fee at which attorneys find it beneficial to take a case. For example $f^{\min}$ could be the fee paid to attorneys who work for the public sector. To simplify the writing, we assume that $f^{\min} = 0$. Clearly, attorneys are best off if the fee is $f = f^{\max}$, whereas clients are best off when $f = f^{\min} = 0$. Therefore, we need to specify a fee-determination mechanism so that $f = f^{\max}$ whenever excess demand for lawyers reaches a peak, and $f = f^{\max}/2$ (the surplus is equally divided between an attorney and his client) whenever the market is at equilibrium, that is, when excess demand is zero. Therefore, we define the attorneys' fee function by

$$f \stackrel{\text{def}}{=} \begin{cases} 0 & \text{if } ED < -2\eta \\ \frac{f^{\max}}{2} + \frac{f^{\max}}{4\eta} ED & \text{if } -2\eta \leq ED \leq 2\eta \\ f^{\max} & \text{if } ED > 2\eta. \end{cases} \tag{11.20}$$

Equation (11.20), which is drawn in Figure 11.7, is clearly an ad hoc (linear) mechanism for fee determination in the presence of a steady situation of excess demand.

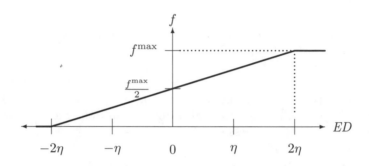

Figure 11.7: Attorney's fee determination.

Substituting (11.19) into (11.20), we obtain the market-determined fee as a function of the exogenously determined supply of attorneys. Therefore,

$$f = \begin{cases} \frac{3f^{\max}}{4} + \frac{f^{\max}}{4\eta}\eta_L & \text{if } 0 \leq \eta_L \leq \eta \\ \frac{5f^{\max}}{4} - \frac{f^{\max}}{4\eta}\eta_L & \text{if } \eta < \eta_L \leq 5\eta \\ 0 & \text{if } \eta_L > 5\eta. \end{cases} \tag{11.21}$$

The market-determined fee function (11.21) is plotted in Figure 11.8. Equation (11.21) and Figure 11.8 yield our main proposition.

Proposition 11.8
Let the number of lawyers satisfy $\eta_L < \eta$. Then, an increase in the supply of lawyers will increase the fee charged by attorneys.

Figure 11.8 also reveals that only when the supply of lawyers reaches η, the population size in our example, fees begin to slowly decline with a further increase in the supply of attorneys. The fee is maximized when $\eta_L = \eta$, i.e., when excess demand reaches 2η.

11.3.3   Variable productivity: A generalization

So far, our analysis assumed that each lawyer can handle only one case (either a prosecution case, a defense case, or handle a case for the legal

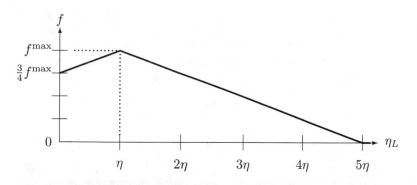

Figure 11.8: Attorney's fees and the supply of attorneys.

system). The purpose of that assumption was to simplify the exposition by identifying the number of lawyers with the demand for legal representations. We now demonstrate that no generality was lost by imposing that assumption and that all our results are easily generalized for the case where each attorney can handle more than one case.

Let ψ ($\psi \geq 1$) denote the number of cases each lawyer can handle (during a certain time period). We refer to ψ (pronounced `psi`) as the attorney's productivity parameter. Thus, an increase in the exogenously given level of ψ corresponds to an improvement in an attorney's ability to handle more cases, which could result from a better training, introducing computerized procedures (e.g., filing forms), and simplifying court's procedures. In what follows, we look at the market for *legal representations* and not the market for attorneys as we did earlier since now we assume that each attorney can handle more than one case. Therefore, the supply and demand for legal representations are now given by

$$S \stackrel{\text{def}}{=} \psi \eta_L \quad \text{and} \quad Q = \begin{cases} \eta + 2\psi \eta_L & \text{if } 0 \leq \eta_L \leq \frac{\eta}{\psi} \\ 3\eta & \eta_L > \frac{\eta}{\psi}. \end{cases} \quad (11.22)$$

Comparing (11.22) with (11.18) reveals that in the present case, with $\psi > 1$, the demand for attorney representations reaches a peak when the supply of attorneys reaches the level of η/ψ which is below the population size.

The excess demand for legal representations is now given by

$$ED = Q - S = \begin{cases} \eta + \psi \eta_L & \text{if } 0 \leq \eta_L \leq \frac{\eta}{\psi} \\ 3\eta - \psi \eta_L & \text{if } \eta > \frac{\eta}{\psi}, \end{cases} \quad (11.23)$$

and is plotted in Figure 11.9. Figure 11.9 extends Figure 11.6 to include

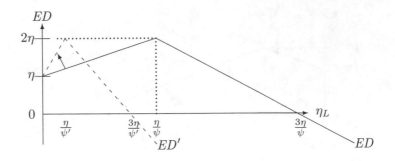

Figure 11.9: Excess demand for attorneys with varying productivity.

the attorneys' productivity parameter ψ. Excess demand peaks when the supply of attorneys reaches η/ψ and then declines with a further increase in η_L. Figure 11.9 captures an increase in attorneys' productivity parameter from an initial level of ψ to ψ', where $\psi' > \psi$, by a shift in the excess demand function from ED to ED' (dashed line). Therefore we can state the following proposition.

Proposition 11.9
As long as the supply of practicing attorneys is sufficiently below η/ψ', an increase in the productivity of attorneys, as measured by an increase in the number of cases each attorney can handle, will increase the shortage (excess demand) for attorneys. In contrast, when the supply of attorneys exceeds η/ψ, an increase in productivity will reduce the excess demand for attorneys.

The intuition behind Proposition 11.9 is that when there are not many attorneys, any increase in productivity will be directed toward filing more law suits, thereby further enhancing the demand for defense attorney and by the legal system. In contrast, when there is a large supply of practicing attorneys, an increase in productivity will reduce excess demand for legal representations since the extra productivity will be directed toward defense cases and the legal system.

If we tie the attorney's fee to the excess demand for legal representations using a rule like the one defined by (11.20) and displayed in Figure 11.7, we can conclude that bar associations should push for a productivity increase whenever the excess demand for representations is large, but should attempt to prevent productivity increase (as well as an increase in the number of attorneys) whenever the excess demand for attorneys is low.

11.4   International Time Coordination

The rotation of the earth, which causes the changes in the amount of light coming from the sun, generates different working time in different parts of the world. If people go to work at 8 A.M. in New York City, people go to sleep in Beijing since it is 8 P.M. in Beijing. With the increase in globalization of production, east-coast companies find hard time communicating with Asian businesses due to the significant time difference. Volatility in Asian stock markets affects the same-day trade in Wall Street. However, volatility in Wall Street, affects Asian markets only a day after.

International time coordination is essential for all international activities. This coordination is most visible in broadcasting where stations like CNN broadcasts from Atlanta and BBC from London to the entire world. How can a broadcasting schedule be constructed in a way in which a Japanese viewer will be to relate to a schedule of a London-based TV station? How can a pilot read a weather map of his destination city if there is no way in which the pilot can relate his departure time with the time of the forecast?

Therefore, broadcasting schedules and weather observations and forecasts are reported in *Universal Coordinated time (UTC)*, which used to be known as Greenwich Mean Time (GMT), that is, the local time at the Greenwich meridian (zero degrees longitude). It is UTC instead of UCT because the abbreviation is based on the initials in French, not English. UTC, therefore, allows weather observations the world over to have the same time stamp.

Most countries establish two adjustment periods each year relative to the UTC which are called *standard time (ST)* and *daylight-saving time (DST)*. The switch from ST to DST takes place on first Sunday of April in the United States and on last Sunday of March in Europe. The switch from DST to ST takes place on the last Sunday of October in the United States and Europe.

The local time at each city in the world is found by adding or subtracting a fixed number of hours (and minutes in rare cases) to or from the UTC. For example, UTC − 11 is the (standard) local time in the Midway Island and Samoa. UTC − 10 is the time in Hawaii. UTC − 9 is the time in Alaska. UTC − 3 is the time in Buenos Aires UTC + 1 is the time in Stockholm. UTC+5:30 is the time in Calcutta. UTC + 9 is the time in Osaka, and UTC + 12 is the time in Fiji.

11.5   Who's Driving on the "Wrong" Side of the Road?

Out of 206 countries, 144 countries (70%) drive on the right-hand side of the road, whereas 62 countries (30%) drive on the left-hand side of the road. The people in the most populated country in the world, China, drive on the right-hand side. The soon-to-become most populated country, India, drives on the left-hand side. The third-most populated country, the United States, drives on the right-hand side. The fourth-most populated country, Indonesia, drives on the left-hand side. Determining which driving side is the wrong one depends on where the reader comes from.

An equally difficult question to ask is driving side is more efficient? The clear advantage of the right-hand side for right-handed people stems from the fact that a right-handed person finds it easier to mount a horse from the left side of the horse, and it would be difficult to do otherwise if wearing a sword (on the left). It is safer to mount and dismount toward the side of the road, rather than in the middle of traffic, so if one mounts on the left, then the horse should be ridden on the left side of the road. In contrast, right-handed horsemen looking for a good fight prefer to keep left of each other in order that their sword arm is nearer to a potential opponent. The choice of sides seems to have been governed by the time of introduction of these different modes of transportation and their relative numbers, as well as by social and political influence. Most often, left-hand riding was the initial standard. In areas where carts and postilion riders became dominant, right-hand driving was adopted. In areas where wagons driven from the vehicle became dominant, left-hand driving remained the norm.

Our interest in driving side patterns stems from the facts that

(a) Driving pattern exerts a strong network externality on other driving, since it is simply to the advantage of each driver to follow the pattern used by other drivers. This externality is also strongly manifested in bike paths, swimming pools, and running paths. In this respect, driving side resembles our analysis of compatibility in the presence of network externalities of Section 2.2, and our analysis of international standardization given in Section 4.3.

(b) Driving pattern exerts a production externality, simply because cars to be shipped to countries that drive on the left-side of the road must have the driver sitting on the right-hand side, whereas the gear-shifting stick must be placed to the left of the driver.

(c) Driving-side differences generates two types of switching costs. First, drivers who drive across countries with a different pattern must increase their concentration as well as slow down in order to avoid traffic accidents caused by mistakenly driving on the wrong side in that country. Also, having to drive a car where the driver seat faces the shoulder rather the center line further complicates the driving. Second, even if the driver rents a local car, the driver has to adjust to driving a car from the side which he is not used to. For example, some U.S. drivers may find it difficult to shift gears manually in a car where the stick must be operated by the left hand.

Kincaid (1986) and Lucas (2000) discuss the problems (switching costs) associated with changing the driving side for an entire country. Several regions in the United States and Canada used to have left-side driving due to the influence of the British colonies. The latest significant switch in driving side took place in Sweden where at 5 A.M. on Sunday, September 3, 1967, Swedish drivers switched from left-side driving to right-side driving. The preparation for an immediate switch took several years, including special books that were circulated in Sweden preparing the drivers for right-side driving (see Exercise 6 at the end of this chapter). Speed limits were significantly reduced and then raised gradually. Most people did not drive for a few days until traffic signs were replaced. Since the switch was planned years in advance, many people began purchasing new cars with a left steering wheel long before the switch took place.

A natural question to ask is why did the Swedish government bothered to switch (while the British did not). Clearly, the Swedish government saw compatibility of driving side (with the rest of Europe) as a step for some integration. Most roads on the Northern part of the countries were very long, so drivers between Norway and Sweden got confused which side of the road they should drive because they could not remember which country they are driving in.

11.6   Exercises

1. Consider the language-acquisition model of Section 11.1.2, but suppose now that there are three languages: English, Spanish, and Hebrew. Initially, there are η_E native-English speakers, η_S native-Spanish speakers, and η_H native-Hebrew speakers, where $\eta_E + \eta_S + \eta_H = \eta$. Suppose that $\eta_E > \eta_S > \eta_H$, and that each individual can learn *only one* second language at the cost of ϕ. Let n_{EH} denote the number of native-English speakers who learn Hebrew, n_{ES} denote the number of native-English speakers who learn Spanish, and so on. Let the utility of a native speaker of language i be given by

$$U_i \overset{\text{def}}{=} \begin{cases} \alpha(\eta_i + n_{ji} + n_{ki}) & \text{if doesn't learn any language} \\ \alpha(\eta_i + \eta_j + n_{ki} + n_{kj}) - \phi & \text{if he learns } j \\ \alpha(\eta_i + \eta_k + n_{ji} + n_{jk}) - \phi & \text{if he learns } k, \end{cases}$$

where $i, j, k = E, S, H$, and $i \neq j \neq k$.

Find the conditions under which $n_{EH} = \eta_E$, $n_{HS} = \eta_H$, and $n_{SE} = \eta_S$ constitute a language acquisition equilibrium. Prove your answer.

2. Consider the democratic religions model analyzed in Section 11.2.2. Suppose now that in this environment there is an equal number of conformists and nonconformists. That is, $\eta^c = \eta^n$. Answer the following questions.

   (a) Draw a believer allocation box similar to the one drawn in Figure 11.3 on page 264.

   (b) Mark the regions for which each religion is open and closed.

   (c) Draw arrow indicating conversions from one religion to another.

   (d) Conclude which believer allocations constitute unequal-size religion equilibria. Explain.

3. Consider the model of profit-making religions analyzed in Section 11.2.3. Suppose now that in a religion with n affiliated believers, a fraction of

$$\lambda(n) = 1 - \frac{1}{n^2},$$

of the n believers are administrators, and that administrators do not pay fees. Assume that each affiliated believer who is not an administrator pays a fixed fee denoted by ϕ. Answer the following questions.

   (a) Calculate the number of administrators in this religion.

   (b) Calculate the number of believers who are not administrators, and conclude how much revenue is collected from the fees.

   (c) Using Definition 11.5 infer whether this religion is efficient or inefficient.

   (d) Suppose that all the revenue collected from the fees is spent on paying wages to administrators. Calculate the wage paid to each administrator. Conclude whether this religion is open or closed to new converts.

4. Answer the previous question assuming that $\lambda(n) = 1/n^2$.

5. Consider the market for attorneys of Section 11.3. Suppose that each attorney can handle only one case (either as a prosecutor or as a defense attorney). In view of (11.18), assume that the demand for attorneys as a function of the supply of attorneys is now given by

$$Q = \begin{cases} \eta + \eta_L & \text{as long as } \eta_L < \eta \\ 2\eta & \text{for } \eta_L > \eta. \end{cases}$$

which means that for every attorney filing a law suit on behalf of a plaintiff, there is a demand for one additional attorney to serve as a defense attorney. That is, unlike the previous analysis where each law suits generated a demand for two attorneys in additional to the prosecutor who is filing the suit on behalf of the plaintiff, here we assume that there is a demand only for one additional attorney to serve on a defense, and that the legal system (judges, clerks, etc.) does not demand attorneys. Answer the following questions.

(a) Write down and plot the excess demand for attorneys as a function of the supply of attorneys. Indicate the levels of η_L at which excess demand is maximized, and the level at which demand for lawyers equals the supply of lawyers.

(b) Suppose that the probability that plaintiffs win a law suit is $\epsilon = 1/2$, and that upon winning the plaintiff is awarded \$120 to be paid by the losing defendant. Using the utility functions (11.16) and (11.17), calculate the maximum fee, f^{max}, which plaintiffs and defendants are willing to pay to an attorney for handling their case. Show your calculations.

(c) Suppose that the market attorney's fee level is determined by

$$
f \overset{\text{def}}{=} \begin{cases} 120 & \text{if } ED > \eta \\ 60 + \frac{60}{\eta} ED & \text{if } -\eta \leq ED \leq \eta \\ 0 & \text{if } ED < -\eta, \end{cases}
$$

where ED is the excess demand for attorneys you calculated in part (a). Calculate the market-determined attorneys' fee level assuming that the population size of this economy is $\eta = 100,000$ and that the supply of attorneys is $\eta_L = 5000$.

(d) Answer the previous question assuming that $\eta_L = 120,000$.

6. Consider the discussion in Section 11.5 of the different driving sides employed by various countries. Answer question (a) below if you come from a country where people drive on the right-hand side or the road (such as in the United States). Answer question (b) if you come from a country where people drive on the left-hand side of the road (such as in Japan). Plot a picture that supports your answer.

(a) Suppose that you are driving a car in Bangkok where people drive on the left side of the road. You are driving on a two-way street and you are standing at an intersection with another two-way street, wishing to make a right turn at a green light.

1. Upon crossing the intersection, should you turn into the close lane or the far lane?

2. Which traffic imposes the more immediate danger, the traffic coming from the right or from the left?

(b) Answer (1) and (2) of question (a) assuming that you are driving a car in Tel Aviv where (most) people drive on the right side of the road and you wish to make a left turn from a two-way street into another two-way street.

11.7   Selected References

Church, J., and I. King. 1993. "Bilingualism and Network Externalities." *Canadian Journal of Economics* 26: 337–345.

Iannaccone, L. 1998. "Introduction to the Economics of Religion." *Journal of Economic Literature* 36: 1465–1495.

Kincaid, P. 1986. *The Rule of the Road: An International Guide to History and Practice.* Greenwood Press.

Lucas, B. 2000. *Which side of the road do they drive on...?* Unpublished note. Available online at `http://www.travel-library.com/general/driving/drive_which_side.html`.

Smith, A. (1965) [1776]. *An Inquiry into the Nature and Causes of the Wealth of Nations.* New York: Modern Library.

Appendix A
Normal-Form Games

A.1   What is Game Theory?

A.1.1   Tools and applications

Game theory (sometimes referred to as "Interactive Decision Theory") is a collection of tools for predicting outcomes for a group of interacting agents, where an action of a single agent directly affects the payoffs (welfare or profits) of other participating agents. The term *game theory* stems from the resemblance these tools have to sports games (e.g., football, soccer, ping-pong, and tennis), as well as to "social" games (e.g., chess, cards, and checkers).

Game theory is especially useful when the number of interactive agents is small, in which case the action of each agent may have a significant effect on the payoff of other players. For this reason, the bag of tools and the reasoning supplied by game theory have been applied to a wide variety of fields, including economics, political science, animal behavior, military studies, psychology, and many more. The goal of a game-theoretic model is to predict the outcomes (a list of actions adopted by each participant), given the assumed incentives of the participating agents. Thus, game theory is extremely helpful in analyzing industries consisting of a small number of competing firms, since any action of each firm, whether price choice, quantity produced, research and development, or marketing techniques, has strong effects on the profit levels of the competing firms.

A.1.2 Classification of games

Our analyzes in this book focus only on noncooperative games. We generally distinguish between two types of game representations: *normal form games* (analyzed in this appendix), and *extensive form games* (analyzed in Appendix B). Roughly speaking, we can say that in normal form games all players choose all their actions simultaneously, whereas in extensive form games agents may choose their actions in different time periods. In addition, we distinguish between two types of actions that players can take: a *pure* action, where a player plays a single action from the player's set of available actions, and a *mixed* action, where a player assigns a probability for playing each action (say by flipping a coin). Our entire analysis in this book is confined to pure actions.

Finally, information plays a key role in game theory (as well as in real life). The most important thing that we assume is that the players that we model are at least as intelligent as economists are. That is, the players that we model have the same knowledge about the structure, the rules, and the payoffs of the game as the economist that models the game does. Also important, our analysis in this chapter is confined to games with *perfect information*. Roughly, this means that in perfect information games, each player has all the information concerning the actions taken by other players earlier in the game that affect the player's decision about which action to choose at a particular time. Games under imperfect information are not used in this book.

A.2 What is a Game?

Our first encounter with games will be with normal form games. In normal form games all the players are assumed to make their moves at the same time. The following definition provides three elements that constitute what we call a game. Each time we model an economic environment in a game-theoretic framework, we should make sure that the following three elements are clearly stipulated:

DEFINITION A.1
*A **normal form game** is described by the following:*

(a) *A set of N players whose names are listed in the set $I \stackrel{\text{def}}{=} \{1, 2, \ldots, N\}$.*

(b) Each player $i, i \in I$, has an **action set** A^i which is the set of all actions available to player i. Let $a^i \in A^i$ denote a particular action taken by player i. Thus, player i's action set is a list of all actions available to player i and hence, $A^i \stackrel{\text{def}}{=} \{a_1^i, a_2^i, \ldots, a_{k_i}^i\}$, where k_i is the number of actions available to player i.

Let $a \stackrel{\text{def}}{=} (a^1, a^2, \ldots, a^i, \ldots, a^N)$ be a list of the actions chosen by each player. We call this list of actions chosen by each player i an **outcome** of the game.

(c) Each player i has a payoff function, π^i, which assigns a real number, $\pi^i(a)$, to every outcome of the game. Formally, each payoff function π^i maps an N-dimensional vector, $a = (a^1, \ldots, a^N)$ (the action chosen by each player), and assigns it a real number, $\pi^i(a)$.

A few important remarks on the definition of a game follow:

1. It is very important to distinguish between an action set A^i, which is the set of all actions available to a *particular* player i, and an outcome a, which is a list of the particular actions chosen by *all* the players.

2. Part b of Definition A.1 assumes that each player has a finite number of actions, that is, that player i has k_i actions in the action set A^i. However, infinite action sets are commonly used in industrial organization. For example, often, we will assume that firms choose prices from the set of nonnegative real numbers.

3. We use the notation $\{list \ of \ elements\}$ to denote a *set* where a set (e.g., an action set) contains elements in which the order of listing is of no consequence. In contrast, we use the notation $(list)$ to denote a vector where the order does matter. For example, an outcome is a list of actions where the first action on the list is the action chosen by player 1, the second by player 2, and so on.

4. The literature uses the term *action profile* to describe the list of actions chosen by all players, which is what we call an *outcome*. For our purposes there is no harm in using the term *outcome* (instead of the term *action profile*) for describing this list of actions. However, if games involve some uncertainty to some players, these two terms should be distinguished since under uncertainty an action profile may lead to several outcomes.

5. In the literature one often uses the term *strategy* instead of the term *action* (and therefore *strategy set* instead of *action set*), since

in a normal form game, there is no distinction between the two terms. However, when we proceed to analyze extensive form games (Appendix B), the term *strategy* is given a different meaning than the term *action*.

The best way to test whether Definition A.1 is clear to the reader is to apply it to a simple example. A simple way to describe the data that define a particular game is to display them in a matrix form. Consider the following game described in Table A.1. We now argue that

		Firm 2		
		LOW PRICE		HIGH PRICE
Firm 1	LOW	100	100	300	0
	HIGH	0	300	200	200

Table A.1: The Low price–High price game.

Table A.1 contains all the data needed for properly defining a game according to Definition A.1. First, we have two players, $N = 2$, called firm 1 and 2. Second, the two players happen to have the same action sets: $A^1 = A^2 = \{$LOW, HIGH$\}$. There are exactly four outcomes for this game: (LOW, LOW), (LOW, HIGH), (HIGH, LOW), (HIGH, HIGH). Third, the entries of the matrix (i.e., the four squares) contain the payoffs to player 1 (on the left-hand side) and to player 2 (on the right-hand side), corresponding to the relevant outcome of the game. For example, the outcome $a = ($LOW, HIGH$)$ specifies that firm 1 charges a low price whereas firm 2 charges a high price. The payoff to player 1 from this outcome is $\pi^1(a) = \pi^1($LOW, HIGH$) = 300$. Similarly, the payoff to player 2 is $\pi^2(a) = \pi^2($LOW, HIGH$) = 0$ since firm 2 is priced out of the market.

In the literature, the game described in Table A.1 is commonly referred to as the *Prisoners' Dilemma* game. Instead of having two firms engaged in a price war, consider two prisoners suspected of having committed a crime, for which the police lack sufficient evidence to convict either suspect. The two prisoners are put in two different isolated cells and are offered a lower punishment (or a higher payoff) if they confess of having jointly committed this crime. If we replace LOW with CONFESS, and HIGH with NOT CONFESS, we obtain the so-called Prisoners' Dilemma game.

In the present analysis we refrain from raising the question whether the game described in Table A.1 is observed in reality or not, or whether the game is a good description of the world. Instead, we ask a different set of questions, namely, given that firms behave like those described in

Table A.1, can we (the economists or political scientists) predict whether the market will end up in having both firms charging a low price or charging high price. In order to perform this task, we need to define *equilibrium concepts*.

A.3 Equilibrium Concepts

Once the game is properly defined, we can realize that games may have many outcomes. Therefore, by simply postulating all the possible outcomes (four outcomes in the game described in Table A.1), we cannot make any prediction of how the game is going to end. For example, can you predict how a game like the one described in Table A.1 would end up? Will there be a price competition, or will both firms maintain a high price? Note that formulating a game without having the ability to predict implies that the game is of little value to the researcher. In order to make predictions, we need to develop methods and define algorithms for narrowing down the set of all outcomes to a smaller set that we call *equilibrium outcomes*. We also must specify properties that we find desirable for an equilibrium to fulfill. Ideally, we would like to find a method that would select only one outcome. If this happens, we say that the equilibrium is *unique*. However, as we show below, the equilibrium concepts developed here often fail to be unique. Moreover, the opposite extreme may occur where a particular equilibrium may not exist at all. A game that cannot be solved for equilibria is of less interest to us since no real-life prediction can be made.

Before we proceed to defining our first equilibrium concept, we need to define one additional piece of notation. Recall that an outcome of the game $a = (a^1, \ldots, a^i, \ldots, a^N)$ is a list of what the N players are doing (playing). Now, pick a certain player, whom we will call player i, (e.g., i can be player 1 or 89 or N, or any player). Remove from the outcome a the action played by player i himself. Then, we are left with the list of what all players are playing except player i, which we denote by a^{-i}. Formally,

$$a^{-i} \stackrel{\text{def}}{=} (a^1, \ldots, a^{i-1}, a^{i+1}, \ldots, a^N).$$

Note that after this minor surgical operation is performed, we can still express an outcome as a union of what action player i plays and all the other players' actions. That is, an outcome a can be expressed as $a = (a^i, a^{-i})$.

A.3.1 Equilibrium in dominant actions

Our first equilibrium concept, called equilibrium in dominant strategies, is a highly desirable equilibrium, in the sense that if it exists, it describes

the most intuitively plausible prediction of what players would actually
do. The following definition applies for a *single* player in the sense that it
classifies actions in a player's action set according to a certain criterion.

DEFINITION A.2

A particular action $\tilde{a}^i \in A^i$ *is said to be a* **dominant action** *for player* i
if no matter what all other players are playing, playing $\tilde{a}^i$ *always maximizes player* i*'s payoff. Formally, for every choice of actions by all players
except* i, $a^{\neg i}$,

$$\pi^i(\tilde{a}^i, a^{\neg i}) \geq \pi^i(a^i, a^{\neg i}), \text{ for every } a^i \in A^i$$
$$\pi^i(\tilde{a}^i, a^{\neg i}) > \pi^i(a^i, a^{\neg i}), \text{ for at least one action } a^i \in A^i.$$

For example,

Proposition A.1

In the game described in Table A.1, the action $a^1 = $ LOW *is a dominant
action* **for player 1**.

Proof. It has to be shown that no matter what firm 2 does, firm 1 is
always better off by setting a low price. Thus, we have to scan over
all the possible actions that can be played by firm 2. If player 2 plays
$a^2 = $ LOW, then

$$\pi^1(\text{LOW, LOW}) = 100 > 0 = \pi^1(\text{HIGH, LOW}).$$

Also, if player 2 plays $a^2 = $ HIGH, then

$$\pi^1(\text{LOW, HIGH}) = 300 > 200 = \pi^1(\text{HIGH, HIGH}).$$

∎

Similarly, since the game is symmetric (meaning that renaming player 1
as player 2 and vice versa, does not change players' payoffs), the reader
can establish that $a^2 = $ LOW is a dominant action for firm 2.

We now turn to defining our first equilibrium concept. An equilibrium in dominant actions is simply an outcome where each player plays
a dominant action. Formally,

DEFINITION A.3

An outcome $(\tilde{a}^1, \tilde{a}^2, \ldots, \tilde{a}^N)$ *(where* $\tilde{a}^i \in A^i$ *for every* $i = 1, 2, \ldots, N$*) is
said to be an* **equilibrium in dominant actions** *if* $\tilde{a}^i$ *is a dominant
action for each player* i.

Clearly, since LOW is a dominant action for each player in the game described in Table A.1, the outcome $(a^1, a^2) = (\text{LOW, LOW})$ is an equilibrium in dominant actions.

Although an equilibrium in dominant actions constitutes a very reasonable prediction of how players may interact in the real world, unfortunately, this equilibrium does not exist for most games of interest to us. To demonstrate this point, let us analyze the following game described in Table A.2.

		Firm 2			
		STANDARD α		STANDARD β	
Firm 1	STANDARD α	200	100	0	0
	STANDARD β	0	0	100	200

Table A.2: Standardization Game (Battle of the Sexes case).

The game described in Table A.2 demonstrates a situation where two firms in an industry can make their products more popular when they design their products to operate on the same standards. For example, if the two products operate on the same voltage (say, 220v), or for the case of video players, both operate on the same video system (say, VHS or the DVD standards). Note that in some markets the game described in Table A.2 is not valid, since in some markets firms make higher profits by differentiating their products by having them operating on different standards (e.g., designing computers operating on different incompatible operating systems). Table A.3 on page 294 demonstrates how a small modification in the players' payoffs can alter the equilibrium outcome of this standardization game.

The game in Table A.2 is often called the Battle of the Sexes, since if we replace firm 1 with a male named John, and firm 2 with a female named Mary, and if we replace STANDARD α by the action GOING TO THE OPERA and STANDARD β by GOING TO FOOTBALL, then we have a description of a couple in love where, despite their heterogeneous preferences for the different forms of entertainment, they prefer to be together rather than splitting. Thus, the Battle of the Sexes is sometimes referred to as a *coordination game*.

We now seek to find some predictions for this game. However, the reader will probably be disappointed to find out that:

Proposition A.2
There does not exist an equilibrium in dominant actions for the game described in Table A.2

Proof. It is sufficient to show that one of the players does not have a dominant action. In this case, there cannot be an equilibrium in dominant actions since one player will not have a dominant action to play. Therefore, it is sufficient to look at firm 1: If firm 2 chooses $a^2 = \alpha$, then firm 1 would choose α because

$$\pi^1(\alpha, \alpha) = 200 > 0 = \pi^1(\beta, \alpha).$$

However, when firm 2 chooses $a^2 = \beta$, then firm 1 would choose β because

$$\pi^1(\beta, \beta) = 100 > 0 = \pi^1(\alpha, \beta).$$

So, we have shown that one player does not have a dominant action, and this suffices to conclude that Definition A.3 cannot be applied; hence, there does not exist an equilibrium in dominant actions. ■

A.3.2   Nash equilibrium (NE)

So far we have failed to develop an equilibrium concept that would select an outcome that would be a "reasonable" prediction for a game like the one described in Table A.2. In 1951, John Nash provided an existence proof for an equilibrium concept (earlier used by Cournot when studying duopoly) that has become the most commonly used equilibrium concept in analyzing games.

DEFINITION A.4
*An outcome $\hat{a} = (\hat{a}^1, \hat{a}^2, \ldots, \hat{a}^N)$ (where $\hat{a}^i \in A^i$ for every $i = 1, 2, \ldots, N$) is said to be a **Nash equilibrium (NE)** if no player would find it beneficial to deviate provided that all other players do not deviate from their strategies played at the Nash outcome. Formally, for every player i, $i = 1, 2, \ldots, N$,*

$$\pi^i(\hat{a}^i, \hat{a}^{-i}) \geq \pi^i(a^i, \hat{a}^{-i}) \quad \text{for every } a^i \in A^i.$$

The general methodology for searching which outcomes constitute a NE is to check whether players benefit from a unilateral deviation from a certain outcome. That is, to rule out an outcome as a NE we need only demonstrate that one of the players can increase the payoff by deviating to a different action than the one played in this specific outcome, assuming that all other players do not deviate. Once we find an outcome in which no player can benefit from any deviation from the action played in that outcome, we can assert that we found a NE outcome.

We continue our discussion of the NE with the investigation of the relationship between Nash equilibrium and equilibrium in dominant actions. To demonstrate the relationship between the two equilibrium concepts, we first search for the NE outcomes for the game described in Table A.1. Recall that we have already found that (LOW, LOW) is an equilibrium in dominant actions, but can this fact help us in searching for a NE for this game? Not surprisingly, yes, it can! Since an equilibrium in dominant actions means that each player plays a dominant action, no player would find it beneficial to deviate no matter how the others play. In particular, no player would deviate if the other players stick to their dominant actions. Hence,

Proposition A.3
An equilibrium in dominant actions outcome is also a NE. However, a NE outcome need not be an equilibrium in dominant actions.

Altogether, we have it that (LOW, LOW) is a NE for the game described in Table A.1. We leave it to the reader to verify that no other outcome in this game is a NE. Therefore, this equilibrium is called unique. The second part of Proposition A.3 follows from the game displayed in Table A.2, where there exist two NE, but there does not exist an equilibrium in dominant actions.

Multiple Nash equilibria

We now demonstrate that a Nash equilibrium need not be unique. For example, applying Definition A.4 to the game of Table A.2:

Proposition A.4
The standardization game described in Table A.2 exactly has two Nash equilibrium outcomes: (α, α) and (β, β).

Proof. To prove that (α, α) is a NE, we have to show that no player would benefit from deviation, given that the other does not deviate. In this game with two players, we have to show that, given that $a^2 = \alpha$, player 1 would play $a^1 = \alpha$; and that given that $a^1 = \alpha$, player 2 would play $a^2 = \alpha$. These two conditions follow from

$$\pi^1(\alpha, \alpha) = 200 \geq 0 = \pi^1(\beta, \alpha) \tag{A.1}$$
$$\pi^2(\alpha, \alpha) = 100 \geq 0 = \pi^2(\alpha, \beta).$$

Using the same procedure, it can be easily shown that the outcome (β, β) is also a NE. Finally, we need to show that the other two outcomes, (α, β) and (β, α) are not NE. However, this follows immediately from (A.1). ∎

Nonexistence of a Nash equilibrium

So far we have seen examples where there is one or more NE. That is, as demonstrated in Table A.2, it is always possible to find games with multiple NE. If the equilibrium is not unique, the model has a low prediction power. In contrast, Table A.3 demonstrates a game where a Nash equilibrium does not exist. Therefore, consider the variant of the game displayed in Table A.2. The intuition behind the game described

		Firm 2			
		STANDARD α		STANDARD β	
Firm 1	STANDARD α	200	0	0	200
	STANDARD β	0	100	100	0

Table A.3: Nonexistence of a NE (in pure actions).

in Table A.3 is that firm 1 earns higher profits when it produces on the same standard adopted by firm 2. In contrast, firm 2 earns higher profits when it differentiates itself from firm 1. Thus, this industry is unlikely to achieve standardization.

Proposition A.5
The game described in Table A.3 does not have a NE.

Proof. We must prove that each outcome is not a NE. That is, in each of the four outcomes, at least one of the players would find it beneficial to deviate.

1. For the (α, α) outcome, $\pi^2(\alpha, \beta) = 200 > 0 = \pi^2(\alpha, \alpha)$. Hence, firm 2 would deviate to $a^2 = \beta$.

2. For the (β, α) outcome, $\pi^1(\alpha, \alpha) = 200 > 0 = \pi^1(\beta, \alpha)$. Hence, firm 1 would deviate to $a^1 = \alpha$.

3. For the (β, β) outcome, $\pi^2(\beta, \alpha) = 100 > 0 = \pi^2(\beta, \beta)$. Hence, firm 2 would deviate to $a^2 = \alpha$.

4. For the (α, β) outcome, $\pi^1(\beta, \beta) = 100 > 0 = \pi^1(\alpha, \beta)$. Hence, firm 1 would deviate to $a^1 = \beta$.

∎

A.4   Best-Response Functions

We now construct players' "best-response" functions that greatly facilitate the search for NE.

DEFINITION A.5

(a) In a two-player game, the **best-response function** of player i is the function $R^i(a^j)$, that for every given action a^j of player j assigns an action $a^i = R^i(a^j)$ that maximizes player i's payoff $\pi^i(a^i, a^j)$.

(b) More generally, in an N-player game, the best-response function of player i is the function $R^i(a^{-i})$, that for given actions a^{-i} of players $1, 2, \ldots, i-1, i+1, \ldots, N$, assigns an action $a^i = R^i(a^{-i})$ that maximizes player i's payoff $\pi^i(a^i, a^{-i})$.

Let us now construct the best-response functions for firm 1 and 2 for the standardization game described in Table A.2. It is straightforward to conclude that

$$R^1(a^2) = \left\{ \begin{array}{ll} \alpha & \text{if } a^2 = \alpha \\ \beta & \text{if } a^2 = \beta \end{array} \right. \quad \text{and} \quad R^2(a^1) = \left\{ \begin{array}{ll} \alpha & \text{if } a^1 = \alpha \\ \beta & \text{if } a^1 = \beta. \end{array} \right. \quad (A.2)$$

That is, if firm 2 standardize on α, firm 1's best response is also to standardize on α. if firm 2 standardize on β, firm 1's best response is also to standardize on β. Clearly, due to the symmetry of this game, firm 2's best-response function is the same.

Now, the importance of learning how to construct best-response functions becomes clear in the following proposition:

Proposition A.6
If $\hat{a}$ is a Nash equilibrium outcome, then $\hat{a}^i = R^i(\hat{a}^{-i})$ for every player i.

Proof. By Definition A.4, in a NE outcome each player does not benefit from deviating from the strategy played in a NE outcome (given that all other players do not deviate). Hence, by Definition A.5, each player is on her best-response function. ∎

That is, in a NE outcome, each player chooses an action that is a best response to the actions chosen by other players in a NE. Proposition A.6 is extremely useful in solving for NE in a wide variety of games and will be used extensively.

The procedure for finding a NE is now very simple: First, we calculate the best-response function of each player. Second, we check which outcomes lie on the best-response functions of all players. Those outcomes that we find to be on the best-response functions of all players constitute the NE outcomes. For example, in the standardization game displayed in Table A.2, (A.2) implies that outcomes (α, α) and (β, β) each satisfy both players' best-response functions and therefore constitute NE outcomes.

A.5   Pareto Comparisons Among Outcomes

So far, our analysis has concentrated on defining equilibrium concepts that enable us to select equilibrium outcomes for predicting how players would end up acting when facing similar games in the real world. However, we have not discussed whether the proposed equilibria yield efficient outcomes. That is, we wish to define an efficiency concept that would enable us to compare outcomes from a welfare point of view. In particular, using the Pareto efficiency criterion, we wish to investigate whether there are outcomes that yield higher payoff levels to some players without reducing the payoffs of all other players. For example, in the price competition game of Table A.1, the outcome (HIGH, HIGH) yields higher payoffs to both players compared with the outcome (LOW, LOW). In this case, we say that the outcome (HIGH, HIGH) Pareto dominates the outcome (LOW, LOW). Formally,

DEFINITION A.6
(a) The outcome $\hat{a}$ **Pareto dominates** the outcome $\bar{a}$ (also called **Pareto superior** to $\bar{a}$) if

1. For every player i, $\pi^i(\hat{a}) \geq \pi^i(\bar{a})$, and

2. there exists at least one player j for whom $\pi^j(\hat{a}) > \pi^j(\bar{a})$.

(b) An outcome a^* is called **Pareto efficient** (also called **Pareto optimal**) if there does **not** exist any outcome which Pareto dominates the outcome a^*.

(c) Outcomes $\bar{a}$ and $\tilde{a}$ are called **Pareto noncomparable** if for some player i, $\pi^i(\bar{a}) > \pi^i(\tilde{a})$; but for some other player j, $\pi^j(\bar{a}) < \pi^j(\tilde{a})$.

For example, in the price competition game described in Table A.1 the outcomes (LOW, HIGH) and (HIGH, LOW) are Pareto noncomparable. In the standardization game of Table A.2, the outcomes (α, β) and (β, α) are Pareto dominated by each of the other two outcomes. The outcomes (α, α) and (β, β) are Pareto efficient and are also Pareto noncomparable.

A.6   Exercises

1. Using Definition A.5,

   (a) Write down the best-response functions for firm 1 and firm 2 for the low price–high price game described in Table A.1 on page 288, and decide which outcomes constitute NE (if there are any).

   (b) Write down the best-response functions for each player in the game described in Table A.3 on page 294, and decide which outcomes constitute a NE (if there are any).

2. Consider the normal form game described in Table A.4. Find the conditions on the parameters $a, b, c, d, e, f, g,$ and h that will ensure that

Firm 2

		STANDARD α		STANDARD β	
Firm 1	STANDARD α	a	b	c	d
	STANDARD β	e	f	g	h

Table A.4: Generalized standardization game.

(a) the outcome (α, α) is a NE;

(b) the outcome (α, α) is an equilibrium in dominant actions;

(c) the outcome (α, α) Pareto dominates all other outcomes;

(d) the outcome (α, α) is Pareto noncomparable to the outcome (β, β).

Appendix B
Extensive-Form Games

Our analysis so far has concentrated on normal-form games where the players are restricted to choosing an action at the same time. In this appendix we analyze games in which players can move at different times and more than once. Such games are called *extensive-form games*. Extensive-form games enable us to introduce timing into the model.

Before going to the formal treatment, let us consider the following example, displayed in Figure B.1. In the game displayed in Figure B.1,

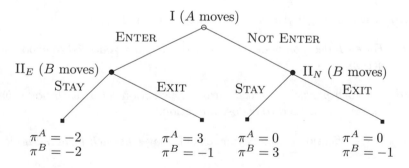

Figure B.1: Entry-exit game with sunk cost: B is the incumbent, A is the potential entrant.

player B is the incumbent (already established) firm. Player A is a potential entrant. Entry into the industry requires sinking a cost of 1 unit of money (consisting of initial market surveys, infrastructure of the firm, legal and registration fees). The major difference between firm A and B is that firm B has already paid the sunk cost, whereas firm A

can still control whether to pay the sunk costs by choosing whether to enter or not.

The game is represented by a *tree*, with a starting decision node (point I), other decision nodes (II_E and II_N), and terminal nodes (end points). Note that in some literature, the term *vertex* (vertices) is used in place of the term *node(s)*. The *branches* connecting decision nodes, and decision nodes to terminal nodes describe actions available to the relevant player on a particular decision node.

The extensive-form game displayed in Figure B.1 has two stages. In stage I, firm A decides whether to enter (sink 1 unit of money) or not. Therefore, in stage II, firm B (the incumbent) may find itself competing with A (node II_E), or maintaining its monopoly power (node II_N). At *each* of these nodes firm B has a node-specific action set. The incumbent's actions set is $A^B_{II_E} = \{\text{STAY, EXIT}\}$ at node II_E, and $A^B_{II_N} = \{\text{STAY, EXIT}\}$ at node II_N.

We can now give a formal definition to extensive-form games with perfect information.

DEFINITION B.1
*An **extensive form game** is:*

(a) *A game tree containing a starting node, other decision nodes, terminal nodes, and branches linking each decision node to successor nodes.*

(b) *A list of $N \geq 1$ players, indexed by i, $i = 1, 2, \ldots, N$.*

(c) *For each decision node, the name of the player entitled to choose an action.*

(d) *For each player i, a specification of i's action set at each node that player i is entitled to choose an action.*

(e) *A specification of the payoff to each player at each terminal node.*

B.1 Defining Strategies and Outcomes in Extensive-Form Games

Our preliminary discussion of extensive-form games emphasized that a player may be called to choose an action more than once and that each time a player chooses an action, the player has to choose an action from the action set available at that particular node. Therefore, we need to define the following term.

DEFINITION B.2
A **strategy** *for player i (denoted by s^i) is a complete plan (list) of actions, one action for each decision node that the player is entitled to choose an action.*

Thus, it is important to note that a strategy is not what a player does at a single specific node but is a list of what the player does at *every* node where the player is entitled to choose an action.

What are the strategies available to the incumbent firm in the game described in Figure B.1? Since the incumbent may end up in either node II_E or II_N, a strategy for the incumbent would be a specification of the precise action he will be taking at *each* node. That is, although it is clear that the incumbent will reach either node II_E or II_N but not both, a strategy for this player must specify what she will do at *each* of the two nodes. Therefore, the incumbent has four possible strategies given by (STAY, STAY), (STAY, EXIT), (EXIT, STAY), (EXIT, EXIT), where the first component refers to the incumbent's action in node II_E, and the second component refers to his action at node II_N.

We now wish to list all the possible outcomes of this game. An outcome of an extensive-form game is a list of all the actions taken by each player at *every* possible node that the player is entitled to make a move. Thus, an outcome for this particular game must take the form of

(*A*'s action at *I*, (*B*'s action at II_E, *B*'s action at II_N)).

Since the potential entrant is restricted to making a move only at node *I*, and since his action set has two possible actions, this game has eight outcomes given by:
(ENTER, (STAY, STAY)), (ENTER, (STAY, EXIT)),
(ENTER, (EXIT, STAY)), (ENTER, (EXIT, EXIT)),
(NOT, (STAY, STAY)), (NOT, (STAY, EXIT)),
(NOT, (EXIT, STAY)), (NOT, (EXIT, EXIT)).

B.2 A Normal-Form Representation for Extensive-Form Games

Now that the game is well defined, we seek to find some predictions. The first step would be to search for a Nash equilibrium. Recalling our definition of Nash equilibrium (Definition A.4), in extensive form games we look for a Nash equilibrium in strategies, where each player cannot increase the payoff by unilaterally deviating from the strategy played at the NE outcome.

It turns out that in many instances transforming an extensive form game into a normal form makes it easier to find the Nash equilibria.

Table B.1 provides the normal form representation for the Entry-Exit game described in Figure B.1. Table B.1 shows that there are three

Firm B

		(STAY,STAY)		(STAY,EXIT)		(EXIT,STAY)		(EXIT,EXIT)	
A	ENTER	-2	-2	-2	-2	3	-1	3	-1
	NOT	0	3	0	-1	0	3	0	-1

Table B.1: Normal form representation of the Entry-Exit game

Nash equilibrium outcomes for this game: (ENTER, (EXIT, STAY)), (ENTER, (EXIT, EXIT)), and (NOT, (STAY, STAY)). Note that here, as in the standardization game of Table A.2 on page 291, multiple NE greatly reduce our ability to generate predictions from this game. For this reason, we now turn to defining an equilibrium concept that would narrow down the set of NE outcomes into a smaller set of outcomes. In the literature, an equilibrium concept that selects a smaller number of NE outcomes is called a *refinement* of Nash equilibrium, which is the subject of the following subsection.

B.3 Subgames and Subgame-Perfect Equilibria

In this subsection we define an equilibrium concept that satisfies all the requirements of NE (see Definition A.4) and has some additional restrictions. This equilibrium concept may be helpful in selecting a smaller set of outcomes from the set of NE outcomes, by eliminating some undesirable NE outcomes.

Before we proceed to the formal part, let us go back to the Entry-Exit game of Figure B.1 and look at the three NE outcomes for this game. Comparing the three NE outcomes, do you consider any equilibrium outcomes to be unreasonable? What would you suggest if the potential entrant (firm A) were to hire you as his strategic adviser? Well, you would probably tell firm A to enter. Why? By looking at the incumbent's payoffs at the terminal nodes in Figure B.1 we can see that if firm A plays ENTER, the incumbent will play EXIT (a payoff of $\pi^B = -1$ compared with $\pi^B = -2$ if she stays), and firm A will gain a payoff of $\pi^A = 3$ compared with a payoff of $\pi^A = 0$ for not entering. Thus, a "smart" potential entrant would be able to look at this game tree and conjecture that the incumbent will avoid a stiff price competition and will exit from the market. From this we conclude that the limitation of the NE concept is that it cannot capture the entrant's ability to predict that the incumbent will not have the incentive to engage in a price competition. More precisely, under the NE outcome (NOT, (STAY, STAY)) does not reflect the entrant's ability to "force" exit on the incumbent by simply sinking her entry costs and making its entry a fact. More precisely, the incumbent's strategy (STAY, STAY) is an *incredible threat*, since the actions will not be taken upon entry of firm A.

We now want to formalize an equilibrium concept that would exclude the unreasonable Nash equilibria. In particular, we look for an equilibrium concept that would exclude outcomes where the potential entrant does not use his *first-mover advantage* in order to force the incumbent to exit. Thus, we seek to define an equilibrium concept where the player who moves first would calculate and take into account how subsequent players (the incumbent in the present case) would respond to the moves of the players who move earlier in the game. Hence, having computed how subsequent players would respond, the first player can optimize by narrowing down the set of actions yielding higher payoffs. In the Entry-Exit example, we wish to find an equilibrium concept that would generate a unique outcome where firm A enters.

We first define a subgame of the game.

DEFINITION B.3

*A **subgame** is a decision node from the original game along with the decision nodes and terminal nodes directly following this node. A subgame is called a **proper subgame** if it differs from the original game.*

Clearly, the Entry-Exit game has three subgames: One is the game itself whereas the other two are proper subgames with nodes II_E and II_N as starting nodes. The two proper subgames are illustrated in Figure B.2.

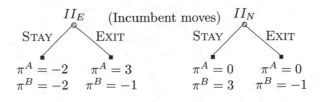

Figure B.2: Two proper subgames.

In 1965, Rheinhard Selten proposed a refinement of the NE concept defined as follows:

DEFINITION B.4

*An outcome is said to be a **subgame perfect equilibrium (SPE)** if it induces a Nash equilibrium in every subgame of the original game.*

Definition B.4 states that a SPE outcome is a list of strategies, one for each player, consisting of players' actions that constitutes a NE at every subgame. In particular, a SPE outcome must be a NE for the original game since the original game is a subgame of itself.

We now seek to apply Definition B.4 in order to solve for a SPE of the Entry-Exit game.

Proposition B.1

The outcome (ENTER, (EXIT, STAY)) *constitutes a unique SPE for the Entry-Exit game.*

Proof. Since a SPE is also a NE for the original game, it is sufficient to look at the three NE outcomes of the original game given by (ENTER, (EXIT, STAY)), (ENTER, (EXIT, EXIT)), and (NOT, (STAY, STAY)). Next, each proper subgame has only one NE, namely, the incumbent plays EXIT at II_E, and plays STAY at II_N. Hence, given that a SPE outcome must be a NE for every subgame, we conclude that the outcomes (ENTER, (EXIT, EXIT)) and (NOT, (STAY, STAY)) are not SPE. Finally, the outcome (ENTER, (EXIT, STAY)) is a SPE since it is a NE for the original game, and the strategy (EXIT, STAY) is associated with the unique NE for every proper subgame. ∎

Thus, we have shown that using the SPE refines the NE in the sense of excluding some outcomes which we may consider unreasonable.

We conclude this discussion of the SPE by describing the methodologies commonly used for finding SPE outcomes. The general methodology for finding the SPE outcomes is to use *backward induction*, meaning that we start searching for NE in the subgames leading to the terminal nodes. Then, we look for NE for the subgames leading to the terminal nodes, taking as given the NE actions to be played in the last subgames before the terminal nodes. Then, continuing to solve backward, we reach the starting node and look for the action that maximizes player 1's payoff, given the NE of all the proper subgames. Note that the backward induction methodology is particularly useful when the game tree is long. Finally, another common methodology is to first find the NE outcomes for the game, say by transforming the extensive form representation into a normal form representation (see section B.2). Then, once we have the set of all NE outcomes, we are left to select those outcomes that are also NE for all subgames. This can be done by trial and error, or, as we do in the proof of Proposition B.1, by ruling out the NE outcomes of the original game that are not NE for some proper subgames.

B.4 Exercises

1. Consider a dynamic version of the standardization game described in Table A.2 on page 291. Assume a two-stage game where firm 1 selects its standard at stage I, while firm 2 selects its standard in stage II, knowing which standard was selected by firm 1.

   (a) Draw the game tree and mark all decision nodes and profit levels at the terminal nodes.

   (b) Solve for SPE of this game (if there are any).

2. Draw the game tree and solve for SPE for the standardization game displayed in Table A.3 on page 294 (if there are any), assuming a two-stage game where firm 1 selects its standard at stage I, while firm 2 selects its standard in stage II, knowing which standard was selected by firm 1.

3. Draw the game tree and solve for SPE for the standardization game displayed in Table A.4 on page 297, assuming that $g > h > f > b > d > a$. Assume a two-stage game where firm 1 selects its standard at stage I, while firm 2 selects its standard in stage II, knowing which standard was selected by firm 1.

The goal of this appendix is to explore the simplest possible differentiated products environment where (pure) Nash-Bertrand equilibrium prices do not exist due to price cycles a la Edgeworth and to suggest an alternative equilibrium concept as better suited to analyzing such environments.

   We develop and characterize a concept called an *Undercut-Proof equilibrium*. In an Undercut-Proof equilibrium, each firm chooses its price so as to maximize profit while ensuring that its price is sufficiently low that any rival firm would *not* find it profitable to set a lower price in order to grab all of the first firm's customers. Thus, unlike the Nash-Bertrand behavior, where each firm assumes that the rival firm does not alter its price, in an Undercut-Proof equilibrium environment, firms assume that rival firms are more sophisticated in that they are "ready" to reduce their prices whenever undercutting and grabbing their rivals' customers is profitable. These beliefs are pervasive amongst firms competing in differentiated products using pricing strategies. Finally, the Undercut-Proof equilibrium can be calculated easily for any number of firms in the industry.

C.1   The Simplest Product Differentiation Model

Consider the following example (see Shilony 1977, Eaton and Engers 1990, and Shy 1996, Ch. 7), of a market with two stores called A and B which sell differentiated brands. Assume that production costs are zero. There are two groups of consumers, type A (called brand A oriented consumers) and type B (called brand B oriented consumers). There are $\eta_A > 0$ type A consumers and $\eta_B > 0$ type B consumers.

Each consumer buys one unit either from store A or store B. Let p_A and p_B denote the prices of the stores and let $\delta \geq 0$ denote the extra distaste cost a consumer bears if he buys his less preferred brand. Altogether, the utilities of consumers of type A and type B are assumed to be

$$U_A \stackrel{\text{def}}{=} \begin{cases} -p_A & \text{buying from } A \\ -p_B - \delta & \text{buying from } B, \end{cases} \tag{C.1}$$

and

$$U_B \stackrel{\text{def}}{=} \begin{cases} -p_A - \delta & \text{buying from } A \\ -p_B & \text{buying from } B. \end{cases}$$

One way of interpreting this example is as a discrete version of the Hotelling (1929) location model where the two stores locate on opposite sides of a lake or high terrain and where crossing from one side to the other requires paying a fixed transportation cost of δ.

Let q_A denote the (endogenously determined) number of consumers buying from store A, and q_B denote the number of consumers buying from store B. Then, (C.1) implies that

$$q_A = \begin{cases} 0 & \text{if } p_A > p_B + \delta \\ \eta_A & \text{if } p_B - \delta \leq p_A \leq p_B + \delta \\ \eta_A + \eta_B & \text{if } p_A < p_B - \delta, \end{cases} \tag{C.2}$$

and

$$q_B = \begin{cases} 0 & \text{if } p_B > p_A + \delta \\ \eta_B & \text{if } p_A - \delta \leq p_B \leq p_A + \delta \\ \eta_A + \eta_B & \text{if } p_B < p_A - \delta. \end{cases}$$

C.2   Nonexistence of a Nash-Bertrand Equilibrium

A Nash-Bertrand equilibrium is the nonnegative pair $\left(p_A^N, p_B^N\right)$ such that, for a given p_B^N, store A chooses p_A^N to maximize $\pi_A \stackrel{\text{def}}{=} p_A q_A$ and, for a given p_A^N, store B chooses p_B^N to maximize $\pi_B \stackrel{\text{def}}{=} p_B q_B$, where q_A and q_B are given in (C.2).

Proposition C.1

There does not exist a Nash-Bertrand equilibrium in pure price-strategies for the differentiated products model.

Proof. To establish a contradiction, suppose that $\left(p_A^N, p_B^N\right)$ is a Nash equilibrium. Then, there are three cases: (1) $|p_A^N - p_B^N| > \delta$, (2) $|p_A^N - p_B^N| < \delta$ and (3) $|p_A^N - p_B^N| = \delta$.

(1) With no loss of generality, suppose that $p_A^N - p_B^N > \delta$. Then (C.2) implies that $q_A^N = 0$, and hence $\pi_A^N = 0$. However, store A can increase its profit by reducing its price to $\tilde{p}_A = p_B^N + \delta$, in which case $q_A = \eta_A$ and $\tilde{\pi}_A = \eta_A(p_B^N + \delta) > 0$; a contradiction.

(2) With no loss of generality, suppose that $p_A^N < p_B^N + \delta$. Then store A can increase its profit by slightly increasing its price to $\tilde{p}_A$ satisfying $p_A^N < \tilde{p}_A < p_B^N + \delta$ to earn a profit level of $\tilde{\pi}_A = \eta_A \tilde{p}_A > \pi_A^N$; a contradiction.

(3) With no loss of generality, suppose that $p_A^N - p_B^N = \delta$. Then, $p_B^N = p_A^N - \delta < p_A^N + \delta$ and store B can increase its profit by slightly raising p_B^N; a contradiction. ∎

C.3   The Undercut-Proof Equilibrium

We first need to provide a precise definition to what we mean by "undercutting."

DEFINITION C.1
*Store i **undercuts** store j, if $p_i \le p_j - \delta$, where $i, j = A, B$, $i \ne j$.*

Thus, undercutting occurs when store i reduces its price to its competitor's price minus the transportation cost. Thus, in some sense undercutting occurs when one store "subsidizes" the transportation costs.

The Undercut-Proof equilibrium is now defined.

DEFINITION C.2
*The **Undercut-Proof equilibrium (UPE)** is the pair of prices $(p_A^U,\ p_B^U)$ satisfying:*

(a) For given p_B^U and q_B^U, firm A chooses the highest price p_A^U subject to

$$\pi_B^U = p_B^U q_B^U \ge (p_A - \delta)(\eta_A + \eta_B).$$

(b) For given p_A^U and q_A^U, firm B chooses the highest price p_B^U subject to

$$\pi_A^U = p_A^U q_A^U \ge (p_B - \delta)(\eta_A + \eta_B).$$

(c) The distribution of consumers between the firms is determined in (C.2).

The first part states that, in an Undercut-Proof equilibrium, firm A sets the highest price it can while preventing firm B from undercutting p_A^U and grabbing firm A's customers. More precisely, firm A sets p_A^U as high as possible without causing B's equilibrium profit level to be smaller than B's profit level when it undercuts by setting $\tilde{p}_B < p_A^U - \delta$, and selling to $\tilde{q}_B = \eta_A + \eta_B$ customers. The above two inequalities therefore hold as equalities which can be solved for the equilibrium prices

$$p_A^U = \frac{(\eta_A + \eta_B)(\eta_A + 2\eta_B)\delta}{(\eta_A)^2 + \eta_A\eta_B + (\eta_B)^2} > \delta \qquad (C.3)$$

and

$$p_B^U = \frac{(\eta_A + \eta_B)(2\eta_A + \eta_B)\delta}{(\eta_A)^2 + \eta_A\eta_B + (\eta_B)^2} > \delta.$$

First note that by setting $p_i \leq \delta$, each firm can secure a strictly positive market share without being undercut. Hence, in an Undercut-Proof equilibrium both firms maintain a strictly positive market share. Substituting (C.3) into (C.2), we have that $q_A^U = \eta_A$ and $q_B^U = \eta_B$.

Figure C.1 illustrates how the Undercut-Proof equilibrium is determined. Figure C.1's left panel, shows how firm A is constrained in

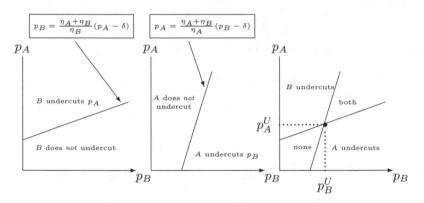

Figure C.1: Undercut-Proof equilibrium.

setting p_A so that firm B cannot benefit from undercutting p_A^U. Figure C.1's middle panel shows how firm B is constrained in setting p_B so that firm A would not benefit from undercutting p_B^U. Figure C.1's right panel displays the region where neither firm finds it profitable to undercut its rival; the Undercut-Proof equilibrium prices maximize profits on this region. It should be emphasized that the curves drawn in Figure C.1 are *not* best response (reaction) functions (see Definition A.5 on page 295), but simply divide the regions into prices that make undercutting profitable or unprofitable for each firm.

C.4   Four Important Properties of the UPE

We now conclude this example with characterizations of the Undercut-Proof equilibrium prices. First, from (C.3), prices rise with distaste (transportation) costs and monotonically decline to zero as distaste costs approach zero, reflecting a situation in which the products become homogeneous.

Second,

$$\Delta p^U \overset{\text{def}}{=} p_B^U - p_A^U = \frac{\left[(\eta_A)^2 - (\eta_B)^2\right]\delta}{(\eta_A)^2 + \eta_A\eta_B + (\eta_B)^2} < \delta. \qquad (C.4)$$

Hence, $\Delta p^U \geq 0$ if and only if $\eta_A \geq \eta_B$. Thus, in an Undercut-Proof equilibrium, the store selling to the larger number of consumers charges a lower price. This result is commonly observed in retailing, where discount stores sell to larger numbers of consumers (e.g., WalMart and Kmart). Note that this result is *not* obtained in the conventional Hotelling linear-city location model which predicts that the store with the higher market share sells at a higher price.

Third,

$$\Delta \pi^U \overset{\text{def}}{=} \pi_B^U - \pi_A^U = p_B^U\eta_B - p_A^U\eta_A = \frac{(\eta_A + \eta_B)^2(\eta_B - \eta_A)\delta}{(\eta_A)^2 + \eta_A\eta_B + (\eta_B)^2}. \qquad (C.5)$$

Hence, $\Delta \pi^U \geq 0$ if and only if $\eta_B \geq \eta_A$. That is, in an Undercut-Proof equilibrium, the firm selling to a larger number of consumers makes a higher profit despite selling at a lower price.

Fourth, under a symmetric distribution of consumers ($\eta_A = \eta_B$), the equilibrium prices are given by $p_A^U = p_B^U = 2\delta$. That is, each firm can mark up its price to twice the level of the distaste (transportation) cost without being undercut.

C.5   Exercises

1. In this exercise we introduce production cost into the model. Suppose that $\eta_A = \eta_B = \eta$ (i.e., there is an equal number of consumers oriented toward each store). The cost of producing one unit by store A is c_A and by store B is c_B, where $0 < c_A < c_B$ (that is, store A is more efficient). Assuming that $c_B - c_A < \delta$ answer the following questions.

   (a) Calculate the UPE prices as functions of η, c_A, and c_B.

   (b) Infer which store charges a higher price, and whether the difference in prices increases or decreases with η, c_A, and c_B. Explain your findings.

2. Your are given the following pieces of information: (a) The price charged by store B is $p_B = 12$, (b) store A has 5 customers, (c) store B has 10 customers, and (d) there are no production costs and prices are determined by an UPE.

   Calculate the transportation cost parameter, δ, associated with traveling between store A and store B; and calculate the price charged by store A.

C.6   Selected References

Eaton, J., and M. Engers. 1990. "Intertemporal Price Competition." *Econometrica* 58: 637–659.

Hotelling, H. 1929. "Stability in Competition." *Economic Journal* 39: 41–57.

Shilony, Y. 1977. "Mixed Pricing in Oligopoly." *Journal of Economic Theory* 14: 373–388.

Shy, O. 1996. *Industrial Organization: Theory and Applications.* Cambridge, Mass.: The MIT Press.

Index